DANISH: A COMPREHENSIVE GRAMMAR

Related titles by Routledge

Colloquial Danish: A Complete Language Course
Danish Dictionary

Colloquial Norwegian: A Complete Language Course
Norwegian: An Essential Grammar
Norwegian Dictionary

Colloquial Swedish: The Complete Course for Beginners
Swedish: A Comprehensive Grammar
Swedish: An Essential Grammar

DANISH: A COMPREHENSIVE GRAMMAR

Robin Allan
Philip Holmes
Tom Lundskær-Nielsen

LONDON AND NEW YORK

First published 1995
by Routledge
2 Park Square, Milton Park, Abingdon, Oxon OX14 4RN

Simultaneously published in the USA and Canada
by Routledge Inc.
270 Madison Avenue, New York, NY 10016

Reprinted with corrections 1988

Reprinted 2002, 2003, 2004 (twice)

Transferred to Digital Printing 2006

Routledge is an imprint of the Taylor & Francis Group

Set in 10/12pt Times New Roman
by Philip Holmes
Printed and bound in Great Britain by TJI Digital, Padstow, Cornwall

British Library Cataloguing in Publication Data
A catalogue record of this book has been requested

Library of Congress Cataloguing in Publication Data
A catalogue record of this book has been requested

ISBN 0–415–08206–4

CONTENTS

PREFACE

Small languages like Danish are often poorly provided with adequate reference material for learners. Our aim with this book has therefore been to make available a substantial work of reference on Danish grammar which may serve as an aid not only to beginners but also to more advanced students and to teachers. Danish obviously counts as a minor European language in terms of the number of speakers, but it is the medium of a rich culture as well as being an official EU language which is both learnt and taught widely in Europe and beyond.

Danish may be small, but it is not perfectly formed; the language is changing quite rapidly in some key areas, and we hope to have been able to demonstrate this in our snapshot of the language in the mid-1990s.

This is both a general and a comparative account concentrating on the areas of Danish which pose problems for English speakers and providing translations of most of the examples. But its starting-point is nearly always Danish rather than English.

We have attempted to strike the difficult balance between accuracy of linguistic description and analysis on the one hand and clarity and usability on the other. The structure of the book is deliberately traditional in order to help users who are often not linguists. Terms that may not be familiar are explained either when they are first used in the text or in the section on Linguistic Terms.

The book contains a hierarchy of detail from the major summary charts and tables provided for ready reference to the minor detail to be found in the Notes. The comprehensive Index is intended to facilitate rapid location of problem areas and details, as the book is most likely to be used from the Index rather than studied chapter by chapter. In Chapter 10, however, users are advised to begin by reading Section A, which lays the foundation for the detailed account of sentence structure that follows in that chapter.

Any work of this kind draws on the labours of the many others who have gone before. The Bibliography lists major sources and provides a guide for those who wish to delve deeper into specific aspects of the language. The authors primarily responsible for the individual chapters of the book are as follows: Chapters 1, 2, 3 (PH), Chapters 4, 5 (TLN), Chapter 6 (RA), Chapters 7, 8 (TLN), Chapters 9, 10 (RA), Chapters 11, 12, 13 (PH).

We wish to acknowledge the generous help and encouragement of many Danes and others. The International Office of the Danish Ministry of Education has, through the good offices of Dinah Bechshøft and Ida Boisen, taken a great interest in this project and has generously provided funds for several research visits to Denmark. The EU through its Lingua programme has helped towards the publication costs of this book.

We owe a particular debt to Ian Hinchliffe, who, with Phil Holmes, did the groundwork in writing *Swedish: A Comprehensive Grammar*, which has provided a firm foundation for the present book.

Our thanks go also to a number of friends and colleagues: Jørgen Bang, Michael Barnes, Joseph Crabtree, Wendy Davies, Kirsten and Glyn Jones, Hans Anton Kofoed, Else and Hans Bekker-Nielsen, Niels Davidsen-Nielsen, Hans Frede Nielsen, Jørgen Højgaard Jørgensen, Bjarne le Fevre Jakobsen, Jannie Roed, Birgitte and Peter Skov-Jakobsen, Georg Søndergaard, Suzanne and Michael Taylor, Karen and Poul Vad, and to Erik Hansen and the staff at Dansk Sprognævn for advice and encouragement.

We are extremely grateful to Henrik Galberg Jacobsen for reading the manuscript and giving invaluable advice, and to Katie Lewis who singlehandedly compiled the Index and made many helpful comments at proof stage.

Finally, the two other authors wish to thank Phil Holmes for undertaking the unenviable and arduous task of setting the entire manuscript for printing.

Robin Allan Philip Holmes Tom Lundskær-Nielsen

London, Hull and Cambridge November 1994

Preface to the Reprint:
This reprint has allowed us to correct a number of errors and to make minor changes to the text. We are especially grateful to Michael Taylor for many helpful suggestions, some of which we have followed. Since the publication of the book in 1995, the new comma has been introduced, which has made it necessary to rewrite paragraphs 1202-04 in order to take account of this. However, for practical reasons, we have preserved the use of the traditional comma in the examples.

SYMBOLS AND ABBREVIATIONS USED IN THE TEXT

Jeg tror, (at) han kommer i dag.	word in brackets may be omitted
kørs(e)len, hundred(e)	letter in brackets may be omitted
låsede/låste	alternatives
...	word(s) omitted
/at/	approximate pronunciation using normal Danish spelling
[di]	phonetic transcription
vent/*ede*	verb stem with inflexional ending
mål/tid	elements in a compound
***Han gik ham en tur.**	incorrect usage
***hjulen**	incorrect form
-e, -er, -r	inflexional endings
-ske, -inde	word ending in the suffixes **-ske, -inde**
x ⇨ y	x changes into y
x ↔ y	y refers to or agrees with x
I, II, III, IV	verb conjugations
en ˈbolig	stress on syllable following mark
en ˈsød, ˈung pige	stress on words

a, A	adverbial positions	NFV	non-finite verb
adj.	adjective	O	object
adv.	adverb	obj.	object(ive)
attrib.	attribute, attributive	OC	object complement
compl.	complement	para.	paragraph
conj.	conjunction, conjugation	prep.	preposition(al)
coord. conj.	coordinating conjunction	RS	real subject
def.	definite	S	subject
DO	direct object	SC	subordinate clause, subject complement
F	front position	SE	second element in a compound
FE	first element in a compound	sub. conj.	subordinating conjunction
FS	formal subject	v, V	verb, verbal positions
FV	finite verb	v1, v2	verb first, verb second clause
IO	indirect object	X_1, X_2	extra positions
MC	main clause		
n, N	nominal positions		

1 NOUNS

101 Introduction

(a) Different types of noun are:

Proper nouns: **Esbjerg**; **Kirsten**; **Politiken** (newspaper); **Tyskland**, Germany

Common nouns: **hus**, house; **kat**, cat; **pige**, girl; **stol**, chair

Types of common noun are:

Count nouns, i.e. concrete things and creatures: **kage**, cake; **lærer**, teacher; **træ**, tree

- Some abstracts are count nouns: **farve**, colour; **glæde**, joy; **sygdom**, illness

Non-count nouns, i.e. substances: **benzin**, petrol; **luft**, air; **vand**, water

- Some abstracts are non-count nouns: **hvidhed**, whiteness; **lykke**, happiness; **musik**, music

(b) Danish has two genders, common and neuter (some grammars use the term 'non-neuter' for common gender). Common gender nouns take the indefinite article **en** and the end article (definite article) **-(e)n** (see 134ff below):

en hånd, a hand	**hånden**, the hand
en pige, a girl	**pigen**, the girl

Neuter nouns take the indefinite article **et** and the end article **-(e)t**:

et hus, a house	**huset**, the house
et æble, an apple	**æblet**, the apple

(c) Danish nouns form their indefinite plural in three main ways, by adding the endings **-(e)r**, **-e** or -zero (i.e. no plural ending) (see 113–18):

en by – byer, town – towns; **en krone – kroner**, crown – crowns; **en stol – stole**, chair – chairs; **et sprog – sprog**, language – languages

For plurals of foreign nouns see 119–22.

(d) There are two cases for Danish nouns: a basic (unmarked) case, and a genitive ending in **-s** (see 132ff):

en pige, a girl	**en piges hånd**, a girl's hand
pigen, the girl	**pigens hånd**, the girl's hand
piger, girls	**pigers hænder**, girls' hands
pigerne, the girls	**pigernes hænder**, the girls' hands

A GENDER RULES

102 Introduction

About 75% of all nouns are common gender. Whilst it is clearly advisable to learn each noun with its gender, the following guidelines should provide some help in predicting gender (for the gender of loans see 108). In many cases either the meaning of the noun or its suffix may provide a clue to its gender.

Gender also determines the form of the adjective and of some pronouns, as these agree in gender and number with nouns (see 209, 401ff):

en stor pige a big girl	**et stort hus** a big house
pigen er stor the girl is big	**huset er stort** the house is big

Note – Old Danish had masculine, feminine and neuter gender, and remnants of this system are occasionally found in poetry and hymns:

dagen – han, the day – he	**natten – hun**, the night – she
månen – han, the moon – he	**solen – hun**, the sun – she

103 Common gender by meaning

The following types of noun are generally common gender by meaning:

(a) Personal names and nouns describing human beings:

en dreng, a boy; **en far**, a father; **en kone**, a woman/wife; **en lærer**, a teacher; **en svensker**, a Swede; **en søster**, a sister; **en udlænding**, a foreigner

Marie er ung endnu.	Marie is still young.

Note 1 – Exceptions: **et barn**, a child; **et bud**, a messenger; **et geni**, a genius; **et individ**, an individual; **et medlem**, a member; **et menneske**, a human being; **et vidne**, a witness

When referring to these neuter nouns the applicable masculine or feminine pronoun is, however, generally used of individuals:

Klubben har fået et nyt medlem. Han/Hun hedder Søren/Marie.
The club has gained a new member. He/She is called Soren/Marie.

Barnet holdt op med at lege. Han/Hun begyndte at græde.
The child stopped playing. He/She began to cry.

But when referring to these nouns in a general sense or when the gender is unknown **det** is used:

Selv når barnet er uartigt, bør man ikke slå det.
Even when the child has misbehaved one should not smack it.

With nouns of common gender describing people the masculine or feminine pronoun is used rather than the common gender pronoun **den** when referring to an individual:

en agent, an agent; **en baptist**, a baptist; **en fætter**, a male cousin; **en gæst**, a guest; **en læge**, a doctor; **en person**, a person; etc.

Lægen var meget sympatisk. Hun var god til at lytte.
The doctor was very understanding. She was a good listener.

Note 2 – Nouns of neuter gender do not alter their gender when used to depict a human being:

Han æder som et svin.	He eats like a pig.
Han er et dyr.	He is a brute.

(b) Words describing animals:

en gås, a goose; **en hund**, a dog; **en kat**, a cat; **en ko**, a cow; **en laks**, a salmon

Note 1 – Exceptions: **et bæst**, a beast; **et dyr**, an animal, and others in **-dyr**: **et pattedyr**, a mammal, etc.; **et egern**, a squirrel; **et føl**, a foal; **et får**, a sheep; **et insekt**, an insect; **et kid**, a kid; **et kreatur**, a cow; **kvæget**, cattle; **et lam**, a lamb; **et møl**, a moth; **et svin**, a pig, and others in **-svin**: **et marsvin**, a guinea pig, etc.; **et æsel**, a donkey.

When referring to family pets, owners often use **han** or **hun** whilst strangers may use **den**.

Note 2 – In fairy tales and children's stories in which animals are given human characteristics they may be referred to as **han** or **hun**.

(c) Words for plants, trees and fruit:

en birk, a birch; **en blomst**, a flower; **en eg**, an oak; **en nød**, a nut; **en plante**, a plant; **en pære**, a pear; **en rose**, a rose

Note – Exceptions: **et bær**, a berry; **et frø**, a seed; **græsset**, the grass; **et løg**, an onion; **et træ**, a tree; **et æble**, an apple; compounds in **-frø**, **-træ**: **et sesamfrø**, a sesame seed; **et grantræ**, a fir tree. Nouns in **-bær** are neuter when denoting the fruit but common gender when denoting the tree or shrub.

(d) Festivals and months:

i julen	at Christmas
i påsken	at Easter
Januar var kold.	January was cold.

Note – The seasons vary, however: **sommeren/vinteren**, the summer/winter. But: **foråret/efteråret**, the spring/autumn; since **år**, year, is neuter.

(e) Lakes and rivers:

en flod, a river; **en strøm**, a stream; **en å**, a river; **Themsen**, the Thames; **den Blå Nil**, the Blue Nile

(f) Nouns derived from cardinal numbers (see also 307):

en toer, a two; **en tier**, a ten

Note – Exceptions: **et ettal**, a one; **et hundred(e)**, a hundred; **et tusind(e)**, a thousand

(g) Fractions ending in **-del** (see also 312):

en fjerdedel, a quarter; **en femtedel**, a fifth

104 Common gender by form

Nouns with the following suffixes are common gender by form:

-ance **en ambulance**, an ambulance; **en balance**, a balance; **en chance**, a chance; **en elegance**, an elegance; **en leverance**, a delivery

-ans **en instans**, an authority; **en substans**, a substance

-ant **en debutant**, a debutante; **en protestant**, a protestant; **en repræsentant**, a representative; **en variant**, a variant

-de **bredden**, the breadth; **dybden**, the depth; **højden**, the height; **længden**, the length

-dom **en ejendom**, a property; **en sygdom**, an illness; **ungdommen**, youth (see also 113(c))

-é **en allé**, an avenue; **en armé**, an army; **en attaché**, an attaché; **en café**, a café; **en idé**, an idea; **en orkidé**, an orchid

Note 1 – Exceptions: **et communiqué**, a communiqué; **et resumé**, a resumé

-else **en bevægelse**, a movement; **en foreteelse**, a phenomenon; **en forsinkelse**, a delay; **en overraskelse**, a surprise; **skabelsen**, the creation; **en skuffelse**, a disappointment; **en tilladelse**, permission

Note 2 – Exceptions: **ragelset**, the junk; **et spøgelse**, a ghost; **et værelse**, a room; but some compounds in which **-værelse** does not mean 'room' have common gender: **en fraværelse**, an absence; **en nærværelse**, a presence; **en tilværelse**, a life

-en Verbal nouns: **Jeg er træt af al den løben**, I'm tired of all this dashing about; **Hold op med den hosten!**, Stop that coughing!; **en uophørlig skraben penge sammen**, a ceaseless scraping together of money; **denne skiften standpunkter**, this shifting of viewpoint; **en bæven**, a trembling; **en formåen**, an ability; **en hilsen**, a greeting; **en hoben**, a heap; **en hvisken**, a whisper; **en indgriben**, an intervention

-ence **en kompetence**, a competence; **en konference**, a conference; **en konkurrence**, a competition; **en reference**, a reference

-ens **en abstinens**, an abstinence; **en frekvens**, a frequency; **kongruensen**, the congruence

-er Occupations: **en bager**, a baker; **en lærer**, a teacher
Others: **en alder**, an age; **en fiber**, a fibre

-hed **ensomheden**, the loneliness; **en hastighed**, a speed; **kærligheden**, the love; **en lejlighed**, a flat; **en nyhed**, a piece of news; **en tavshed**, a silence; **trætheden**, the fatigue

-ik **etikken**, ethics; **en grammatik**, a grammar; **komikken**, the comedy; **en kritik**, a criticism; **musikken**, the music; **trafikken**, the traffic (see also 113(c))

-ing, -ling, -ning **en parkering**, a car park; **en stilling**, a position; **en yngling**, a young person; **en bygning**, a building; **en slægtning**, a relative

-isme **fascismen**, fascism; **kommunismen**, communism; **socialismen**, socialism; **vegetarianismen**, vegetarianism

-ist **en ateist**, an atheist; **en idealist**, an idealist; **en kapitalist**, a capitalist; **en metodist**, a Methodist; **en realist**, a realist

-sion, *-tion* **en diskussion**, a discussion; **en pension**, a pension; **en situation**, a situation

-tet **elektriciteten**, the electricity; **en identitet**, an identity; **en lokalitet**, a locality; **en popularitet**, a popularity; **en solidaritet**, a solidarity

Note 3 – Exceptions: **et fakultet**, a faculty; **et universitet**, a university

-or Occupations: **en direktør**, a director; **en frisør**, a hairdresser; **en konduktør**, a guard; **en massør**, a masseur

Note 4 – Nouns in **-ør** which are not occupations are neuter: **et eksteriør**, an exterior; **et interiør**, an interior; **et humør**, a mood

Feminines with the suffixes ***-esse,-inde, -ske, -ose,*** (see also 110(b),(c)):

en baronesse, a baroness; **en veninde**, a girl friend; **en husholderske**, a housekeeper; **en massøse**, a masseuse;

105 Neuter by meaning

The following types of noun are generally neuter by meaning:

(a) Words for many substances (but see also 112):

brød, bread; **glas**, glass; **guld**, gold; **jern**, iron; **kød**, meat; **papir**, paper; **snavs**, dirt; **sølv**, silver; **vand**, water

Note – Exceptions: **jorden**, the earth; **luften**, the air; **regnen**, the rain; **sneen**, the snow; **ulden**, the wool; **vinen**, the wine

(b) Areas and localities:

et amt, a county; **et distrikt**, a district; **et kontinent**, a continent; **et land**, a country; **et område**, an area; **et sogn**, a parish; **et torv**, a square

Note 1 – Exceptions: **en by**, a village; **en gård**, a farm; **en verden**, a world; **en ø**, an island

This rule also applies to proper nouns for geographical locations found in a definite noun phrase:

det lille Danmark, little Denmark; **det gamle Rom**, ancient Rome; **det nye København**, the new Copenhagen; **det økonomisk tilbagestående Sicilien**, the economically backward Sicily

When adjectives qualify proper nouns for countries and pronouns are used to refer back to the names of countries, these have neuter form, as the word **(et) land** is understood:

Vi bor i England. Det er grønt.	We live in England. It is green.
(Cf. **Landet er grønt.**	The country is green.)
Vi bor i Amerika. Det er stort.	We live in America. It is big.

When adjectives qualify proper nouns for mountains and oceans and when pronouns are used to refer back to the names of mountains and oceans, these have neuter form, as the words **(et) bjerg** and **(et) hav** are understood:

Vi så det sneklædte Ben Nevis. Det var smukt.	We saw the snow-covered Ben Nevis. It was beautiful.
(Cf. **det sneklædte bjerg**)	
Snowdon er kun 1100 m højt.	Snowdon is only 1,100 metres high.

Note 2 – When pronouns and adjectives are used to refer back to the names of towns and islands there is a tendency to use the common gender form, as **(en) by**, **(en) ø** are understood and the noun is regarded as common gender:

København er stor. Copenhagen is big. (Cf. **Byen er stor.**)
But: **det store København**

Odense – Aldersmæssigt kan den måle sig med Ålborg.
Odense – In age it can compete with Ålborg.

Note 3 – In the names of seas, lakes and rivers there is a tendency to use the common gender form, as **(en) sø**, **(en) flod**, **(en) å** are either explicit or understood, and the noun is treated as common gender:

den smukke Bodensø, beautiful Lake Constance; **den lange Donau**, the long Danube; **Gudenåen**, the Gudenå; **Nilen**, the Nile; **Themsen**, the Thames

(c) Names of letters of the alphabet (the noun **(et) bogstav**, a letter, is understood):

et langt u, a long u

(d) Other word classes used as nouns:

et hvorfor, a why; **jeget**, the ego; **et nej**, a no

Note – When the infinitive is used as a noun, a predicative adjective is inflected as if the infinitive has neuter gender. (See 528(c).)

(e) Many collectives nouns:

et folk, a people; **et følge**, a company; **et hold**, a team; **et selskab**, a society

Note – Exceptions: **en forsamling**, an assembly; **en gruppe**, a group

(f) Languages derived from adjectives (the noun **(et) sprog**, a language, is understood):

Jeg har glemt mit engelsk, I have forgotten my English; **det ældste dansk**, the oldest Danish

Note – A few of these take the end article **-en**:

dansken, the Danish language; **tysken**, the German language

106 Neuter by form

Nouns with the following suffixes are neuter gender by form:

-domme **et herredømme**, a mastery; **et hertugdømme**, a duchy; **et omdømme**, a reputation

-ed **et hoved**, a head; **et marked**, a market; **linnedet**, the linen; **lærredet**, the canvas

Note 1 – Exceptions: **en foged**, a bailiff; **en fælled**, a common; **en måned**, a month; **en ørred**, a trout

-em **et diadem**, a diadem; **et fonem**, a phoneme; **et system**, a system

-ende **et udseende**, an appearance; **et velbefindende**, a well-being

Note 2 – Exceptions: Some persons: **en gående**, a pedestrian; **en logerende**, a lodger; **en studerende**, a student; and also: **en ende**, an end; **en legende**, a legend. See also 529(b)(ii).

-ri **et bageri**, a bakery; **et batteri**, a battery; **et havari**, a shipwreck; **et menageri**, a menagerie

-(t)iv **et direktiv**, a directive; **et stativ**, a stand

Note 3 – Exception: **en kursiv**, an italic. Grammatical terms in **-iv** vary: Cases are common gender: **en akkusativ**, an accusative; **en genitiv**, a genitive; word classes are neuter gender: **et adjektiv**, an adjective; **et substantiv**, a noun

-um **et gymnasium**, a Sixth Form College; **et laboratorium**, a laboratory; **et museum**, a museum

B MISCELLANEOUS POINTS OF GENDER

107 Particularly difficult suffixes

It is best to check in a good dictionary the gender of dubious nouns such as the following.

(a) Nouns ending in the following suffixes are usually common gender but there are a number of exceptions:

-al **en filial**, a branch; **en kapital**, capital; **en lineal**, a ruler; **en original**, an original/an eccentric

But: **et areal**, an area; **et ideal**, an ideal; **et interval**, an interval; **et signal**, a signal

-ar People: **en aktuar**, an actuary; **en antikvar**, an antique dealer; **en bibliotekar**, a librarian; **en notar**, a notary
Others: **en hangar**, a hangar; **en hektar**, a hectare; **en katar**, catarrh

But: **et eksemplar**, a copy; **et honorar**, an honorarium; **et inventar**, an inventory; **et pessar**, a pessary; **et virvar**, a mess

-el **en bagatel**, a trifle; **en model**, a model; **en propel**, a propeller

But: **et hotel**, a hotel; **et kapel**, a chapel; **materiellet**, the equipment; **personellet**, the personnel

-ent People: **en agent**, an agent; **en docent**, a lecturer; **en klient**, a client; **en konsulent**, a consultant; **en konsument**, a consumer; **en patient**, a patient; **en student**, a student
Others: **en accent**, an accent; **cementen**, the cement

But: **et argument**, an argument; **et departement**, a department; **et dokument**, a document; **et eksperiment**, an experiment; **et element**, an element; **et instrument**, an instrument; **et kontinent**, a continent; **et moment**, a factor; **et ornament**, an ornament; **et patent**, a patent

-i **en epidemi**, an epidemic; **en fantasi**, an imagination; **en filosofi**, a philosophy; **fotografien**, photography; **en industri**, an industry; **(en) sympati**, sympathy

But: **et demokrati**, a democracy; **et fotografi**, a photograph; **et geni**, a genius; **et konditori**, a café; **et parti**, a political party; **politiet**, the police

(b) Nouns ending in **-at** are usually neuter but there are a number of exceptions:

et antikvariat, a second-hand bookshop; **et certifikat**, a certificate; **et format**, a format; **et internat**, an approved school; **et koncentrat**, a concentrate; **et konsulat**, a consulate

But: Some words for people: **en advokat**, a lawyer; **en delegat**, a delegate; **en demokrat**, a democrat
Some words for plants, etc.: **en salat**, a salad; **en tomat**, a tomato
Some others: **en automat**, a vending machine; **en undulat**, a budgerigar

(c) Nouns with the following suffixes may have either gender:

-sel Concrete: **et bidsel**, a bridle; **brænds(e)let**, the fuel; **et fængsel**, a prison; **et gidsel**, a hostage; **et hængsel**, a hinge
Abstract: **en advarsel**, a warning; **kørs(e)len**, driving; **en rædsel**, a terror; **en tilførsel**, a supply; **en trussel**, a threat

-skab Neuter: **et forfatterskab**, an authorship; **et fællesskab**, a community; **et medlemskab**, a membership; **et mesterskab**, a championship; **et redskab**, an implement; **et selskab**, a society; **et slægtskab**, a relationship; **et venskab**, a friendship; **et ægteskab**, a marriage

Common: **en dårskab**, a madness; **en egenskab**, a quality; **en galskab**, a madness; **en klogskab**, a wisdom; **en lidenskab**, a passion; **en troskab**, a loyalty; **en videnskab**, a science

108 Gender of abbreviations and nouns of foreign origin

(a) There are no hard and fast rules for genders of abbreviations in Danish. For indigenous words and words treated as indigenous the gender is often the same as for the unabbreviated noun:

> **en bh (en brystholder/busteholder)**, a bra; **et tv (et fjernsyn)**, a TV; **et wc** (cf. **et kloset**), a WC

When the original is no longer obvious there is a tendency to treat the abbreviation as a neuter singular concept:

> **det statsdrevne DSB** (cf. **Danske Statsbaner**), the state-run Danish Railways

Foreign abbreviations, especially English ones, are often treated as neuter singular:

> **det britiske BBC**, the British BBC
> **det magtesløse FN**, the powerless United Nations
> **det store USA**, the big United States of America

Note – **en/et pH**, a pH value

(b) Most recent loans into Danish are from English, which, unlike e.g. Latin, Greek or German, possesses no grammatical gender or formal clues, and is thus not able to guide Danes in the choice of gender. The following general principles apply to the gender of loans:

(i) People and animals

Most nouns for persons and animals are common gender in line with indigenous nouns (cf. 103(a),(b)):

> **en bodyguard**; **en fan**; **en kænguru**, a kangaroo; **en orangutang**; **en playboy**; **en stand-in**

(ii) Form

In some cases the final syllable of a noun determines the gender.

Nouns in **-um**: The Latin neuter has long been established in Danish:

> **et faktum**, a fact; **et gymnasium**, a Sixth Form College

Nouns in **-ment**:

et fundament, a foundation; **et regiment**, a regiment

Nouns in **-erie**: The Greek feminine determines the Danish gender:

en arterie, an artery; **en materie**, a substance

Sometimes this system is disturbed.

Nouns in **-tek**: A Greek feminine ending, but neuter in Danish:

et apotek, a chemist's shop; **et bibliotek**, a library; thus by analogy new words in **-tek** are neuter: **et diskotek**, a discotheque; **et videotek**, a videotheque

New nouns in **-er**, **-ing**, **-or**, **-tion** tend to be of common gender:

en computer, en sightseeing, en editor, en sales promotion

These two principles are paramount, but there are some other tendencies that operate in specific cases ((iii)–(vi) below):

(iii) Formal similarity to a Danish noun

If a loan clearly resembles an indigenous noun there is a strong tendency to adopt the gender of that noun by analogy:

	By analogy with:
et college	**et kollegium**, a student hall of residence
et mart	**et marked**, a market
et party (social gathering)	**et parti**, a (political) party
et showroom	**et rum**, a space

(iv) By analogy with a group of Danish words of similar meaning (cf. 105(b), notes 2, 3):

- Clothes are often common gender: **en cardigan, en jumper, en sweater** (cf. **en bluse, en trøje**)
- Boats are often common gender: **en brig, en skonnert**, a schooner (cf. **en båd**)

- Types of dance and music are often common gender: **en blues, jazzen** (cf. **en dans, musikken**)
- Types of car are often common gender: **en BMW, en jeep** (cf. **en bil**)
- Types of dog are often common gender: **en bulldog, en collie** (cf. **en hund**)

(v) Actions

Nouns that indicate actions or events and are derived from verb stems tend to be neuter in Danish:

at råb/e ⇨ **et råb**, a shout; **at løb/e** ⇨ **et løb**, a run

In the same way, most nouns borrowed from English verb stems are neuter:

et check (but: **en (bank)check**); **et ræs**, a race

(vi) The closest translation

The gender of the closest Danish synonym appears to play a role in determining gender in some cases:

et band	cf. **et orkester**
en suit-case	cf. **en kuffert**
et team	cf. **et hold**

109 Compound nouns

Compound nouns nearly always take the gender of the second element of the compound, as it is onto this that the inflexional endings are added:

en skole + et køkken	⇨	**et skolekøkken**, a school kitchen
et køkken + en maskine	⇨	**en køkkenmaskine**, a kitchen appliance

Exceptions are often found when the second element loses its original meaning:

et bogstav, a letter of the alphabet	cf. **en stav**, a stave
en gråskæg, a grey-beard	cf. **et skæg**, a beard
et måltid, a meal	cf. **en tid**, a time

Some plants:

en okseøje, an oxeye daisy	cf. **et øje**, an eye
en tornblad, a gorse bush	cf. **et blad**, a leaf

110 Masculines and feminines

See also 103(a).

(a) Generally speaking, lexical distinctions are nowadays employed to distinguish male and female:

andrik, drake	**and**, duck
dreng, boy	**pige**, girl
enkemand, widower	**enke**, widow
fætter, male cousin	**kusine**, female cousin
hane, cock	**høne**, hen
hingst, stallion	**hoppe**, mare
konge, king	**dronning**, queen
tyr, bull	ko, cow

(b) Until quite recently matrimonial feminines were common, and were indicated by a feminine suffix, but they are now rarely encountered:

amtmand, prefect of a county	**amtmandinde**, prefect's wife
bisp, bishop	**bispinde**, bishop's wife
general, general	**generalinde**, general's wife
oberst, colonel	**oberstinde**, colonel's wife
pastor, pastor	**pastorinde**, pastor's wife
professor, professor	**professorinde**, professor's wife
rektor, headmaster	**rektorinde**, headmaster's wife

A few are still current, however:

baron, baron	**baronesse**, baroness
greve, count	**grevinde**, countess
hertug, duke	**hertuginde**, duchess
prins, prince	**prinsesse**, princess

Without any matrimonial link:

abbed, abbot	**abbedisse**, abbess

(c) Functional titles

(i) Functional feminines in **-inde**, **-ske**, **-trice**, etc., have been severely curtailed in recent years, and nowadays men and women often have the same titles:

lærer and **lærerinde** ⇨ **lærer**, teacher
forretningsindehaver and **forretningsindehaverske** ⇨ **forretningsindehaver**, proprietor (of a business)

nabo and **naboerske** ⇨ **nabo**, neighbour
direktør and **direktrice** ⇨ **direktør**, director

This also applies to some nationality words:

englænder and **englænderinde** ⇨ **englænder**, Englishman, Englishwoman

Note 1 – **En nordmand**, Norwegian (of either gender); **en franskmand**, Frenchman or French woman.

A few titles considered 'sexist' have been provided with feminine equivalents:

formand ⇨ **forkvinde**, chairwoman

Some new neutral titles have also appeared in recent years to avoid using 'sexist' titles:

folketingsmand ⇨ **folketingsmedlem**, MP
tillidsmand ⇨ **tillidsrepræsentant**, shop steward

However, some feminine job titles have not been masculinized:

flyværtinde, **stewardesse**, (male or female) member of cabin crew; **sygeplejerske**, nurse (both male and female) and others in **-plejerske**

Note 2 – **En sygeplejer** is a nursing auxiliary of either gender.

Some job titles in **-mand** still apply equally to women, where necessary with the word **kvindelig** (female, woman) in front:

amtsrådsformand, chairman of county council; **ombudsmand**, ombudsman; **styrmand**, first officer; **vognmand**, haulier

(ii) In some cases forms with the feminine suffix are retained where the gender of the person is significant:

elsker	**elskerinde**	lover
helt	**heltinde**	hero(ine)
samlever	**samleverske**	live-in partner

ven	**veninde**	(boy/girl) friend
vært	**værtinde**	host(ess)

(iii) In a few cases forms with the feminine suffix are sometimes seen in titles:

husholderske, housekeeper; **sangerinde**, singer; **skuespillerinde**, actress; **tiggerske**, beggar

Note 3 – The animal names: **løvinde**, lioness; **ulvinde**, female wolf

111 Double forms

A number of nouns possess double forms. In the examples below the more usual gender is given first. There are a number of different reasons for this vagueness as to gender.

(a) The noun is generally used in a form without the article:

(et) besvær, trouble

Jeg ville ikke volde dig besvær.	I didn't want to cause you any trouble.
Det er ikke meget besvær.	It's not much trouble.
al den/alt det besvær	all this trouble

sigt -en, sight, may be either gender in phrases: **på lang(t) sigt**, in the long term

Other indigenous nouns that have double gender are: **djævelskab**, nuisance; **efterskrift**, postscript; **gavn**, benefit; **men**, injury; **sjov**, fun; **tant**, vanity; **tidsfordriv**, pastime; **urede**, mess; **vemod**, sadness

This especially applies to words for substances, otherwise often neuter (cf. 105(a)). See also 112.

(b) The noun **en slags** is partitive and unstressed and often acquires the gender of the noun following:

en slags abe, a kind of ape	cf. **en abe**
et slags menneske, a kind of human being	cf. **et menneske**

But:

Den slags mennesker afskyr jeg.	I detest that kind of person.

(c) Some foreign loans may vary in gender:

approach -en (-et); en (et) hardware

Others: **bacon**; **carte blanche**; **cirkus**; **city**; **domino**; **enfant terrible**; **fokus**; **fond**, fund; **game**; **harakiri**; **katalog**; **kitsch**; **patois**; **sample**; **software**; **species**; **swing**; **understatement**

(d) A few nouns have a different gender when used in set phrases (see also (a) above):

et gab, a gap	**Døren står på vid gab**. The door stands wide open.
et minut, a minute	**på minutten/minuttet**, precisely

Notice also:

ensporet, single-track	cf. **et spor**, a track
enøjet, one-eyed	cf. **et øje**, an eye

But:

enbenet/etbenet, one-legged	cf. **et ben**, a leg
en etårig kontrakt, a one-year contract	

Notice also:

et enetages hus, a one-storey building	cf. **en etage**
Colloquially **et etetages hus**	
en etværelses lejlighed, a one-room flat	cf. **et værelse**
Colloquially **en enværelses lejlighed**	

See also 302.

112 Gender and substances

See also 105(a), 210(b).

(a) Many nouns denoting substances are neuter:

brødet, the bread; **jernet**, the iron; **papiret**, the paper; **saltet**, the salt

Some are common gender:

cementen, the cement; **jorden**, the soil; **stenen**, the rock; **ulden**, the wool; **vinen**, the wine

Some, however, have double gender:

gummi-en (-et), the rubber; **jod-et (-en)**, the iodine; **kanel-en (-et)**, the cinnamon; **klister-et (-en)**, the glue; **klor-et (-en)**, the chlorine

Others include: **flødeskum**, whipped cream; **koffein**, caffein; **kokain**, cocaine; **lak**, lacquer; **malt**, malt; **nylon**, nylon; **plast**, plastic; **polystyren**, polystyrene; **svovl**, sulphur; **zink**, zinc

(b) Notice the possible use of a neuter article or adjective with a common gender noun when denoting type or selection:

fedfattig(t) mælk, low fat milk	cf. **mælk-en**
det/den bedste mad, the best food	cf. **mad-en**
det/den bedste landbrugsjord, the best agricultural soil	cf. **jord-en**

Note 1 – Some common gender nouns for substances are used with the neuter form of the pronoun:

Vi får noget sne.	We'll get some snow.
Alt det regn vi fik ...	All the rain we got ...
Han har meget fantasi.	He has a lot of imagination.
Vil du tørre det mælk op!	Will you mop up that milk!

Note 2 – In some Jutland dialects all non-count nouns consistently have neuter gender and all count nouns common gender:

det sne, the snow; **det regn**, the rain; but: **den æg**, the egg; **den træ**, the tree

(c) Rather more unusually, and often in technical or trade jargon, some neuter nouns denoting substances can be common gender when used of a specific type or quantity:

en billig lærred, a cheap (type of) canvas	cf. **lærredet**
den danske salt, Danish salt	cf. **saltet**

This also applies to some nouns with double gender under (a) above.

(d) Some neuter nouns that may be regarded as either non-count or count may be common gender when used as countables:

en øl, a (bottle or glass of) beer	cf. **øllet**
en vand, a (bottle or glass of) soft drink	cf. **vandet**
en rugbrød med leverpostej a slice of rye bread with liver pâté	cf. **brødet**

C PLURAL NOUN FORMS

113 Plural of indigenous nouns

(a) Danish has three indigenous ways of forming the plural of nouns, and Danish nouns are divided into declensions according to the way in which the plural is formed.

First Declension		*Second Declension*		*Third Declension*	
Ending in -(e)r		*Ending in -e*		*Zero ending* (no plural form)	
en by a town	**to byer** two towns	**en krig** a war	**to krige** two wars	**en fejl** a mistake	**to fejl** two mistakes
et menneske a human being	**to mennesker** two human beings	**et land** a country	**to lande** two countries	**et flag** a flag	**to flag** two flags

(b) These declensions are outlined in 115–17. There are also some irregular plural forms detailed in these paragraphs. Some nouns in current usage loaned from foreign languages have retained their own foreign plural endings, and these are dealt with in 119ff. For some clues as to how to predict the plural forms of nouns see 114.

(c) It is worth noting the general orthographical rule (explained in 1305) that Danish consonants are doubled between two vowels when the first of these is a short stressed vowel. This affects the plural and definite forms of some nouns:

en bus a bus	**bussen** the bus	**busser** buses	**busserne** the buses
et bær a berry	**bærret** the berry	**bær** berries	**bærrene** the berries

This also applies to the following consonants after unstressed vowels: **-p**, **-t**, **-k**, **-g** (pronounced [g]), and the suffix **-dom**:

sennep	**senneppen**	**sennepper**	**sennepperne**, mustard
idræt	**idrætten**	**idrætter**	**idrætterne**, sport
sygdom	**sygdommen**	**sygdomme**	**sygdommene**, illness

114 Nouns – plural indefinite forms: predictability

(a) Although it is impossible to provide hard and fast rules, the plural forms of Danish nouns are to some extent predictable. Approximately 60% of indigenous nouns have plurals in **-(e)r**, and 25% in **-e**, while 15% have a zero plural (i.e. have the same form in the plural as they do in the singular). The decisive factors in the choice of a plural ending are listed below, but note that these only represent general rules and that there are some exceptions.

(b) Complexity

Monosyllables that are common gender and end in a consonant add **-e**:

en vej – veje, road

Monosyllables that are neuter and end in a consonant have zero plural:

et æg – æg, egg

Polysyllabic nouns ending in **-e** take **-r**:

en rose – roser, rose

Polysyllabic nouns that are not compounds (and do not end in **-e**) take **-er**:

et køkken – køkkener, kitchen

(c) Stress

Polysyllabic nouns with stress on the last syllable (often loanwords) take **-(e)r**:

en a'vis – aviser, newspaper

Nouns ending in a stressed vowel take **-(e)r**:

en by – byer, town

Nouns with stress shift (loans) take **-er**:

en ˈlektor – lekˈtorer, lecturer

Nouns ending in unstressed **-er** take **-e**:

en lærer – lærere, teacher

(d) Origin

Foreign loans often take **-er**:

en eksport – eksporter, export

(e) Derivatives with certain endings

Nouns ending in **-dom** take **-e** (with doubling of the **m**, cf. 113(c)):

en sygdom – sygdomme, illness

Nouns ending in **-hed** take **-er**:

en svaghed – svagheder, weakness

Nouns ending in **-i** take **-er**:

et bageri – bagerier, bakery

Nouns ending in **-ion** take **-er**:

en station – stationer, station

Nouns ending in **-skab** take **-er**:

et venskab – venskaber, friendship

(f) Proper nouns and words from other word classes used as nouns take **-(e)r** (cf. 115 (a)(iii), but see also 133(c)):

to Sørener og tre Marianner, two Sørens and three Mariannes
alle men'er og hvis'er, all the ifs and buts

115 The first declension: plural in -(e)r

(a) The first declension includes:

(i) Almost all nouns ending in a vowel. These are of two types.

1 Nouns ending in unstressed **-e** take **-r** (see below):

> **en krone – kroner**, a crown; **en lampe – lamper**, a lamp; **et billede – billeder**, a picture; **et menneske – mennesker**, a human being; **et vindue – vinduer**, a window

2 Nouns ending in a stressed vowel (or unstressed **-a**) take **-er**:

> **en by – byer**, a town; **et drama – dramaer**, a drama; **en kollega – kolleg(a)er**, a colleague; **en ske – skeer**, a spoon; **en sky – skyer**, a cloud; **et tema – temaer**, a theme; **en villa – villaer**, a detached house; **en å – åer**, a small river; **en ø – øer**, an island

Note – Exceptions: The following have zero plural: **et frø – frø**, a seed; **en sko – sko**, a shoe; **et strå – strå**, a straw. See 117.

(ii) Most polysyllabic nouns, especially derivatives and loanwords. Many of these have end stress:

> **en a'vis – aviser**, a newspaper; **et biblio'tek – biblioteker**, a library; **et kon'tor – kontorer**, an office; **et pa'pir – papirer**, a piece of paper; **en para'ply – paraplyer**, an umbrella; **en ro'man – romaner**, a novel; **en sol'dat – soldater**, a soldier; **en sta'tion – stationer**, a station; **en tele'fon – telefoner**, a telephone; **en tu'rist – turister**, a tourist; **et universi'tet – universiteter**, a university

This group includes all nouns ending in **-hed**, **-skab** (cf. 107(c)):

> **berømtheder**, celebrities; **dumheder**, idiocies; **dårskaber**, follies; **enheder**, units; **landskaber**, landscapes; **selskaber**, societies; **skønheder**, beauties; **venskaber**, friendships; **videnskaber**, sciences; **vittigheder**, jokes

(iii) Personal names and place names (see 133(c)):

> **Der var flere Marier og Larser.**
> There were several Maries and Larses.

Hvor mange Nykøbinger er der i Danmark?
How many Nykøbings are there in Denmark?

i de to Amerikaer
in the two Americas

(b) Basic rules:

First declension nouns add the plural ending **-er** to the stem:

en blomst	flower	**blomster**	**et sted**	place	**steder**
en by	town	**byer**	**et træ**	tree	**træer**

This group includes all nouns ending in **-ed** and most bisyllabic nouns ending in an unstressed syllable:

en fælled	common	**fælleder**	**en ˈbolig**	home	**boliger**
et marked	market	**markeder**	**et ˈbryllup**	wedding	**bryllupper**
			(cf. 113(c))		

First declension nouns ending in unstressed **-e** add **-r** to the stem:

en kvinde	woman	**kvinder**	**et menneske**	human being	**mennesker**

Others include: **en dame**, a lady; **et frimærke**, a postage stamp; **en færge**, a ferry; **en kirke**, a church; **en myre**, an ant; **en pige**, a girl; **en rejse**, a journey; **en skole**, a school; **en uge**, a week; **en vare**, a product; **en åre**, an oar

(c) Nouns ending in unstressed **-el** often drop the **-e-** of the stem before adding the plural ending in **-er**:

en cykel	cycle	**cykler**

Common gender: **en aksel**, an axle; **en artikel**, an article; **en bibel**, a bible; **en cirkel**, a circle; **en fabel**, a fable; **en kedel**, a kettle; **en længsel**, a longing; **en onkel**, an uncle; **en regel**, a rule; **en snabel**, a snout; **en titel**, a title

Neuter: **et eksempel**, an example; **et fængsel**, a prison; **et kabel**, a cable; **et mirakel**, a miracle; **et møbel**, a piece of furniture; **et spektakel**, a spectacle; **et stempel**, a stamp; **et tempel**, a temple; **et varsel**, a warning; **et æsel**, an ass

Some nouns drop a consonant, as a double consonant cannot precede **-l**, **-n**, **-r**: **en gaffel – gafler**, fork; **en kartoffel – kartofler**, potato; **et middel – midler**, means; **en pukkel – pukler**, hump; **en seddel – sedler**, note; **en skammel – skamler**, footstool

Note 1 – Exceptions that do not drop the stem **-e-** include:

en kennel – kenneler, a kennel; **en tunnel – tunneler**, a tunnel

Note 2 – Nouns in stressed **-el** are rare, but they do not drop the stem **-e-**:

et hotel – hoteller, hotel; **en propel – propeller**, propeller

Note 3 – A few nouns for religious concepts ending in unstressed **-el** take a plural in **-e**:

en apostel – apostle, apostle; **en discipel – disciple**, disciple; **en djævel – djævle**, devil; **en engel – engle**, angel; **en himmel – himle**, heaven, sky

(d) Most nouns in **-en** do not drop the stem **-e-** before adding the plural ending **-er**:

en eksamen – eksamener (or **eksaminer**), examination; **en helgen – helgener**, saint; **et køkken – køkkener**, kitchen; **et pronomen – pronomener** (or **pronominer**), pronoun; **en præ(di)ken – præ(di)kener**, sermon; **verden – verd(e)ner**, world

Note – Exceptions: A few may, however, optionally drop the stem **-e-** in the plural as for nouns in **-el**:

en figen – fig(e)ner, fig; **en frøken – frøk(e)ner**, unmarried woman; **en hilsen – hils(e)ner**, greeting; **et lagen – lag(e)ner**, sheet

(e) Some nouns modify the root vowel before adding the plural ending **-(e)r**:

Vowel change:

A > Æ:	**and – ænder**, duck; **kraft – kræfter**, power; **nat – nætter**, night; **stang – stænger**, pole; **tand – tænder**, tooth; **tang – tænger**, pair of tongs
A > Æ with vowel lengthening:	**stad – stæder**, city
O > Ø:	**bog – bøger**, book; **bonde – bønder**, farmer; **klo – kløer**, claw; **ko – køer**, cow; **so – søer**, sow

O > Ø with vowel shortening: **fod – fødder**, foot; **rod – rødder**, root

Å > Æ: **hånd – hænder**, hand; **rå – ræer**, yard (on ship); **tå – tæer**, toe

(f) Some neuter nouns ending in **-ium** drop the **-um** before adding the plural ending **-er**:

et gymnasium	**gymnasier**	Sixth Form College

Like **gymnasium** are: **akvarium**, aquarium; **evangelium**, gospel; **kollegium**, hall of residence; **kompendium**, compendium; **kriterium**, criterion; **laboratorium**, laboratory; **medium** (or **medie**), medium; **ministerium**, ministry; **privilegium**, privilege; **seminarium**, teachers' training college; **stadium**, stage; **studium**, study; **terrarium**, terrarium

Notice also some nouns in **-(e)um** that drop **-um**:

et museum	**museer**	museum
et verbum	**verber**	verb

Cf. plurals in **-a** in (g) below and in 121, 137(e).

(g) Some nouns in **-um**, **-us** have two alternative forms, the Latin plural in **-a** and the Danish plural in **-er** (cf. 121):

et forum	**fora/forum(m)er**	forum
et feminimum	**feminina/femininer**	feminine
en/et virus	**vira/virus/virus(s)er**	virus

Notice also:

et kursus	**kursus/kurser**	course

(h) Some nouns ending in **-a** either add the **-er** to the original singular form or alternatively drop the **-a** and add **-er** (cf. 121):

en kollega	**kollegaer/kolleger**	colleague

But:

et firma	**firmaer**	firm

(i) Most nouns in **-or** with plurals in **-er** have stress shift:

en ´motor	**mo´torer**	engine
en ´pastor	**pa´storer**	pastor

Like **motor** are: **elevator,** lift; **faktor,** factor; **junior,** junior; **professor,** professor; **rektor,** headmaster; **senior,** senior; **traktor,** tractor

Note 1 – **En kon´ditor – kon´ditorer,** baker, does not have stress shift.

Note 2 – In colloquial Danish some of these nouns do not have stress shift in the plural:

´motorer, ´traktorer

Note 3 – The English loans **bachelor, tutor,** among some academic titles, conform to this pattern.

(j) Vowel lengthening occurs in some monosyllabic nouns ending in a short vowel plus **-d**:

en gud	**guder**	god
en rad	**rader**	line
en stad	**stæder**	city
et sted	**steder**	place

(k) The ‘stød’ (marked ’), i.e. the glottal stop, is generally retained in the plural of nouns, but is lost in the plural of some nouns, including:

(i) those ending in **-l-**, **-n-**, **-r-** plus a consonant:

byl’t	**bylter**	bundle
prin’s	**prinser**	prince
sor’g	**sorger**	grief

(ii) those ending in **-l**, **-n**, and **-nd**, **-rd** where the **d** is silent:

fræv’l	**trævler**	thread
bøn’	**bønner**	prayer
stund’	**stunder**	while
jord’	**jorder**	land

(l) The ‘stød’ is added before the plural ending of all foreign loans with a plural in **-er** and of other word classes used as nouns:

et drama	**drama'er**	drama
et ja	**ja'er**	yes

(m) For plural definite forms see 138.

116 The second declension: plural in **-e**

(a) The second declension includes:

(i) Many monosyllabic common gender nouns ending in a consonant:

en del – dele, part; **en dreng – drenge**, boy; **en fugl – fugle**, bird; **en krig – krige**, war; **en løgn – løgne**, lie; **en stol – stole**, chair; **en vej – veje**, road

(ii) Some monosyllabic neuter nouns:

et bord – borde, table; **et brev – breve**, letter; **et hus – huse**, house; **et land – lande**, country

(iii) All nouns ending in unstressed **-er** (see also (c) below):

en arbejder – arbejdere, worker; **en kunstner – kunstnere**, artist; **en lærer – lærere**; teacher; **en russer – russere**, Russian; **en svensker – svenskere**, Swede; **en århusianer – århusianere**, inhabitant of Århus

(iv) All nouns ending in **-dom**:

These double the **-m** in the plural: **en ejendom – ejendomme**, property; **en sygdom – sygdomme**, illness (cf. 113(c)).

(b) Basic rule:

Second declension nouns add the plural ending **-e** to the stem:

et bord	a table	**borde**	tables
et brev	a letter	**breve**	letters
en kat	a cat	**katte**	cats
en sang	a song	**sange**	songs

(c) Nouns in **-er** often keep (or can keep) the **-e** of the stem in the plural:

en bager – bagere, baker; **en kælder – kæld(e)re**, basement; **en køber – købere**, buyer; **en revolver – revolvere**, revolver

But many drop the stem **-e** in the plural (common gender except where indicated):

brødre, brothers (cf. **en bro(de)r**); **fibre**, fibres; **filtre** (n.), filters; **fingre**, fingers; **fædre**, fathers (cf. **en fa(de)r**); **hylstre** (n.), cases; **klostre** (n.), convents; **ministre**, ministers; **orkestre** (n.), orchestras; **skuldre**, shoulders; **svogre**, brothers-in-law; **søstre**, sisters; **teatre** (n.), theatres; **vintre**, winters

Where two identical consonants would otherwise be followed by another consonant, one of them is dropped:

en datter	**døtre**	daughter
et nummer	**numre**	number
et offer	**ofre**	victim
en sommer	**somre**	summer

(d) This declension includes some common gender nouns denoting people and ending in **-ing**:

flygtninge, refugees; **islændinge**, Icelanders; **lærlinge**, apprentices; **nævninge**, jury members; **oldinge**, old men; **slægtninge**, relatives; **udlændinge**, foreigners; **ynglinge**, youngsters

The following nouns have alternative forms: **dødninge(r)**, ghosts; **hedninge(r)**, heathens; **høvdinge(r)**, chieftains; **opkomlinge(r)**, parvenus; **uslinge(r)**, wretches

Note – Exceptions: Many other words ending in **-ing**, **-ling** take **-er**:

forretninger, businesses; **indledninger**, introductions; **meninger**, opinions; **muslinger**, mussels

This is also true of some words for people:

arvinger, heirs; **dronninger**, queens; **kællinger**, old women; **tvillinger**, twins

It is also true of the names of some types of fish:

brislinger, sprats; **fjæsinger**, greater weever fish; **hvillinger**, whiting

(e) This declension includes some nouns denoting family relationships that change the stem vowel before adding the plural in **-e**:

en bror (broder)	**brødre**	brother
en datter	**døtre**	daughter
en far (fader)	**fædre**	father
en mor (moder)	**mødre**	mother

(f) Notice the following irregular plural:

et øje	**øjne**	eye

(g) Vowel lengthening occurs in the plurals of monosyllabic nouns ending in a short vowel plus **-d** or **-v** (cf. 136(g)).:

et blad	**blade**	leaf
et hav	**have**	ocean
en lov	**love**	law

(h) Nouns with a 'stod' (marked ') usually lose this in the plural form in **-e**:

en de'l	**dele**	part
en fu'gl	**fugle**	bird
et hu's	**huse**	house
en skov'	**skove**	wood
en sto'l	**stole**	chair

(i) For plural definite forms see 138.

117 The third declension: zero plural

These nouns do not add a plural ending.

(a) The third declension includes:

(i) Many monosyllabic neuter nouns:

et brød – brød, (loaf of) bread; **et bær – bær**, berry; **et dyr – dyr**, animal; **et flag – flag**, flag; **et folk – folk**, people; **et glas – glas**, glass; **et hjem – hjem**, home; **et kort – kort**, card; **et liv – liv**, life; **et lys – lys**, light; **et mål – mål**, goal; **et par – par**, pair; **et pas – pas**, passport; **et skæg – skæg**, beard; **et sprog – sprog**, language; **et tal – tal**, number; **et uvejr – uvejr**, storm; **et æg – æg**, egg; **et år – år**, year

Note – **Et tog**, a train, has two possible plural forms: **tog/toge**.

(ii) Some polysyllabic nouns ending in a consonant:

et fjernsyn – fjernsyn, television; **et forhold – forhold**, relationship; **et forsøg – forsøg**, attempt; **et spørgsmål – spørgsmål**, question

(iii) Some monosyllabic common gender nouns:

en fejl – fejl, mistake; **en fisk – fisk**, fish; **en mus – mus**, mouse; **en sko – sko**, shoe; **en sten – sten**, stone; **en ting – ting**, thing; **en tvivl – tvivl**, doubt

(iv) Some nouns ending in **-ende** (many of them denoting temporary occupations and formed from the present participles of verbs):

en gående – gående, pedestrian; **en rejsende – rejsende**, traveller; **en studerende – studerende**, student; **en troende – troende**, believer

(v) The noun **et tilfælde**, pl. **tilfælde** (coincidence) fits into no pattern.

(b) Basic rule:

Third declension nouns add no plural ending:

en sko	a shoe	**sko**	shoes
et æg	an egg	**æg**	eggs

(c) Some nouns show plural by changing the stem vowel in the plural:

et barn	a child	**børn**	children
en gås	a goose	**gæs**	geese
en mand	a man	**mænd**	men

(d) For plural definite forms see 138.

118 Plurals and compound nouns

Normally only the second element in a noun compound takes the plural ending:

en skolepige – skolepiger	**en pigeskole – pigeskoler**
a schoolgirl	a girls' school

There are a few exceptions, however, in which both elements take (or may take) the plural form:

et barnebarn – børnebørn	a grandchild
en barnefødsel – barnefødsler/børnefødsler	childbirth

Like **en barnefødsel** are: **barnehoved**, child's head; **barneseng**, child's bed; **barnesko**, child's shoe; **barneskole**, children's school; **barnestol**, child's chair

Note 1 – Some compounds with **barne-** have an alternative singular form in **børne-**:

barnecykel/børnecykel – barnecykler/børnecykler, child's bicycle

In new formations there is a tendency only to use **børne-** as the first element:

et børnebibliotek, children's library; **børnebegrænsning**, family planning; **børnepenge**, child maintenance; **en børnehave**, a kindergarten; **en børnelæge**, a paediatrician

Note 2 – When the compound only refers to one child, however, the first element is **barne-**:

barnestørrelse, child's size; **barnetro**, childhood faith

This also applies to some fixed cases: **barnedåb**, infant baptism; **barnepige**, nanny; **barnevogn**, pram

Some compounds in **bonde-** have alternative plural forms:

en bondedreng – bondedrenge or **bønderdrenge**	country boy
en bondepige – bondepiger or **bønderpiger**	country girl

Some other compound nouns have a plural form in the first element:

mødrehjem, home for mothers; **mødrerum**, room for nursing mothers; **Mødrehjælpen**, the National Council for the Unmarried Mother and her Child; **Brødremenigheden**, The Moravian Brethren

119 Plurals of loans

Over recent years efforts have been made on the part of language planners to encourage the replacement of foreign plural endings so as to allow the adaptation of loan-words into the Danish inflexional pattern. There is now a consistent policy for this adaptation, but in some cases foreign plurals are still in common use, not least in advertising and the media. For genders of loans see 108.

120 English loans with original plurals in **-s**

(a) Most nouns borrowed from foreign languages, and especially those from English – many of which previously had a plural in **-s** – now have plural forms in **-(e)r**, **-e** or zero. The **-s** plural declension frequently offers a temporary refuge to loan words which are later adapted to Danish inflexional patterns:

en baby – babyer; en bar – barer; en bus – busser; en film – film; en folder – foldere; en lift – lifte(r); et job – job; en single – singler; et trip – trip

(b) English nouns with a stem ending in **-er** generally take the plural ending **-e**:

en bestseller – bestsellere; en computer – computere; en container – containere; en gangster – gangstere; en manager – managere; en reporter – reportere; en pullover – pullovere; en sweater – sweatere; en trailer – trailere

(c) A few loans with **-s** plurals have an alternative zero ending:

heats/heat; tricks/trick

(d) A small group of nouns with plurals in **-s** remains, including:

(i) Nouns occurring mostly in plural or collective (non-count) forms. (These have a definite plural in **-ene**. See 137.)

cornflakes, jeans, odds, pickles, shorts

(ii) Others where alternative Danish endings are found:

checks/check, cocktails/cocktail, cowboys/cowboyer, fotos/fotoer, jeeps/jeeper, shows/show, tests/test

(e) For plural definite forms see 137.

121 Latin loans ending in **-um**, **-ium**, **-us**, **-a**

(a) Some Latin loans ending in **-um**, **-us** retain their original Latin plurals in **-a**, **-i** (see 115(f),(g)):

et faktum	**fakta**	fact
et maksimum	**maksima**	maximum
et genus	**genera/genus**	gender

en musikus	**musici**	musician

(b) A few nouns have alternative plural forms, i.e. Latin or Danish:

en/et femininum	**feminina/femininer**	feminine
et referendum	**referenda/referendum(m)er**	referendum
et serum	**sera/serum(m)er**	serum

Note – **Et medium – medier** (medium) retains the Latin plural **media** when used of the mass media.

(c) The Danish inflexion is on occasion found added to the original singular:

et drama	**dramaer**	drama
en farao	**faraoner/faraoer**	pharaoh
en kollega	**kolleg(a)er**	colleague
et tema	**temaer**	theme

(d) Some loans in **-um** drop the **-um** and add the Danish plural ending **-er** (see also 115(f)):

et amfibium	**amfibier**	amphibian
et centrum	**centrer**	centre
et glossarium	**glossarier**	glossary
et kriterium	**kriterier**	criterion
et museum	**museer**	museum
et observatorium	**observatorier**	observatory
et territorium	**territorier**	territory

Four nouns ending in **-ium** have alternative singular forms in **-ie**:

et kranium/kranie	**kranier**	cranium
et medium/medie	**medier**	medium
et ovarium/ovarie	**ovarier**	ovary
en/et spatium/spatie	**spatier**	space

Some other nouns are found in **-ie** in the singular in colloquial Danish but these forms are not yet accepted as good written Danish:

et gymnasium/gymnasie	**gymnasier**	Sixth Form College
et imperium/imperie	**imperier**	empire
et solarium/solarie	**solarier**	solarium

This can be explained not only by analogy with the plural indefinite form in **-ier**, but also with the definite singular in **-iet** and the compound form in **-ie**:

akvarier	aquaria
seminariet	the teachers' training college
kollegieværelse	student room

(e) Notice also two nouns ending in **-en** that have plurals in **-er** with alternative plural forms where the stem changes from **-en** to **-in**:

eksamen	**eksaminer/eksamener**	examination
pronomen	**pronominer/pronomener**	pronoun

122 Loans ending in -o

(a) Most loans ending in **-o**, from whatever source, have only Danish inflexion in which the **-o** is retained:

en avocado	**avocadoer**
en cello	**celloer**

Others include: **bistro**, **espresso**, **fiasko**, **ghetto**, **libretto**, **logo**, **memento**, **piano**, **radio**, **video**

Note 1 – Some nouns have alternative plural forms in **-os**:

cigarilloer/cigarillos, desperadoer/desperados, fotoer/fotos

These have plural definites in **-oerne**: **fotoerne**.

Note 2 – Two currencies ending in **-o** have no Danish plural in the indefinite form: **pesos, escudos**.

Note 3 – **En fresko – freskoer** (fresco) has a Danish alternative: **en freske – fresker**.

(b) Some loans, mostly in the fields of banking and music, have both an original Italian plural and a Danish alternative where **-er** is added to the Italian singular form:

et intermezzo	**intermezzi/intermezzoer**	intermezzo
en konto	**konti/kontoer**	account
en risiko	**risici/risikoer**	risk
en saldo	**saldi/saldoer**	balance
en solo	**soli/soloer**	solo
et tempo	**tempi/tempoer**	tempo

Note – In a few cases a form in **-ier** is found:

en impresario	**impresari(o)er**
et scenario	**scenari(o)er**

(c) For plural definite forms see 137.

123 Nouns – plural indefinite forms: summary chart

Alternative forms are shown with oblique slashes. Numbers refer to paragraphs.

Para.	*Singular*	*Plural*	*Plural ending*	*Meaning*
115 FIRST DECLENSION			**-er**	
COMMON GENDER				
	en sky	**skyer**		cloud
	en motor	**motorer**		engine
	en artikel	**artikler**		article
	en måned	**måneder**		month
	en fod	**fødder**		foot
	en hånd	**hænder**		hand
NEUTER				
	et møbel	**møbler**		(piece of) furniture
	et køkken	**køkkener**		kitchen
	et museum	**museer**		museum
	et drama	**dramaer**		drama
115 FIRST DECLENSION			**-r**	
COMMON GENDER				
	en uge	**uger**		week
NEUTER				
	et billede	**billeder**		picture
116 SECOND DECLENSION			**-e**	
COMMON GENDER				
	en dag	**dage**		day
	en lærer	**lærere**		teacher
	en ejendom	**ejendomme** (113(c))		property
	en datter	**døtre**		daughter
NEUTER				
	et bord	**borde**		table
	et hus	**huse**		house

Para.	Singular	Plural	Plural ending	Meaning
117 THIRD DECLENSION			zero	
COMMON GENDER				
	en sko	**sko**		shoe
	en gående	**gående**		pedestrian
	en mand	**mænd**		man
NEUTER				
	et år	**år**		year
	et barn	**børn**		child
120 ENGLISH PLURALS			**-s**	
	et show	**shows**		show
	en drag	**drags**		drag artist
121 LATIN PLURALS			**-a**	
	et faktum	**fakta**		fact
122 ITALIAN & SPANISH PLURALS			**-i/-s**	
	en konto	**konti/kontoer**		account
	en desperado	**desperados/desperadoer**		

D NOUNS WITH NO PLURAL FORM OR NO SINGULAR FORM, COLLECTIVES AND QUANTITY

124 Nouns with no plural form

The following categories of noun generally have no plural form:

(a) Verbal nouns describing an action:

Verbal nouns in **-en: grublen**, brooding; **nysen**, sneezing; **viden**, knowledge

Nouns in **-en** formed from a verb phrase: **fremtræden**, appearance; **hensyntagen**, consideration; **indskriden**, intervention; **indtræden**, commencement

(b) Abstract nouns:

adel, nobility; **ansvar**, responsibility; **fattigdom**, poverty; **godhed**, goodness; **kulde**, cold; **lykke**, happiness; **sødme**, sweetness; **troskab**, loyalty

Plurals of abstract nouns express a countable quantity:

Hans døtre var skønheder.	His daughters were beauties.
Hun har få glæder.	She has few pleasures.
hendes længslers mål	the goal of her dreams

(c) Substances and materials (cf. 112):

garn, yarn; **guld**, gold; **kød**, meat; **kul**, coal; **luft**, air; **mad**, food; **mælk**, milk; **nylon**, nylon; **olie**, oil; **sne**, snow; **tobak**, tobacco; **vand**, water; **vin**, wine; **øl**, beer

Plurals of such words are, however, used to indicate types or makes of a substance:

garner, wools; **teer**, teas; **vine**, wines

Note – Colloquially these are found as count nouns: **madder**, sandwiches; **vander**, soft drinks; **øller**, beers (i.e. glasses or bottles of beer)

(d) Collective nouns:

afkom, progeny; **folk**, people; **kvæg**, cattle

(e) Weights and measures, which usually have a zero plural form after cardinal numbers (cf. English '6 foot tall'; see also 127ff):

tre meter lang, three metres long

(f) Some nouns which 'borrow' a plural form:

besvær	**besværligheder**	trouble
dåb	**dåbshandlinger**	baptism
død	**dødsfald**	death
gæld	**gældsposter**	debt
løn	**lønninger**	salary
spøg	**spøgefuldheder**	joke

Notice one noun with an unrelated 'borrowed' plural:

dåd	**bedrifter**	deed

In all these cases the plural form 'borrowed' has a corresponding singular form, e.g. **et dødsfald**.

125 Nouns with no singular form

The following nouns are usually encountered only in the plural:

(a) Many words for articles of clothing: **bukser** (trousers), **jeans**, **shorts**, **slacks**, **slippers**, **trusser** (knickers)

Note that **pyjamas** is regarded as singular: **pyjamas – pyjamas(s)en – pyjamas (pyjamas(s)er)**

Note – **En buks** (a trouser), **en trusse** (a pair of knickers) are used in the clothing trade.

(b) Collectives denoting people: **forældre**, parents; **søskende**, brothers and sisters; **småbørn**, infants

Singulars have been formed in the case of **en forælder** (a parent), **en søskende** (a brother or sister), but there is still resistance to them in some quarters.

(c) Other collectives (see also 126): **briller**, spectacles; **cinders**, furnace coke; **finanser**, finances; **grejer**, things; **indvolde**, entrails; **klæder**, clothes; **viktualier**, victuals

Note – **En brille** (a pair of spectacles) is used in the ophthalmic trade.

(d) Some illnesses: **kopper**, smallpox; **mæslinger**, measles; **røde hunde**, German measles

(e) Some place names: **Alperne**, the Alps; **Færøerne**, the Faroes; **Nederlandene**, the Netherlands

(f) Words for decades: **tred(i)verne**, the Thirties; **fyrrene**, the Forties

(g) Others: **fagter**, gestures; **løjer**, high jinks

126 Collectives

(a) The noun **mand** may remain in the singular form in expressions of numerical strength:

en gruppe på 20 mand — a group of 20 men
en officer og ti mand — one officer and ten men
en besætning på 500 mand — a crew of 500 men

Notice also:

Alle mand på dæk! — All hands on deck!

(b) A small number of other nouns possess a separate collective plural form:

Singular	*Collective plural*	*Count plural*
orm worm	**orm** worms (infestation)	**orme** worms
sten stone	**sten** stone(s)	**stene** stones
øje eye	**øjne** eyes	**øjer** 'eyes'
øl beer	**øl** beers, i.e. types	**øller** beers, i.e. bottles or glasses

Note 1 – **Stene** = gemstones or gravestones.

Note 2 – **Øjer** is used only in compounds:

katteøjer, reflectors on bicycles; **koøjer**, portholes; **nåleøjer**, eyes of needles

127 Nouns expressing quantity

In expressions such as those given below, the noun indicating the measure of quantity usually has a zero plural. Notice that in these cases the English 'of' has no equivalent in Danish:

en fod — one foot
to fod — two feet (or: foot)
et kilo (smør) — one kilo (of butter)
fire kilo (smør) — four kilos (of butter)
en kilometer — one kilometre
halvtreds kilometer — fifty kilometres
en liter (mælk) — one litre (of milk)
tre liter (mælk) — three litres (of milk)

en meter (tøj)	one metre (of cloth)
tre meter (tøj)	three metres (of cloth)
en mil	one Danish mile (= 4.7 Eng. miles)
to mil	two Danish miles
(det koster ikke) en øre	(it doesn't cost) an øre
(det koster) halvtreds øre	(it costs) fifty øre

Note 1 – The noun **krone** does, however, possess a separate plural form:

en krone	one crown (unit of currency)
to kroner	two crowns
Det koster ti kroner.	It costs ten crowns.

Note 2 – Less common are the following nouns for measurements:

en favn træ	one cord of wood
to favne træ	two cords of wood
en skæppe havre	one bushel of oats
to skæpper havre	two bushels of oats

Alternative plural forms of some of these nouns are occasionally encountered when the measure of quantity rather than the quantity expressed is of prime importance:

Man må regne kilometrene ud.
We have to work out the mileages.

Jeg har to femogtyveører. cf. **femogtyve øre**, 25 øre
I have two twenty-five øre pieces.

tusinder af mennesker cf. **flere tusind mennesker**
thousands of people several thousand people

E DIFFERENCES IN NUMBER BETWEEN ENGLISH AND DANISH

128 Nouns which are singular in English but plural in Danish

In addition to those nouns listed in 125 which have no singular form in Danish, there are a number of differences in usage between the two languages. The Danish nouns below often possess a singular form:

(a) There was no furniture in the room.
... ingen møbler.

But: I bought a new piece of furniture.
... et nyt møbel.

(b) I have my information from a reliable source.
Jeg har mine oplysninger fra en pålidelig kilde.
But: A piece of information ...
En oplysning ...

(c) My income and expenditure ...
Mine indtægter og udgifter ...
But: He has a large income.
... en god indtægt.

(d) A good knowledge of Danish ...
Gode kundskaber i dansk ...
But: The tree of knowledge ...
Kundskabens træ ...

(e) The news is on TV every night.
Nyhederne ...
But: I have got some news (a piece of news) for you.
... en nyhed ...

(f) I did some good business.
... gode forretninger.
But: A good piece of business ...
En god forretning ...

(g) I need some good advice.
... gode råd.
But: A good piece of advice ...
Et godt råd ...

(h) I have conclusive proof.
Jeg har afgørende beviser.
But: A piece of evidence ...
Et bevis ...

(i) I have a lot of money/cash.
Jeg har mange penge/kontanter.

129 Nouns which are singular in Danish but plural in English

(a) Danish has a number of singular nouns which correspond to plural ideas in English:

aske ashes
indhold contents
løn wages
middelalderen the Middle Ages
middelklassen the middle class(es)
protokol minutes (of a meeting)
rigdom riches
sprit spirits
tolden Customs
i udkanten af on the outskirts of
udseende looks

These cases include a number of English nouns ending in '-ics':

atletik athletics
fysik physics
gymnastik gymnastics
lingvistik linguistics
matematik mathematics
politik politics
statistik statistics
økonomi economics

They also include cases where English has 'a pair of':

en knibtang (a pair of) pliers
en passer (a pair of) compasses
en pincet (a pair of) tweezers
en saks (a pair of) scissors
en trappestige (a pair of) steps, a stepladder
en vægt (a pair of) scales

Notice that 'several pairs of tongs' = **flere tænger**, and so on.

(b) In Danish, singular nouns are used in reciprocal constructions:

Skal vi bytte plads? Shall we change places?

Vi gav hinanden hånden.	We shook hands.

(c) Danish uses a singular noun in some expressions where English has a possessive with a plural noun:

Mændene mistede livet.	The men lost their lives.
De skiftede mening.	They changed their minds.
Han stod med hånden i lommen.	He was standing with his hands in his pockets.

(d) A singular noun is used in a few expressions with numerals:

halvandet år	18 months; one and a half years
to og en halv måned	2½ months
i det 15. og 16. århundrede	in the 15th and 16th centuries
i kapitel 6 og 7	in chapters 6 and 7

F SOME DANISH NOUN HOMONYMS

130 List of Danish noun homonyms

Some Danish nouns have two or more very different meanings, often reflected either in different genders or in different plural forms, or both. The following is a list of the most frequent homonyms.

Singular	*Plural*	*Meaning*
en ark	**arker**	ark
et ark	**ark**	piece of paper
en bid	**bidder**	morsel, bite to eat
et bid	**bid**	bite
en brud	**brude**	bride
en brud	**brude**	weasel
et brud	**brud**	break
brug-en	–	use
et brug	**brug**	farm
en buk	**bukke**	billy-goat
et buk	**buk**	bow
fotografi-en	–	photography
et fotografi	**fotografier**	photograph

Singular	*Plural*	*Meaning*
en frø	**frøer**	frog
et frø	**frø**	seed
en fyr	**fyrre**	pine
en fyr	**fyre**	chap
et fyr	**fyr**	lighthouse
et fyr	**fyr**	furnace, boiler
en følge	**følger**	sequence
et følge	**følger**	retinue
en gran	**graner**	spruce
et gran	**gran**	particle, pinch (e.g. of salt)
en klap	**klapper**	flap
et klap	**klap**	pat
en kok	**kokke**	chef
en kok	**kokke**	cockerel
en lap	**lapper**	patch
en lap	**lapper**	Lapp, Sami
en led	**led(d)er**	side, direction
et led	**led**	joint
et led	**led**	gate
en leje	**lejer**	rent
et leje	**lejer**	couch; village (e.g. **fiskerleje**, fishing village)
en læg	**lægge**	calf, shank
et læg	**læg**	pleat
en lod	**lodder**	fate, share
et lod	**lodder**	lead weight, lottery ticket
et mål	**mål**	aim, goal
et mål	**mål**	dialect
en nød	**nødder**	nut
nød-en	–	distress
en nøgle	**nøgler**	key
et nøgle	**nøgler**	ball of yarn
en pil	**pile**	willow
en pil	**pile**	arrow
pust-en	–	breath
et pust	**pust**	puff of wind

Singular	*Plural*	*Meaning*
ris-en	**ris**	rice
et ris	**ris**	rod
et råd	**råd**	piece of advice
råd-det	–	rot
en sigte	**sigter**	sieve
et sigte	**sigter**	sight, aim
en skrift	**skrifter**	handwriting
et skrift	**skrifter**	publication
en søm	**sømme**	hem
et søm	**søm**	nail
en ting	**ting**	thing
et ting	**ting**	parliament, court
tryk-ken	–	print
et tryk	**tryk**	press, squeeze

G THE GENITIVE

131 The form of the genitive

(a) Basic rule:

> To form the genitive, - is added to the indefinite or definite singular or to the indefinite or definite plural form, i.e. to the basic form:

Indefinite singular	*Definite singular*
en piges, a girl's	**pigens**, the girl's
et barns, a child's	**barnets**, the child's
Indefinite plural	*Definite plural*
pigers, girls'	**pigernes**, the girls'
børns, children's	**børnenes**, the children's

Proper nouns also take this ending:

Mozarts Requiem; **Svends sommerhus**, Svend's summer cottage; **Grundtvigs salmer**, Grundtvig's hymns; **Carlsbergs ledelse**, the board of Carlsberg; **Danmarks statsminister**, the Prime Minister of Denmark

Other genitive endings are listed below, but there are also many periphrastic forms of the genitive (see 732(b),(c)).

(b) Unlike in English, there is generally no apostrophe before the genitive **-s**:

et barns ansigt	a child's face

(c) After proper names ending in **-s**, **-x** or **-z** there are two equally viable methods of indicating the genitive:

1 An apostrophe + **s**:

Lars's lejlighed	Lars's flat
Columbus's opdagelse af Amerika	Columbus's discovery of America
ris's kogetid	the cooking time for rice
Bordeaux's gode vine	the good wines of Bordeaux
Marx's bøger	Marx's books
Schweiz's hovedstad	the capital of Switzerland

2 An apostrophe alone:

Lars' lejlighed	Lars' flat
Columbus' opdagelse af Amerika	Columbus' discovery of America
ris' kogetid	the cooking time for rice
Bordeaux' gode vine	the good wines of Bordeaux
Marx' bøger	Marx's books
Schweiz' hovedstad	the capital of Switzerland

3 + **es**:

There is a third (and more rarely used) colloquial possibility with nouns whose final -**s** is pronounced:

Larses lejlighed
Schweizes hovedstad, etc.

This method is, therefore, not used with words like **Bordeaux**.

Note – The method with apostrophe alone is not used with nouns ending in **-s** + consonant:

***president Bush' tale** should be **president Bushs tale**, President Bush's speech

(d) After abbreviations without a full stop, an apostrophe + **s** is added:

USA's hær	the US Army
DSB's problemer	DSB's problems
tv's underholdningsprogrammer	TV's entertainment programmes

When an abbreviation can be pronounced as a word, **-s** alone may be added as an alternative to apostrophe + **s**:

Natos (Nato's) generalsekretær	the Secretary General of NATO

For abbreviations ending in **-s**, **-x**, **-z**, the same rules apply as above:

SAS's/SAS' priser	SAS's prices

Note – There is a tendency in Denmark, especially on shop signs, to adopt the English apostrophe:

***Jensen's Bageri** (Jensen's Bakery) should be **Jensens Bageri**

(e) After abbreviations with a full stop, no apostrophe should be used, but this rule is often ignored:

Christian 4.s regeringstid	the reign of Christian IV
B.T.s/ B.T.'s sportsider	the sports pages of B.T.
en cand. mag.s beskæftigelses-muligheder	a graduate's employment prospects

(f) In two-noun place names a first noun ending in **-havn**, **-holm** or **-land** takes a genitive **-s**:

Københavns Slot, Copenhagen Castle; **Frederiksholms Kanal**; **Holmslands Klit**, Holmsland's Cliff

In some other two-noun place names this only applies when the second noun is qualified (in which case it begins with a small letter):

Roskildes smukke domkirke	Roskilde's beautiful cathedral

Otherwise the first noun often does not take **-s**:

> **Roskilde Domkirke**, Roskilde Cathedral; **Christiansborg Slot**, Christiansborg Castle; **Odense Kommune**, Odense Local Authority; **Vejle Amt**, Vejle County

(g) Adjectival nouns may also take an **-s** genitive (see also 221ff):

> **den gamles/de gamles sparepenge**, the old man's/old people's savings; **det godes sejr**, the victory of good

(h) There are many remnants of the older Danish genitive case after the preposition **til** (see 716(a)):

(i) With a genitive in **-s**:

> **til alters**, to the altar; **til bords**, to table; **til bys**, to town; **til fods**, on foot; **til havs**, by sea; **til lands**, by land; **til sengs**, to bed; **til skibs**, aboard; **til skovs**, to the woods; **til søs**, by sea; **til vands**, by water; **til vejrs**, aloft; **spørge til råds**, ask someone's advice

(ii) With a genitive in **-e**:

> **til døde**, to death; **til punkt og prikke**, to the letter; **til spilde**, to waste; **til stede**, present; **til syne**, into view; **tage til orde**, speak; **have til huse**, be housed

Note – The following have an old Danish dative case ending in **-e**:

> **ad åre**, some time; **fra borde**, from the table; **i drømme**, in one's dreams; **i live**, alive; **i senge**, in bed; **i søvne**, in one's sleep; **over borde**, overboard

(i) Latin genitives are used in some names:

Mariæ bebudelsesdag	the feast of the Annunciation
Kristi himmelfartsdag	Ascension Day
Jesu liv	Jesus's life
Skt. Annæ Plads	St Anne's Square

(j) In older Danish both the noun stem and the end article were inflected. A few relic forms are found in fixed expressions:

af livsens kræfter	with all one's strength

på havsens bund	at the bottom of the sea

132 The use of the genitive

(a) Danish uses the genitive in **-s** much more often than English uses the genitive in 's or s'.

(b) After a noun in the genitive form the noun following never takes an end article:

the top of the hill	**bakkens top**
the headmaster of the school	**skolens rektor**
the girls' parents	**pigernes forældre**

This often involves a conscious transformation from the English:

Cf. the end of summer	⇨	*lit.* the summer's end **sommerens afslutning**
Definite article No article		*Definite article No article*

Note – A rare exception is where the noun is a title or proper noun:

Jeg kan godt lide Kirks *Fiskerne*.	I like Kirk's 'The Fishermen'.

(c) If a name comprises a group of words, the genitive is usually placed on the last word of the group, the 'group genitive':

Svend Andersens far	Svend Andersen's father
Anders Bodelsens romaner	Anders Bodelsen's novels
professor Nils Nielsens forelæsninger	Professor Nils Nielsen's lectures
firmaet Hansen & Søns fabrik	the firm of Hansen & Son's factory
Kongen af Danmarks bolsjer	the King of Denmark's sweets
en af mine venners datter	the daughter of one of my friends

This also applies to adjectival nouns:

mange gamles største problem	the greatest problem for many old people
de tos kærlighed	the couple's love
Gorm den Gamles høj	Gorm the Old's mound

(d) A noun in apposition often takes the same case as the noun to which it refers, in these examples the genitive:

Vi afventer universitetets rektors, professor Søndergårds, svar.
We are awaiting the University Vice-Chancellor, Professor Søndergård's, reply.

However, also possible here is the group genitive:

Vi afventer universitetets rektor, professor Søndergårds, svar.

In cases of apposition with relatively fixed expressions there is no need for agreement in case:

den nuværende dronning, Margrethes, regeringstid
the present queen, Margrethe's, reign

(e) Particularly in spoken Danish there are many prepositional genitive expressions involving different prepositions or no genitive marker at all, which correspond to the English genitive construction with 'of'. For a detailed account of these see 732.

133 The **-s** genitive

The **-s** genitive is very frequent in Danish, especially in the written language, and corresponds both to English genitive constructions with 's or s' and to expressions with 'of':

the boy's father	**drengens far**
the boys' father	**drengenes far**
the King of Kings	**kongernes konge**
the discovery of America	**Amerikas opdagelse**
the life of Shakespeare	**Shakespeares liv**
the death of a hero	**en helts død**
the Queen of England	**Englands dronning**
the capital of Denmark	**Danmarks hovedstad**
the owner of the farm	**gårdens ejer**

Notice, however, the following special uses of the **-s** genitive in Danish:

(a) The genitive of measurement:

et par timers søvn	a couple of hours' sleep
en toliters vinflaske	a two-litre wine bottle
et tietages højhus	a ten-storey high building

et fyrreminutters tv-program	a 40-minute TV programme
en tomils spadseretur	a nine-mile walk
en tidages rejse	a 10-day journey
to måneders husleje	2 months' rent
en femtenårs dreng	a 15-year-old boy
et femårs fangenskab	5 years' captivity
et firekrones frimærke	a 4-kroner stamp
en fireværelses lejlighed	a 4-room flat

(b) Genitives in surnames, referring to 'family' or 'shop':

Der var ingen hjemme hos Olsens.
There was no-one at home at the Olsens'.

Jeg køber altid hos Larsens.
I always shop at Larsen's.

(c) To indicate a quality:

Det var fandens godt gjort.	That was damned well done.
et herrens vejr	awful weather
tre satans kønne piger	three devilishly pretty girls
en helvedes karl	a devil of a chap

Such words are now regarded as indeclinable adjectives.

(d) The **-s** genitive corresponding to English superlative + 'in':

Danmarks rigeste mand	the richest man in Denmark

H THE FORM OF THE INDEFINITE ARTICLE

134 The indefinite article

The indefinite article in Danish is **en** for common gender nouns and **et** for neuter nouns:

en mand, a man	**en kvinde**, a woman
et hus, a house	**et æble**, an apple

See 302 for the numeral **en**.

I THE FORM OF THE DEFINITE ARTICLE

135 Introduction

In Danish the definite article (or end article) singular is added to the end of the noun as a suffix: **-(e)n** for common gender nouns and **-(e)t** for neuter nouns. See 113(c) for doubling of the consonant before the end article.

The end article plural is **-ne** for both common gender and neuter nouns with a plural indefinite in **-e** or **-(e)r**, and **-ene** for nouns with a plural indefinite in zero.

However, where the noun has a prepositioned adjective attribute, a front (or adjectival) article (**den, det** or **de**) replaces the end article (see 216ff).

Noun alone:

Singular:	-EN/-ET	-N/-T
Common	**manden**, the man	**kvinden**, the woman
Neuter	**hus*et***, the house	**æble*t***, the apple

Note – The **-t** of the end article is usually pronounced [ð].

Plural:	-NE	-ENE
Common	**kvinder*ne***, the women	**mænd*ene***, the men
Neuter	**hus*ene***, the houses	**sprog*ene***, the languages

Noun with prepositioned adjective attribute (see 216ff):

Singular:

Common	**den gamle mand** the old man	**den gamle kvinde** the old woman
Neuter	**det gamle hus** the old house	**det gamle æble** the old apple

Plural:

	de gamle kvinder the old women	**de gamle æbler** the old apples

---

136 The form of the definite singular with end article

(a) Basic rule:

Most Danish nouns add the end article **-en** or **-et** according to gender:

Common:

en hånd	a hand	**hånden**	the hand
et barn	a child	**barnet**	the child

Neuter:

en by	a town	**byen**	the town
et træ	a tree	**træet**	the tree

(b) Exceptions:

Nouns of either gender ending in unstressed **-e** add **-n** or **-t** according to gender:

en uge	a week	**ugen**	the week
et billede	a picture	**billedet**	the picture

Examples:

– Common gender nouns in **-e** take **-n** in the definite form:

frikadelle-n, the meatball; **kage-n**, the cake; **kone-n**, the wife; **krone-n**, the crown; **maskine-n**, the machine; **pige-n**, the girl; **pære-n**, the pear; **skole-n**, the school; **stue-n**, the room; **time-n**, the hour

– Neuter nouns in **-e** take **-t** in the definite form:

arbejde-t, the work; **frimærke-t**, the stamp; **hjørne-t**, the corner; **menneske-t**, the human being; **stykke-t**, the piece; **vindue-t**, the window; **værelse-t**, the room; **æble-t**, the apple; **øje-t**, the eye

(c) Nouns (common gender) ending in a stressed **-e** retain **-en** in the definite form:

en café	a café	**caféen**	the café
en idé	an idea	**idéen**	the idea

Others: **allé-en**, the avenue; **entré-en**, the entrance; **fe-en**, the fairy; **moské-en**, the mosque; **rosé-en**, the rosé wine; **ske-en**, the spoon; **sne-en**, the snow; **te-en**, the tea

(d) Some nouns ending in unstressed **-el**, **-en**, **-er** either must or may drop the **-e** of the stem before adding the end article **-en** or **-et** (cf. 115(c),(d), 116(c)).

(i) A few always lose the vowel:

en artikel	**artiklen**	article
et mirakel	**miraklet**	miracle
en titel	**titlen**	title

(ii) Many have alternative forms with and without the vowel:

en aften – aft(e)nen	(pl. **aft(e)ner**)	evening
en cykel – cyk(e)len	(pl. **cykler**)	bicycle
et eksempel – eksemp(e)let	(pl. **eksempler**)	example
en frøken – frøk(e)nen	(pl. **frøk(e)ner**)	unmarried woman
en gaffel – gaf(fe)len	(pl. **gafler**)	fork
en hilsen – hils(e)nen	(pl. **hils(e)ner**)	greeting
et køkken – køk(ke)net	(pl. **køk(ke)ner**)	kitchen
et lagen – lag(e)net	(pl. **lag(e)ner**)	sheet
et orkester – orkest(e)ret	(pl. **orkestre**)	orchestra
et teater – teat(e)ret	(pl. **teatre**)	theatre

There are, however, many exceptions: **adel – adelen**, nobility; **en alder – alderen** (pl. **aldre**), age; **en englænder – englænderen**, Englishman; **en finger – fingeren** (pl. **fingre**), finger; **en fætter – fætteren** (pl. **fætre**), cousin; **en kennel – kennelen**, kennel; **et lager – lageret** (pl. **lagre**), store; **en sommer – sommeren** (pl. **somre**), summer; **en søster – søsteren** (pl. **søstre**), sister; **en tunnel – tunnelen**, tunnel

Note – The noun **verden**, world, which historically already possesses an end article, is often found in its basic form, except in compounds:

hele verden	the whole world
kunstnerverdenen	the world of the artist

(e) Latin and Greek loans ending in **-eum**, **-ium** drop the **-um** before adding the end article:

et museum	**museet**	museum
et kollegium	**kollegiet**	hall of residence

et studium	**studiet**	study

Notice also:

en amanuensis	**amanuensen** (or **amanuensis(s)en**)	amanuensis

Cf. 115(f), 121(d).

Note – Compare **et studie** (a radio or TV studio), **en/et studie** (a sketch) and **et studium – studiet** (a study).

(f) After a short stressed vowel the final consonant of the noun is doubled before adding the end article singular (see also 113(c), 1305):

en bus	**bussen**	bus
en hat	**hatten**	hat
et hotel	**hotellet**	hotel
et læs	**læsset**	load
et stakit	**stakittet**	fence
en søn	**sønnen**	son
en ven	**vennen**	friend

(g) Short stressed vowels are lengthened in pronunciation when the end article singular is added to monosyllables in **-d**, **-v**:

et blad	**bladet**	leaf
et hav	**havet**	sea
en lov	**loven**	law

Other examples: **fad**, dish; **fred**, peace; **had**, hatred; **mad**, food; **rad**, row; **smed**, smith; **stad**, city

Note – Exceptions are also found: **skov – skoven**, forest; **skud – skuddet**, shot

(h) In all simple nouns pronounced without 'stod' (marked ') this is introduced in pronunciation in the form with end article:

bogstav	**bogsta'vet**	letter (of the alphabet)
søn	**søn'nen**	son
tøj	**tøj'et**	clothes

In many of the cases under (g) above 'stod' is, therefore, introduced in the form with end article:

bad	**ba'det**	(pl. **bade**)	bath

gud	**gu'den**	(pl. **guder**)	god
sted	**ste'det**	(pl. **steder**)	place

137 Choice of the definite plural ending

For plural indefinite forms of nouns see 113–23. The major factor in determining the choice of the plural article form is the form of the plural indefinite.

(a) Plurals ending in **-e**, **-er** (both genders) add **-ne**:

en by	**byen**	**byer**	**byerne**	town
en gade	**gaden**	**gader**	**gaderne**	street
en stol	**stolen**	**stole**	**stolene**	chair
et bord	**bordet**	**borde**	**bordene**	table

Note – In a very few nouns with plural indefinite forms in **-er**, the **-r** is optional in the plural definite:

housecoate(r)ne, the housecoats; **menneske(r)ne**, the people

(b) Zero plurals (both genders) take **-ene**:

en mus	**musen**	**mus**	**musene**	mouse
en sko	**skoen**	**sko**	**skoene**	shoe
et år	**året**	**år**	**årene**	year
et barn	**barnet**	**børn**	**børnene**	child
en mand	**manden**	**mænd**	**mændene**	man

(c) In recent years there has been a tendency in spoken Danish to avoid the ending **-ene** in a number of polysyllabic words by inserting an **-r** before **-ne**. This is now becoming acceptable as an alternative form:

Spoken form	*Written form*	
agernerne	**agernene**	acorn
asterserne	**asterse(r)ne**	aster
egernerne	**egerne(r)ne**	squirrel
østerserne	**østerse(r)ne**	oyster

(d) Plurals of foreign loans ending in -s

(i) Where the only possible plural is **-s** these nouns add **-ene** but may drop the **-s**:

Singular	*Plural*	*Plural definite*	
jeans	**jeans**	**jeansene**	jeans
joke	**jokes**	**jokene**	joke
kiks	**kiks**	**kiksene**	biscuit

(ii) Where the alternative plural indefinite forms are **-s** or **-er** these nouns either add **-ne** to the **-er** plural or drop the **-s** and add **-ene**:

cowboy	**cowboys/cowboyer**	**cowboyerne**	cowboy
jeep	**jeeps/jeeper**	**jeepe(r)ne**	jeep

(iii) Where the alternative plural indefinite forms are **-s** or zero plural these nouns drop the **-s** and add **-ene**:

heat	**heats/heat**	**heatene**

(iv) Where the indefinite plural forms end in **-ers** these nouns add **-e(r)ne**:

en kippers	**kippers**	**kippersene**	
–	**cinders**	**cinderse(r)ne**	furnace coke

(e) Foreign loans ending in **-a** or **-i** add **-ene** to the plural indefinite:

datum	**data**	**dataene**	data
faktum	**fakta**	**faktaene**	fact
musikus	**musici**	**musiciene**	musician

Some have alternative Danish plural forms:

konto	**konti/kontoer**	**kontiene/ kontoerne**	account

138 Nouns – forms with end article: summary

Paragraph	*Common gender*	*Paragraph*	*Neuter*
Singular			
136(a)	**mand-en**	136(a)	**dyr-et**
136(a)	**ko-en**	136(a)	**drama-et**
136(b)	**pige-n**	136(b)	**menneske-t**
136(c)	**café-en**		–
136(d)	**artikl-en** (from **artikel**)	136(d)	**eksemp(e)l-et** (from **exempel**)
136(d)(i)	**finger-en**	136(d)(i)	**lager-et**
136(d)(ii)	**cyk(e)l-en** (from **cykel**)	136(d)(ii)	**mirakl-et** (from **mirakel**)
136(e)	–	136(e)	**gymnasi-et** (from **gymnasium**)
136(f)	**hat-ten**	136(f)	**hotel-let**
Plural			
137(a)	**skoler-ne**	137(a)	**køk(ke)ner-ne** (from **køk(ke)ner**)
137(a)	**stole-ne**	137(a)	**huse-ne**
137(b)	**sten-ene**	137(b)	**børn-ene**
137(b)	**gæs-sene**	137(b)	**glas-sene**
137(c)	**egerne(r)-ne** (from **egerner**)	137(e)	**fakta-ene**

J THE USE OF THE INDEFINITE AND DEFINITE ARTICLE

139 Introduction

In most cases the same principle applies in Danish as in English, namely that concepts familiar from the context take a definite article whilst unfamilar concepts take an indefinite article:

> **De havde købt et nyt hus. Huset lå ved en sø. Søen var lille, men den var dyb. Den dybe sø var meget smuk.**
> They had bought a new house. The house lay by a lake. The lake was small but it was deep. The deep lake was very beautiful.

What follows is a brief general outline of Danish article use, followed by specific comparisons with English use. Danish article use may be seen as a series of contrasts or choices between three forms of the noun.

(a) Noun without article

For count nouns the form without article (**bil, hus**) is contrasted both with the form with indefinite article (**en bil, et hus**) and with the form with definite article (**bilen, huset**). Use of count nouns without an article tends to imply an abstract sense, concentrating on the content or idea behind the noun rather than indicating one specific case of the noun:

Generality:	*Specific example:*
Har I bil? Have you got a car?	**Har I en bil?** Have you got a car?
Vi fik kylling til middag. We had chicken for lunch.	**Vi fik en kylling til middag.** We had a chicken for lunch.
Fru Lund var på rejse. Mrs Lund was travelling.	**Fru Lund var på en rejse.** Mrs Lund was on a journey.
Du må læse lektier til i morgen. You must do your homework for tomorrow.	**Du må læse lektierne til i morgen.** You must do the homework for tomorrow.

(b) Noun with indefinite article

This is usually found in the case of count nouns for concepts unfamiliar from the context (see examples above):

Generality:	*Type or sort:*
Bonden fandt kun sten på markerne. The farmer found only stone in his fields.	**Peter fandt en sten på stranden.** Peter found a stone on the beach.

With count nouns indicating substances, etc., the use of the indefinite form indicates a limitation of the generality and stresses a type or sort:

Granit er en hårdfør sten.
Granite is a resistant rock.

In contrast with the noun without article, it may also have a figurative sense:

Literal:	*Figurative:*
Olivier var skuespiller.	**Din lille pige er en skuespiller.**
Olivier was an actor.	Your little girl is an actress.

(c) Nouns with definite article

The listener is usually sure which example or occasion is referred to, e.g. **krigen** to a Dane today might mean **anden verdenskrig** (the Second World War), but to a Dane in the 1930s it would have meant **første verdenskrig** (the Great War).

When there is assumed common knowledge of a context, Danish often has the definite form even in many cases where English does not:

Han er i byen.	He is in town.

(d) In accordance with these general principles, a whole species or family may be denoted by either definite singular or indefinite plural:

Elgen/Elge findes over hele Sverige.
The elk/Elk is/are to be found throughout Sweden.

In the cases outlined in 140ff below, the two languages differ in their use of the articles.

140 Definite article in Danish – no article in English

(a) Abstract nouns and nouns in a generic sense:

livet i det moderne samfund	life in modern society
den danske industri	Danish industry
den offentlige mening	public opinion
Hvor tiden går!	How time flies!
tilbage til naturen	back to nature
livet efter døden	life after death

(i) This applies particularly to nouns depicting aspects of human life and thought:

> **alderdommen**, old age; **arbejdet**, work; **evigheden**, eternity; **forureningen**, pollution; **himlen**, heaven; **jorden**, earth; **kvinden**, woman; **krigen**, war; **kærligheden**, love; **litteraturen**, literature; **livet**, life; **lykken**, happiness; **manden**, man; **menneskeheden**, humanity; **mennesket**, mankind; **skæbnen**, fate; **ungdommen**, youth

(ii) Set phrases include:

i virkeligheden	in reality
traditionen tro	in keeping with tradition

Note – When writing about cultural personalities with a title or job description:

> **maleren Jens Jensen**, painter JJ; **forfatteren Klaus Rifbjerg**, author KR; **komponisten og dirigenten Leonard Bernstein**, composer and conductor LB

(b) Many proverbs:

Mennesket spår, men Gud råder.	Man proposes but God disposes.
Historien gentager sig.	History repeats itself.
Livet er kort, kunsten er lang.	Life is short, art is long.

(c) Some idiomatic phrases for location:

Han er i byen/tager til byen.	He's in town/going to town.
Søren går på universitetet.	Søren is at university.
Hun ligger i sengen/på hospitalet.	She's in bed/in hospital.
(But: **Hun går i seng/i kirke/i skole/ på arbejde.**	She goes to bed/church/school/ work.)

(d) Some idiomatic phrases for time:

om vinteren/om mandagen	in winter/on Mondays
om dagen	by day
om natten	by night
i julen/påsken	at Christmas/Easter
i skumringen	at dusk
før/efter mørkets frembrud	before/after dark
til foråret	next spring

Note – Exceptions: **ved solopgang/daggry**, at sunrise/dawn; festivals ending in **-aften**: **juleaften**, Christmas Eve; **nytårsaften**, New Year's Eve; **Mortensaften**, St Martin's Eve; **-dag**: **første juledag**, Christmas Day; **grundlovsdag**, Constitution Day; **-morgen**: **påskemorgen**, Easter morning

(e) Types and groups in a collective sense:

Mennesket er kun en nøgen abe.	Man is merely a naked ape.
Priserne er stigende.	Prices are rising.

(f) Many expressions with **flest**, **mest**, most:

de fleste studerende	most students
det meste øl	most beer

(g) Other phrases:

komme gennem tolden	go through Customs
med posten	by post
til udlandet	abroad
give én hånden	shake hands
i fjernsynet	on (the) TV

(h) Names of some public places:

Frederiksstaden, **Rådhuspladsen**, **Sjællandsbroen**, **Slotsholmen**, **Strøget**,

Note – There are many exceptions including most street names: **Nytorv**, **Vesterbro**, **Nørre Voldgade**, **Botanisk Have**

(i) Names of some geographical locations:

Himmelbjerget, **Limfjorden**, **Victoriasøen**

Note – Names generally drop the end article when used as the first element in compounds:

Atlanten, the Atlantic	cf. **Atlantpagten**, the Atlantic Pact
Themsen, the Thames	cf. **Themsmundingen**, the mouth of the Thames

(j) The names of some countries and regions:

Algeriet, Algeria; **Mongoliet**, Mongolia; **Normandiet**, Normandy; **Tyrkiet**, Turkey

141 Definite article in Danish – indefinite article in English

This is often found in expressions indicating frequency of occurrence:

ti gange om ugen/måneden/året
ten times a week/month/year

De tjener hundrede kroner i timen.
They earn a hundred kroner an hour.

Han drikker mindst fem øl om dagen.
He drinks at least five bottles of beer a day.

At abonnere koster 50 kr. i kvartalet.
It costs 50 kroner a quarter to subscribe.

142 No article in Danish – definite article in English

(a) With certain adjectives which often have the definite form (see 220(d)):

Samme aften kom vi hjem.	The same evening we arrived home.
Næste dag var det dejligt vejr.	The next day the weather was beautiful.
Første/Sidste gang jeg mødte ham ...	The first/last time I met him ...
De bor på øverste etage.	They live on the top floor.
Vi traf hende forleden dag.	We met her the other day.
nærværende forfatter	the present writer
på rette tid og sted	at the right time and place
på rette vej	on the right track

(b) In some phrases involving instruments and pastimes, where the verb is unstressed:

De hører radio.	They listen to the radio.
Bodil spiller klaver/violin.	Bodil plays the piano/the violin.
Mor læser avis.	Mother is reading the paper.

Note – Forms with the article are, however, common when referring to a specific object:

Han skal stemme klaveret.	He is going to tune the piano.

(c) With proper names:

Vi spiste middag hos Jensens.	We had dinner at the Jensens.

Note – This is also the case when using English proper names in Danish:

Jeg har læst det i Guardian.	I've read it in the Guardian.
Han boede på Grand.	He stayed at the Grand.
De studerede på British Museum.	They studied at the British Museum.

(d) With many linguistic terms and other words from Latin:

i præsens/futurum/imperativ	in the present/future/imperative
i singularis/pluralis	in the singular/plural
i neutrum	in the neuter

This also applies to their Danish equivalents:

i nutid/fremtid	in the present/future
i ental/flertal	in the singular/plural
i intetkøn	in the neuter

Other Latin loans often used in the indefinite form only are:

centrum, the town centre; **kursus**, the course; **publikum**, the public

(e) With compass points:

Solen står op i øst og går ned i vest.
The sun rises in the east and sets in the west.

(f) With superlatives which are usually in the definite form in English:

Hvilken vin smager bedst?	Which wine tastes (the) best?
Hvem er mest intelligent?	Who is the brightest?
Hvilket engelsk amt er størst?	Which English county is the biggest?

(g) With some river names:

Donau, the Danube; **Loire**, the Loire; **Mississippi**, the Mississippi; **Po**, the River Po

Note – Exceptions are many, and include many well-known European or Danish rivers:

Elben, the Elbe; **Rhinen,** the Rhine; **Themsen,** the Thames; **Gudenåen; Kongeåen; Ejderen,** the Ejder; **Nilen,** the Nile

(h) In many set phrases:

Hun er forfatter til mange bøger. She is the author of a lot of books.
Hun er datter af en præst. She is the daughter of a priest.
i håb(et) om in the hope of
med undtagelse af with the exception of
under indflydelse af under the influence of

See also 143.

(i) In phrases after (unstressed) **have** (have):

have lejlighed til have the opportunity to
have lyst til have the desire to
have ret til have the right to

143 No article in Danish – indefinite article in English

(a) With nouns denoting nationality, profession, trade, religion or political belief:

Marie er dansker. Marie is a Dane.
Jørgen er lærer. Jørgen is a teacher.
Preben er præst. Preben is a priest.
Vibeke er katolik. Vibeke is a Catholic.
Coco var klovn. Coco was a clown (in the circus).

However, the indefinite article must be used in the following cases:

(i) When the noun is preceded by a qualifier:

Han er en dygtig læge. He is a good doctor.

(ii) When the noun is qualified by a following (restrictive) relative clause:

Han var en studerende, der brugte mange penge.
He was a student who spent a lot of money.

(iii) When the noun is used in a figurative sense, or is a personal attribute that is not a profession, etc. (cf. examples above):

Jens var en klovn.	Jens was a clumsy fool.
Han er en løgner/et geni/en helt.	He is a liar/a genius/a hero.
Han er en arbejdshest.	He is a (hard) worker.
(Cf. **Han er arbejder.**	He is a (manual) worker.)
Hun er en mor for dem.	She is a mother to them.
(Cf. **Hun er mor til fem børn.**	She is the mother of five children.)

Skuespilleren Erik Eriksen er en sagfører.
The actor EE is (i.e. plays the role of) a lawyer.

(Cf. **Erik Eriksen er sagfører.**
Erik Eriksen is a lawyer.)

(b) When the noun follows **som** (= 'in the capacity of'):

Som professor var han meget imponerende.
As a professor he was very impressive.

Som ung mand var han uhyre grim.
As a young man he was terribly ugly.

(c) In cases with singular count nouns when the general idea is inferred rather than a specific example. All nouns must be unqualified:

Har han hus? Han har slot!	Has he got a house? He has a castle!
De venter barn.	They are expecting a child.
De går på café/restaurant.	They are going to a café/restaurant.
Han sad på vinstue.	He sat in a wine bar.
Har Birgit fået pels?	Has Birgit got a fur coat?
Han skulle gå med hat.	He should wear a hat.
Vi spiste middag.	We ate dinner.
(Cf. **Vi spiste en middag med fire retter.**	We had a four-course dinner.)

(d) In other idiomatic phrases:

vente/få brev	expect/receive a letter
have/køre bil	own/drive a car
ryge pibe	smoke a pipe
bestille plads	book a place

bestille billet	book a ticket
have feber	have a (high) temperature
have hovedpine	have a headache
have svar på alt	have an answer to everything
have tanke for	give/have a thought to
have hastværk	be in a hurry
gøre nar af	make a fool of
det er synd	that's a shame
med høj stemme	in a loud voice
i dårligt humør	in a bad mood

(e) The Danish equivalents to 'a little, a few, a lot' function as adjectives:

få:	**kun få modstandere**	only a few opponents
lidt:	**lidt brød**	a little bread
meget:	**meget øl**	a lot of beer

For 'a hundred, a thousand' see 304(a).

144 Indefinite article in Danish – no article in English

Notice the following expressions that use **en** meaning 'about, approximately, some':

en tre-fire timer	some three or four hours
for en fem år siden	some five years ago

145 Use of the definite article to indicate possession

Where possession is obvious with clothes or parts of the body, Danish often uses the end article in preference to the possessive pronoun:

Hun frøs om hænderne/fødderne.	Her hands/feet were cold.
Han tog hende i hånden.	He took her hand.
Børnerne vaskede hænderne.	The children washed their hands.
hjælpe én på benene	to help someone onto their feet
De gik med hinanden under armen.	They walked arm in arm.
Solen skinnede mig i øjnene.	The sun shone into my eyes.
Jeg skar mig i fingeren.	I cut my finger.
Tag hatten af!	Take your hat off!

Han rystede på hovedet over det, han havde hørt.	He shook his head at what he had heard.

Note – Exceptions: Where it is necessary to indicate the precise ownership of an article of clothing or part of the body:

Hun lagde sin hånd i min.	She put her hand in mine.
Tyven stak sin hånd ned i min lomme.	The thief put his hand into my pocket.

See also 420.

146 Difference in the position of the article in Danish and English

Notice the following differences in word order involving articles:

en halv liter	half a litre
Man kan se det med et halvt øje.	One can see it with half an eye.
den halve tid	half the time
en lige så fin forestilling	as fine a performance
en ganske kort tid	rather a short time
hele familien	the whole family

2 ADJECTIVES

201 Introduction to forms and use

Adjectives are inflected in Danish. Both attributive and predicative adjectives change form according to the gender and number of the noun or pronoun with which they agree. The indefinite forms of the adjective are used both attributively and predicatively, while the definite forms are only used attributively:

	Indefinite	*Definite*
Attributive	**varm luft** warm air	**den varme luft** the warm air
	varmt vand warm water	**det varme vand** the warm water
	varme vinde warm winds	**de varme vinde** the warm winds
	en ung pige a young girl	**den unge pige** the young girl
	unge piger young girls	**de unge piger** the young girls
	et stort hus a big house	**det store hus** the big house
	store huse big houses	**de store huse** the big houses

Predicative	**pigen er ung** the girl is young	**pigerne er unge** the girls are young
	huset er stort the house is big	**husene er store** the houses are big

(a) Notice that the definite declension of the adjective usually employs the front article **den, det, de** (see 216ff).

(b) After verbs like **være, blive,** i.e. copulas, the adjective constitutes a predicative complement and usually inflects according to the subject or object to which it refers (see 209).

A FORM AND ORDER

202 The basic rule

(a) There is no distinctive marker for the common gender singular indefinite (basic or dictionary) form of the adjective, but the neuter singular form adds **-t**, and both the plural indefinite and the definite (singular and plural) add **-e**. The basic rule is shown for the adjective **fin** (fine):

Common gender singular indefinite
(Basic form)

fin

Neuter singular indefinite	*Plural (and definite of both genders)*
fint	**fine**

Notice that there is no distinction made between common gender and neuter plural form.

Examples:

en fin bog, et fint tæppe, fine bøger/fine tæpper
a fine book, a fine carpet, fine books/fine carpets

(b) The basic rule (shown in this form for comparison with 203ff):

	Common gender	*Neuter*	*Plural/definite*	*Meaning*
Ending:	**-zero**	**-t**	**-e**	
	bleg	**blegt**	**blege**	pale
	rolig	**roligt**	**rolige**	quiet

The large group of adjectives which inflects according to this pattern includes:

(i) Many monosyllabic adjectives ending in a consonant or consonant group:

bar, bare; **dyb**, deep; **dyr**, dear; **høj**, high; **jævn**, even; **klog**, wise; **kold**, cold; **lang**, long; **lav**, low; **lys**, light; **mørk**, dark; **pæn**, pretty; **rig**, rich; **sjov**, funny; **skøn**, lovely; **stærk**, strong; **svag**, weak; **ung**, young; **varm**, hot

(ii) Polysyllabic adjectives ending in **-al**, **-bar**, **-el**, **-ig**, **-iv**, **-ær**, **-(i)øs**:

legal, legal; **minimal**, minimal; **social**, social
brugbar, usable; **dyrebar**, precious; **holdbar**, durable
essentiel, essential; **industriel**, industrial; **kontroversiel**, controversial
dygtig, capable; **dårlig**, bad; **flittig**, hard-working
depressiv, depressive; **intensiv**, intensive; **naiv**, naive
cirkulær, circular; **regulær**, regular; **vulgær**, vulgar
kuriøs, quaint; **pompøs**, pompous; **seriøs**, serious

203 Variations – singular indefinite forms

(a) Some Danish adjectives possess no special neuter form in **-t**. Note that they do, however, take a plural/definite ending in **-e** (see also 217). The adjectives that do not always inflect in the neuter singular include:

(i) Adjectives ending in **-(i)sk**:

Common gender	*Neuter*	*Plural*
en dansk skole	**et dansk skib**	**danske skoler/skibe**
a Danish school	a Danish ship	Danish schools/ships

Other examples:

freudiansk, Freudian; **fynsk**, of Funen; **himmelsk**, heavenly; **medicinsk**, medicinal; **musikalsk**, musical

arkæologisk, archaeological; **automatisk**, automatic; **demokratisk**, democratic; **elektrisk**, electrical; **fascistisk**, fascist; **økonomisk**, economic

This group includes most adjectives denoting nationality or location or deriving from a personal name:

amerikansk, American; **engelsk**, English; **fransk**, French; **indisk**, Indian; **kinesisk**, Chinese; **portugisisk**, Portuguese; **russisk**, Russian; **tysk**, German; **andersensk**, of (Hans Christian) Andersen; **bangsk**, of (Herman) Bang; etc.

Some monosyllabic adjectives ending in **-sk** do not denote nationality or geographical location and do not derive from names. With these the neuter **-t** ending is optional but may always be omitted:

barsk(t), harsh; **besk(t)**, bitter; **fersk(t)**, fresh; **fjendsk(t)**, hostile; **frisk(t)**, fresh; **harsk(t)**, rancid; **lumsk(t)**, crafty; **rask(t)**, quick; **skælmsk(t)**, roguish

et frisk(t) brød	a fresh loaf

Note 1 – This also applies when the monosyllabic adjective ending in **-sk** forms part of a compound:

et børnefjendsk(t) par	a couple who hate children
et morgenfrisk(t) bad	an early morning bath(e)/swim

(ii) Adjectives already ending in **-t**:

Common gender	*Neuter*	*Plural*
en sort kat	**et sort hul**	**sorte katte/huller**
a black cat	a black hole	black cats/holes

This group includes: **flot**, posh; **glat**, smooth; **halt**, lame; **kort**, short; **let**, light; **mæt**, replete; **skidt**, bad; **smart**, smart; **stolt**, proud; **strikt**, strict; **tæt**, close

Many polysyllabic loanwords end in **-t**, including a number in **-at**, **-ant**, **-ent**:

abstrakt, adækvat, akkurat, arrogant, desperat, distinkt, elegant, excellent, frekvent, intakt, korrekt, latent, nonchalant, permanent, privat, relevant, tolerant

(iii) A few adjectives ending in a vowel + **d** [ð]:

et glad budskab	a glad tiding
et fremmed sprog	a foreign language

Note 2 – Many adjectives ending in a vowel + **-d** do, however, inflect in the neuter, including:

– Some very common adjectives: **død – dødt**, dead; **hvid – hvidt**, white; **kåd**, playful; **lad**, lazy; etc.

– Loan adjectives ending in **-id**: **et solidt firma**, a well-founded company

Others include: **fluid – fluidt; frigid – frigidt; hybrid – hybridt; rapid – rapidt; rigid – rigidt; timid – timidt**

Notice that all of these adjectives in **-id** are pronounced [ið'] or [i'ð] in the basic form and [ið'd] in the neuter form, except **solidt** [-id], cf. (iii) above.

(iv) A few adjectives which end in a consonant + **d** where the final **d** is pronounced [d]:

et absurd drama	an absurd drama
et lærd selskab	a learned society

Note 3 – In contrast, those cases where the final **–d** after a consonant is silent (and replaced by a 'stød') usually inflect in the neuter:

fuld – fuldt, full; **hård – hårdt**, hard; **kold – koldt**, cold; **mild – mildt**, mild; **rund – rundt**, round; **tynd – tyndt**, thin

(v) In spoken Danish some adjectives in **-(l)ig** (where the **-g** is silent in the basic form):

et rigtig svar	a correct answer
et skriftlig memorandum	a written memo
et rigelig udbud	a wide selection
stort årlig udsalg	great annual sale
Det er mærkelig.	That's strange.

This is not recommended in written Danish.

(vi) See also 207 for indeclinable adjectives.

(b) The consonant is unvoiced before the neuter ending **-t** in some adjectives whose basic form ends in **-v**:

en grov stemme a coarse voice	**et groft brød** a coarse bread	**grove brædder** coarse boards
en stiv finger a stiff finger	**et stift ben** a stiff leg	**stive fingre/ben** stiff fingers/legs

(c) Some adjectives add the ending **-er** (common gender), **-e** (neuter gender):

In a very few expressions older Danish endings are found, often used in a humorous way:

en flinker mand, a clever man	cf. also **flink**
en grimmer sag, a nasty case	cf. also **grim**

Some forms are derived from dialects, notably those of Jutland:

et slemme menneske, a bad person	cf. also **slemt**
et skønne vejr, beautiful weather	cf. also **skønt**

Of the forms in **-e** only two are current in modern standard Danish:

en skønne dag, one/some day
i ramme alvor, in deadly earnest

204 Variations – plural/definite form

In the following cases the plural form varies from the basic rule in 202 above.

(a) The adjective **lille** borrows a plural form:

Common gender	*Neuter*	*Plural*
en lille pige a small girl	**et lille barn** a small child	**små piger/børn** small girls/children
den lille pige the small girl	**det lille barn** the small child	**de små piger/børn** the small girls/children

Lille and **små** are indeclinable and, unlike English 'little, small', are not interchangeable.

(b) The adjectives **blå**, **grå** and others ending in **-å** do not add **-e** to form the plural or definite:

Common gender	*Neuter*	*Plura/Definite*
en blå skjorte	**et blåt halstørklæde**	**(de) blå bukser**
a blue shirt	a blue scarf	(the) blue trousers

(c) See 207 for indeclinable adjectives.

(d) Adjectives ending in unstressed **-el**, **-en**, **-er** drop the **-e** of the stem before adding the plural **-e**:

Common gender	*Neuter*	*Plural*
en gammel kone	**et gammelt hus**	**gamle koner/huse**
an old woman	an old house	old women/houses
en moden pære	**et modent æble**	**modne pærer/æbler**
a ripe pear	a ripe apple	ripe pears/apples
en lækker kage	**et lækkert wienerbrød**	**lækre kager/wienerbrød**
a tasty cake	a tasty pastry	tasty cakes/pastries

See 225(c) for comparative forms.

This group also includes:

simpel, simple; **sjofel**, dirty; **ædel**, noble; and many loans in **-abel**: **diskutabel**, **fashionabel**, **kapabel**, and in **-ibel**: **fleksibel**, **plausibel**

doven, idle; **ulden**, woollen; **voksen**, adult; **åben**, open

bitter, bitter; **fager**, fair; **mager**, lean; **sikker**, sure

Note 1 – Adjectives with a double consonant in the stem drop one consonant as well as the -e- of the stem in the plural form:

bitter – bitre, bitter; **sikker – sikre**, certain

Note 2 – Adjectives in stressed **-el** double the final **-l** before adding the plural ending (cf. 206):

industriel – industrielle, industrial; **officiel – officielle**, official

(e) Adjectives in **-et** change the **-t** to **-d** when adding **-e** in the plural (and definite) form:

Common gender	*Neuter*	*Plural*
en tosset film	**et tosset spørgsmål**	**tossede film/spørgsmål**
a silly film	a silly question	silly films/questions

This group includes **broget**, multicoloured, and many past participles: e.g. **elsket**, loved; **forlovet**, engaged; **malet**, painted; **pakket**, packed; **repareret**, repaired; **slukket**, extinguished

(f) Some past participles have alternative plural forms in **-ne/-de**:

bedragen/bedraget	**bedragne/bedragede**	deceived
henreven/henrevet	**henrevne/henrevede**	carried away
overdragen/overdraget	**overdragne/overdragede**	transferred

Others include: **besveget, hensovet, iagttaget, inddraget**

See also 530.

205 Variations – adjectives ending in **-en/-et**

(a) Adjectives ending in **-en** usually add **-t** in the neuter form:

en åben forretning	**et åbent vindue**
an open shop	an open window

Others include: **erfaren**, experienced; **gedigen**, genuine; **gylden**, golden; **kneben**, narrow; **kræsen**, fussy; **lunken**, lukewarm; **moden**, ripe; **muggen**, mouldy; **nyfigen**, inquisitive; **nøgen**, naked; **vissen**, withered

Note – **egen** (own) has the neuter form **eget**, but if it means 'peculiar' it can have the form **egent**.

This group includes most adjectives originally derived from past participle forms where the forms are no longer associated with the original verb:

en forfalden villa	**et forfaldent hus**
a ramshackle detached house	a ramshackle house
en vågen betjent	**et vågent øje**
a vigilant policeman	a watchful eye

(b) When used as a verb (expressing the result of activity) the past participle only has the **-et** form irrespective of the gender of the subject:

Bilen er stjålet. The car has been stolen.	cf. **Uret er stjålet.** The watch has been stolen.
en maskinskrevet meddelelse a typewritten message	cf. **et maskinskrevet brev** a typewritten letter

But when the past participle depicts a state either **-en** (**-ne**) or **-et** are technically possible:

en stjålet (or **stjålen**) **bil** a stolen car	cf. **et stjålet ur** a stolen watch
Bilerne er stjålet (or **stjålne**). The cars have been stolen.	**cf. Urene er stjålet** (or **stjålne**). The watches have been stolen.

In these cases the **-et** form is more modern and is stylistically unmarked, while the **-en/-ne** form is more formal and archaic.

Some other past participles which possess an adjectival form in **-en** are:

overdreven, exaggerated; **rusten**, rusty; **sprukken**, cracked; **sulten**, hungry; **uopdragen**, ill-mannered; **voksen**, grown-up

Some weak verbs also have two possible forms for the plural:

Bilen er lejet. The car is hired.	**Bilerne er lejet** (or **lejede**). The cars are hired.

In some rare cases a distinction is made in the singular between a verbal use of the past participle (literal) in **-et** and an adjectival use (figurative) in **-ent** (cf. (a) above):

et stjålet ur a stolen watch	**et stjålent blik** a furtive glance
slebet glas polished glass	**et slebent væsen** a polished manner
kødet er svedet the meat is burned	**et svedent smil** a knowing smile

For use with the verbs **have, være, blive** see 530.

206 Variations – adjectives doubling the final consonant

Adjectives ending in a short stressed vowel + consonant double the final consonant when adding the plural (and definite) ending **-e**:

Common gender	*Neuter*	*Plural*
en morsom bog	**et morsomt foredrag**	**morsomme historier**
an amusing book	an amusing lecture	amusing stories

Many adjectives do this, e.g. **dum – dumme**, stupid; **flot – flotte**, posh; **grim – grimme**, ugly; **grøn – grønne**, green; **langsom – langsomme**, slow; **let – lette**, light; **mæt – mætte**, replete; **slem – slemme**, nasty; **smuk – smukke**, pretty; **tom – tomme**, empty; **træt – trætte**, tired; **tyk – tykke**, fat; **tør – tørre**, dry

See 225(b) for comparative forms.

207 Indeclinable adjectives

The following types of adjective are indeclinable, i.e. do not add an inflexional ending in either the indefinite or definite declension, but see also 228 for comparative forms.

(a) Adjectives ending in **-e**:

Indefinite

Common gender	*Neuter*	*Plural*
en moderne bil	**et moderne hus**	**moderne mennesker**
a modern car	a modern house	modern people

Definite

Common gender	*Neuter*	*Plural*
den moderne bil	**det moderne hus**	**de moderne mennesker**
the modern car	the modern house	the modern people

Indefinite

Common gender	*Neuter*	*Plural*
en ventende mor	**et elskende par**	**rasende anfald**
an expectant mother	a loving couple	furious attacks

Definite

Common gender	*Neuter*	*Plural*
den ventende mor	**det elskende par**	**de rasende anfald**
the expectant mother	the loving couple	the furious attacks

This group includes: **bange**, afraid; **lige**, equal; **stille**, calm; **øde**, deserted; and some ordinal numbers and present participles: **tredje**, third; **fjerde**, fourth; **irriterende**, irritating; **larmende**, noisy; **levende**, living; **tilsvarende**, corresponding; **velhavende**, well-to-do; **vidtspændende**, wide-ranging

(b) Many adjectives ending in a vowel:

en snu mand	**et snu vidne**	**snu forretningsmænd**
a wily man	a wily witness	wily businessmen

This group includes: **ekstra**, extra; **gaga**, gaga; **kry**, cocky; **lilla**, lilac-coloured; **prima**, first-rate; **rosa**, pink; **sky**, shy; **tro**, faithful; **ædru**, sober

Note 1 – Exceptions: The following adjectives ending in a stressed vowel inflect according to the basic rule but have an optional **-e** in the definite and plural forms:

fri – frit – fri(e), free; **ny – nyt – ny(e)**, new

Note 2 – Exceptions: **blå** and **grå** do take a **-t** form but do not inflect in the plural/definite: **et gråt hav – det grå hav – grå have**

(c) Adjectives ending in **-s**:

en fælles sag	**et fælles køb**	**fælles venner**
a common cause	a joint purchase	mutual friends

This group includes: **afsides**, remote; **dagligdags**, everyday; **ens**, identical; **gammeldags**, old-fashioned; **nymodens**, new-fangled

Some of these adjectives are formed from other word classes, e.g. adverbs: **forgæves**, in vain, or nouns: **stakkels**, poor

Note 1 – Exceptions: adjectives ending in a long vowel + **s** inflect according to the basic rule:

løs – løst – løse, loose

Others ending in **-øs** and **-løs**: **nervøs**, nervous; **religiøs**, religious; **fantasiløs**, lacking in imagination

Note 2 – Adjectives ending in **-vis** have an optional **-t** in the neuter form (for adverbs in **-vis**, see 602(c) note, 611):

et gradvis(t) tilbagetog, a partial climbdown

For **vis**, certain, see 449.

208 The order of adjective attributes

(a) The order of adjective attributes is very largely the same as in English:

en sød, ung pige, a pretty young girl
den solide, danske arbejder, the solid Danish worker
en rar, gammel mand, a lovely old man

But occasionally differences of emphasis do occur:

et nyt, stort hus, a big new house
en gammel, hvidhåret mand, a white-haired old man

(b) Significant differences in word order from English are found in only a few specific cases (cf. 146):

'First', 'Last':

de tre første dage, the first three days

cf.

De sidste ti år har vi boet i Århus.
For the last ten years we have lived in Århus.

and:

De ti sidste år af sit liv skrev han ingen digte.
For the last ten years of his life he wrote no poems.

When the superlative is relative ('last' = 'most recent') it precedes the numeral; when it is an absolute superlative ('last' = 'final') it follows the numeral. See also 234.

'Worth/y':

Arbejderen er sin løn værd.
The labourer is worth his pay.

Det er intet værd.
It's not worth anything.

'Such':

When used adjectivally the order with **sådan** is different from English:

en sådan begivenhed, such an occurrence
et sådant hus, such a house

But the use of **sådan et**, etc., is very common:

sådan et hus, such a house/a house like that

'Half':

en halv time, half an hour

(c) Adjective attributes in postposition:

It is unusual in modern Danish to find the adjective positioned immediately after the noun. This order is, however, occasionally found in poetry and in relict forms which have now become fixed:

barnlille, little one; **morlille**, little old woman

In e.g. **en mundfuld** (a mouthful) there is ellipsis: **en mund, fuld af mad**, a mouth, full of food

cf. **et stort fad, fuldt af æbler**, a large bowl, full of apples

B THE INDEFINITE DECLENSION

209 Use of the indefinite form

(a) The indefinite form of the adjective is used attributively with no article or pronoun preceding the adjective + noun if the noun is non-count (see 101(a)) or plural:

Common gender	*Neuter*	*Plural*
god mad	**fint vejr**	**lange, lige veje**
good food	fine weather	long, straight roads

(b) The indefinite form of the adjective may be used attributively after:

1 The indefinite article **en, et** (a/an) and cardinal numbers in the plural

2 The following indefinite pronouns: **noget, nogle** (some); **ikke nogen, ikke noget, ikke nogen** (no); **ingen, intet, ingen** (no); **en anden, et andet, andre** ((an)other)

3 The following emphatic pronouns: **sådan en, sådant et, sådan noget, sådan nogle** (such (a)); **sikken en, sikket et, sikke nogle, sikke** (such (a))

4 The following interrogative pronouns: **hvilken, hvilket, hvilke** (which); **hvad for en, hvad for et, hvad for nogle** (which)

5 The following indefinite pronouns: **alle** (all), **flere** (several), **få** (few), **mange** (many)

	Common gender	*Neuter*	*Plural*
1	**en ny bil** a new car	**et nyt hus** a new house	**to nye biler/huse** two new cars/houses
2	**ikke nogen morsom fortælling** not an amusing story	**noget varmt brød** some hot bread	**nogle saftige æbler** some juicy apples
	ikke nogen god idé no good idea	**ikke noget nyt forslag** no new proposal	**ikke nogen gode idéer** no good ideas
	en anden ung mand another young man	**et andet ungt barn** another young child	**andre unge piger** other young girls
3	**sådan en dyr jakke** an expensive jacket like that	**sådan et stærkt tov** a strong rope like that	**sådan nogle store sko** big shoes like that
	sikken en kold blæst what a cold wind	**sikket et fint vejr** what beautiful weather	**sikke nogle mørke skyer** what dark clouds
4	**hvilken ung mand** what young man	**hvilket stort slot** what big castle	**hvilke nye møbler** what new furniture
5	–	–	**mange onde gerninger** many evil deeds
	–	–	**alle unge mennesker** all young people

(c) The indefinite form of the adjective may be used predicatively:

(i) As a subject complement:

Romanen er svær.	The novel is difficult.
Dramaet er svært.	The drama is difficult.
Romanerne/Dramaerne er svære.	The novels/dramas are difficult.
Hun bliver aldrig tyk.	She will never get fat.
Det bliver aldrig rigtigt.	It will never be right.
De bliver aldrig gamle.	They will never grow old.

(ii) As an object complement:

Han malede stolen grøn, bordet gult og væggene hvide.
He painted the chair green, the table yellow and the walls white.

Hun kunne ikke holde maden varm.
She couldn't keep the food hot.

(iii) As a predicative attribute:

Snefnuggene faldt tætte og tunge.
The snowflakes fell dense and heavy.

Hun sad i sofaen, tavs og dyster.
She sat on the sofa, silent and gloomy.

210 Agreement and lack of agreement

(a) Adjectives agreeing with some abstract nouns formed from verbs take the neuter ending.

Adjectives usually agree with the noun they qualify:

Bilen er stor. The car is big.	**Huset er stort.** The house is big.

But some common gender abstract nouns formed from verbs require the neuter ending on the adjective:

Rygning er skadeligt.	Smoking is harmful.

Svømning er dejligt. Swimming is marvellous.

This also applies to infinitive phrases that are used as postponed real subject where the adjective agrees with the pronoun **det**. Here the neuter form is the unmarked form, i.e. the form used naturally if there is no common gender or plural noun present:

Det er skadeligt at ryge. (cf. **At ryge er skadeligt.**)
It is harmful to smoke.

Det er dejligt at svømme. (cf. **At svømme er dejligt.**)
Swimming is marvellous.

(b) Nouns used in a generalized sense take the neuter.

In cases where the subject has a general, abstract or collective sense, the neuter indefinite form of the adjective is often used (as an unmarked form) irrespective of the gender or number of the subject:

Frugt er sundt.	Fruit is healthy.	cf. **frugt-en**
Fisk er dyrt.	Fish is expensive.	cf. **fisk-en**
En lille pause ville være skønt.	A short break would be nice.	cf. **pause-n**

In these cases it is not, for example, the fruit, etc., itself that is healthy, but the abstract idea of eating fruit. Expressions of this type may, therefore, be regarded as ellipted forms:

Det er sundt at spise frugt.	It is healthy to eat fruit.
Det er dyrt at købe fisk.	It is expensive to buy fish.
Det ville være skønt med en lille pause.	It would be nice to have a short break.

(c) Past participles emphasizing an action may inflect according to their inherent meaning in the plural. Compare the following:

(i) Past participles used as predicative complements after the verbs **være/blive** usually agree with a plural subject:

Bilerne er rød*e*/importere*de*. The cars are red/imported.
ADJ/PAST PARTICIPLE

(ii) But past participles of some verbs only agree with a plural subject when depicting a state (adjectival), and have the basic form in **-et** when emphasizing an action (verbal):

Action	*State*
Stolene er (blevet) malet.	**Stolene er malede.**
The chairs are (have been) painted.	The chairs are painted (as opposed to unpainted).
Musikerne er (blevet) engageret til en koncert.	**De unge mennesker var alle stærkt engagerede.**
The musicians were engaged for a concert.	The young people were all deeply involved.
Alle dørene er (blevet) aflåst.	**Dørene er altid aflåste efter kl. 18.**
The doors have been locked.	The doors are always locked after 6 p.m.

Other examples of the verbal past participle emphasizing action are:

Priserne er faldet.	Prices have fallen.
De var draget bort.	They had left.
Syv dage er gået siden ...	A week has passed since ...
15 demonstranter blev arresteret.	15 demonstrators were arrested.
Alle eleverne var samlet.	All the pupils had assembled.
Pengene er brugt.	The money has been used up.

Other examples of the adjectival past participle emphasizing state are:

Jørgen er død, vi er alle rystede.	Jørgen is dead, we are all shaken.
Kufferterne skal være mærkede med navn og adresse.	The cases should be marked with name and address.

See also 530.

(d) There is a growing tendency in the case of certain adjectives to abandon congruence, especially when the adjective is found in the predicative position:

Bordet står klar.
The table is ready.

(Cf. **Det står klart for mig, at han er skyldig.**
It is clear to me that he is guilty.)

Det har vi ikke været opmærksom på.
We have not been aware of this.

(e) In cases of neuter nouns denoting persons, agreement may be according to their meaning (reflected by common gender) rather than their grammatical gender (neuter gender):

Barnet er fuld af visdom.	The child is full of wisdom.
Vidnet blev så hvid som et lagen.	The witness went as white as a sheet.
Postbudet var blevet gammel.	The postman had grown old.

(f) Notice the following idiomatic phrases which do not generally show congruence:

være ked af	**Vi er ked af politikere.** We are bored with politicians.
være ... lig	**Børnene er deres far lig.** The children are like their father.
være læk	**Skibet var læk.** The ship was leaky.
være parat	**Vi er parat til at gøre det.** We are ready to do it.
være vant	**Vi er vant til det.** We are used to it.
være nogen noget skyldig	**De var os tak skyldig.** They owed us a debt of gratitude.
bryde løs	**Uvejret brød løs.** A storm broke.
gå løs	**Svinet gik løs.** The pig was loose.
slippe løs	**Hønsene slap løs.** The hens got loose.
fare vild	**Børnene for vild.** The children got lost.

slippe uskadt	**Turisterne slap uskadt fra jordskælvet.** The tourists survived the earthquake unharmed.
have nogen kær	**Vi har børnene kær.** We love the children.
bliver nogen kvit	**Vi blev endelig de ubudne gæster kvit.** We finally got rid of the uninvited guests.
gøre nogen opmærksom på noget	**De gjorde os opmærksom på fejlen.** They made us aware of the fault.

211 Coordinated subjects

(a) When the subject consists of two or more coordinated elements, the complement is usually in the plural form (but see also 210(c),(d)):

Svend og Anders var forfærdelig snavsede.
Svend and Anders were terribly dirty.

Dronningen og prinsen er populære.
The Queen and Prince are popular.

Note – With two infinitives used as the subject the complement is in the neuter singular:

At arbejde og at hvile er lige nødvendigt. (To) work and (to) rest are equally necessary.

(b) There are some cases where the form of the adjective is determined by the meaning of the subject:

(i) When the coordinated subject is one indivisible idea:

Lov og ret er truet. Law and order are threatened.

(ii) **Både ... og ...** Here two entities are implied and a plural complement is therefore required:

Både han og hun var kedelige. Both he and she were boring.

(iii) **Såvel ... som ...** Again the presence of two entitites renders a plural complement necessary:

Såvel barnet som moderen var grimme og tykke.
Both the child and the mother were ugly and fat.

(iv) **Enten ... eller ... ; hverken ... eller ...** :

1 If each subject is singular then the complement will be singular:

Hverken han eller hun var venlig.	Neither he nor she was kind.
Enten du eller jeg er gal.	Either you or I am mad.

2 If the subject comprises both singular and plural then the complement assumes the number and gender of the subject placed nearest to it:

Hverken læreren eller børnene var trætte.
Neither the teacher nor the children were tired.

Enten vinduerne eller en dør må stå åben.
Either the windows or a door must remain open.

212 Constructions according to meaning

In these cases the inherent meaning of the subject overrides the grammatical number, in other words sense overrides form (cf. 210(e)). Therefore, with subjects denoting a collective, the complement is often found in the plural.

(a) The pronoun **man** is singular, but is found with a plural complement, especially in spoken Danish, when it corresponds to 'they' or 'we' in English:

Man var uenige.	They had a difference of opinion.
Man kan ikke alle være intelligente.	We can't all be intelligent.

When **man** corresponds to English 'one' it is singular:

Man bliver syg, hvis man spiser for meget chokolade.
One will become ill if one eats too much chocolate.

(b) The pronoun **ingen** may be either singular or plural:

Ingen har været syg.	No one has been ill.
Nu er ingen af dem raske.	Now none of them are well.

(c) **Par** is plural:

Brudeparret var lykkelige.	The bridal couple were happy.

(d) Collective nouns such as **hold** (team) and **regering** (government) may indicate either a group (and the complement is singular) or a number of individuals (and the complement is plural):

Holdet er stærkt.	The team is strong.
Holdet var glade for sejren.	The team were delighted with the win.
Regeringen er uenig/uenige.	The government is/are divided.

(e) Titles of published books and newspapers which are plural are regarded as common gender singular for purposes of agreement:

***Syv fantastiske fortællinger* er ikke lettilgængelig.**
Seven Gothic Tales is not easily understood.

213 Words indicating measurement or degree

These cases are rather similar to those in 211. Here adjective agreement with the plural noun is the rule:

En del af bøgerne er læselige.	Some of the books are readable.
(Cf. **En del af landskabet er fladt.**	Part of the landscape is flat.)

Størstedelen af/Størsteparten af eleverne er flittige.
The majority of the pupils are hard-working.

214 The independent adjective

The adjective is normally used either attributively or predicatively, and is subordinated to the noun. Sometimes, however, it functions independently. There are various intermediate stages between adjective and noun (see 221–23), but one or two types of independent adjective are always found in the neuter form:

(a) Colours:

Søren så rødt.
Søren saw red.

Jeg har det sort på hvidt.
I have it in black and white (i.e. in writing).

(b) Nominalized adjective retaining its adjectival ending (always in the neuter form):

Jeg holder mere af surt end af sødt.
I prefer savoury (things) to sweet (things).

Other idioms using the nominalized adjective are:

Hvad nyt?
What's new?

Pigen har ondt i maven.
The girl has a stomach-ache.

Jeg fik hverken vådt eller tørt.
I got neither food nor drink.

De fulgtes ad igennem tykt og tyndt.
They stayed together through thick and thin.

Ordet skal skrives med stort.
The word is written with a capital letter.

Vi har svært ved det.
We have some difficulty with it.

215 The indefinite use of adjectives: summary

Common gender	*Neuter*	*Plural*	*Paragraph*
ATTRIBUTIVE			
1 When no word precedes adjective + noun:			209(a)(b)
god mad good food	**fint vejr** fine weather	**nye bøger** new books	

Common gender	*Neuter*	*Plural*	*Paragraph*
2 When one of the following articles or pronouns precedes adjective + noun:			209(b)
en **stor dreng** = a/two	***et*** **stort hus**	***to*** **store drenge/huse**	
– = a/some/any	***noget*** **stort hus**	***nogle*** **store drenge/huse**	
ikke nogen **stor dreng** = no	***ikke noget*** **stort hus**	***ikke nogen*** **store drenge/huse**	
ingen **stor dreng** = no	***intet*** **stort hus**	***ingen*** **store drenge/huse**	
en anden **stor dreng** = another/other	***et andet*** **stort hus**	***andre*** **store drenge/huse**	
sådan en **stor dreng** = such (a)	***sådant et*** **stort hus**	***sådan nogle*** **store drenge/huse**	
sikke(n) en **stor dreng** = such (a)	***sikke(t) et*** **stort hus**	***sikke nogle*** **store drenge/huse**	
hvilken **stor dreng** = which	***hvilket*** **stort hus**	***hvilke*** **store drenge/huse**	
hver **stor dreng** = each	***hvert*** **stort hus**	–	
–	–	***mange*** **store drenge/huse** = many	
–	–	***flere*** **store drenge/huse** = several	
lidt **god mad** = a little	***lidt*** **godt øl**		
al **god mad** = all	***alt*** **godt øl**	***alle*** **gode tanker**	
–	–	***få*** **store drenge/huse** = few	
–	–	***adskillige*** **store drenge/huse** = several	
PREDICATIVE			
Drengen er stor. The boy is big.	**Huset er stort.** The house is big.	**Drengene/Husene er store.** The boys/houses are big.	209(c)
Rygning er skadeligt. Smoking is harmful.			210(a)
Fisk er dyrt. Fish is expensive.			210(b)
Stolen er malet. The chair has been painted.			210(c)
Bordet står klar. The table is ready.			210(d)
Postbudet var blevet gammel. The postman had grown old.			210(e)

C THE DEFINITE DECLENSION

216 The definite form of the adjective

(a) The ending used to indicate the definite form of the adjective is the same as that for the indefinite plural, i.e. **-e** is added to the basic form.

Compare:

Indefinite		*Definite*	
Singular	*Plural*	*Singular*	*Plural*
en ung pige	**unge piger**	**den unge pige**	**de unge piger**
a young girl	young girls	the young girl	the young girls
et stort hus	**store huse**	**det store hus**	**de store huse**
a big house	big houses	the big house	the big houses

Notice that there is no distinction made in the definite declension between gender in the common and neuter singular, or between singular and plural, unlike the situation in the indefinite declension.

(b) Without a special definite form are:

(i) Adjectives ending in unstressed **-e**: **stille**, calm; **øde**, deserted; **tredje**, third; **levende**, living

(ii) Some adjectives ending in a stressed vowel (cf. 207(b)): **blå**, blue; **sky**, shy. But notice: **fri(e)**, **ny(e)**, see 207(b) note.

(iii) Some adjectives in **-s** (cf. 207(c)): **fælles**, common; **gammeldags**, old-fashioned

Note – Exceptions: the following adjectives in **-s** take **-e**:

hvas, sharp; **konfus**, confused; **løs**, loose; **nervøs**, nervous; **tilfreds**, contented

(c) The end article **-(e)n**, **-(e)t** is not used in definite constructions (Type 1 in 217f), but is replaced by a front article, **den (det, de)**, which is identical to one type of demonstrative pronoun (see 421):

manden, the man ⇨ **den gamle mand**, the old man

217 Use of the definite form

There are three types of definite construction in which adjective and noun can be combined.

Common gender	*Neuter*	*Plural*
TYPE 1 After the front article **den, det, de** and the demonstratives **den, det, de, denne, dette, disse** (218):		
den røde dør the/that red door	**det røde tag** the/that red roof	**de røde vægge** the/those red walls
denne nye båd this new boat	**dette nye skib** this new ship	**disse nye færger** these new ferries
TYPE 2 After genitives and possessive pronouns (219):		
Karens store gård Karen's big farm	**familiens fattige hjem** the family's poor home	**pigens gamle sko** the girl's old shoes
min varme jakke my warm jacket	**mit varme tørklæde** my warm scarf	**mine varme sokker** my warm socks
vores grønne vase our green vase	**vores hvide spisebord** our white dining table	**vores sorte stole** our black chairs
TYPE 3 With no word preceding the adjective + noun (220):		
Kære ven! Dear friend!	**ovennævnte brev** the above–mentioned letter	**omtalte forfattere** the aforementioned authors

218 The definite form after the front article **den (det, de)** and the demonstratives **den (det, de), denne (dette, disse)**

When an adjective is used before a noun in the definite, the end (definite) article is replaced by a front article **den, det, de** or a demonstrative **den (det, de), denne (dette, disse)**:

Common gender	*Neuter*	*Plural*
sygdommen the illness	**vejret** the weather	**æblerne** the apples

but:

den alvorlige sygdom the/that serious illness	**det dårlige vejr** the/that bad weather	**de røde æbler** the/those red apples
denne alvorlige sygdom this serious illness	**dette dårlige vejr** this bad weather	**disse røde æbler** these/those red apples

These are the most frequent uses of the definite declension. The noun is defined twice, by the front article in the singular and by the definite ending on the adjective.

219 The definite form after genitives and possessive pronouns

(a) The word preceding the adjective in this case is either a noun in the genitive (i.e. usually ending in **-s**) or a possessive pronoun:

Common gender	*Neuter*	*Plural*
Genitive		
Eriks gule cykel Erik's yellow bicycle	**Gittes røde tørklæde** Gitte's red scarf	**Sørens smarte bukser** Søren's smart trousers
firmaets gamle fabrik the firm's old factory	**værelsets store vindue** the room's large window	**byens smalle gader** the town's narrow streets
Possessive		
min dygtige elev my clever pupil	**vores gamle tæppe** our old carpet	**hendes gode venner** her good friends

(b) There are several major exceptions to this rule. In these exceptional cases the adjective remains in the indefinite even when found in what might appear to be a definite construction:

(i) After some genitives of measurement:

flere timers hårdt arbejde	several hours' hard work

(ii) After **en slags**:

en slags hjemmelavet vin	a kind of home-made wine

(iii) After a genitive or a possessive pronoun the adjective **egen** follows the indefinite declension (**zero,-t,-e**):

mors egen lille Svend	mummy's own little Svend
Han har købt sit eget store hus.	He has bought his own big house.
De har deres egne ski.	They have their own skis.

220 The definite form when no article or pronoun precedes the adjective

These constructions are of two different types:

1 The end article is impossible (as in (a) below), or omitted (as for types 1 and 2 (in 217) as in (b)–(f) below).

2 The end article is added after **hele** and **selve** (in (g) below).

The following are common constructions of this kind:

(a) Some forms of address with proper nouns and other expressions denoting relationships:

Kære far/Peter/professor Hansen	Dear father/Peter/Professor Hansen
gamle Lars	old Lars
unge Svend	young Svend

Note 1 – Occasionally the adjective is compounded with a following common noun:

storesøster, big sister; **lillebror,** little brother

Note 2 – In earlier titles the adjective and front article were placed after the proper noun:

Knud den Store, King Canute; **Gorm den Gamle,** King Gorm the Old; **Olav den Hellige,** Saint Olav

(b) Some other uses in place names:

Store Kongensgade; Gamle Carlsberg; Vestre Fængsel

(c) Some expressions with the superlative:

med største fornøjelse	with great pleasure
i højeste grad	to the highest degree
efter bedste evne	to the best of one's ability

(d) Some expressions with the words **første, sidste, bedste,** (and indeclinable) **forrige** and **næste**:

første gang	the first time
kærlighed ved første blik	love at first sight
sidste forestilling	the last performance
for sidste gang	for the last time
sidste måned/år	last month/year
forrige uge/måned/år	last week/month/year
næste søndag/morgen/måned/år	next Sunday/morning/month/year
samme størrelse	the same size

Note 1 – **Næste** meaning 'following' can take a front article:

det næste år, the following year
den næste dag, the following day

Note 2 – **Forrige** meaning 'previous' can take a front article:

det forrige år, the previous year

Note 3 – Strictly speaking, when 'last' means 'latest' Danish should use **senest,** and when it means 'absolutely final' **sidst,** but this distinction does not always hold in practice:

kommitéens seneste møde, the committee's last (latest) meeting
øverste sovjets sidste møde, the last (final) meeting of the Supreme Soviet

But: **sidste nyt,** the latest news

(e) Some expressions with participial forms in bureaucratic and legal language:

ovennævnte kontrakt	the above-mentioned contract
omtalte firma	the aforementioned firm
vedlagte lille pakke	the enclosed small package
Jeg, undertegnede, erklærer ...	I, the undersigned, declare ...

(f) Increasingly in popular newspaper language the front article is omitted for the sake of brevity in temporary epithets:

sexede Brigitte, sexy Brigitte; **otteårige Anders**, eight-year-old Anders; **folkekære Uffe**, popular Uffe

(g) The end article is added to the noun in some expressions with **hele** and **selve**:

hele tiden	all the time
hele dagen/natten/året	all day/night/year
selve paven	the Pope himself
drikke af selve flasken	drink straight from the bottle

Note – However, the front article is used in: **det hele**, all of it; **det halve**, half of it; **det meste**, most of it.

See also 413.

D ADJECTIVAL NOUNS

221 Use of adjectival nouns

(a) There are three cases in which adjectives are used as nouns:

(i) When a noun is omitted to avoid repetition:

Han foretrækker dansk mad for fremmed (mad).
He prefers Danish food to foreign (food).

Min jakke er gammel, så jeg køber en ny (jakke).
My jacket is old, so I'm buying a new one.

Et stort (juletræ) og et lille juletræ.
A large Christmas tree and a small one.

Du skal få bogen byttet for en anden (bog).
You will have the book exchanged for another one.

Notice that Danish, unlike English, does not require a word for 'one'.

(ii) When a noun is merely understood (these are usually thought of as quintessential adjectival nouns):

De unge (mennesker) begriber ikke de gamle.
The young do not understand the old.

Som ung (mand) var han køn.
As a young man he was handsome.

Som attenårig (pige) blev hun gravid.
As an eighteen-year-old she got pregnant.

(iii) Independent use with no noun understood (see 214):

Valget stod mellem grønt og blåt.
The choice was between green and blue.

(b) Danish uses adjectival nouns in the definite plural in much the same way as English, largely to describe people:

de arbejdsløse, the unemployed; **de fattige**, the poor; **de rige**, the rich; **de retfærdige**, the just; **de syge**, the sick; **de sårede**, the wounded

Notice that adjectival nouns can have a genitive in **-s**:

de unges verden, the world of the young

(c) The plural indefinite is used independently only of people:

fremmede	strangers
levende og døde	the quick and the dead
rejsende	travellers
voksne	adults

(d) Danish also uses the common gender indefinite singular form of the adjective as a noun to describe a person, often unlike English:

en ansat, an employee; **en fremmed**, a stranger; **en gal**, a madman; **en lille**, a baby; **en lærd**, a scholar; **en nyfødt**, a new-born baby; **en sagkyndig**, an expert; **en syg**, a sick person; **en voksen**, an adult

(e) In some cases Danish also uses the neuter definite singular form of the adjective:

gøre sit bedste, do one's best; **det er det fine ved ham**, that's the nice thing about him; **i det fri**, in the open air

Other examples are:

det latterlige	the ridiculous thing
det mærkelige	the strange thing
det overnaturlige	the supernatural
det umulige	the impossible
det væsentlige	the essential thing
i det store og hele	on the whole
ligge på sit yderste	be at death's door

(f) The use of the definite singular form of the adjectival noun in Danish may occasionally correspond to that in English:

(den) afdøde	the deceased
(den) anklagede	the accused

(g) In many cases where Danish has a definite adjectival noun, English has a common noun:

den dannede	the educated person
den dømte	the convicted person
den myrdede	the murder victim
den sidste	the last person
den troende	the believer
den uskyldige	the innocent person
de ansatte	the employees
de Grønne	the Greens
de hvide, de sorte	the whites, the blacks
de kongelige	the royals
de Konservative	the Conservatives
de kristne	the Christians
de nygifte	the newly-weds
de overlevende	the survivors
de rejsende	the travellers
de sørgende	the mourners

(h) Neuter adjectival nouns in Danish may correspond to abstract nouns in English:

det kloge/ukloge	the wisdom/inadvisability
det nødvendige	the necessity

det passende the suitability

(i) In a few cases Danish uses the definite form of the adjective without an article as a noun to describe people (cf. 217, Type 3) in intimate direct address:

elskede, love; **kæreste**, dearest

(j) Numerals are occasionally used in the definite form without article in Danish:

Jeg bor på fjerde (sal). I live on the fourth (floor).
Frederik skal op i sjette (klasse). Frederik is going into the sixth class.

222 Nationality words

Whereas English often uses adjectival nouns such as 'the English, the French' to express nationality, Danish always has a proper noun, e.g. **englænderne**, **franskmændene**. Some Danish nationality words are listed below.

Country	*Adjective*	*Inhabitant noun (sg./pl.)*	*Meaning of adjective*
Amerika	**amerikansk**	**amerikaner-e**	American
USA, De Forenede Stater			
Belgien	**belgisk**	**belgier-e**	Belgian
Danmark	**dansk**	**dansker-e**	Danish
England	**engelsk**	**englænder-e**	English
(Storbritannien	**britisk**	**brite-r**	British)
Estland	**estisk**	**estlænder-e, ester -e**	Estonian
Finland	**finsk**	**finne-r**	Finnish
Frankrig	**fransk**	**franskmand, -mænd**	French
Færøerne	**færøsk**	**færing-er**	Faroese
Grønland	**grønlandsk**	**grønlænder-e**	Greenlandic
Grækenland	**græsk**	**græker-e**	Greek
Holland	**hollandsk**	**hollænder-e**	Dutch
Irland	**irsk**	**irer-e, irlænder-e**	Irish
Island	**islandsk**	**islænder-e, islænding-e**	Icelandic
Italien	**italiensk**	**italiener-e**	Italian
Japan	**japansk**	**japaner-e**	Japanese
Kina	**kinesisk**	**kineser-e**	Chinese

Country	*Adjective*	*Inhabitant noun (sg./pl.)*	*Meaning of adjective*
Letland	**letlandsk**	**lette-r**	Latvian
Litauen	**litauisk**	**litauer-e**	Lithuanian
Luxemb(o)urg	**luxemb(o)urgsk**	**luxemb(o)urger-e**	Luxemburgish
Nederland(ene)	**nederlandsk**	**nederlænder-e**	Dutch
Norge	**norsk**	**nordmand, -mænd**	Norwegian
Portugal	**portugisisk**	**portugiser-e**	Portuguese
Rusland	**russisk**	**russer-e**	Russian
Spanien	**spansk**	**spanier-e, spaniol-er**	Spanish
Sverige	**svensk**	**svensker-e**	Swedish
Tyskland	**tysk**	**tysker-e**	German
Europa	**europæisk**	**europæer-e**	European

Note 1 – For the use of capital letters with nationality words see 1308–11.

Note 2 – Usually there is no separate female form for inhabitants, but see 110(c)(i).

223 Nominalization of adjectives

(a) Complete nominalization of the adjective (i.e. where an adjective has taken on noun inflexion) is found in the following words:

Adjective:	*Noun:*		
bekendt -e, familiar	**en bekendt**, aquaintance	–	**bekendte**
dyb -t -e, deep	**et dyb**, depth	**dybet**	**dyb**
fed -t -e, fat	**et fedt**, fat	**fedtet**	**fedter**, kinds of fat
god -t -e, good	**en godte**, a sweet	**godten**	**godter**
	et gode, a benefit	**godet**	**goder**
hvid -t -e, white	**en hvide**, white (of egg)	**hviden**	**hvider**
kær(est), dear(est)	**en kæreste**, sweetheart	**kæresten**	**kærester**
næste, next	**en næste**, neighbour	**næsten**	–
ond -t -e, evil	**et onde**, evil	**ondet**	**onder**
vild -t -e, wild	**et vildt**, game	**vildtet**	–

Notice also: **en fuldmægtig – fuldmægtige** (principal in a ministry or firm), from a now archaic adjective **fuldmægtig**.

(b) Note the forms of the following two nominalized adjectives:

(i) **Lille** (indeclinable adj.) – **få/vente en lille**, have/expect a baby; **den lille**, the baby

(ii) **Død -t -e**, dead – **en død**, a dead person; **den døde**, the dead person; **de døde**, the dead (people)
cf. **en død**, a death; **døden**, death

E COMPARISON OF ADJECTIVES

224 Introduction

(a) Danish adjectives possess a basic (positive) form which is inflected according to number, gender and species (definite/indefinite, see Sections A–C), a comparative form which is uninflected and a superlative form which is inflected according to species alone (indefinite or definite declension).

Comparison implies that two objects or circumstances are contrasted or that one is contrasted with itself at a different juncture:

Ib er højere end sin far.
Ib is taller than his father.

Vejret er bedre i dag end i går.
The weather is better today than yesterday.

(b) There are four different methods of comparison in Danish. See paragraph:

(i) The endings **-ere**, **-est** are added to the basic form: 225

Basic	*Comparative*	*Superlative*
pæn	**pænere**	**pænest**
nice	nicer	nicest

(ii) The endings **-(e)re**, **-(e)st** are added to the basic form and its root vowel is modified: 226

Basic	*Comparative*	*Superlative*
ung	**yngre**	**yngst**
young	younger	youngest

(iii) Irregular comparison. A different stem is used: 227

god	**bedre**	**bedst**
good	better	best

(iv) The words **mere, mest** are used with the basic form: 228

snavset	**mere snavset**	**mest snavset**
dirt	dirtier	dirtiest

(c) The superlative (and not the comparative) is used to compare between two:

Hvilket er det smukkeste af de to billeder?
Which is the more/most beautiful of the two pictures?

Erik er den ældste af de to søskende.
Erik is the elder of the two siblings.

225 Comparison with the endings -ere, -est

Basic	*Comparative*	*Superlative*
glad	**gladere**	**gladest**
happy	happier	happiest

(a) Most adjectives compare in this way, including many monosyllabic adjectives, e.g.:

dyr, expensive; **dyb**, deep; **fin**, fine; **fri**, free; **høj**, high; **hård**, hard; **kold**, cold; **kort**, short; **lav**, low; **lys**, light; **mørk**, dark; **ny**, new; **pæn**, beautiful; **sjov**, fun(ny); **tung**, heavy; **tynd**, thin

(b) Adjectives ending in a consonant after a short stressed vowel often double the final consonant when adding the comparative and superlative endings:

Basic	*Comparative*	*Superlative*
let	**lettere**	**lettest**
easy	easier	easiest
skøn	**skønnere**	**skønnest**
lovely	lovelier	loveliest

Basic	*Comparative*	*Superlative*
smuk beautiful	**smukkere** more beautiful	**smukkest** most beautiful

See also 206.

(c) Adjectives ending in **-el**, **-en**, **-er** drop the **-e-** of the stem before adding the comparative and superlative endings:

sjofel shabby	**sjoflere** shabbier	**sjoflest** shabbiest
doven lazy	**dovnere** lazier	**dovnest** laziest
mager lean	**magrere** leaner	**magrest** leanest

See also 204(d).

(d) **Nær** has deviant forms:

nær close	**nærmere** closer	**nærmest** closest

Note – When **nær** = 'intimate' it compares **nærere, nærest.**

(e) Adjectives in **-(l)ig**, **-agtig**, **-som** and some in **-rig** add **-ere**, **-st** to the basic form:

hyppig frequent	**hyppigere** more frequent	**hyppigst** most frequent
livagtig lifelike	**livagtigere** more lifelike	**livagtigst** most lifelike
voldsom violent	**voldsommere** more violent	**voldsomst** most violent

Like this go: **dejlig**, lovely; **farlig**, dangerous; **fattig**, poor; **fordelagtig**, advantageous; **langsom**, slow; **morsom**, funny; **talrig** (notice: **talrig(e)st**), numerous

226 Comparison with the endings **-(e)re**, **-(e)st** plus modification of the root vowel

(a) Four adjectives compare in this way:

Basic	*Comparative*	*Superlative*	
få	**færre**	**færrest**	few
lang	**længere**	**længst**	long
stor	**større**	**størst**	big
ung	**yngre**	**yngst**	young

(b) However, there are a number of comparative and superlative forms of this kind, originally derived from adverbs of place but now regarded as deficient in a basic form (see also 607(f), 616):

(ind)	**indre**	**inderst**	inner, innermost
(ud)	**ydre**	**yderst**	outer, outermost
(over)	**øvre**	**øverst**	upper, uppermost
(ned)	**nedre**	**nederst**	lower, lowest
(under)	–	**underst**	at the bottom
(bag)	–	**bagest**	hindmost
(frem)	–	**fremmest**	foremost
(før)	–	**først**	first
(midt)	–	**midterst**	in the middle
(mellem)	–	**mellemst**	in the middle

227 Irregular comparison

(a) Six adjectives have comparative and superlative forms that adopt a new stem:

Basic	*Comparative*	*Superlative*	
dårlig, ond, slem	**værre**	**værst**	bad, evil
gammel	**ældre**	**ældst**	old
god	**bedre**	**bedst**	good
lille	**mindre**	**mindst**	small
mange	**flere**	**flest**	many
megen, meget	**mere**	**mest**	much

(b) 'Worse, worst'

(i) **Værre, værst** often indicates more of a bad quality:

Hendes dårlige finger er blevet værre.
Her bad finger has got worse.

Hendes slemme hoste er blevet værre.
Her bad cough has got worse.

Det onde diktatur i landet er blevet værre.
The evil dictatorship in the country has got worse.

(ii) **Dårligere, dårligst** often indicates less of a good quality:

Kartoflerne er blevet dårligere.
The potatoes have got worse.

(c) 'More, most'

(i) **Flere, flest** are plural forms used with count nouns (see 101):

Vi har ikke købt flere bøger.
We haven't bought more books.

De fleste bøger er dyre.
Most books are expensive.

(ii) **Mere, mest** are singular forms used with non-count nouns (see 101):

Vil du have mere kaffe?
Would you like some more coffee?

Det meste sukker kommer fra Vestindien.
Most sugar comes from the West Indies.

With numbers alone **mere end** is used: **mere end 100**, more than 100. This is now usually applied to numeral + noun:

Der var mere end 100 mennesker til stede.
There were more than 100 people present.

228 Comparison with mere, mest

This group includes a number of different types.

(a) Most present and past participles and most longer adjectives:

Basic	*Comparative*	*Superlative*
iøj(n)efaldende striking	**mere iøj(n)efaldende** more striking	**mest iøj(n)efaldende** most striking
spændende exciting	**mere spændende** more exciting	**mest spændende** most exciting
velkendt well-known	**mere velkendt** more well-known	**mest velkendt** most well-known

(b) All adjectives in **-et**:

interesseret interested	**mere interesseret** more interested	**mest interesseret** most interested

Like this go: **forvirret**, confused; **langhåret**, longhaired; **skuffet**, disappointed; **snavset**, dirty; **tosset**, foolish; **velnæret**, well-nourished

Cf. 204(e).

(c) All adjectives with the suffix **-isk**:

praktisk practical	**mere praktisk** more practical	**mest praktisk** most practical

Like this go: **fantastisk**, fantastic; **høvisk**, courteous; **jordisk**, earthly; **komisk**, comical; **krigerisk**, warlike; **realistisk**, realistic; **rytmisk**, rhythmical; **typisk**, typical

Cf. 203(a)(i).

Note – This does not apply to monosyllabic adjectives ending in **-sk**. These take inflexional comparative endings (but see 229, note 1):

besk	**beskere**	**beskest**
bitter	more bitter	most bitter

Others are: **barsk**, harsh; **fersk**, fresh (with **vand**); **frisk**, fresh, new

(d) Some adjectives in **-en**:

sulten	**mere sulten**	**mest sulten**
hungry	more hungry	most hungry

Like this go: **gnaven**, irritable; **kræsen**, choosy; **regelbunden**, regular; **skrækslagen**, terrified; **velbeholden**, safe; **voksen**, adult; **vågen**, awake; **åben**, open

Cf. 204(d), 205.

(e) Some adjectives in unstressed **-e** and short adjectives ending in a vowel:

bange	**mere bange**	**mest bange**
afraid	more afraid	most afraid

Like this go: **stille**, peaceful; **grå**, grey; **ædru**, sober

Cf. 207(a).

Note – Exceptions: **fri – friere – friest**, free; **ny – nyere – nyest**, new; **nøje – nøjere – nøjest**, precise; **ringe – ringere – ringest**, poor (of quality)

(f) Some adjectives ending in **-s**:

gammeldags	**mere gammeldags**	**mest gammeldags**
old-fashioned	more old-fashioned	most old-fashioned

Others: **afsides**, remote; **gængs**, current; **kompleks**, complex; **nymodens**, new-fangled

See also 207(c).

(g) Some loan words:

intellektuel	**mere intellektuel**	**mest intellektuel**
intellectual	more intellectual	most intellectual

Like this go: **desperat**, desperate; **handy**, handy; **resistent**, resistant; **senil**, senile; **sporty**, sporty

(h) Cases where two different adjectives are compared:

Han er mere smart end ærlig.	He is more smart than honest.

229 Adjectives which do not normally compare

Some adjectives do not usually compare when used in a concrete sense. These include adjectives whose sense is either absolute (i.e. always occurs in the same way) or complex (i.e. denotes specific circumstances):

arbejdsløs, unemployed; **barnløs**, childless; **daglig**, daily; **dansk**, Danish; **død**, dead; **evig**, eternal; **firkantet**, rectangular; **halt**, lame; **hel**, whole; **ligbleg**, deathly pale; **lige**, equal, straight; **socialdemokratisk**, Social Democratic; **stum**, dumb; **åben**, open

Note 1 – When some of the above adjectives are used metaphorically they do compare:

Hun er den dødeste sild, jeg kender.	She is the most boring person (*lit.* the deadest herring) I know.
Han er noget af det mest danske.	He is terribly Danish.

Note 2 – Colours may be compared:

Dine øjne er mere blå end hans.	Your eyes are bluer than his.
de rødeste roser	the reddest roses

230 The comparative is indeclinable

The comparative retains the same form for both indefinite and definite irrespective of gender and number:

Hun har en ældre søster.	She has an older sister.
Hun er min ældre søster.	She is my elder sister.
Den ældre søster hedder Mette.	The older sister is called Mette.
De har et ældre hus.	They have a rather old house.
Det ældre hus ligger ved søen.	The older house is by the lake.
de ældre søstre/huse	the older sisters/houses

Cf. Indeclinable adjectives in **-e**, 207(a).

231 Inflexion of the superlative

(a) Like the basic form of the adjective, the superlative also has a definite form in **-e**:

lettest – det letteste	**hyppigst – det hyppigste**	**ældst – de ældste**
light – the lightest	frequent – the most frequent	oldest – the oldest

(b) When used predicatively the superlative is either left uninflected (indefinite declension) or inflected (definite declension):

Dine roser er smukkest. *Indefinite*
Your roses are most beautiful.

Dine roser er de smukkeste i byen. *Definite*
Your roses are the most beautiful in the town.

(c) When used attributively the superlative is always inflected (definite declension):

Common gender	*Neuter*	*Plural*
den smukkeste rose	**det smukkeste digt**	**de smukkeste billeder**
the most beautiful rose	the most beautiful poem	the most beautiful pictures

(d) In superlatives when the front article precedes **mest** plus the basic form of the adjective, the adjective takes the definite ending:

Det var den mest fantastiske forestilling.
It was the most fantastic performance.

Han er den mest berejste journalist.
He is the most widely travelled journalist.

Hun er den mest velkendte politiker.
She is the best-known politician.

Jette er den mest temperamentsfulde pige.
Jette is the most temperamental girl.

Note – The present participle already ends in **-e**:

Det var den mest spændende film.	It was the most exciting film.
Det var det mest intetsigende svar.	It was the most inane reply.

(e) The superlatives are sometimes used in the definite form without the front article in **bedst, først, sidst**. See 220(c),(d).

232 Similarity, dissimilarity and reinforcement

(a) Phrases with **som** or **så ... som** are used to link two elements that are similar:

De taler samme sprog som os.
They speak the same languages as us.

De nye studerende er lige så flittige som de gamle.
The new students are just as hard-working as the old ones.

De seneste romaner er ikke (lige) så interessante som de tidlige.
The latest novels are not as interesting as the early ones.

See 408 for pronouns in these expressions.

Note – Subordinate clauses expressing similarity often begin with **som om**:

Manden lyder, som om han er fuld.	The man sounds as if he is drunk.
Det ser ud, som om der vil komme sne.	It looks as though there's going to be snow.

(b) The adverb **lige** is used with the basic form of the adjective to express similarity:

Børnene er lige intelligente.
The children are equally intelligent.

Hun er mindst lige så gammel som ham.
She is at least as old as him.

See 408 for pronouns in these expressions.

(c) With comparatives the particle **end** is often used:

Whisky er stærkere end øl.	Whisky is stronger than beer.
Han kører bedre end dig.	He drives better than you.

See 408 for pronouns in these expressions.

(d) The adjectives **forskellig, anden** and **anderledes** express dissimilarity:

De to børn er meget forskellige.
The two children are very different.

Han er en ganske anden mand, end han tidligere var.
He is a very different man from what he was previously.

De er anderledes end andre mennesker.
They are different from other people.

(e) In order to reinforce the comparative and superlative, the words **stadig, endnu** and the amplifying prefix **aller-** are used:

Hun bliver stadig bedre.	She is getting better and better.
Hun bliver endnu bedre.	She is going to be even better.
Søren var min allerbedste ven.	Søren was my very best friend.

(f) 'The more ... the more' is expressed in Danish by the bracketing expression **jo (mere) ... jo (mere)** or **jo (mere) ... des/desto (mere)**:

Jo mere han tjente, jo/des(to) mere brugte han.
The more he earned, the more he spent.

See also 918(d).

233 The absolute comparative

(a) When the second part of the comparison is not stated in Danish, the element of comparison may in part or in whole disappear. This is known as an absolute comparative, as opposed to a relative comparative. The Danish construction is often translated into English as 'rather X', 'quite Y'. Only a limited number of adjectives are used in this way.

Relative comparative:
Den sum penge, han vandt, var større, end han troede.
The sum of money he won was larger than he thought.

Absolute comparatives:
Han har vundet en større sum penge i lotteriet.
He has won quite a large sum on the lottery.

De brugte en mindre formue på rejser.
They spent a small fortune on travel.

De har købt en mindre villa.
They have bought quite a small detached house.

Han skal ikke være her i længere tid.
He is not staying for very long.

Dette er hændt i nyere tid.
This has happened recently.

Han fik sig en værre omgang.
He got a real hiding.

Thomas er en værre Don Juan.
Thomas is a proper Don Juan.

Digtet er skrevet i højere stil.
The poem is written in an elevated style.

Hun kommer kun i højere kredse.
She only moves in the higher circles.

Vi satser på den højere uddannelse.
We are investing in higher education.

Compare: **en gammel dame**, an old lady — **en ældre dame**, an elderly lady
en ung mand, a young man — **en yngre mand**, a youngish man

Note 1 – Informal English uses the suffix '-ish' in some of these cases:

et mindre hus, a smallish house; **en længere færd**, a longish journey; **en bedre middag**, a goodish dinner

Note 2 – Some absolute comparatives in English have no equivalent in Danish:

Greater Copenhagen	**Storkøbenhavn**
lower lip	**underlæbe**
the Upper House	**Overhuset**

(b) Other idiomatic phrases using the absolute comparative include:

Jeg morede mig ikke videre.	I didn't enjoy myself much.
Der er ingen større skade sket.	No great harm is done.

ved oftere gentagne forsøg	in frequently repeated attempts

234 The absolute superlative

(a) The superlative usually implies a comparison (relative superlative). The absolute superlative is used, however, when the speaker/writer wishes to show that something possesses a quality to a very high degree, without directly comparing it to anything else. The use of the superlative in this way is an exaggeration:

Relative superlative:
Ib og Michael er de bedste studerende i denne årgang.
Ib and Michael are the best students in this year group.

Absolute superlatives:
Ib og Michael er de bedste venner (af verden).
Ib and Michael are the best of friends.

Hun har den største uorden i sine papirer.
Her papers are in great disarray.

(b) Other idiomatic phrases employing the absolute superlative:

med de venligste hilsener	kindest regards
med største fornøjelse	with very great pleasure
med den venligste mine	with a very friendly appearance
på det bestemteste	most definitely
i det mindste	at least
på det sidste	lately
den vidunderligste udsigt	the most wonderful view
Det gør ikke det mindste.	That doesn't matter in the least.
Der var det mest rørende forhold mellem dem.	The relationship between them was very moving.

Note – **Venligst** is often used adverbially corresponding to the English 'please':

Send venligst tres kroner.	Please send 60 kroner.

235 Adjectives – use of the basic, comparative and superlative: summary

	Attributive	*Predicative*
A BASIC		
Indefinite (202–15)	**en livlig pige** **en interesseret elev** **et morsomt program** **frisk vind**	**Pigen er livlig.** **Eleven er interesseret.** **Programmet er morsomt.** **Vindene er friske.**
Definite (216–20)	**den livlige pige** **den interesserede elev** **det morsomme program** **de friske vinde**	
B COMPARATIVE		
Indefinite (224–33)	**en livligere pige** **en mere interesseret elev** **et mere imponerende resultat** **livligere piger** **mere interesserede elever** **morsommere programmer** **mere imponerende resultater**	**Pigen er livligere.** **Eleven er mere interesseret.** **Resultatet er mere imponerende.** **Pigerne er livligere.** **Eleverne er mere interesserede.** **Programmerne er morsommere.** **Resultaterne er mere imponerende.**
Definite	**den livligere pige** **den mere interesserede elev** **det mere imponerende resultat** **de livligere piger** **de mere interesserede elever** **de morsommere programmer** **de mere imponerende resultater**	
C SUPERLATIVE (224–34)		
Indefinite		**Pigen/Pigerne er livligst.** **Eleven/Eleverne er mest interesseret/ interesserede.** **Resultatet/Resultaterne er mest imponerende.**
Definite	**den livligste pige** **den mest interesserede elev** **det mest imponerende resultat** **de livligste piger** **de mest interesserede elever** **de mest imponerende resultater**	

F COMPOUND ADJECTIVES

236 Introduction

(a) Adjectives and participles may be prefixed by various word classes to form compound adjectives (see also 1113ff):

Compounded with:	*Examples:*
NOUN	**ordblind**, dyslexic; **fremgangsrig**, successful; **idiotsikker**, idiotproof; **børnevenlig**, child-friendly
ADJECTIVE	**dybfrossen**, deep frozen; **kortsigtet**, shortsighted. Shades of colour: **mørkeblå**, dark blue; **gyldenrød**, golden red
VERB	**vaskeægte**, colour-fast
PRONOUN	**selvoptaget**, self-absorbed
NUMERAL	**enetages**, single-storey
ADVERB	**velholdt**, well-kept
PREPOSITION	**overophedet**, overheated

(b) Only the final element inflects as an adjective (but see 237(c)):

et mørkegrønt træ	a dark green tree
flere krympefrie skjorter	several non-shrink shirts
de synskadede børn	the visually impaired children

237 Comparison of compound adjectives

Compound adjectives compare in one of three ways:

(a) Generally they follow the pattern for the adjective that is second element in the compound (see 224–28):

Basic	*Comparative*	*Superlative*
godmodig good-natured	**godmodigere** more good-natured	**godmodigst** most good-natured

Basic	*Comparative*	*Superlative*
kortvarig	**kortvarigere**	**kortvarigst**
brief	briefer	briefest

(b) In some cases the compound is compared with **mere**, **mest**:

dybfrossen	**mere dybfrossen**	**mest dybfrossen**
deep frozen	more deep frozen	most deep frozen
formfuldendt	**mere formfuldendt**	**mest formfuldendt**
elegant	more elegant	most elegant
kortfattet	**mere kortfattet**	**mest kortfattet**
concise	more concise	most concise
opsigtsvækkende	**mere opsigtsvækkende**	**mest opsigtsvækkende**
sensational	more sensational	most sensational
svenskvenlig	**mere svenskvenlig**	**mest svenskvenlig**
Sweden-friendly	more Sweden-friendly	most Sweden-friendly

(c) In a few cases of adjective + adjective compounds, the first element alone may compare:

tætbefolket	**tættere befolket**	**tættest befolket**
densely populated	more densely populated	most densely populated

3 NUMERALS

A FORMS OF NUMERALS

301 List of cardinal and ordinal numbers

	Cardinal numbers		*Para.*	*Ordinal numbers*	*Paragraph*
0	**nul**	zero	301*n*10		
1	**en/et**	one	302	**første**	311(a)
2	**to**	two, etc.	303	**anden, andet**	311(b)
3	**tre**			**tredje**	301*n*11

	Cardinal numbers	Para.	Ordinal numbers	Para.
4	**fire**		**fjerde**	301*n*11
5	**fem**		**femte**	301*n*11
6	**seks**		**sjette**	301*n*11
7	**syv**		**syvende**	301*n*11
8	**otte**		**ottende**	
9	**ni**		**niende**	
10	**ti**		**tiende**	
11	**el(le)ve**		**el(le)vte**	301*n*11
12	**tolv**		**tolvte**	
13	**tretten**		**trettende**	
14	**fjorten**		**fjortende**	
15	**femten**		**femtende**	
16	**seksten**		**sekstende**	
17	**sytten**		**syttende**	
18	**atten**		**attende**	
19	**nitten**		**nittende**	
20	**tyve**		**tyvende**	
21	**enogtyve**	301*n*1	**enogtyvende**	
22	**toogtyve**		**toogtyvende**	
30	**tred(i)ve**		**tred(i)vte**	
40	**fyrre**		**fyrretyvende**	
50	**halvtreds**	305	**halvtredsindstyvende**	
60	**tres**	305	**tresindstyvende**	
70	**halvfjerds**	305	**halvfjerdsindstyvende**	
80	**firs**	305	**firsindstyvende**	
90	**halvfems**	305	**halvfemsindstyvende**	
100	**(et) hundred(e)**	304	**hundrede**	
101	**(et) hundred(e) (og) en/et**			
125	**(et) hundred(e) (og) femogtyve**			
200	**to hundred(e)**	301*n*3		
1 000	**(et) tusind(e)**	304	**tusinde**	
1 000 000	**en million -er**	304	**millionte**	
1 000 000 000	**en milliard -er**	304	**milliardte**	
1 000 000 000 000	**en billion -er**	304	**billionte**	

Note 1 – The order of the words in compound numbers above 20 is different from English. Danes place the units first and link them to the tens with an **og** (cf. German 'einundzwanzig'):

femogtyve twenty-five

The word **og** may be omitted in some cases, but in others it must be present. To avoid mistakes it is best to include **og**:

5 346 **fem tusind (og) tre hundrede (og) seksogfyrre**
8 030 **otte tusind og tred(i)ve**
1 055 **tusind og femoghalvtreds**

Note 2 – Numerals under 100 are written as one word (for the use of figures or letters to express numbers see 1314):

46 **seksogfyrre**

50 **halvtreds**

Numerals under 100 are also written as one word when they are part of a larger number:

457 **fire hundrede og syvoghalvtreds**
95 000 **femoghalvfems tusind**

Note 3 – Numerals over 100 are often written as separate words:

200 **to hundred(e)**
235 **to hundred(e) femogtred(i)ve**
5 000 **fem tusind**
7 000 000 **syv millioner**
4 337 **fire tusind (og) tre hundred (og) syvogtred(i)ve**

Note 4 – The gap (or full stop) between the thousands in numbers written as figures corresponds to the English comma:

Danish **13 014 (13.014)** English 13,014
Danish **1 000 000 (1.000.000)** English 1,000,000

Note 5 – Numbers over 1,000 may, as in English, be pronounced in two ways:

1 354 either: **et tusind tre hundrede og fireoghalvtreds**
or: **tretten hundrede og fireoghalvtreds**

Note 6 – In practice large numbers are often written as one word:

ettusindtrehundredefireoghalvtreds

Note 7 – In dates the word **hundrede** is in some cases optional (cf. 315):

år tretten (hundrede) fireoghalvtreds, the year 1354

Note 8 –**Million** and **milliard** are nouns that inflect in the plural:

to millioner indbyggere two million inhabitants
fire milliarder kroner four billion kroner

Note 9 – Cardinal numbers may take a genitive in **-s**:

disse tres store præstation the great achievement of these three

Note 10 – **Nul** translates variously as 'nought, zero, oh, nil, love, duck', and takes a plural noun:

nul grader zero degrees
nul sekunder zero seconds

Note 11 – Ordinal numbers are derived from cardinal numbers by adding the suffixes **-dje**, **-de**, **-te**, **-nde**. Occasionally this requires some modification of the stems, e.g. **elleve - ellevte/elvte**.

302 En, et, én, ét, ene

(a) To distinguish the numeral from the indefinite article (cf. 134) the numeral usually has an acute accent, but this is omitted where there is no likelihood of confusion. The choice of **én** or **ét** to translate English 'one' is determined by the gender of the following noun if there is one. See 101ff.

én bus, ét tog	one bus, one train

cf.

Der kommer en bus/et tog.	A bus/A train is coming.

Note – Before 1955 these numerals were written **een, eet.**

(b) **Én** (not **ét**) is used in general counting and calculating:

én, to, tre ... énogtyve ... hundrede og én
one, two, three ... twenty-one ... a hundred and one

(c) The word **én** is usually indeclinable in compound numerals:

énogtred(i)ve kilo	31 kilos

However, it does agree with a following neuter noun when this comes immediately after the numeral:

to hundrede og ét år	two hundred and one years

(d) **Ét** is used in the following kinds of expressions:

Klokken er ét.	It's one o'clock.
fjende nummer ét	public enemy number one
nummer trehundrede (og) ét	number three hundred and one
linie ét	(bus) line number one
side tohundrede (og) ét	page two hundred and one
hovedvej ét	Highway 1

In the last three examples above the word **nummer** would appear to be understood.

(e) **En** has the definite form **ene**:

den ene af dem	(the) one of them
Han mistede det ene ben.	He lost one of his legs.

Note the following expressions:

den ene efter den anden	one after another/the other
det ene med det andet	one thing and another
døv på det ene øre	deaf in one ear

(f) **En** is also used unstressed to express 'approximately':

en seks-syv stykker	about six or seven

303 To, tve-, etc.

(a) The usual word for 'two' is **to**, and this is also a common prefix, often corresponding to English 'bi-':

todækker, double decker; **tohundredårsdag**, bicentenary; **tosidet**, bilateral; **tosproget**, bilingual

(b) Occasionally the archaic words **tvende** and **trende** are found for 'two' and 'three' in poetic or humorous style.

(c) The prefix **tve-** also indicates 'two':

tvelyd, diphthong; **tvetydig**, ambiguous; **tveægget**, two-edged

(d) The prefix **dobbelt-** is also common:

dobbelthage, double chin; **dobbeltradet**, double-breasted; **dobbeltslebet**, bifocal; **dobbeltstik**, two-way adaptor

(e) The prefix **bi-** is also found, meaning 'two', 'secondary', etc.:

bierhverv, sideline; **bifag**, subsidiary subject; **biseksuel**, bisexual

(f) Notice also **et par**, which means both 'a couple' and 'a few', 'one or two':

om et par dage/uger/måneder/år
in a couple of days/weeks/months/years

304 Hundred(e), tusind(e), etc.

(a) Form and inflexion

The words **hundred(e), tusind(e), million, milliard** and **billion** are all nouns with plurals in **-(e)r**.

Both the long and short forms given above are acceptable, but:

(i) In some compounds the **-e** drops out:

hundredvis, hundreds; **tusindtal**, thousands; but: **attenhundred(e)tallet,** 19th century (see 314).

(ii) In fractions and ordinals (see 311(f), 312) the **-e** must, however, be retained:

to hundrededele, two hundredths; **for hundrede gang**, for the hundredth time

The word **et** may be omitted in numerals with **et hundred(e)** or **et tusind(e)**:

100 personer	**(et) hundred(e) personer**
115	**(et) hundredefemten**
1300	**(et) tusind (og) tre hundred(e)**

In this last example either **et** or **og** must be present:

tusind og tre hundred(e) or **et tusind tre hundred(e)**

(b) To express exact hours by the 24-hour clock the word 'hundred' is translated as **nul nul**:

15.00	fifteen hundred hours	**femten nul nul**

(c) Notice the following expressions:

have hundrede og sytten ting at gøre	to have a hundred and one things to do
århundred(e)	century
tusind år, årtusind(e)	millennium
tusindben	millipede
en tusindkunstner	a Jack of all trades

305 Danish numerals for 20–99 and the 'titalsord'

For a list of numerals see 301.

(a) The Danish cardinal numbers for 40–90 possess older long forms which are more emphatic and formal and are now fast disappearing:

	Modern form:	*Older form:*
40	**fyrre**	**fyrretyve**
50	**halvtreds**	**halvtredsindstyve**
60	**tres**	**tresindstyve**
70	**halvfjerds**	**halvfjerdsindstyve**
80	**firs**	**firsindstyve**
90	**halvfems**	**halvfemsindstyve**

These long forms reveal the derivation of the numerals, which are based on scores (20s) and half scores:

halvtre	**+d**	**sind s**	**tyve**	= 50
2 ½		times	20	
tre		**sind s**	**tyve**	= 60
3		times	20	
halvfjerd		**sind s**	**tyve**	= 70
3 ½		times	20	
fir(e)		**sind s**	**tyve**	= 80
4		times	20	
halvfem		**sind s**	**tyve**	= 90
4 ½		times	20	

Note 1 – **Fyrretyve** (forty) is an exception, the **-tyve** here meaning 'ten'. This longer form is occasionally still used for emphasis.

Note 2 – **Sind** (time, occasion) is still found in the adverbs: **ingensinde**, never; **nogensinde**, ever.

These obscure numerals are unusual among European languages (cf. French 'quatre-vingt', however) and cause problems for foreign learners and for other Scandinavians, especially when spoken at speed, e.g. in telephone numbers which are always given in pairs:

56 72 91	=	**seksoghalvtreds**	**tooghalvfjerds**	**enoghalvfems**
		fifty-six	seventy-two	ninety-one

(b) But Danish also possesses another system which employs the suffix **-ti** like the other main Nordic languages (cf. Swedish and Norwegian 'tretti', thirty):

	Cardinal numbers	*Ordinal numbers*
20	**toti**	**tyvende**
21	**totien**	**tyvendeførste**
30	**treti**	**tretiende**
35	**tretifem**	**tretifemte**
40	**firti**	**firtiende**
43	**firtitre**	**firtitredje**
50	**femti**	**femtiende**
60	**seksti**	**sekstiende**
70	**syvti**	**syvtiende**
80	**otti**	**ottiende**
90	**niti**	**nitiende**

The **tital** forms of the '-ty' words from 20 to 90 are used on cheques, money orders, receipts, contracts, etc., and on the 50-kroner (**femti kroner**) note (since 1957). Whilst in Denmark these are popularly supposed to come from Swedish, they are in fact older Danish forms that were supplanted in everyday use during the last century by the system of scores and half scores. The **-ti** system was revived in commerce after the decimalization of the Scandinavian currencies in 1875, but has never established itself in spoken Danish.

The order of the tens and units with these short forms is unlike the usual Danish order (or that in German), but is the same as in English. Compare the list above with its equivalent in 301.

Although these shorter written forms are rarely used in speech, Danes have been encouraged by linguists to adopt them to aid inter-Nordic understanding. One of several arguments adduced (unsuccessfully) for their more widespread adoption is that the traditional ordinal forms of the present numerals from 40 to 90 are clumsy and are increasingly avoided (see 301).

306 Some other expressions for numerical quantities

(a) et dusin = tolv

et dusin søm	a dozen nails
et halvt dusin lommetørklæder	half a dozen handkerchiefs

(b) **en snes = tyve**

en snes æg	20 eggs
en halv snes jakker	10 jackets
fire snese år gammel	80 years old

Snes, halv snes are often used to indicate approximate number:

en halv snes	about 10

(c) **et gros** = 144

et gros tegnestifter	a gross of drawing pins

(d) Approximate numbers (see also (b) above):

nogle og tred(i)ve	thirty-something
et par og fyrre	forty-two-ish

B THE USE OF CARDINAL NUMBERS

307 Notes on the use of cardinal numbers

(a) Nouns are formed from cardinal numbers by the addition of the suffix **-(e)r** (pl. **-e**): **en ener/etter**, a one; **en toer**, a two.
Others: **en firer, en femmer, en sekser, en syver, en otter, en nier, en tier, en elver, en tolver**; etc.

These indicate the following:

(i) Number, e.g. 'a five', especially in currency:

Stik mig en femmer/tier!	Give me a five/ten (5/10 kroner coin)!

This is also written **5'er/10'er**.

The figure itself is given by adding **-tal**:

Hans syvtaller kan let forveksles med hans firtaller.
His sevens can easily be confused with his fours.

Note – **Et nul – nuller** can also mean 'a nonentity'.

(ii) Number of bus, train, class or ward:

Vi tager en firer til arbejdet.
We take a number four to work.

Etteren går gennem centrum.
The number one goes through the town centre.

en 68'er
bus number 68 (or a person from the 1968 generation)

(b) The following nouns are derived from cardinal numbers:

et årti -er	**et tiår** pl. -	a decade
et århundred(e) -r	**et hundredår** pl. -	a century
et årtusind(e) -r	**et tusindår** pl. -	a millennium

(c) The noun **stykker** (sing. **stykke**, which also means 'a piece') is often inserted after numerals when used alone:

Jeg vil have tre stykker, tak.	I would like three, please.
en fire-fem stykker	four or five
nogle stykker	some

(d) **Gang -en, -e** is used to indicate frequency:

fem/adskillige gange	five/several times
denne gang	this time
en anden gang	another time, on another occasion

(e) 'Twofold', 'threefold', etc.: multiplication of this kind is indicated by employing the suffix **-dobbelt**, i.e. **tredobbelt**, triple; **fir(e)dobbelt**, quadruple, four-fold; etc.

dobbelt så mange ulykker	double the/twice as many accidents
det fir(e)dobbelte af min gage	four times my salary
det seksdobbelte beløb	six times the amount

308 Age

There are a number of different ways of expressing age:

Jesper er tre år (gammel). Jesper is three years old.

Also:

Jesper er en treårig dreng. Jesper is a three-year old boy.
Jesper, i en alder af tre år, ... Jesper, at the age of three, ...
Jesper, et barn på tre år, ... Jesper, a child of three, ...

Note 1 – For approximate age see 306(d).

Note 2 – **Else er i 60'erne/70'erne.** (See also 314(b).) Else is in her 60s/70s.

309 Temperature

+5°C

Termometeret viser 5 plusgrader.
The thermometer is showing (plus) 5.

Det er 5 graders varme.
It is 5 degrees (above).

-5°C

Termometeret viser, at det fryser 5 grader.
Termometeret viser, at det er 5 graders frost.
Termometeret viser, at det er 5 minusgrader.
The thermometer is showing 5 degrees below.

Notice:

Han har 40 graders feber/40 i feber.
He has a temperature of 40°C (104°F).

Han har meget høj feber.
He has a very high temperature.

Skal du tage hans temperatur nu?
Are you going to take his temperature now?

Temperaturen stiger/falder.
The temperature is rising/falling.

310 Mathematical expressions

Notice the differences in mathematical symbols:

Danish	*English*	*Danish*
$4 + 5 = 9$	$4 + 5 = 9$	**fire plus fem er ni**
$12 \div 2 = 10$	$12 - 2 = 10$	**tolv minus to er ti/to fra tolv er ti**
$6 \cdot 3 = 18$	$6 \times 3 = 18$	**seks gange tre er atten**
$10:5 = 2$	$10 \div 5 = 2$	**ti divideret/delt med fem er to/ fem op i ti er to**
$2^2 = 4$	$2^2 = 4$	**kvadratet af to er fire/ to i anden (potens) er fire**
$10^3 = 1000$	$10^3 = 1000$	**ti i/ophøjet til tredje potens er tusind**
$\sqrt{16} = 4$	$\sqrt{16} = 4$	**kvadratroden af seksten er fire**
%	%	**procent**
‰	‰	**promille**

Note 1 – **200 x 45** is in Danish a measurement of area (200 by 45).

Note 2 – The decimal point in English is a decimal comma in Danish, e.g. **2,5; 3,5**

C THE USE OF ORDINAL NUMBERS

311 Notes on the use of ordinal numbers

(a) Ordinal numbers are found with the front article, or after a possessive or a noun with the **-s** genitive:

Det er den første i dag.	It's the first today.
Eva er hans anden kone.	Eva is his second wife.
Det er Jans tredje bil.	It is Jan's third car.

Note – The following expressions with **første, anden**:

første juledag, Christmas Day; **anden juledag,** Boxing Day
for det første/andet, firstly, in the first place /secondly, in the second place
med det første, soon
ikke med det første, not for a while

(b) **Anden, andet** means 'second', but also 'other', in which case it has a plural form **andre**:

for anden gang	a second time
intet andet sted	nowhere else
de andre børn	the other children

To avoid confusion Danes often use **nummer to** for the ordinal 'second':

Eva er Prebens kone nummer to.	Eva is Preben's second wife.

(c) Figures are often used instead of words for ordinals, notably in the names of rulers and popes:

Pius den Tolvte	**Pius 12./Pius XII**
Christian den Fjerde	**Christian 4./Christian IV**

Note 1 – The method of mixing numbers and letters, i.e. **1ste, 2den, 3dje**, etc., is now archaic in Danish.

Note 2 – Numbers are often used for ordinals, in which case a full stop comes after the Arabic numeral but not after Roman numerals, cf. above.

(d) Ordinal numbers are used to indicate frequency of occurrence:

en gang hvert tred(i)vte minut	once every 30 minutes/thirtieth minute
en gang hver fjortende dag	once every 14 days/fortnight
en gang hvert sjette år	once every 6 years/sixth year

(e) Notice also the following expressions:

first name	**fornavn**
first night	**premiere**
first thing (tomorrow)	**straks i morgen tidlig**

(f) Most fractions are formed from ordinal numbers (see 312).

D FRACTIONS

312 Fractions

(a) The numerator in fractions is a cardinal number and the denominator an ordinal number to which is added the noun **-del(-e)**:

en femtedel	= 1/5
tre femtedele	= 3/5
en femtedel liter	= 1/5 litre

(b) The long forms of the numerals are used to form the ordinals from 40th to 99th and therefore also the fractions from these:

1/73 = **en treoghalvfjerdsindstyvendedel**

But 'short' forms are now occasionally seen: **en treoghalvfjerdsendedel.** Cf. 305(b).

313 **Halv**, half, one and a half, quarter

(a) Halv inflects:

en halv side	half a page
tre halve sider	three half pages
den halve side	the half page
den halve tid	half the time
et halvt æble	half an apple
det halve æble	the half apple (apple is cut in two)
Forstod du det halve af, hvad han sagde?	Did you understand half of what he said?
to (og) en halv kilometer	two and a half kilometres
halvanden liter	one and a half litres

Notice the different idioms in English and Danish:

halvandet år/et og et halvt år	18 months
et halvt år	6 months

Note 1 – **Halv-** in compounds is often rendered by 'semi' in English:

halvautomatisk	semiautomatic
halvkreds	semicircle
halvtone	semitone

But note:

halvleg	half (of a match), half time

Note 2 – The forms **halvtredje, 2 ½; halvfjerde, 3 ½**, etc, are now archaic.

(b) The usual words for 'quarter' as a fraction are **en fjerdedel -e** or **en kvart -er**. **Et kvarter** is generally used to indicate 'a quarter of an hour' (except in expressions of time such as **kvart i to**, a quarter to two, see 317).

E DATES

314 Centuries and decades

(a) The suffix **-tal** is now used for specific centuries:

attenhundred(e)tallet/1800-tallet	the 19th century

It is increasingly replacing **århundred(e)** in this sense:

det nittende/19. århundred(e)	the 19th century

But **århundrede** is retained in a more general sense:

et halvt århundred(e)	half a century
i århundreder	for centuries
vort århundred(e)	our century

Et sekel, pl. **sekler** (century), is now rare in everyday use.

Note – **-tal** is also used for the figure itself (see 307(a)).

(b) Decades are expressed by forming a noun from a cardinal number plus **-(e)r (-ne)**:

i attenhundrede og halvfemserne/1890'erne	in the 1890s
tyvernes danske litteratur	Danish literature of the 1920s

de glade halvfemsere	the naughty nineties
Hun er i fyrrerne/40'erne.	She is in her forties.
Han er i tresserne/60'erne.	He is in his sixties.

315 Years

Years are usually written in figures in Danish (cf. 1314), but when written out in full they follow the same rules as other numerals (see 301, Notes 2,3). There is no **og** between the hundreds and tens but there is an **og** between the units and tens over 20. The word **hundrede** may be omitted.

1995	**nitten(hundrede)femoghalvfems**	ninteteen ninety-five
1215	**tolvhundredeogfemten**	twelve fifteen

Danes use **tusind(e)** in dates only for the years 1000–1099, 2000–2099, etc.

Island blev kristnet i år 1000 (tusind).
Iceland became Christian in the year 1000.

316 Months, days

(a) Months of the year do not have a capital letter in Danish unless they begin a sentence (see also 1308(b)):

januar	**maj**	**september**
februar	**juni**	**oktober**
marts	**juli**	**november**
april	**august**	**december**

All months are common gender and do not possess a plural form:

en kold januar	a cold January
en grå november	a grey November

(b) As in English the corresponding ordinal number is used to express the date. Notice that Danish no longer possesses any equivalent to 'th', 'rd' or 'st' in English dates such as: 17th, 23rd, 31st, or to the word 'of ' before the month in English idiom (but see 311(c) note 1):

Ålborg, (den) 3. (tredje) februar 1995
Ålborg, 3rd February 1995

Han er født den 27. (syvogtyvende) april.
He was born on the 27th of April.

The preposition 'on' before dates in English has no equivalent in Danish:

Vi mødtes sidst den 9. (niende) juni.
We last met on the ninth of June.

(c) Days of the week do not have a capital letter in Danish unless they begin a sentence (see 1308(b)):

søndag, mandag, tirsdag, onsdag, torsdag, fredag, lørdag

Days of the week are common gender and have a plural in **-e**.

F THE TIME

317 The time

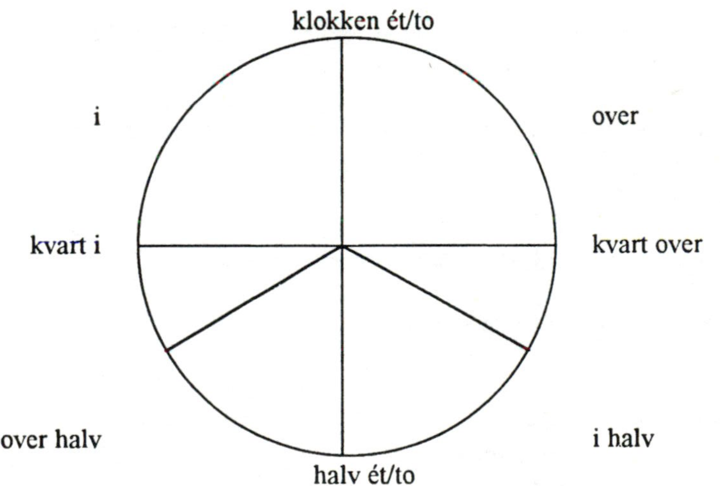

(a) 'What is the time?'; etc.

Hvad er/Hvor mange er klokken?	What's the time?
Klokken er ti.	It's ten o'clock.
Klokken/Den er (præcis) ti.	It's (exactly) ten o'clock.
Klokken er ti minutter over tre.	It's ten past three.

Klokken er syv minutter i fem.	It's seven minutes to five.
Klokken er kvart/(et) kvarter i/ over tolv.	It's a quarter to/ past twelve.
Klokken er mange.	It's late.
Hvad tid kører toget?	What time does the train leave?
klokken seks	at six (o'clock)

Note 1 – The word **minutter** is still usually retained in Danish, unlike e.g. English 'twenty to three'.

Note 2 – Danish has no equivalent to 'a.m.' or 'p.m.' and expresses this by **om morgenen, om formiddagen, om eftermiddagen, om aftenen, om natten.**

Note 3 – The Danish **et døgn** = a day, i.e. 24 hours beginning at midnight.

Note 4 – The international clock is commonly used in Denmark:

13.00 (tretten nul nul)	thirteen hundred (hours), i.e. 1 p.m.
17.30 (sytten tred(i)ve)	5.30 p.m.

(b) 'Half past' an hour in English is always expressed as 'half (to)' the next hour in Danish:

Klokken/Den er halv syv.	It's half past six.
Klokken er halv ét.	It's half past twelve.

(c) The most commonly used way of expressing time from 21 minutes past the hour to 21 minutes to the hour is relative to the half-hour:

Klokken er fire minutter i halv syv.	It's twenty-six minutes past six.

Another method is:

Klokken er seksogtyve minutter over seks.

(d) Some other useful expressions of time:

fjorten dage	a fortnight
klokken fem præcis	at 5 o'clock sharp
Mit ur går for langsomt/stærkt/ Mit ur taber/vinder.	My watch is slow/fast.
omkring kl. 8	around 8 o'clock
om otte dages tid	in a week's time
ved midnat/daggry/solopgang	at midnight/dawn/sunrise
i skumringen/ved solnedgang	at dusk/sunset

4 PRONOUNS

A PERSONAL PRONOUNS

401 Personal, reflexive and possessive pronouns – forms, table

Singular	*Subjective case*	*Objective case*	*Reflexive pronouns*	*Possessive pronouns*
1st person	**jeg** I	**mig** me	**mig** myself	**min/mit/mine** my, mine
2nd person – informal	**du** you	**dig** you	**dig** yourself	**din/dit/dine** your, yours
2nd person – formal	**De** you	**Dem** you	**Dem** yourself	**Deres** your, yours
3rd person – masculine	**han** he	**ham** him	**sig** himself	**hans/sin** his

Singular	*Subjective case*	*Objective case*	*Reflexive pronouns*	*Possessive pronouns*
3rd person – feminine	**hun** she	**hende** her	**sig** herself	**hendes/sin** her
3rd person – common gender	**den** it	**den** it	**sig** itself	**dens/sin** its
3rd person – neuter	**det** it	**det** it	**sig** itself	**dets/sin** its
Plural				
1st person	**vi** we	**os** us	**os** ourselves	**vores** **(vor/vort/vore)** our, ours
2nd person – informal	**I** you	**jer** you	**jer** yourselves	**jeres** your, yours
2nd person – formal	**De** you	**Dem** you	**Dem** yourselves	**Deres** your, yours
3rd person	**de** they	**dem** them	**sig** themselves	**deres** their, theirs

Note – The 2nd person pronouns **I, De, Dem, Deres** are always written with a capital letter to distinguish them from the preposition **i** (in) and the 3rd person plural pronouns, respectively.

402 Function and reference of personal pronouns

(a) Function

As in English, the main function of personal pronouns is to replace nouns or noun phrases:

Lise hjalp den gamle mand.	Lise helped the old man.
Hun hjalp ham.	She helped him.

The neuter pronoun **det** can also replace infinitives and clauses (see 406).

(b) Reference

(i) When personal pronouns replace nouns/noun phrases, they represent or refer to the latter. There are three main types of reference: anaphoric, cataphoric and deictic.

1 Pronouns have *anaphoric* reference when they refer to a previously mentioned noun/noun phrase. Thus **han** refers back to the noun **drengen** in:

Drengen tændte for fjernsynet, da han kom hjem.
The boy turned on the television when he came home.

This is by far the most common type of reference.

2 Pronouns have *cataphoric* reference when they refer to a following noun/noun phrase. Thus **hun** refers to the following noun phrase **den gamle dame** in:

Hun er virkelig rar, den gamle dame.
She is really nice, the old lady.

This kind of usage is usually found in the spoken language.

3 Pronouns have *deictic* reference when they identify, or 'point to', an object in the speaker's immediate surroundings ('deixis' is the Greek word for 'pointing'):

Han skal være vores næste formand. (With a nod towards a man.)
He is going to be our next chairman.

Pronouns with deictic reference belong to the spoken language and are always stressed.

(ii) However, the reference of personal pronouns is inherently vague, i.e. without a context it is often impossible to be sure precisely what a given pronoun refers to. For example, the personal pronoun **han** is three-way ambiguous in a sentence like the following:

Min bror smilede, da han trådte ind i stuen.
My brother smiled as he entered the living-room.

It has anaphoric reference if **han** refers *either* to **min bror** *or* to another previously mentioned male person, but it has deictic reference if the speaker somehow indicates another man in the room. In most cases, though, the context in which the pronoun appears will make its reference clear.

B THE USE OF SUBJECTIVE AND OBJECTIVE FORMS

403 The first person – **jeg/mig, vi/os**

(a) The singular

Jeg (subjective case) and **mig** (objective case) refer to the speaker in the singular.

(i) The subjective form **jeg** is used as subject, including before an apposition:

Jeg hedder John.	I am called John.
Det vidste jeg ikke.	I didn't know that.
Jeg arme stakkel!	Poor thing that I am!
Jeg, en gammel officer ...	An old officer like me ...

(ii) The objective form **mig** is used as object (both direct and indirect) and as prepositional complement:

John slog mig.	John hit me.
Chefen gav mig et nyt job.	The boss gave me a new job.
Hunden løb efter mig.	The dog ran after me.

(iii) **Mig** is also used as subject complement:

Det er mig.	It's I/me.
Det var mig, der spildte mælken.	It was I/me who spilt the milk.

While the subjective case is an option here in English, only the objective case is possible in Danish.

Notice, however, that the kind of verb used may be of importance:

1 When **hvem**-questions contain a lexical verb (usually a verb of action), the answer will take one of two forms, either:

Det + (a form of) **være** + the *objective* case

or

Det + (a form of) **gøre** + the *subjective* case

Hvem tog blyanten?	**Det var mig. / Det gjorde jeg.**
Who took the pencil?	It was I/me. / I did.

(Cf. the cleft sentence: **Det var mig, der tog blyanten,** I was I/me who took the pencil, where the *lexical* verb appears in the relative clause.)

For cleft sentence see 1032.

2 **Hvem**-questions with a form of **være** or **blive** as the main verb usually produce one of the following two types of answer:

A. When the **hvem**-question has a noun phrase as subject complement, the answer will take the following form:

Det + (a form of) **være/blive** + the *subjective/objective* case

Hvem er anføreren?	**Det er jeg. / Det er mig.**
Who is the team captain?	I am. / It's I/me.
Hvem blev den nye kasserer?	**Det blev jeg. / Det blev mig.** (or: **Det gjorde jeg.**)
Who became the new treasurer?	I did. / It was me.

Cf. the cleft sentences:

Det er mig, der er anføreren.	I'm the team captain.
Det var mig, der blev den nye kasserer.	I became the new treasurer.

where **være/blive** appears in the relative clause.

B. When the **hvem**-question has an adjective (phrase) as subject complement, only the *subjective* case is used:

Hvem er den ældste i klassen?	**Det er jeg.**
Who is the oldest in the class?	I am.
Hvem blev mest flov?	**Det blev jeg. / Det gjorde jeg.**
Who became most embarrassed?	I did.

(iv) The objective form **mig** can be said to be the 'unbound' or 'free' form of the pronoun (cf. French 'moi', etc., see 412). This is often seen in examples where the speaker expresses an element of surprise (whether genuine or feigned) at being singled out:

Teacher: **Du dernede på sidste række!** You on the back row!
Pupil: **Hvem? Mig?** Who? Me?

Parent: **Har du spist kagen?** Have you eaten the cake?
Child: **Mig? Hvordan kan du tro det?** Me? How can you think that?

(v) In colloquial language, the objective form **mig** is sometimes used as subject (see also 412). This happens mostly in coordination with a noun phrase, irrespective of the order of the two (or more) coordinated elements, though it is felt to be even more informal when the personal pronoun appears in first place, often with a humorous effect. We can thus establish a scale of formality:

1 Formal:

Min bror og jeg er gode venner. My brother and I are good friends.

2 More informal:

Min bror og mig er gode venner. My brother and me are good friends.

3 Colloquial and child language:

Mig og min bror er gode venner. Me and my brother are good friends.
mig og kongen/generalen, etc. me and the King/general, etc.
mig og min bamse me and my teddy-bear

Most of the **jeg/mig** distinctions mentioned above also occur in the use of subjective vs. objective case in the 1st person plural and in the 2nd and 3rd person. The treatment of the function of these forms below will therefore be more cursory where their uses do not differ from those of **jeg/mig**.

See also 408.

(b) The plural

Vi (subjective case) and **os** (objective case) refer to the speaker plus one or more other persons (or animals). They can, but need not, include the listener(s).

(i) The subjective form **vi** is only used as subject:

Min kone og jeg har lige været i Paris. Vi elsker at rejse.
My wife and I have just been to Paris. We love travelling.

Farvel, vi må snart mødes igen.
Goodbye, we must meet again soon.

Jeg har en lille hund. Vi går tur hver dag.
I've got a little dog. We go for a walk every day.

(ii) The objective form **os** is used as object (both direct and indirect) and as prepositional complement:

Værtinden behandlede os godt.	The hostess treated us well.
Vores søn sendte os et langt brev.	Our son sent us a long letter.
Du kan regne med os.	You can count on us.

Since the mid-1980s there has been a growing tendency to use **vi** rather than **os** in conjunction with **andre** or with an adjective specifying a group when the two words together act as complement of certain prepositions. Although this is strictly speaking ungrammatical, it can be found even in the written language. For example:

Der bliver aldrig noget tilbage til vi andre.
Nothing is ever left for the rest of us.

Der gøres ikke nok for vi gamle.
Not enough is done for us old people.

This type of construction may be slightly more complex than appears at first glance, for whereas a similar distribution (including breaches of it) is found in the 2nd person plural, this is not the case in the 3rd person plural.

(iii) The plural pronoun (**vi/os**) is sometimes used in situations where the notion of plurality is either absent or dubious:

1 The so-called 'royal we' as used by a royal or other prominent personage (meaning the 'august' person him/herself):

Vi alene vide ... (attributed to King Frederik VI)	We alone know ...

A polite version of this is the 'we' of lecturers (meaning the lecturer him/herself, where 'I' is felt to be too direct):

Vi har lige talt om, at ...	We have just talked about ...

2 The 'editorial we', as used by authors, journalists, etc. (meaning the reader):

Som vi så på foregående side ...	As we saw on the previous page ...

This can come close to the 'we' of lecturers:

Vi omtalte tidligere, at ...	We mentioned earlier that ...

3 The 'collective we', as used by a speaker to claim membership of a group, a nation, etc. (meaning the group, nation, etc. as a whole, even in the past):

Vi blev europamestre i fodbold.	We became European football champions.
Vi mistede Sønderjylland i 1864.	We lost southern Jutland in 1864.

4 The 'condescending we', as used to children, patients, old people, etc. (meaning the person addressed):

Hvordan har vi det i dag?	How are we today?
Har vi sovet godt i nat?	Did we sleep well last night?

404 The second person – **du/dig**, **De/Dem**; **I/jer**, **De/Dem**

(a) The basic use of second person pronouns

There are two pairs of 2nd person personal pronouns. In the singular, **du** (subjective) and **dig** (objective) are the informal/colloquial forms, while **De** (subjective) and **Dem** (objective) are the formal versions. The informal/colloquial plural forms are **I** (subjective) and **jer** (objective), with **De** (subjective) and **Dem** (objective) in formal usage, as in the singular. Note that all these forms are rendered by the form 'you' in English. The distribution of subjective vs. objective forms corresponds to that of the 1st person (see 403(a)):

Du/De må love mig at komme til mødet.
You must promise me to come to the meeting.

Har I/De nogen børn?
Have you any children?

Jeg så dig/Dem i byen i går.
I saw you in town yesterday.

Vi vil gerne invitere jer/Dem til vores fest.
We would like to invite you to our party.

Har John vist dig/Dem sin nye bil?
Has John shown you his new car?

Vi sender jer/Dem snart et brev om det.
We'll send you a letter about it soon.

Det var dejligt at høre fra dig/Dem igen.
It was lovely to hear from you again.

Hvordan går det med jer/Dem?
How are you these days?

Jeg er glad for, at jeg ikke er dig.
I'm glad that I'm not you.

Er det dig, Anne?
Is that you, Anne?

Note – **Stakkels dig!** Poor you!

(b) Formal versus informal usage

(i) The situation before the 1960s

Up to the 1960s, the choice between formal and informal pronouns was roughly parallel to that found in German ('du/Sie, ihr/Sie') and French ('tu/vous'). Generally speaking, there were three possibilities if we consider conversational exchanges.

1 Mutual use of the formal pronouns, as a mark of politeness and respect, was found between people who were not on very intimate or familiar terms. This was, for instance, the norm in asymmetric relationships such as those between subordinates and superiors in factories and offices, between shop assistants and customers, between students and university teachers, and of course when addressing strangers:

Customer: **Har De kjolen i en anden farve?**
Have you got the dress in a different colour?

Shop assistant: **Ja, hvis De vil følge med, skal jeg vise Dem én.**
Yes, if you come this way, I'll show you one.

2 Mutual use of the informal pronouns was usually restricted to family and friends, as well as certain peer groups, e.g. at workplaces and within sports communities, though this could vary considerably from place to place, often according to tradition and social status:

Child: **Far, kan du låne mig en tier?**
Daddy, can you lend me ten kroner?

Father: **Har du allerede brugt dine lommepenge?**
Have you already spent your pocket money?

3 The third possibility, viz. that of formal usage by one conversation partner and informal use by the other, was chiefly found in interchanges between children/young people and non-related adults. This could be observed, in particular, in schools and other educational institutions, at least up to higher education:

Pupil: **Undskyld, jeg forstod ikke det sidste, De sagde.**
Excuse me, sir, I didn't understand the last thing you said.

Teacher: **Så skal jeg forklare jer det én gang til!**
Then I'll explain it to you once more!

(ii) The present situation

This intricate, and potentially very subtle, system of 2nd person pronoun usage underwent a radical change from the 1960s onwards, to the extent that the informal pronouns **du/dig, I/jer** are now used in all but a very limited range of contexts, such as very official interchanges, situations where one may be in doubt about the expected form of address or where people are worried about offending the person addressed. The informal way of addressing people has thus been extended to most areas of conversation where previously only the polite forms would have been possible. This includes, for example, the whole of the educational sector (pupils to teachers, etc.), the media, most private and public workplaces (whatever people's position in the hierarchy), neighbours, and often complete strangers:

Pupil: **Vil du godt gentage, hvad du lige sagde?**
Would you repeat what you just said?

Teacher: **Ja, men så skal I også være stille.**
Yes, but then you must be quiet.

Interviewer: **Hvilke interesser har du ud over politik?**
What interests do you have besides politics?

Minister: **Hvorfor spørger du mig om det?**
Why do you ask me that?

One could point to a number of reasons for this change, such as a breakdown of many social barriers, a decrease in people's respect for the authorities and a general trend towards greater egalitarianism in Danish society from the 1960s onwards. It is therefore only to be expected that the use of the informal pronouns should be more widespread among the generations who grew up in the 1960s and later than among people of previous generations. The best policy for foreign speakers is to use the polite forms when in doubt, but if addressed as **du** to respond in the same way.

(c) Nowadays many speakers, particularly the younger generations, use **du** rather than the more formal indefinite pronoun **man** when referring to people in general (cf. German 'man'). This is no doubt largely due to influence from English where 'you' performs both functions, but it is advisable not to exaggerate this usage. This substitution is only possible when the addressee is somehow included in the sphere of action:

For at komme til Tivoli herfra skal du/man gå over Rådhuspladsen.
To get to Tivoli from here you must cross the Town Hall Square.

(?Du/)Man kan aldrig vide, hvad der vil ske.
You never know what is going to happen.

I Kina har (*du)/man andre traditioner end i Danmark.
In China they have other traditions than in Denmark.

(d) **Du** may be used (informally) in direct address to people, either on its own or pre-/postmodified by one or more adjectives. Some of these constructions belong to the sphere of intimate relationships:

Du, kom lige her!
You, come over here!

Hør nu lige her, du!
Now listen ...

Hej du, har du set en blå cykel?
Hi you there, have you seen a blue bike?

Søde, lille du, hvor har jeg savnet dig!
My little darling, how I have missed you!

Kom maj, du søde, milde ... (from a song)
Come May, you sweet and mild (i.e. month) ...

Stakkels lille du!
Poor little you!

Compare the last example with the following idiomatic phrase (using the objective case) (cf. (a) above and 412(d) Note):

Stakkels dig!
Poor you!

(e) **Du** may also form part of clearly idiomatic expressions (usually indicating surprise, and only roughly translatable by a similar idiom):

Du godeste!	Goodness!
Du milde Moses!	Good Lord!
Du store kineser!	Great Scot!

But see 418 for constructions with possessive pronoun (+ adjective) + noun, such as **din store idiot**, you big idiot.

(f) A special form of **du** – **dus** (meaning to be on informal or first-name terms with someone and therefore using **du** as the form of address, cf. the German verb 'duzen'), can collocate with a few verbs to form idiomatic expressions:

være dus med én	be on first-name terms with someone
blive dus med én	get on first-name terms with someone
drikke dus med én	to seal getting on first-name terms with someone by drinking to it

The meaning of some of these idioms can be extended to a feeling of familiarity with animals, things or even abstract notions:

Dus med dyrene (a TV programme)
On friendly terms with animals

Jeg er endnu ikke dus med min computer.
I have still not got to grips with my computer.

Jeg kan ikke blive dus med tanken om at skulle flyve.
I can't get used to the idea of having to fly.

Note – A parallel form of **De** – **Des** also exists:

Vi er Des. We are on formal terms with each other.

405 The third person – han/ham, hun/hende, den, det, de/dem

The 3rd person singular displays more gender distinctions than are found in any other area of Danish grammar. Thus it distinguishes masculine gender: **han/ham**; feminine gender: **hun/hende**; common gender (i.e. what is neither specifically masculine/feminine nor neuter): **den**; and neuter: **det**.

The 3rd person plural forms are **de/dem**.

(a) The singular

(i) Masculine forms: **han** (subjective) and **ham** (objective):

1 The masculine gender forms are chiefly used to refer to people of the male sex:

Jeg har lige mødt John. Han er på ferie.
I have just met John. He is on holiday.

Kommer John ikke snart? Jeg har ikke talt med ham siden jul.
Isn't John coming soon? I haven't talked to him since Christmas.

2 In the case of 'higher animals', it is possible to use **han/ham** when the animal is known to be male, but this use of masculine forms is not as common as in English, and it is never compulsory. As in English, the closer one feels to the animal in question, the stronger the inclination to refer to it as **han**:

Han er nu en dejlig hund.
He really is a lovely dog.

Jeg vil ikke sælge min hest. Han har vundet mange pengepræmier.
I won't sell my horse. He has won a lot of prize money.

(ii) Feminine forms: **hun** (subjective) and **hende** (objective):

1 The feminine gender forms are chiefly used to refer to people of the female sex:

Johns mor er ved at blive gammel. Hun fylder 75 på tirsdag.
John's mother is getting old. She will be 75 on Tuesday.

Min søster bor i Frankrig, så jeg besøger hende hver sommer.
My sister lives in France, so I visit her every summer.

2 It is possible to refer to 'higher animals' by means of the feminine pronouns if the animal is known to be female. The same circumstances apply as with the masculine forms above, and similar examples could be cited, substituting **hun** for **han**:

Sikke en sød hund! Hvor længe har du haft hende?
What a nice dog! How long have you had her?

3 In male-dominated communities or workplaces, certain objects (in particular vehicles such as ships, cars, etc.) have traditionally been referred to as female, using **hun/hende**. This usage with its sexual connotations is now in decline, in tune with a growing awareness of sexist language:

Se, hvor roligt hun ligger på vandet. (said of a ship)
Look how calmly she lies on the water.

(iii) Masculine or feminine forms?

See also 103(a).

Most Danish common gender nouns denoting a person are neutral as to the sex of the person referred to (e.g. **ejeren**, the owner; **gæsten**, the guest; **læseren**, the reader; etc.). This is also true of a few neuter nouns (e.g. **barnet**, the child; **mennesket**, the human being) (for these see (iv)(2) below). This causes no problems when the identity of the individual is known, but when such a noun is used with general reference, the choice of pronoun becomes less obvious. On its own, neither **han** nor **hun** seems satisfactory, although in the past the masculine form was often used as the common form, as for example in:

Bogen stiller store krav til læseren. Han skal være ...
The book makes great demands on the reader. He must be ...

In the absence of a common form for masculine and feminine, five courses of action are possible to circumvent the problem:

1 Use both gender pronouns together, i.e. **han eller hun** (he or she) or **han/hun**. This is probably the most clear-cut solution, but it strikes many people as rather clumsy:

Ansøgeren skal kunne tysk. Han/Hun må også kunne ...
The applicant must know German. He/She should also know ...

2 Avoid pronouns, if possible, by repeating the noun (or using a synonym):

Ansøgeren skal kunne tysk. Ansøgeren må også kunne ...
The applicant must know German. The applicant should also know ...

3 Use another gender-neutral word:

Ansøgeren skal kunne tysk. Vedkommende må også kunne ...
The applicant must know German. The person in question should also know ...

4 Use a passive construction (see 541–43):

Ansøgeren skal kunne tysk. Der forudsættes også kundskaber i ...
The applicant must know German. Knowledge of ... is also required.

5 Use a plural form:

Ansøgere skal kunne tysk. De må også kunne ...
Applicants must know German. They should also know ...

(iv) Common gender/neuter: **den/det**

1 Common gender:

The common gender has only one form: **den**. **Den** can never refer to a noun denoting a person, but is used to refer to other common gender nouns, including animals:

Pas på tyren! Den er på vej herover.
Look out for the bull! It is on its way over here.

Hvor er bogen? Jeg lagde den på bordet.
Where is the book? I put it on the table.

Stenen er for hård til, at du kan hvile hovedet på den.
The stone is too hard for you to rest your head on it.

Hvad er klokken? Den er tre.
What time is it? It is three o'clock.

In some idiomatic expressions, **den** does not have any obvious reference:

Den er fin.	That's great.
Den er gal.	There is something wrong.
Hvad er den af?	What's the matter?
Er du med på den?	Do you see? / Are you game?
Tag den med ro!	Take it easy!

2 Neuter:

Like the common gender, neuter has only one form: **det**. **Det** is used to refer to neuter nouns, including those denoting a person if the sex is not known or irrelevant (cf. (iii) above):

Barnet græder. Prøv, om du kan trøste det.
The child is crying. Try and comfort it.

Darwin sagde om mennesket, at det nedstammer fra aberne.
Darwin said of mankind that it descends from the apes.

Vi fangede et rådyr, men vi lod det løbe igen.
We caught a deer, but we let it run away again.

Bordet passer ikke til stuen; det har ikke den rigtige farve.
The table doesn't match the room; it hasn't got the right colour.

For other functions of **det** see 406.

(b) The plural:

(i) The 3rd person plural has two forms: **de** (subjective) and **dem** (objective), which refer to one or more plural nouns, or two or more singular nouns, irrespective of gender:

Lokalet var fuldt af mennesker, og de så alle glade ud.
The room was full of people and they all looked happy.

Jeg har mange bøger. De fylder meget, men jeg behøver dem.
I have got many books. They take up a lot of space, but I need them.

Fjern billederne! Jeg kan ikke lide dem.
Take away the paintings! I don't like them.

Teltene er så store, at der kan bo 5–6 mennesker i dem.
The tents are so big that 5 or 6 people can stay in them.

(ii) When a 3rd person pronoun refers to a so-called collective noun (i.e. a noun with singular form and singular or plural meaning), the choice between singular **den/det** and plural **de** may vary. Most of these collective nouns denote a grouping of people who form some kind of entity (e.g. **befolkningen**, the population; **byrådet**, the town council; **familien**, the family; **holdet**, the team; **parret**, the couple; **regeringen**, the government; etc. With most of these nouns, the choice of number depends on whether one wants to emphasize the collective unity (singular) or the individual members (plural) of the group.

Familien skulle til Odense, men den/de kørte den forkerte vej.
The family was/were going to Odense, but it/they went the wrong way.

Holdet syntes selv, at det/de havde spillet dårligt.
The team themselves thought that they had played badly.

In some cases, the notion of the individuals dominates; hence only the plural seems possible:

Et ungt par blev standset i toldet. (*Det)/De kom fra Århus.
A young couple were stopped at the customs. They came from Århus.

In others the concept of a unitary body prevails; here the singular is clearly favoured:

Regeringen har lige ophævet en lov, som den/(*de) tidligere vedtog.
The government has just repealed an Act which it previously passed.

For **den/det/de** as demonstrative pronouns see 421ff.

406 The major uses of **det**

(a) The primary use of **det** is to refer to a previously mentioned neuter noun in the singular, as we saw in 405(a)(iv)(2):

Jeg har et skrivebord. Det er stort.	I have a desk. It is big.

However, **det** has several other functions in Danish. In most of these, but not all, **det** corresponds to English 'it'.

(b) **Det** is used as a demonstrative pronoun (see 421ff).

(c) **Det** is used in connection with the copulas **være** and **blive**:

Hvad er det?	What is it?
Det blev sent.	It got late.
Er det dig, John?	Is it you, John?

When **være/blive** has a noun phrase or a pronoun as subject complement, **det** is used with identifying function regardless of the gender and number of the noun/pronoun:

Hvad er det? Det er en hund.
What is it? It is a dog.

Hvem slog dig? Det gjorde de store drenge.
Who hit you? It was the big boys.

Hvad mærke er hans bil? Det er en Ford.
What brand is his car? It is a Ford.

Det blev strenge tider.
Times became hard.

(d) **Det** is used as a formal subject in sentences with the verbs **være/blive** + an adjective followed by an infinitive or an **at**-clause. The adjective agrees with **det** and appears in the neuter indefinite form (with the ending **-t**) (see also 1003). The real subject in these constructions is the infinitive clause or the **at**-clause, respectively:

Det er svært at være ung nu om dage.
It is difficult to be young nowadays.

Det kan blive kedeligt at spise ude hver dag.
It can get boring to eat out every day.

Det er synd, at du ikke kan komme til min fødselsdag.
It is a pity that you can't come on my birthday.

(e) **Det** is used to refer to an infinitive (with or without modifications) or a clause:

At dyrke sport er ofte sundt, men det kan også være farligt.
To do sport is often healthy, but it can also be dangerous.

"Vi behøver flere medhjælpere." "Hvorfor det?"
'We need more assistants.' 'Why?'

Du sagde, at han stadig går i skole, men det gør han ikke.
You said that he still goes to school, but he doesn't.

Notice the conversational use of **det** as object of verbs like 'think','believe', 'hope', 'say', etc., in answer to a preceding question. In such cases, **det** usually appears in front position and corresponds to 'so' in English:

A: **Rejser han i morgen?** B: **Det tror jeg./Det håber jeg./Det sagde han.**
A: Is he leaving tomorrow? B: I think so./I hope so./He said so.

Note – The expression **det ... også** corresponds to the English construction 'so' + 'be/have/do' + subject:

Ole er træt. Det er jeg også.	Ole is tired. So am I.
De har et hus. Det har vi også.	They have a house. So have we.

(f) **Det** is used as the subject complement of **være/blive** or as the object of **have** and the modals, in answers to questions formulated with one of these verbs. Here **det** usually has no equivalent in English, and as in (e) above, **det** usually appears in the front position in the clause:

A: **Er du syg?**	B: **Ja, det er jeg.**
A: Are you ill?	B: Yes, I am.
A: **Har hun set huset?**	B: **Ja, det har hun.**
A: Has she seen the house?	B: Yes, she has.
A: **Blev det færdigt?**	B: **Ja, det blev det.**
A: Was it finished?	B: Yes, it was.

A: **Kan du russisk?**	B: **Nej, det kan jeg ikke.**
A: Do you know Russian?	B: No, I don't.

Note that **gøre**, like 'do' in English, replaces lexical verbs (i.e. verbs that are neither auxiliaries nor modals) and that other verbs such as **synes/tro** (think) and **vide** (know) also appear in responses of this kind:

A: **Så du filmen?**	B: **Nej, det gjorde jeg ikke.**
A: Did you see the film?	B: No, I didn't.
A: **Kender du Michael?**	B: **Ja, det gør jeg.**
A: Do you know Michael?	B: Yes, I do.
A: **Skal vi invitere ham?**	B: **Ja, det synes jeg.**
A: Shall we invite him?	B: Yes, I think so.
A: **Kommer du sent hjem?**	B: **Nej, det tror jeg ikke.**
A: Will you be home late?	B: No, I don't think so.
A: **Hvad er klokken?**	B: **Det ved jeg ikke.**
A: What's the time?	B: I don't know.

(g) A variation of (f) occurs when a speaker confirms or denies an allegation or a suggestion. **Være** usually appears as the verb of this confirmation or denial:

Han opførte sig som en slyngel, og det er han også.
He behaved like a scoundrel, and that's what he is.

Det forekommer ganske uskadeligt, men det er det ikke.
It seems quite innocuous, but it isn't.

(h) **Det** is used as the subject in cleft sentences, which are more frequent in Danish than in English (see 1032):

Det var mig, der tog tasken.	I took the bag.
Det er ham, der er den skyldige.	He is the guilty one.
Det er Anne, jeg bedst kan lide.	Anne is the one I like best.

(i) Like 'it' in English, **det** is used as a formal subject in a number of impersonal constructions (see also 1003(a)):

det forekommer/hænder/sker, at ..., it happens that ...; **det ser ud til, at ...**, it looks as if ...; **det synes, som om ...**, it seems as if ...; etc.

This is particularly common with verbs that refer to weather conditions:

det blæser, it's windy; **det fryser**, it's freezing; **det hagler**, it's hailing; **det klarer op**, it's clearing up; **det lyner**, there is lightning; **det regner**, it's raining; **det sner**, it's snowing; **det tordner**, it's thundering; **det tør**, it's thawing; etc.

(j) **Det** is used as a formal object in some fixed expressions with an adjective. Note that the adjective agrees in gender with **det** by having the neuter singular ending **-t**:

at have det godt/dårligt	to feel good/bad
at have det let/svært	to find things easy/difficult
at have det morsomt/sjovt	to have fun
at have det kedeligt	to be bored
at tage det roligt	to take it easy

407 Der and det

Though **der** when used as a formal subject and as subject in impersonal constructions is strictly speaking not a pronoun, it has affinities with **det** in these roles. (For **der** as a relative see 431; for **der/dér** as a locative adverb see 609(c).) However, in most cases **der** and **det** do not occur in the same types of construction; for example, unlike **det**, **der** can never refer to something outside the clause. In general, **der** corresponds to 'there' in English and **det** to 'it'. The chief uses of **der** as (formal) subject are listed in (a)–(d) below, and in (e) comparisons are made with **det**:

(a) In existential sentences, **der + være/findes** (be/exist) or **mangle** (be missing) postulates the existence, or non-existence, of the real subject in the predicate position:

Der findes løver i Afrika.	There are lions in Africa.
Der er ikke bjerge i Danmark.	There are no mountains in Denmark.
Der mangler 10 kroner.	There are 10 kroner missing.

(b) Der + være is used in expressions specifying distance of time or space. In most of these, English uses 'it' + 'be':

Der er længe til eksamen.	It's a long time before the exam.
Der er tre måneder til jul.	Christmas is three months off.
Er der langt til hotellet?	Is it far to the hotel?

Der er kun 30 km til Roskilde. It's only 30 kilometres to Roskilde.

(c) Der can combine not only with **være** but also with many other verbs plus a real subject (see 1003). This construction occurs much more frequently in Danish than in English, for example with verbs indicating position such as **ligge** (lie), **sidde** (sit) and **stå** (stand). **Der** is also retained in questions, where it appears immediately after the verb:

Der er udsigt til regn. Rain is expected.
Der bor millioner i Kina. There are millions living in China.
Der kommer nye varer i morgen. New deliveries are due in tomorrow.
Der ligger en butik på hjørnet. There is a shop on the corner.
Der sidder en dame på sofaen. A woman is sitting on the sofa.
Der står to mænd udenfor. There are two men standing outside.
Skete der noget i aftes? Did anything happen last night?

(d) **Der** often occurs with verbs in the passive form (see 541(c)):

Der hørtes hurraråb fra salen. Cheers were heard from the hall.
Der gøres for lidt for de ældre. Too little is done for the elderly.
Der blev sendt bud efter lægen. The doctor was sent for.
Der fødes for mange børn. Too many children are born.

Der + passive verb sometimes occurs in impersonal constructions without any indication of the 'real' subject or 'agent'. This is not usual in English:

Der blev danset hele natten. There was dancing all night.
Der blev banket på døren. There was a knock on the door.
Der tales om valg. There is talk of an election.
Der må ikke ryges. Smoking is not allowed.

(e) Comparison between **der** and **det**

As indicated above, **der** and **det** are generally separated in ways similar to 'there' and 'it' in English. However, there are certain impersonal constructions (mostly with the passive form of the verb) where they seem to be interchangeable:

Der/Det påstås, at han skal fyres. It is claimed that he is to be fired.
Der/Det siges, at hun er gift. It is said that she is married.
Der/Det vides ikke, om det passer. It is not known if it is true.
Der/Det er varmt i Italien. It is hot in Italy.

Furthermore, **der** and **det** can appear in similar constructions, but with a difference in meaning. Unlike **det**, **der** can never refer to something outside the clause:

Der synes at være en fejl.	There appears to be a mistake.
Det synes at være en fejl.	It appears to be a mistake.
Der er dejligt i Danmark.	It's lovely in Denmark.
Det er dejligt at være i Danmark.	It's lovely to be in Denmark.

408 Personal pronouns in comparative constructions with end and som

In Danish, as in English, it is common to omit the finite verb after **end** (than) or **som** (as) in comparative clauses. If this second comparative element consists of a personal pronoun, the objective case of the pronoun is normally used in Danish, whereas English can have either the subjective or the objective form (depending on the level of formality):

Du er yngre end mig.	You are younger than I/me.
Hun er kønnere end ham.	She is prettier than he/him.
Han er lige så stor som dig.	He is just as tall as you.
Er I lige så rige som dem?	Are you as rich as they/them?

If, however, the finite verb after **end/som** is retained, we have two clauses. Hence the second comparative element – being the subject of a finite verb – must appear in the subjective case (as in English):

Du er yngre, end jeg er.	You are younger than I am.
Han er lige så stor, som du er.	He is just as tall as you are.

For the use of **sin (sit, sine)** in similar constructions see 417(i).

409 The ethical dative

The term 'ethical dative' refers traditionally to a very restricted use of 1st or (more rarely) 2nd person objective pronouns which are only loosely connected with the rest of the clause and add very little to the meaning. It merely implies a certain evaluation on the part of the person referred to, such as 'I think', 'in my opinion', etc. Although characteristic of colloquial style, it now has a rather old-fashioned ring. (Since Danish does not have distinct dative forms, the term 'ethical dative' is borrowed from more case-oriented languages, such as Latin and German.)

See also 410(e).

Du er mig den rette person til jobbet.
I think you are the right person for the job.

Han ser mig noget træt ud.
He looks rather tired to me.

Det var dig nok en stor fornøjelse.
I suppose that was a great pleasure for you.

The difference between an 'ethical dative' and an indirect object may be seen from the following examples:

Du er mig en stor hjælp. You are a great help to me.
Du er mig en stor klovn! You really are a clumsy clot!

In the first example, **mig** is the indirect object ('to me'); in the second, **mig** is an almost redundant addition ('really, in my view') and hence an 'ethical dative'.

C REFLEXIVE PRONOUNS

410 The use of reflexive pronouns

In the 1st and 2nd person, reflexive pronouns are identical to the objective forms of the personal pronouns. Only the 3rd person has a separate reflexive form **sig** (in both the singular and the plural).

For a list of the reflexive forms see 401.

(a) As the name suggests, the main function of reflexive pronouns is to 'reflect' or refer back to a noun/pronoun in the same clause, which is usually the subject of the clause (but see (c) below). A reflexive pronoun can appear as direct/indirect object and as prepositional complement, but never as subject.

Note that there is no one-to-one relationship between the Danish reflexive pronouns and the English '-self ' forms. Where Danish has a reflexive pronoun, English often uses a personal pronoun or an intransitive verb. This is at least the norm in non-emphatic use:

Jeg klædte mig hurtigt på. I dressed quickly.

Føler du dig syg?	Are you feeling ill?
De bør skynde Dem hjem, frue.	You ought to hurry home, madam.
Han tog bøgerne med sig hjem.	He took the books home with him.
Karen så ud til at more sig.	Karen seemed to be enjoying herself.
Løven hvilede sig i solen.	The lion rested in the sun.
Det fortager sig med alderen.	One grows out of it.
Vi satte os ned og ventede.	We sat down and waited.
Jeg håber, I føler jer hjemme.	I hope you feel at home.
De har alle ventet Dem for meget.	You have all expected too much.
De tog for sig af retterne.	They tucked into the food.
Katte elsker at slikke sig.	Cats love licking themselves.

In all these examples the reflexive pronoun refers back to the subject of the clause in question.

(b) The existence of a separate 3rd person reflexive form makes it possible in Danish to distinguish between different 3rd person referents in cases where English is unable to do so. This happens above all when the reflexive pronoun follows a preposition in non-emphatic use; here English normally uses the objective form of the personal pronoun. Such examples are therefore formally ambiguous in English, but not in Danish:

Han lukkede døren efter sig. (i.e. himself)	He closed the door behind him. (i.e. himself or another man)
Soldaterne anbragte to bomber foran sig. (i.e. themselves)	The soldiers placed two bombs in front of them. (i.e. themselves or some other people)

(c) It was mentioned in (a) above that the reflexive pronoun usually refers to the subject of the clause. This is not only so in simple finite clauses, such as those found in the examples in (a), (b) above, but also in non-finite complement clauses (in the form of so-called 'accusative + infinitive' constructions). Consider the following example:

Han bad dem lukke døren efter sig.

←————→

He asked them to close the door behind them.

Here **sig** (for most speakers) does not refer to the subject **han** of the finite verb **bad**, but to **dem**, which is the subject of the infinitive **lukke**. The non-finite clause **dem lukke ...** can be transformed into a finite subordinate clause:

Han bad dem, om de ville lukke døren efter sig.
←→
He asked them if they would close the door behind them.

where **sig** refers to the subject (**de**) in the subordinate clause. This construction is particularly common with some verbs of perception (**føle**, feel; **høre**, hear; **se**, see/watch):

John hørte sin ven beklage sig.
←→
John heard his friend complaining.

De så soldaterne forsvare sig tappert.
←→
They watched the soldiers defend themselves bravely.

If a personal pronoun is used instead of a reflexive pronoun, it will refer either to the subject of the finite verb (i.e. **John/De**) or to a third party:

John hørte sin ven beklage ham.
John heard his friend pity him.

De så soldaterne forsvare dem tappert.
They watched the soldiers defend them bravely.

Note that in the examples above, the subject of the infinitive is overtly expressed, unlike in (d) below.

(d) The reflexive pronoun can also refer to the implied subject of an infinitive, which is often identical with the subject of the finite verb:

De forsøgte at forsvare sig.
←— [de] —→
They tried to defend themselves.

But in impersonal constructions, the subject of the infinitive usually does not appear at all and must be deduced from the context. In such cases, the subject of the infinitive will have general reference:

Det er vigtigt at kunne forsvare sig.
[X] ←→
It is important to be able to defend oneself.

(Cf. **Man kan forsvare sig.** One can defend oneself.)

(e) The reflexive pronoun is sometimes used as a rather 'loose' indirect object, denoting that the action specified in some way involves or is of interest to the referent. This use is somewhat reminiscent of the 'ethical dative' (see 409), and is often confused with the latter. Though the construction is not unknown in English, it is far more widespread in Danish. The following examples do not contain a reflexive verb of the form: verb + **sig**, corresponding to the examples used above (e.g. **forsvare sig**, defend oneself; **hvile sig**, rest; **skynde sig**, hurry; etc.):

Han fik sig en lur.	He had a nap.
Hun er sig sit udseende bevidst.	She is conscious of her looks.
De gav sig god tid.	They took their time.

(f) In emphatic use, i.e. with contrastive emphasis, the word **selv** is usually added to **sig**. This comes closest to the use of '-self ' forms in English (see 413):

Hun slog sig selv i hovedet.	She hit herself on the head.
Han roste sig selv til skyerne.	He praised himself to the skies.

(g) **Sig** appears in some idiomatic constructions, mostly as the complement of a preposition. Some of them have parallels in the 1st and 2nd person with use of the corresponding reflexive form:

Jeg/Du/Han er ikke bange af mig/dig/sig.
I am/You are/He is not afraid (by nature).

But others only exist with the 3rd person **sig**:

I burde bo hver for sig.	You ought to live separately.
Vi/De bor hver for sig.	We/They each live on our/their own.
i og for sig	in/by itself, actually
Rygtet har ikke noget på sig.	There is nothing in the rumour.

Note the difference in meaning between the following examples of the verb **vente** (wait) with a reflexive pronoun:

Hvad venter du dig af din søn?	What do you expect of your son?
Du kan bare vente dig!	You just wait!
Venter du dig?	Are you expecting (a baby)?

411 Reciprocal pronouns

Hinanden functions as a reciprocal pronoun in Danish and denotes a mutual action, feeling, etc. between two or more individuals. The notion of reciprocity implies that it must refer to a plural noun/pronoun. It corresponds to 'each other/one another' in English. It can appear in the genitive with the **-s** ending:

I går så vi hinanden for første gang.
Yesterday we saw each other for the first time.

Så giv hinanden hånden derpå!
Then shake hands on it!

De har elsket hinanden i lang tid.
They have loved each other for a long time.

Vi har alle brug for hinanden.
We all need one another.

Hvorfor skulle man ikke kunne hjælpe hinanden?
Why shouldn't people be able to help each other?

De kan lide hinandens selskab.
They like each other's company.

The strict logic of mutuality is not always applied. Consider this example:

De stod i kø efter hinanden.
They were queuing one behind the other.

Each person in the queue must have been standing *either* in front of *or* behind the next one, but not both.

Note 1 – **Hverandre**, which was previously used as a reciprocal pronoun referring to more than two, has now virtually disappeared from the modern standard language, but is still found in dialectal and very formal use:

Bønderne hjalp hverandre med høsten.
The farmers helped one another with the harvest.

Note 2 – Some Danish verbs can take on a reciprocal meaning by adding an **-s** to all their forms (see 540). Consequently, these forms do not occur together with **hinanden**:

Vi ses i morgen.	We'll see each other tomorrow.
De skændtes i timevis.	They quarrelled for hours.

D EMPHATIC PRONOUNS

412 Personal pronouns with emphatic use

A stressed version of the objective form of the personal pronouns can in certain surroundings be used for emphasis (corresponding to French 'moi', etc., see 403(a)(iv)). Pronouns may receive such emphasis under the following three circumstances:

(a) When the pronoun appears independently:

> **Hvem sagde det? Ham dér!**
> Who said that? That man!
>
> **Har du slået min søn? Hvem, mig?**
> Have you beaten my son? Who, me?

(b) When the pronoun is modified by a prepositional phrase; in this case it can function as subject (see also 403(a)(iv)):

> **Ham med skægget er min nabo.**
> The man with the beard is my neighbour.
>
> **Hende på cyklen har travlt.**
> That woman on the bike is in a hurry.

(c) When the pronoun is highlighted in a cleft sentence:

> **Var det dig, der tog min taske?**
> Was it you who took my bag?
>
> **Alligevel var det hende, der fik rollen.**
> And yet she was the one who got the part.

(d) In other cases when the pronoun receives contrastive stress; note that the subjective form may also be stressed:

> **'Hun har ikke noget at klage over; havde det været hendes mor ...**
> 'She has nothing to complain about; if it had been her mother ...
>
> **'Ham kan jeg ikke lide, men hans bror er sød.**
> I don't like 'him, but his brother is nice.

Ham kan 'jeg ikke lide, men min bror kan.
'I don't like him, but my brother does.

Note – The use of the emphatic objective form of the pronoun after **stakkels** as an expression of sympathy (see 404(a),(d)) is not confined to the 2nd person singular:

Stakkels mig/dig/ham/hende, etc.	Poor me/you/him/her, etc.

413 Selv

(a) **Selv** is not restricted to modifying reflexive pronouns (see 410(f)), but can equally well refer to nouns/pronouns in general. The word **selv** is indeclinable and always stressed, and like the English '-self' forms it can occur in different positions in relation to the noun/pronoun which it refers to:

Man skal være god ved sig selv.	One should be nice to oneself.
Du kan selv bestemme menuen.	You can decide the menu yourself.
Han selv sagde ingenting.	He himself said nothing.
Hun påtog sig opgaven selv.	She took on the task herself.

(b) **Selv** may occur in front position in the clause in order to add extra emphasis to the noun/pronoun that it refers to. This can happen in two different types of construction:

(i) Like other clausal constituents, **selv** can be 'fronted' and thus cause inversion of subject and verb (see 1022). **Selv** in this position usually has negative connotations and therefore tends to occur with a negation (**ikke**, not; **aldrig**, never, etc.):

Selv tør jeg aldrig modsige ham.	I myself dare never contradict him.
Selv kan de ikke huske meget.	They themselves can't remember much.
Selv har kongen ringe magt.	The king himself has little power.

(ii) As an adverb, **selv** (in the sense of 'even') may immediately precede a noun/pronoun (if it is a common noun, this must appear in the definite form). In this construction the main stress shifts from **selv** to the noun/pronoun. Compare the following examples with those in (i) above and note the difference in meaning:

Selv jeg tør aldrig modsige ham.	Even I dare never contradict him.
Selv de kan ikke huske meget.	Even they can't remember much.

Selv kongen har ringe magt. Even the king has little power.

It also occurs with the objective case:

Selv ham vil hun ikke kysse. She won't kiss even him.
Han vil ikke betale selv for hende. He won't pay even for her.

(c) A variant form **selve** is used immediately preceding a noun (in the definite form) to emphasize the latter very strongly:

Selve huset er ikke meget værd. The house itself isn't worth much.
Selve biskoppen kommer på besøg. The bishop himself is paying a visit.
Vi bor i selve København. We live in Copenhagen itself.

(d) An even more intensifying form **selveste** may occasionally be used as in (c). This signifies that the speaker is suitably impressed:

Vi blev inviteret til middag hos selveste direktøren.
We were invited to dinner with the managing director himself.

Selveste dronningen tog imod os. The Queen herself welcomed us.

(e) Some idiomatic expressions with **selv**:

Lad mig være mig selv et øjeblik. Let me be alone for a moment.
Du er ikke helt dig selv i dag. You are not quite yourself today.
Hun er noget for sig selv. She is a bit special.
Det siger sig selv. It is self-evident.
Det må du selv om! Suit yourself!
Det kan du selv være! So are you, too!
at være sig selv nok to be self-sufficient

Note in particular:

A: **Tak for i aftes.** Thank you for (the party, etc.) last night.

B: **Selv tak!** Thank ′you! (With stress on 'you'.)

E POSSESSIVE PRONOUNS

414 Possessive pronouns - forms, table

In English, there is a formal distinction between possessive pronouns with (a) determinative function ('my', 'your', etc.) and (b) independent function ('mine', 'yours', etc.). Such a distinction does not exist in Danish. In this section, 'possessive pronoun' will be used as a common term to include both these functions.

	Common gender	*Neuter*	*Plural*
Singular			
1st person	**min** my, mine	**mit**	**mine**
2nd person – informal	**din** your, yours	**dit**	**dine**
2nd person – formal	**Deres** your, yours	**Deres**	**Deres**
3rd person – masculine	**hans/sin** his	**hans/sit**	**hans/sine**
3rd person – feminine	**hendes/sin** her, hers	**hendes/sit**	**hendes/sine**
3rd person – common gender	**dens/sin** its	**dens/sit**	**dens/sine**
3rd person – neuter	**dets/sin** its	**dets/sit**	**dets/sine**
Plural			
1st person	**vores (vor)** our, ours	**vores (vort)**	**vores (vore)**
2nd person – informal	**jeres** your, yours	**jeres**	**jeres**
2nd person – formal	**Deres** your, yours	**Deres**	**Deres**
3rd person	**deres** their, theirs	**deres**	**deres**

(a) Only four of the possessive pronouns (**min, din, sin** plus **vor**) inflect for gender and number, according to the noun(s) which they modify. Their inflection mirrors that of adjectives. The rest are formally genitives and thus indeclinable.

(b) **Din (dit, dine)** corresponds to the informal 2nd person singular personal pronoun **du/dig**, just as **jeres** corresponds to the informal 2nd person plural personal pronoun **I/jer**.

Note – The informal 2nd person plural forms **jer/jert/jere** are now archaic and have been superseded by **jeres**.

(c) **Deres** (always written with capital letter) corresponds to the formal 2nd person singular and plural personal pronoun **De/Dem**.

Note – The formal 2nd person forms **eder, eders** are now archaic and only found in liturgical language.

(d) In addition to the regular 1st person plural form **vores**, the forms **vor, vort, vore** can still be found. However, whilst the plural form **vore** is still used by some speakers, mostly in formal style, the singular forms **vor, vort** are now increasingly rare. Certain well-established phrases retain these pronouns, e.g. **i vor tid**, in our time; **i vore dage**, nowadays. Cf. **Vor Herre** or **Vorherre**, our Lord. Elsewhere, the indeclinable **vores**, which until recently was considered rather colloquial, has replaced the inflected forms.

(e) **Sin (sit, sine)** has reflexive function and usually refers to the subject in the same clause (but see 417). It does not normally occur in predicative position:

Han tog sin frakke.	He took his coat.
Frakken er hans / *sin.	The coat is his.

415 The use of possessive pronouns

(a) The choice of possessive pronoun is determined by the noun/pronoun representing the possessor. The form (where there is more than one possibility) is determined by the gender and/or number of the noun representing the possession:

Jeg har en bil. I have a car.	**Min bil er rød.** My car is red.	**Bilen er min.** The car is mine.
Du har et hus. You have a house.	**Dit hus er stort.** Your house is big.	**Huset er dit.** The house is yours.

Anne har to katte.	**Hendes katte er grå.**	**Kattene er hendes.**
Anne has two cats.	Her cats are grey.	The cats are hers.

(b) On many occasions, Danish has the definite article where English uses a possessive pronoun. See 145, 420.

(c) A possessive pronoun performs the function of a determiner, like for instance a genitive and the definite article. Adjectives preceded by a possessive pronoun therefore appear in the definite form (cf. 219):

min røde bil	my red car
dit store hus	your big house

(d) Possessive pronouns (in the neuter form, where this exists) are sometimes used idiomatically without an attached noun:

Jeg har gjort mit til, at han består eksamen.	I have done my best to ensure that he will pass the exam.
Du har dit på det tørre.	You are on the safe side.
Vi har også vores at se til.	We have problems of our own.

See also 417(k).

Note – The English formulaic greetings in letters 'Yours faithfully', 'Yours sincerely', 'Yours truly', etc. are usually rendered in Danish by **Venlig hilsen, Med venlig hilsen**.

416 Hans or sin? – Basic use

The English 3rd person singular possessive pronouns ('his', 'her(s)', 'its') each have two possible renderings in Danish:

Either: **hans, hendes, dens/dets**, respectively

Or: **sin (sit, sine)**

There are, on the whole, clear rules about how **hans** (etc.) and **sin** are to be used in each instance. Failure to observe these rules is almost certain to cause confusion.

(a) The basic use of **hans, hendes, dens/dets**

Hans (etc.) is used under *one* or *both* of the following conditions:

1 **Hans** (etc.) modifies (and forms part of) the subject of the clause.
2 **Hans** (etc.) refers to an individual or entity which is not the subject of the clause.

Examples:

Han og hans datter var i byen.	He and his daughter were in town.

(**Hans** modifies (and forms part of) the subject of the clause (condition 1).)

Hun læste hendes nyeste roman.	She read her latest novel.

(**Hendes** cannot refer to the subject of the clause (condition 2), so it must refer to another woman; note that 'her' in the English sentence is ambiguous.)

John troede, at Peter elskede hans kone.	John thought that Peter loved his wife.

(**Hans** cannot refer to the subject of the clause (i.e. 'Peter'), so it must refer either to 'John' (the subject of the superordinate clause) or to some other man. Thus **hans** is ambiguous (even though 'Peter' is ruled out as a referent), whereas in the English sentence 'his' is three-way ambiguous since John, Peter or someone else can be the referent.)

John er Peters ven. Han passer hans have.
John is Peter's friend. He tends his garden.

(**Hans** cannot refer to **han** (i.e. 'John'), so, since **han** refers to 'John', **hans** must refer to 'Peter' or some other man. Although 'his' will presumably be understood in the same way, once again it is formally ambiguous.)

(b) The basic use of **sin (sit, sine)**

Sin (sit, sine) agrees in gender and/or number with the noun it modifies. **Sin (sit, sine)** is used when *both* of the following conditions are fulfilled:

1 The possessive pronoun must refer to the subject of the clause (i.e. to the 'possessor'), which must be third person singular.
2 The possessive pronoun must modify a constituent other than the subject of the clause (e.g. the direct/indirect object, the subject complement or a prepositional complement).

Examples with direct object (common gender, neuter, plural):

Anne	**elsker sin**	**mand.**
←――――→	←――→	
Anne	loves her	husband.

The possessive pronoun refers to the subject **Anne** (the 'possessor') — The possessive pronoun modifies the object **mand** (common gender, sing.; hence **sin**)

Anne	**elsker sit**	**barn.**
←――――→	←――→	
Anne	loves her	child.

The possessive pronoun refers to the subject **Anne** (the 'possessor') — The possessive pronoun modifies the object **barn** (neuter, sing.; hence **sit**)

Anne	**elsker sine**	**børn.**
←――――→	←――→	
Anne	loves her	children.

The possessive pronoun refers to the subject **Anne** (the 'possessor') — The possessive pronoun modifies the object **børn** (plural; hence **sine**)

Examples with indirect object, subject complement and prepositional complement:

Anne	**gav sit**	**hus en gang maling.**
←――――→	←――→	
Anne	gave her	house a coat of paint.

The possessive pronoun refers to the subject **Anne** (the 'possessor') — The possessive pronoun modifies the indirect object **hus** (neuter, sing.; hence **sit**)

Anne	**er sin egen**	**værste fjende.**
←――――→	←――→	
Anne	is her own	worst enemy.

The possessive pronoun refers to the subject **Anne** (the 'possessor') — The possessive pronoun modifies the subject complement **fjende** (common gender, sing.; hence **sin**)

Anne **kigger på sine bøger.**

←——————→ ←→

Anne looks at her books.

The possessive pronoun	The possessive pronoun
refers to the subject	modifies the prepositional complement
Anne (the 'possessor')	**bøger** (plural; hence **sine**)

The above rules also apply when **sin (sit, sine)** precedes the subject to which it refers, as part of the constituent it modifies:

I sin bog omtaler han krigen.	In his book he talks about the war.
Sit arbejde nævner hun sjældent.	She rarely mentions her work.

(c) The importance of choosing correctly

(i) As shown above, the choice of **hans** (etc.) or **sin (sit, sine)** often changes the meaning of the clause. Consider the following examples:

John elsker sin kone.
John loves his (own) wife.

Tim elsker også sin kone.
Tim loves his (own) wife too.

Peter elsker også hans kone.
Peter loves his (i.e. John's or Tim's) wife too.

Anne stryger aldrig sit tøj.
Anne never irons her (own) clothes.

Lisa stryger heller aldrig sit tøj.
Lisa never irons her (own) clothes either.

Ulla stryger heller ikke hendes tøj.
Ulla doesn't iron her (i.e. Anne's or Lisa's) clothes either.

(ii) Extra care is required when a sentence consists of more than one clause, since **sin (sit, sine)** cannot have a referent outside the clause to which it belongs:

Min far tror ikke, at chefen kan lide sit arbejde.
My father doesn't think that the boss likes his work.

Here **sit** can only refer to **chefen** – the subject of the subordinate clause in which the possessive pronoun appears; not to **min far** – the subject of the superordinate clause. 'His', of course, can refer to either.

(iii) There are, however, situations where the use of **sin (sit, sine)** is more likely to give rise to ambiguity in the interpretation of sentences than the use of **hans** (etc.) since it does not distinguish between masculine and feminine gender. Compare these sentences:

Hun gav ham hans penge.	She gave him his money.
Hun gav ham sine penge.	She gave him his/her money.

By its form **hans** could not refer to the subject **hun**, whereas **sine** could refer to either **hun** or **ham**. Although gramatically **sine** can only refer to the subject **hun**, there is often uncertainty among native speakers in such cases.

(d) Other 3rd person pronouns with **sin (sit, sine)** in reflexive use

The 3rd person singular pronouns listed below all use **sin (sit, sine)** to refer to them when they function as subject. Where a separate genitive form exists, this is listed too. The distinction between **hans** (etc.) and **sin** remains the same as stated above. More details about these pronouns are found in the paragraphs referred to:

Pronoun	*Paragraph*	*Genitive*	*Possessive pronoun*
enhver	442	**enhvers**	**sin, sit, sine**
hvad	425(c), 434	–	**sin, sit, sine**
hvem	425(b), 433	**hvis**	**sin, sit, sine**
ingen	443	**ingens**	**sin, sit, sine**
man	445	**ens**	**sin, sit, sine**
nogen	448	**nogens**	**sin, sit, sine**

417 Other uses of sin (sit, sine)

There are a number of situations where the relationship between **sin (sit, sine)** and its referent is more complex and consequently less clear-cut than those in 416. In general one may say that the greater the complexity of construction, the more uncertainty in the choice between **hans** (etc.) and **sin (sit, sine)**.

(a) Sin (sit, sine) and complement clauses with an infinitive

Under the basic rule (see 416), **sin (sit, sine)** refers to the subject of its clause. This is certainly the case in simple clauses, but in more complex ones there are sometimes complications. The most notable exception occurs in non-finite complement clauses – the so-called 'accusative + infinitive' constructions (cf. the equivalent rule for the use of the reflexive pronoun **sig** in 410(c)). In this type of construction **sin (sit, sine)** will usually refer to the subject of the infinitive, whereas **hans** (etc.) may be used to refer to the subject of the finite verb. This phenomenon is known as 'attraction', i.e. **sin (sit, sine)** is 'attracted' to the nearest 'subject':

John så ham sparke sin hund. John saw him kick his (own) dog.

At first sight, the use of **sin** to refer to **ham** seems to be at odds with the basic rule as set out in 416 above, in that **John** – and not **ham** – is the subject of the clause. However, the sentence can be transformed so as to show the true relationship between the possessive pronoun and its referent:

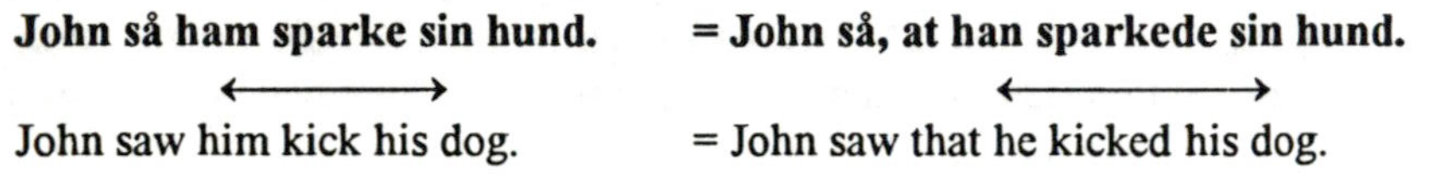

John så ham sparke sin hund. **= John så, at han sparkede sin hund.**

John saw him kick his dog. = John saw that he kicked his dog.

In other words, **sin** refers to the subject of the infinitive.

Further examples with complement clauses containing an infinitive:

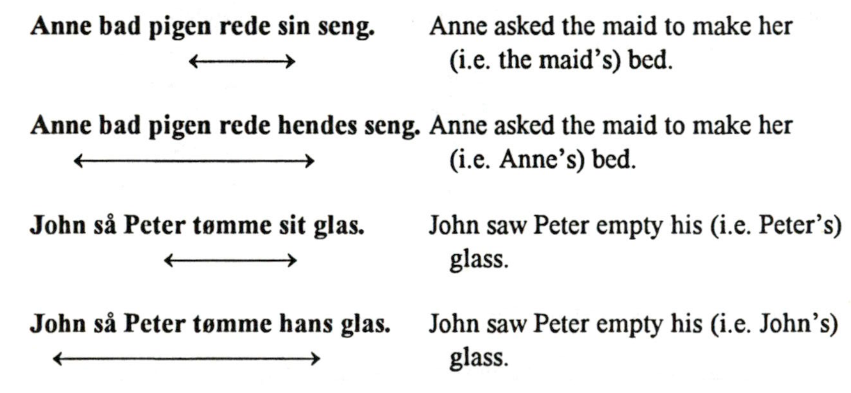

Anne bad pigen rede sin seng. Anne asked the maid to make her (i.e. the maid's) bed.

Anne bad pigen rede hendes seng. Anne asked the maid to make her (i.e. Anne's) bed.

John så Peter tømme sit glas. John saw Peter empty his (i.e. Peter's) glass.

John så Peter tømme hans glas. John saw Peter empty his (i.e. John's) glass.

In this way **hans** (etc.) versus **sin (sit, sine)** in complement clauses may be said to conform to the basic rule, although many native speakers find such examples ambiguous.

(b) Sin (sit, sine) and complement clauses with a participle

(i) Past participle:

Instead of an infinitive, a complement clause may contain a past participle, as in:

Billedet viser en mand omgivet af sin familie.
The picture shows a man surrounded by his family.

This too may be seen as a contracted version where in this case relative **som/der** (who) + a finite form of the verb **være** have been omitted from the sentence, and so the choice of **sin** is easily explainable:

Billedet viser en mand, der er omgivet af sin familie.

↔↔

The picture shows a man who is surrounded by his family.

Sin then refers to the subject of the subordinate clause **der**, which in turn represents **en mand** – the object of the main clause.

Examples like these often contain a passive construction:

Faderen krævede sønnen straffet for sin ulydighed.

↔

= **Faderen krævede, at sønnen blev straffet for sin ulydighed.**

↔

The father demanded that his son be punished for his disobedience.

(ii) Present participle:

Equally, a complement clause may contain a present participle, as in:

Jeg fandt ham siddende på sit værelse.

↔

I found him sitting in his room.

This could be transformed into:

Jeg fandt ham; han sad på sit værelse.

↔

I found him; he was sitting in his room.

Or:

Jeg fandt, at han sad på sit værelse.

⟷

I found that he was sitting in his room.

(c) **Sin (sit, sine)** and complement clauses with an adjective

Instead of a non-finite verb form, a complement clause may contain an adjective. The use of **sin (sit, sine)** here is similar to that in (a)–(b) above. Thus:

Moderen gjorde Anne ked af sin beslutning.

⟷

= **Moderen gjorde, at Anne blev ked af sin beslutning.**

⟷

The mother made Anne (feel) sorry about her decision.

(d) **Sin (sit, sine)** and complement clauses with a prepositional phrase:

John fik øje på bageren med sit lille barn i hånden.

⟷

John caught sight of the baker with his little child hand in hand.

If we replace the preposition **med** with **der havde** (who had), we have a sentence similar to **Billedet viser ...** in (b)(i) above and can postulate the same kind of relationship between the possessive pronoun and its referent. However, native speaker judgement varies in examples of this kind, and one will frequently find uncertainty in the choice between **hans** or **sin**.

(e) **Sin (sit, sine)** with a genitive referent

Consider the following example:

Annes had til sin chef viser hendes stærke følelser.

⟷

Anne's hatred of her boss shows her strong feelings.

This use of **sin** is slightly at odds with the basic rule, insofar as **sin** here refers not to the subject of the clause **had**, but to **Annes** – a genitive modifying the subject. But note that **sin** is part of a prepositional phrase which modifies the subject and that the possessive pronoun attached to the object **følelser** is not **sine**, but **hendes**. This use of **sin** can be justified by transforming the sentence in such a way that it demonstrates the true relationship between **sin** and its referent

Annes, while at the same time showing that **hendes**, which also refers to **Annes**, cannot be replaced by **sine**:

> **Det had, som Anne føler mod sin chef, viser hendes stærke følelser.**
>
> The hatred that Anne feels towards her boss shows her strong feelings.
>
> Cf. **Anne hader sin chef. Anne føler et stærkt had mod sin chef.**
>
> Anne hates her boss. Anne feels a strong hatred towards her boss.

(f) **Sin (sit, sine)** in a prepositional phrase as part of the subject:

> **Landmanden med sin store gæld har sine egne problemer.**
>
> The farmer with his big debt has his own problems.

As in the example in (e) above, **sin** is part of a prepositional phrase which modifies the subject **landmanden**, though here, unlike in (e), the referent is the subject itself, quite in accordance with the rule. Similarly, **sine** in the object noun phrase has **landmanden** as its referent; the use of **hans** for **sine** would therefore be ungrammatical.

(g) **Sin (sit, sine)** in passive sentences

The use of **sin (sit, sine)** in passive sentences follows the basic rule. However, this often means a change of possessive pronoun from the corresponding active sentence. Compare, for instance, the active sentence:

1 **Hans ven hentede ham på stationen.**
His friend met him at the station.

with its passive equivalent:

2 **Han blev hentet på stationen af sin ven.**
He was met at the station by his friend.

Note that **hans ven** – the subject in 1 – becomes **sin ven** in 2, with **sin** now referring to the passive subject **han**.

(h) **Sin (sit, sine)** in constructions with an implied subject

In the following examples:

At glemme sin kones fødselsdag kan næppe undskyldes.
Forgetting one's wife's birthday can hardly be excused.

Det er ikke altid let at holde sine løfter.
It is not always easy to keep one's promises.

there is no overt referent for **sin, sine**. Nevertheless, in each a subject of the infinitive – **at glemme, at holde** – is clearly implied (e.g. **for én**, for one), though it should be emphasized that this implied subject must be in the singular to justify the use of **sin (sit, sine)**, as opposed to **deres**.

(i) **Sin (sit, sine)** in comparative constructions with **end** and **som**

As part of the comparative element that follows **end** or **som** in comparative constructions, **sin (sit, sine)** is largely used in accordance with the basic rule. Thus when the finite verb following the second comparative element is omitted, the construction is perceived as one clause and the normal rules apply:

Hun er ældre end sin søster.
She is older than her (own) sister.

John er lige så dum som hans bror.
John is just as stupid as his (i.e. someone else's) brother.

If, however, the finite verb after **end/som** is retained, we have two clauses. In that case, **sin (sit, sine)** cannot be used since the referent will be in another (i.e. the first) clause:

Hun er ældre, end hendes søster er.
She is older than her sister is.

John er lige så dum, som hans bror er.
John is just as stupid as his brother is.
(Note that **hendes/hans** are now as ambiguous as the English forms.)

In some comparative constructions where two objects (or groups of objects) are compared by an animate subject, the choice between **hans** (etc.) and **sin (sit, sine)** can influence the meaning. Compare:

1 **Hun elsker sine børn mere end hendes mand.** (= **end hendes mand gør**)
She loves her children more than her husband (does).

2 **Hun elsker sine børn mere end sin mand.** (= **end hun elsker sin mand**)
She loves her children more than (she loves) her husband.

This difference in use and meaning actually comforms to the basic rule, in that **hendes mand** in 1 is perceived as the subject of another clause (in which the verb **gør** has been omitted), whereas **sin mand** in 2 is an object in the clause in which **hun** is both the subject and the referent for **sine** and **sin**.

See also 408.

(j) Hver sin (sit, sine)

The idiomatic term **hver sin (sit, sine)** is used emphatically to indicate distribution, corresponding to 'each' in English. As a result, it must refer to a plural subject. This seems to contravene the rule that **sin (sit, sine)** can only have a referent in the singular, but the fact that **hver sin (sit, sine)** can also refer to 1st and 2nd person subjects shows how idiomatic, and thus how little rule-governed, its use is.

Vi gik hver sin vej.	We went our separate ways.
Havde I hver sit soveværelse?	Did you each have your own bedroom?
De købte hver sine bøger.	They each bought their own books.

There is, however, some uncertainty among native speakers, and it is quite common to find respectively **vores, jeres, deres** in the 1st, 2nd and 3rd person used instead of **sin (sit, sine)**, when combining with a plural noun:

De har hver deres problemer.	They have each got their own problems.

(k) Sin (sit, sine) in idiomatic expressions without an attached noun:

Vi svarede enhver sit.	We paid everyone their due.
Hun tænkte sit derved.	She had her own thoughts on the subject.
Fanden hytter sine.	The devil looks after his own.
Han holder på sit.	He sticks to his own view.

Cf. 415(d).

Note also the following expressions without a referent:

i sin tid	at that time, at a certain time
på sine steder	in certain places
på sin vis	in a way
til sin tid	in due course

418 Possessive pronouns in emotional expressions

In colloquial language, possessive pronouns are used idiomatically in emotional expressions addressed directly to a person (cf. 404(e)). Here English uses the personal pronoun. Only the forms of the 2nd person singular (informal), i.e. **din/dit**, are possible, and despite the idiomatic flavour, this type of construction is still productive:

Dit fjols!	You fool!
Din store idiot!	You big idiot!
Din stakkel!	You poor thing!
Din dejlige tøs!	You lovely wench!
Din dovne hund!	You lazy dog!
Dit heldige asen!	You lucky devil!

Note – When similar emotions are expressed in the 1st person singular and the 1st and 2nd person plural, the personal rather than the possessive pronoun is used:

Jeg store klods!	What a clumsy clot I am!
Vi gamle fjolser!	We old fools!
I søde fyre!	You nice chaps!

419 'A friend of mine'

Danish has no direct equivalent of the possessive pronoun construction of the type: 'a friend of mine', 'a sister of theirs', etc. These are expressed in different ways in Danish:

He is a friend of mine.	**Han er en ven af mig.**
	Han er en af mine venner.
She is a sister of theirs.	**Hun er søster til dem.**
	Hun er deres søster.
They have no children of their own.	**De har ingen børn selv.**
	De har ikke selv nogen børn.

Note also:

He is a friend of us all.	**Han er ven med os alle. /** **Han er vores alle sammens ven.**
There are only three of us.	**Vi er kun tre.**
That's no business of yours!	**Det angår/rager ikke dig!**

420 Possessive pronoun in English – definite article in Danish

See also 145.

Where English uses possessive pronouns to modify nouns denoting parts of the body or articles of clothing, Danish uses the definite article instead, when the ownership is not in question:

I have broken my arm.	**Jeg har brækket armen.**
Take your shoes off!	**Tag skoene af!**
He put his hand in his pocket.	**Han stak hånden i lommen.**
She has got something in her eye.	**Hun har fået noget i øjet.**
Are your legs hurting?	**Har du ondt i benene?**

The same difference can be found with nouns denoting parts or qualities of inanimate objects:

Some trees shed their leaves.	**Nogle træer taber bladene.**
The diamonds have lost their sparkle.	**Diamanterne har mistet glansen.**

F DEMONSTRATIVE PRONOUNS

421 Demonstrative pronouns – forms, table

	Common gender singular	*Neuter singular*	*Plural*	*Meaning*
'Near'	**denne (her), den her**	**dette (her), det her**	**disse (her), de her**	this (one), these
'Distant'	**den (der)**	**det (der)**	**de (der)**	that (one), those

Note 1 – In each case, the choice of form (i.e. gender and/or number) is determined by the gender and/or number of the referent.

Note 2 – There is no gender distinction in the plural.

Note 3 – The forms with **her/der** are characteristic of colloquial language. When **den/det/de** are used to indicate 'near' they must be followed by **her**, whereas the use of **der** after **den, det, de** indicating 'distant' is optional. This use often implies the speaker's approval or disapproval of an item:

Har du læst den her nye bog, som alle folk taler om?
Have you read this new book that everybody is talking about?

Den (der) radio virker ikke.
That radio doesn't work.

Note 4 – Even more colloquial is the addition of **hersens** or **dersens** to the demonstratives:

denne hersens oplukker	this bottle opener
det dersens nye stykke	that new play

422 The use of demonstrative pronouns

There are two series of demonstrative pronouns, which are formally distinct and which differ semantically in their deictic reference (cf. 402 and below). They correspond roughly to 'this/these', 'that/those' in English, though there are differences in their use. With certain limitations, demonstrative pronouns can appear both attributively (i.e. modifying a noun/noun phrase) and independently (i.e. without being attached to a noun/noun phrase), and in contrast to the personal pronouns and the front article they are always stressed.

(a) Deictic and anaphoric function

(i) The deictic nature of these pronouns is seen from the fact that **denne/dette/disse (den/det/de her)** are used to refer to objects or entities at a relatively short distance from the speaker, in space or time, while **den/det/de (der)** refer to objects or entities at a greater distance from the speaker. That is, as deictics they have an identifying or 'pointing' function. Deictic use of demonstratives is not context-determined; the physical/temporal situation is in itself sufficient to enable the meaning to be deduced:

Physical distance

Denne bog er værd at læse.	This book is worth reading.
Lad være med at ridse i det bord!	Don't scratch that table!
Nej, jeg mener disse sten.	No, I mean these stones.
Glem de mærkelige idéer, du har!	Forget those strange ideas of yours!

Temporal distance

Vi får travlt i denne uge.	We'll be busy this week.

Nej, i den uge skal jeg til Rom.	No, that week I'm going to Rome.
Jeg sidder i møde i dette øjeblik.	I'm in a meeting at this moment.
I det øjeblik hørte han braget.	That moment he heard the bang.

Note that in temporal use the distance from the 'moment of speaking' can be either in the future or in the past.

The perception of what constitutes a short distance may vary according to context and circumstances, but for a speaker to use the series that indicates close proximity the distance must be relatively short in comparison with other objects in his/her immediate physical or temporal world. It would, therefore, under normal circumstances, be ungrammatical to use **denne/dette/disse** in sentences like the following, since the use of **denne/dette/disse** would usually presuppose that the objects in question were within the speaker's reach:

***Kom herover med denne kop!**	Bring this cup over here!
***Ræk mig lige dette blad!**	Please hand me this magazine!

(ii) Unlike deictic use, anaphoric use of demonstratives is context-determined, in that they have a referent in a previous clause (cf. 402(b)(i)). For cataphoric reference see (c)(iii) below.

Jeg har én is tilbage, men den får du ikke.
I've got one ice-cream left, but you won't get that.

Du sagde, at vi skulle til stranden, men det løfte har du ikke holdt.
You said we were going to the seaside but you haven't kept that promise.

In the last example the referent is the preceding complex clause (**Du sagde, at vi skulle til stranden**).

Note – **Hin (hint, hine)**, which previously formed a contrast to **denne (dette, disse)** by referring to objects at some distance from the speaker in space and time, is now archaic and has been superseded by **den (det, de)**.

(b) Attributive use

The demonstratives can be used attributively to refer to animate and inanimate nouns, including words for people and abstract nouns:

Denne dreng er faret vild.	This boy has got lost.
Den sang kender jeg ikke.	I don't know that song.
Jeg kan ikke lide dette bord.	I don't like this table.

De idéer er farlige. Those ideas are dangerous.

They can even modify proper nouns that have been mentioned previously:

Hvem er i grunden denne fru Hansen?
Who is this Mrs Hansen actually?

Hvad vil den hr. Larsen her?
What does that Mr Larsen want here?

(c) Independent use

(i) The demonstratives can all be used without an attached noun, but one will normally be 'understood'. They assume the gender and number of this implied noun. In this use they can all refer to inanimate nouns. In the spoken language, **her** and **der** respectively are commonly attached to them, functioning almost like a substitute noun (cf. 'one' in English):

Den vase synes jeg ikke om, men denne her er pæn.
I don't like this vase, but that one is nice.

Disse kager er for søde, men de der er pragtfulde.
These cakes are too sweet, but those are delicious.

(ii) On their own, **denne** and its plural form **disse** can also refer to people, though this use is felt to be rather stilted. They are often rendered in English by 'the latter':

Jeg hilste også på chefen. Denne/Ham havde jeg aldrig mødt før.
I also shook hands with the boss. I had never met him before.

De talte om deres syge elever. Disse/De havde ikke været med på turen.
They talked about their sick pupils. The latter hadn't been on the trip.

In this use they both have the genitive form in **-s**:

Dennes børn var store nu.
This person's children were now big.

Disses forventninger var høje.
These people's expectations were high.

Den too can be used about human beings in a general sense, either in proverbial sayings or in coordinated constructions with the pronoun repeated:

Den, der kommer først til mølle, får først malet.
Approx: First come, first served.

Den, der ikke vil høre, må føle.
He who will not listen must be made to feel.

Først var hun forlovet med den og så med den ...
First she was engaged to one person and then to another ...

Tag dig ikke af, hvad den og den mener.
Don't take any notice of what so-and-so thinks.

Note – **Den og den** and **det og det** are both used idiomatically about non-humans, as in:

på den og den dag	on such and such a day
på det og det tidspunkt	at such and such a time

(iii) The neuter forms **dette** and **det** can be used with cataphoric reference, i.e. pointing forward (cf. 402(b)(i)), in front of an infinitive or a subordinate **at**-clause. In the former case (**det(te)** + infinitive), English would just have an infinitive or a gerund ('to go/going ...', etc.), while the latter case (**det(te) at ...**) corresponds to constructions with 'the fact (etc.) that ...':

Det at lege med sine børn er ikke noget, han ynder.
Playing with his children is not something he is fond of.

Dette, at han har snydt kunderne, kan ikke undskyldes.
The fact that he has cheated his customers cannot be excused.

(d) Demonstrative pronouns, personal pronouns and the front article

In most cases demonstrative pronouns, personal pronouns and the front article are easily distinguished. However, the forms **den/det/de** appear with all three functions, which can occasionally lead to some confusion between, on the one hand, a demonstrative and a personal pronoun, and on the other hand, a demonstrative pronoun and the front article:

(i) Demonstratives and personal pronouns

When the demonstrative forms **den/det/de** occur independently, there is sometimes an overlap in function with the same forms used as personal pronouns. In the spoken language, demonstratives are always stressed and personal pronouns usually unstressed. But in the written language this useful clue is missing. We can therefore be in doubt in examples like the following, where the second **den** can be pronounced with or without stress:

Se den lille hundehvalp! Er den ikke sød?
Look at the little puppy! Isn't it/that sweet?

When the pronoun in question is an object or a prepositional complement, the word order may help to differentiate between demonstratives in front position and personal pronouns placed after the verb:

Demonstrative pronoun (with stress):
Familien Jensen har også fået en ny bil, men ˈden har jeg ikke set.
The Jensens have also got a new car, but that I haven't seen.

Nej, men vi har et træ i haven; ˈdet må du gerne klatre i.
No, but we have got a tree in the garden; you may climb that.

Personal pronoun (without stress):
Familien Jensen har fået en ny bil, men jeg har ikke set den.
The Jensens have got a new car, but I haven't seen it.

Peter har allerede set træet. Han må gerne klatre i det.
Peter has already seen the tree. He is allowed to climb it.

However, personal pronouns too can be both fronted and stressed, as in:

Der er kommet en ny professor, men ˈham har jeg ikke mødt endnu.
There is a new professor, but I haven't met him yet.

I to kan godt få en nøgle til huset, for ˈjer stoler jeg på.
You two can have a key to the house because I trust you.

In other words, there is a certain amount of overlap here.

(ii) Demonstratives and the front article

When the demonstrative pronouns **den/det/de** appear before an adjective (+ noun), they are formally identical to the front article, which is used in precisely these surroundings. Here, even more than in (i) above, stress can be a useful guide in the spoken language since demonstratives are always stressed, while the definite article is always unstressed:

det gamle træ (front article without stress)
the old tree

'det gamle træ (demonstrative pronoun with stress)
that old tree

In the written language the distinction is less clear. However, a demonstrative cannot have a referent that is placed too far from it, whereas article + adjective (+ noun) can be found at some distance from its referent. Thus **det** in the following example must be the front article:

John sad i sit dejlige, store kontor og arbejdede. /.../ Det store kontor havde flere udgange.
John was sitting working in his lovely big office. /.../ The big office had several exits.

(e) Double definiteness

Denne, **dette** and **disse** can appear in a noun phrase in front of a genitive or a possessive pronoun and thus cause what we may call 'double definiteness'. This construction is now old-fashioned and is mainly found in rather stilted, formal language:

denne min yndlingsbeskæftigelse	this favourite occupation of mine
dette hans væsentligste bidrag	this, his most important contribution
disse folkemængdens vrede udbrud	these angry shouts from the crowd

Note 1 – The genitive form **dennes** is used in formal business correspondence in much the same way as 'instant' (abbreviated to inst. = of this month) in English:

I Deres brev af den 14. dennes ... In your letter of the 14th inst. ...

Note 2 – The formal Danish equivalent of the English construction 'the former ... the latter' is **(den) førstnævnte ... (den) sidstnævnte.**

G INTERROGATIVE PRONOUNS

423 Interrogative pronouns – forms, table

Common gender	*Neuter*	*Plural*	*Genitive*
hvem who(m)	**hvad** what	**hvem** who(m)	**hvis** whose
hvilken which/what	**hvilket** which/what	**hvilke** which/what	–
hvad for en which (one)	**hvad for et/noget** which (one)	**hvad for nogle** which (ones)	–

424 The use of interrogative pronouns

When a speaker asks an addressee something, using an interrogative pronoun, he/she tries to persuade the addressee to fill in correctly the place held by the interrogative pronoun. The main function of interrogative pronouns is thus to specify to the addressee what kind of information is requested. They can introduce both direct and indirect questions:

Hvem tog min frakke? John (tog min frakke).
Who took my coat? John (took my coat).

Hvad så hun i København? (Hun så) Tivoli.
What did she see in Copenhagen? (She saw) Tivoli.

Jeg spurgte hende, hvad hun så i København.
I asked her what she saw in Copenhagen.

425 Hvem, hvad, hvis

(a) The interrogative pronoun **hvem** has three forms: **hvem** (common gender) and **hvad** (neuter) are chiefly nominal, i.e. used independently, whereas the genitive form **hvis** is used attributively with determinative function or independently with an implied noun phrase:

Hvem så du?	Who(m) did you see?
Hvad gjorde han?	What did he do?
Hvis (bil) er det?	Whose (car) is it/that?

(b) **Hvem** can introduce direct and indirect questions. It can refer to human beings only, and it can be associated with both singular and plural. The number may or may not be clear from the context:

Singular	
Hvem er den nye redaktør?	Who is the new editor?
Hvem er sur?	Who is in a bad mood?
Plural	
Hvem er dine forældre?	Who are your parents?
Hvem er sure?	Who are in a bad mood?
Number unspecified	
Hvem kommer i aften?	Who is/are coming this evening?
Hvem traf han i byen?	Who(m) did he meet in town?

Hvem can function as subject, subject complement, direct and indirect object, and prepositional complement. When it appears as prepositional complement, the preposition is usually placed at the end of the clause since a preposed preposition seems excessively formal:

Hvem har taget min blyant?	Who has taken my pencil?
Hvem er han?	Who is he?
Hvem skal vi vælge?	Who(m) shall we elect?
Hvem har du givet nøglen?	Who(m) have you given the key to?
Hvem er hun gift med?	Who(m) is she married to?

In indirect questions, **hvem** must be followed by **der** when it is subject, but not in other uses:

Ved du, hvem der har boet i det hus?
Do you know who has lived in that house?

Fortæl mig, hvem du mistænker.
Tell me who(m) you suspect.

Kan I gætte, hvem jeg tænker på?
Can you guess who(m) I am thinking of?

Hvem can modify a few indefinite pronouns in the plural:

Hvem andre har du mødt?	Who else have you met?
Hvem flere har de inviteret?	Who else have they invited?

Note – **Hvem der** can introduce a sentence that expresses the speaker's wishful thinking and as such represents an 'if only I ...' type of utterance:

Hvem der havde en kold øl lige nu!	If only I had a cold beer right now!
Hvem der bare havde et hus ved Middelhavet!	If only I had a house by the Mediterranean!

(c) Hvad is a neuter singular pronoun with non-animate reference. Like **hvem**, it can introduce direct and indirect questions and has the same range of functions, except that it does not normally appear as indirect object. As subject it must be supported by **der** in indirect questions:

Direct questions
Hvad forårsagede ulykken?
What caused the accident?

Hvad hedder du?
What is your name?

Hvad har hun købt?
What has she bought?

Hvad tænker du på?
What are you thinking of?

Indirect questions
De ved ikke, hvad der forårsagede ulykken.
They don't know what caused the accident.

Jeg siger ikke, hvad hun hedder.
I won't say what her name is.

Fortæl din mor, hvad du har købt.
Tell your mother what you have bought.

Jeg gad vide, hvad han tænker på.
I wonder what he is thinking of.

In examples like the following **hvad** may be analysed as subject complement rather than as subject:

Hvad er det?	What is that?
Hvad er dit navn?	What is your name?

In colloquial language, **hvad** is sometimes used attributively as a synonym for **hvilken (hvilket, hvilke)**:

Hvad vej skal du?	Which way are you going?
Hvad farve er din cykel?	Which colour is your bike?

Hvad can modify some comparative adjectives in the singular:

Hvad mere forlanger du?	What more do you ask?
Hvad yderligere kan der gøres?	What further can be done?

Some idiomatic expressions with **hvad**:

Hvad?	What? Pardon?
Hvad så?	Then what (happens)?
(Nå) ja, hvad så?	So what?
Åh hvad (lad ham gå!)	Never mind (let him go!)
Ved du hvad?	Do you know what?
Hvad kommer det mig ved?	What do I care?
Hvad enten du vil eller ej!	Whether you want to or not!

Note 1 – Colloquially, **hvad med** followed by a noun/pronoun or an infinitive corresponds to 'what/how about' in English:

Hvad med ham/min ven?	What about him/my friend?
Hvad med at gå en tur?	How about going for a walk?

With more or less the same meaning, we find **hvad om** + a clause:

Hvad om du tog dig lidt sammen?	How about pulling yourself together a bit?

Note 2 – Since **hvem** is used for human beings and **hvad** for inanimate objects, there is a gap in the semantic field covered by these two interrogative pronouns which excludes animals. It is thus equally ungrammatical to use **hvem** and **hvad** in the following question:

Et dyr må have lavet disse spor. *Hvem/*Hvad er det?/Hvad er det for et? (Cf. 427)
An animal must have made these tracks. Who/What is it?/What sort (of animal) is it?

Note 3 – Notice the idiomatic expression: **Hvadbehager?** (Pardon?)

Note 4 – In emotive spoken language, both **hvem** and **hvad** can combine with a number of expletives for greater emphasis:

Hvem søren/dælen/pokker/fanden/satan (etc.) **har gjort det?**
Who on earth/the bloody hell (etc.) has done that?

Hvad søren/dælen/pokker/fanden/satan (etc.) **foregår der her?**
What on earth/the bloody hell (etc.) is going on here?

(d) The genitive form **hvis** is indeclinable. It is mainly used attributively in front of a noun phrase, but can appear independently with the noun phrase omitted but implied. It has animate reference only:

Hvis gamle taske er det?	Whose old bag is that?
Hvis bur er det? Det er fuglens.	Whose cage is that? It is the bird's.
Hvis er det?	Whose is it/that?
Han spurgte, hvis bil det var.	He asked whose car it was.

426 Hvilken (hvilket, hvilke)

This pronoun has three forms: the singular forms **hvilken** (common gender) and **hvilket** (neuter) plus the plural form **hvilke**. It can appear both attributively and independently but sounds increasingly old-fashioned in independent use. Its form is determined by the noun which it modifies, even in independent use, where such a noun is always implied. **Hvilken** typically has the association, 'out of a limited number':

Attributive use
Hvilken kandidat er mest egnet?
Which candidate is best suited?

Hvilket hus er varmest?
Which house is the warmest?

Hvilke regler gælder her?
Which rules apply here?

Independent use
Her er fem oste. Hvilken vil du helst have?
Here are five cheeses. Which (one) would you rather have?

Hvilket er det største dyr i skoven?
Which is the largest animal in the forest?

Se alle de blomster! Hvilke vil passe bedst til stuen?
Look at all those flowers! Which will go best with the living-room?

Like **hvem** and **hvad**, it must be supported by **der** when it is the subject in indirect questions:

Ved du, hvilken der er dyrest?
Do you know which is the most expensive one?

Har du hørt, hvilket våben der blev brugt?
Have you heard which weapon was used?

Hvilken can refer to animate and inanimate objects, but is not used very often about human beings, especially without an attached noun. In such cases **hvem** is preferred:

Hvem/*Hvilken er din nye ven? Who is your new friend?

Hvem/*Hvilken i klassen bor længst fra skolen?
Which one in the class lives furthest away from the school?

Hvilken can be used to ask for either identification or description:

Identification
Hvilken kage vil du have? — **Den dér i hjørnet.**
Which cake do you want? — That one in the corner.

Description
Hvilken (slags) kage vil du have? — **En med masser af flødeskum.**
What kind of cake do you want? — One with lots of whipped cream.

Even with its prime function, i.e. attributively about a limited amount or number, **hvilken** predominantly belongs to a fairly formal style of language. Here it often occurs after a preposition:

I hvilket omfang er det udtryk for en ændret holdning hos regeringen?
To what extent is it evidence of a change in the government's attitude?

Note – **Hvilken** is found in slightly archaic exclamations:

Hvilken morgen! What a morning!
Se hvilket menneske! What a man! (Cf. Latin: 'Ecce homo!')

For **hvilket** as a relative pronoun see 436.

427 Hvad for en (et, nogle)

The construction **hvad for en/et/nogle** usually functions as an interrogative pronoun. It corresponds to English 'what' or 'what kind of ...' and belongs to the spoken language or an informal written style. In attributive use the last part of it **(en)** is the indefinite article and inflects in the normal way (**en, et**) (see 134). In independent use it has more in common with the cardinal number **én/ét** (see 302). In addition, it makes use of the neuter singular form **noget** and the plural form **nogle** of the indefinite pronoun **nogen** (see 448):

Hvad for en bog?	What (kind of) book?
Hvad for et bord?	What (kind of) table?
Hvad for noget mælk?	What (kind of) milk?
Hvad for nogle sange?	What (kind of) songs?

In several ways **hvad for en** resembles **hvilken**.

(a) It appears both attributively and independently. As subject in indirect questions it must be supported by **der**:

Hvad for en cykel har hun?	What kind of bike does she have?
Hvad for et kan du bedst lide?	Which one do you like best?
Ved du, hvad for en der er størst?	Do you know which one is the biggest?

(b) In independent use it cannot refer to human beings:

Jens og Per kommer til middag. *Hvad for en/Hvem vil du have til bords?
Jens and Per are coming for dinner. Which one do you want to sit next to?

(c) It can be used to ask for either identification or description:

Identification
Hvad for nogle bøger bruger I på kurset? Dem ovre på reolen.
What books do you use on the course? Those over there on the shelf.

Description
Hvad for nogle bøger bruger I på kurset? Nogle gamle, kedelige romaner.
What (kind of) books do you use on the course? Some boring old novels.

Hvad for noget is always used with non-count nouns, where **hvad for en/et**

would be impossible:

Hvad for noget tapet skal vi sætte på væggen i soveværelset?
What kind of wallpaper shall we put on the walls in the bedroom?

(d) In very colloquial language, **hvad for en** can appear not only as a unit but also discontinuously in the form of **hvad ... for en**, where **for en** moves to final position in the clause:

Hvad for en dug skal jeg lægge på? Which cloth shall I put on the table?
Hvad skal jeg lægge på for en dug?

Hvad for nogle glas skal vi bruge? What (kind of) glasses shall we use?
Hvad skal vi bruge for nogle glas?

Sometimes the discontinuous form seems more natural with questions of description than with questions of identification:

Hvad er han for en fyr? What sort of chap is he?
(Not equivalent to: **Hvem er han?** Who is he?)

Note the following idiomatic expressions:

Hvad er det for noget?	What sort of thing is that?
Hvad er nu det for noget?	*Approx.*: What have you done?
Hvad er du for en?	What/Who are you? (To a child or a small animal)

However, discontinuous order is not possible after a preposition:

I hvad for et hus har du boet? (*I hvad har du boet for et hus?)
In what house have you lived?

(e) Hvad for can also combine directly with a plural noun without **nogle**. This can cover both identification and description:

Hvad for planer har I for ferien?
What plans have you got for the holidays?

Hvad for bøger har du købt for nylig?
What (kind of) books have you bought recently?

Hvad for frimærker samler han på?
What kind of stamps does he collect?

428 Table of interrogative pronouns in direct and indirect questions

In main clauses, i.e. direct questions	*In subordinate clauses, i.e. indirect questions*		*Para.*
(a) independent use			
hvem	**hvem der**	(subj.)	425
	hvem	(obj.)	
hvad	**hvad der**	(subj.)	425
	hvad	(obj.)	
hvis	**hvis**		425
hvilken (etc.)	**hvilken** (etc.) **der**	(subj.)	426
	hvilken (etc.)	(obj.)	
hvad (...) for en (etc.)	**hvad (...) for en** (etc.) **der**	(subj.)	427
	hvad (...) for en (etc.)	(obj.)	
(b) attributive use			
hvad + adj./noun	**hvad** + adj./noun + **der**	(subj.)	425
	hvad + adj./noun	(obj.)	
hvis + noun	**hvis** + noun		425
hvilken (etc.) + noun	**hvilken** (etc.) + noun + **der**	(subj.)	426
	hvilken (etc.) + noun	(obj.)	
hvad (...) for en (etc.) + noun	**hvad (...) for en** (etc.) + noun + **der**	(subj.)	427
	hvad (...) for en (etc.) + noun	(obj.)	

H RELATIVE PRONOUNS

429 Relative pronouns – forms, table

Relative pronouns introduce relative clauses. They refer back to an antecedent in the preceding clause (with which they agree in gender and number) and they function as a constituent in the relative clause (which determines their case). The antecedent may be a noun phrase or a clause. There are six members of this class: **der, som, hvad, hvem, hvis** and **hvilken/hvilket/hvilke.**

Subject	*Object*	*Prepositional complement*	*Genitive*	*Reference (style)*
der who/which/that			**hvis** whose/of which	Animate or inanimate noun phrase
som who/which/that	**som** who(m)/which/that	**som** who(m)/which/that	**hvis** whose/of which	Animate or inanimate noun phrase

Subject	*Object*	*Prepositional complement*	*Genitive*	*Reference (style)*
	hvem who(m)	**hvem** who(m)	**hvis** whose	Personal noun or noun phrase (formal)
hvad der which	**hvad** which/what/that			Clause, indefinite
hvilket which	**hvilket** which	**hvilket** which		Clause (formal)
		hvilken/hvilket/hvilke which		Animate or inanimate noun phrase (formal)

Note – For the relative adverb **hvor** (where) and its compounds see 612(b), 921(d)..

430 The two types of relative clause

There are two types of relative clause: *restrictive* and *non-restrictive*. In a restrictive relative clause, the relative pronoun (whether it is present or implied) defines or modifies its antecedent (which can never be a clause) in an important way, and such a relative clause could therefore not be omitted without changing the meaning of the whole sentence or rendering it meaningless. In a non-restrictive relative clause, the relative pronoun (which can never be omitted) merely provides extra or supplementary information about its antecedent (which may be a whole clause), and such a relative clause can therefore be omitted without seriously affecting the meaning of the whole sentence. In Danish, the use of the traditional comma offers no clue as to the type of relative clause, whereas the use of the new comma does (se 1203).

Restrictive relative clauses
Den bygning, der hæver sig i baggrunden, er rådhuset.
The building that rises in the background is the town hall.

Der er noget, som jeg må tale med dig om.
There is something which/that I need to talk to you about.

Non-restrictive relative clauses
Min far, som fylder tres år på søndag, har fået et nyt job.
My father, who will be sixty on Sunday, has got a new job.

Jeg begik en fejl, hvilket ikke var særlig heldigt.
I made a mistake, which was not very fortunate.

431 Der

Der is indeclinable. It is only used as subject of the relative clause. Its antecedent may be animate or inanimate, but it cannot be a clause. **Der** can appear in both restrictive and non-restrictive relative clauses (see 430).

Restrictive relative clauses
Der er mange mennesker, der ikke har tag over hovedet.
There are many people who haven't got a roof over their heads.

Det er ham, der er den skyldige.
He is the one who is the culprit.

De plader, der sælges nu om dage, er ikke alle af høj kvalitet.
The records that are sold nowadays are not all of high quality.

Non-restrictive relative clauses
Bogen, der kunne være mere spændende, er allerede udsolgt.
The book, which could be more exciting, is already sold out.

Peter, der endnu ikke går i skole, har fået en lille cykel.
Peter, who does not go to school yet, has been given a small bike.

Since **der** can only function as subject, it can never be omitted. But even as subject, it is not used in the second of two coordinated relative clauses. Here it is replaced by **som**:

Firmaet søger en person, der er velkvalificeret, og som kan klare arbejdspresset.
The firm is looking for a person who is well-qualified and who can cope with the pressure of the job.

Der is felt to be less formal than **som** and therefore, despite its syntactic restrictions, appears very frequently in colloquial language.

Note – Because of the extensive use of existential **der** in Danish (see 1003(b)), there is often confusion between existential and relative **der**:

Hvem tror du, der har gjort det?	Who do you think has/have done it?
Hvem siger du, der kommer?	Who do you say is/are coming?

In fact, there is a respectable tradition within Danish grammatical description which denies **der** pronominal status altogether. (Cf. **som** below.)

432 Som

(a) **Som**, like **der**, is indeclinable. Syntactically as well as semantically, it is the most versatile of all the relatives. It is used as subject, direct and indirect object, and prepositional complement. When it is governed by a preposition, the latter cannot precede **som** but must be placed at the end of the clause. It can have both animate and inanimate antecedents and appear in restrictive and non-restrictive relative clauses alike. In its functions **som** most closely resembles 'that' among the English relatives although, depending on the context, it may be rendered by 'who(m)' and 'which' as well:

Her er to æbler, som skal skrælles.
Here are two apples that have to be peeled.

Den familie, som vi besøgte i foråret, er flyttet.
The family that we visited in the spring have moved.

Er det den gave, som du gav Eva?
Is that the present that you gave Eva?

Der ligger hotellet, som jeg boede på.
There is the hotel that I stayed in.

Min mor, som jeg besøger hver dag, er ikke rigtig rask.
My mother, who(m) I visit every day, isn't very well.

John holdt en tale, som vi godt kunne have undværet.
John made a speech, which we could easily have done without.

(b) In restrictive relative clauses, **som** may be omitted when it is not the subject. In this respect, too, **som** behaves like 'that' in English:

Giv mig den kniv, som ligger på stolen. (Subject)
Give me the knife that is lying on the chair.

Kjolen, (som) jeg viste dig i går, er for lang. (Object)
The dress (that) I showed you yesterday is too long.

Græsset, (som) vi sad på, var endnu vådt. (Prepositional complement)
The grass (that) we were sitting on was still wet.

(c) In non-restrictive clauses **som** can never be omitted, whereas 'that' cannot be used in English:

Vi tog i Tivoli, som vores gæster aldrig havde besøgt.
We went to Tivoli, *that/which our guests had never visited.

In non-restrictive clauses **som** can even have the whole of the preceding clause as its antecedent. In this use **som** acts as an informal alternative to **hvilket** and **hvad**:

Jensens har haft indbrud, som/hvad/hvilket du nok ved.
The Jensens have been burgled, as you probably know.

(d) Som is used to correlate with **samme** (same):

Det er den samme gave, som jeg fik sidste år.
That is the same present (as/that) I got last year.

Vi ankom samme dag, som John tog afsted.
We arrived on the same day (as/that) John set off.

It is notable that **som** here correlates with **samme** rather than with the head of the noun phrase **dag**. This construction forms a transition to the full use of **som** as an element of comparison, usually with **lige så** as its correlative: **lige så ... som** (just as ... as):

Peter er lige så stor som sin far.
Peter is just as tall as his father.

Note – It is sometimes argued that **som** (like 'that' in English) is not an integral part of the relative clause structure and thus not a genuine relative pronoun. One of the arguments used in favour of this view is the fact that in colloquial language and dialects one finds **der** or even **at der** inserted after a subject **som**. This should not be imitated:

Det er den familie, som der lige er flyttet ind ved siden af.
That is the family that has just moved in next door.

Der er den mand, som at der var her i morges.
There is the man who was here this morning.

433 Hvem

The use of **hvem** as a relative pronoun is on the decline. It must have a personal antecedent and it cannot function as the subject of the relative clause. When it is governed by a preposition, it can either follow the preposition or the latter appears in final position. It belongs to the formal language:

Hun svigtede de personer, hvem hun skyldte så meget.
She let down the people whom she owed so much.

Jeg mødte hans bror, hvem jeg har kendt længe.
I met his brother, whom I have known for a long time.

Han er gift med Ulla, hvem jeg ofte taler med.
He is married to Ulla, whom I often talk to.

Han er gift med Ulla, med hvem jeg ofte taler.
He is married to Ulla, with whom I often talk.

In the spoken and informal written language, **som** is nearly always used instead of **hvem**, though it cannot follow a preposition (cf. 432(a)).

434 Hvad

The use of **hvad** as a relative is rather limited.

(a) In a non-restrictive relative clause, **hvad** can have the preceding clause as its antecedent. When it functions as subject, **hvad** must be supported by **der**. In this use **hvad** corresponds to 'which' in English:

Han gik sin vej, hvad der virkede meget barnligt.
He walked away, which seemed very childish.

De ville være danmarksmestre, hvad de også blev.
They wanted to be Danish champions, which they did manage to become.

Hun kom ikke til festen, hvad man godt kan forstå.
She didn't come to the party, which one can well understand.

(b) **Hvad** can be an indefinite relative in connection with certain verbs. In such cases **hvad** has no obvious antecedent and corresponds to 'what' in English:

Politiet gjorde, hvad de kunne for at fange forbryderen.
The police did what they could to catch the criminal.

Du skal bare spise, hvad du kan.
You just eat what you can.

(c) **Hvad** is used idiomatically after the indefinite pronoun **alt** (cf. English 'all that ...'):

Fortæl mig alt, hvad du ved.
Tell me all that you know.

Alt, hvad han rører ved, bliver forvandlet til guld.
All that he touches turns to gold.

(d) **Hvad** is used with cataphoric reference in the same way as 'what' is in English:

Men hvad du ikke har sagt, er, at du dumpede.
But what you haven't said is that you failed the exam.

Og hvad der var endnu bedre, var, at hun fik et job.
And what was even better was that she got a job.

Note – **Hvad** appears in the idiom **hvad (...) angår** (as far as ... is/are concerned):

Hvad angår børnene, så bliver de hos deres mor.
As far as the children are concerned, they will stay with their mother.

Hvad skolen angår, er Jens ikke særlig interesseret.
As far as school is concerned, Jens is not very interested.

For **hvad som helst** see 450.

435 Hvis

The indeclinable genitive form **hvis** can have both animate and inanimate antecedents. Since it is associated with 'possession', it mainly refers to noun phrases that denote people, animals or material objects, but even abstract nouns can act as antecedents. As a relative, **hvis** is never used independently, but must modify a noun. A preposition can precede **hvis** + noun. **Hvis** corresponds to 'whose' and (in formal style) 'of which' in English:

Politiet søger en person, hvis alder er uvis.
The police are looking for a person whose age is uncertain.

Hunden, hvis hale logrede meget, begyndte at gø.
The dog, whose tail was wagging a lot, began to bark.

Bordet, hvis ben var dækket af dugen, så smukt ud.
The table, whose legs were covered by the cloth, looked splendid.

Han følte et had, hvis styrke ingen kendte.
He felt a hatred, the power of which nobody knew.

Hun var den person, på hvis skuldre ansvaret hvilede.
She was the person on whose shoulders the responsibility rested.

436 Hvilken (hvilket, hvilke)

This is the only relative pronoun that can inflect for gender and number: **hvilken** (singular, common gender), **hvilket** (singular, neuter), **hvilke** (plural).

(a) **Hvilken** and **hvilke** are now hardly ever used independently as subject or object. However, **hvilket** can have the preceding clause as its antecedent and thus be a slightly more formal equivalent of **hvad (der)** (cf. 434). The English equivalent is 'which':

Han påstod, at han var uskyldig, hvilket ingen troede på.
He claimed that he was innocent, which nobody believed.

Til sidst opgav han jobbet, hvilket ikke kom som en overraskelse.
In the end he gave up his job, which didn't come as a surprise.

(b) **Hvilken (hvilket, hvilke)** is used independently or attributively in formal style when governed by a preposition. The preposition usually precedes **hvilken** (etc.) (+ noun). The antecedent may be animate or inanimate. Here the English equivalent is 'whom' or 'which':

Hun er en af de få, med hvilken de ansatte kan tale.
She is one of the few, with whom the employees can talk.

Det er den pen, med hvilken traktaten blev underskrevet.
That is the pen with which the treaty was signed.

"Jeg vil ikke," sagde han. Med hvilke ord han rejste sig og gik.
'I won't,' he said. With which words he got up and left.

Det var det valg, efter hvilket der skete store forandringer.
That was the election after which great changes took place.

Note – A special use is found in the idiomatic expression indicating vacillation: **til hvilken side hver anden gang** (now one way, now the other):

A: Er han konsekvent?	A: Is he consistent?
B: Nej, det er nærmest til hvilken side hver anden gang.	B: No, it is more a matter of now one way, now the other.

I INDEFINITE PRONOUNS

437 Introduction

This is a very heterogeneous group of pronouns. Many of them have universal or partitive meaning and they often function as determiners. In the following paragraphs, the form and uses of the most important indefinite pronouns are dealt with in alphabetical order.

438 Al (alt, alle)

The forms **al, alt, alle** represent common gender, neuter and plural, respectively. They may combine with a noun with or without the end article. In English, this corresponds to the use of 'all' + noun (indefinite form) and 'all the' + noun (definite form). In addition, the forms **alt** and **alle**, but not **al**, may be used nominally.

(a) Attributive use

(i) **Al (alt, alle)** + noun without the end article has universal application. **Al (alt, alle)** agrees in gender and number with the following noun:

Al magt til folket!	All power to the people!
Alt kød er udsolgt.	All meat is sold out.
Alle dyr bør beskyttes.	All animals should be protected.

Al/alt + singular count noun without the end article often corresponds to 'every' in English:

De har al udsigt til succes. They have every prospect of success.

(ii) **Al (alt, alle)** has specific application when followed by the definite form of the noun, or by a demonstrative or a possessive pronoun + a noun:

Alle spillerne spillede dårligt. All the players played poorly.
Du får al den hjælp, du behøver. You'll get all the help you need.
Jeg inviterede alle mine venner. I invited all my friends.

(b) Nominal use

The common gender singular form **al** has no nominal use.

(i) **Alt**

1 As subject, object or prepositional complement, corresponding to English 'everything':

Alt er ved det gamle. Everything is as it used to be.
Hun fortalte mig alt. She told me everything.
Han var utilfreds med alt. He was dissatisfied with everything.

2 **Alt** is sometimes synonymous with **alting**:

Alt/Alting ser lyst ud. Everything is looking bright.
Han ved alt/alting om sport. He knows everything about sport.

However, when combining with an adjective, **alt** is preferred:

Han elsker alt dansk. He loves everything Danish.
alt godt fra havet all kinds of seafood

Alt and **alting** are rarely interchangeable in idiomatic expressions:

Du er mit ét og alt. You are everything to me.
Gør det for alt i verden ikke! Don't do it on any account!
Hvorom alting er ... However that may be ...
Når enden er god, er alting godt. All's well that ends well.

3 **Alt sammen** can replace **alt** for greater emphasis:

Det lykkedes alt sammen. It all succeeded.

Note that **alt** is used adverbially (often ironically) in rather archaic expressions like:

Alt så tidligt oppe?	Up already?

(ii) Alle

1 As subject, object or prepositional complement, corresponding to English 'everyone/everybody':

Alle vil have lønforhøjelse.	Everybody wants a pay rise.
Jeg mistænker alle.	I suspect everyone.
Han hilste på alle.	He shook hands with everybody.

2 As specifier (corresponding to 'all'):

In this role, **alle** occurs in the position of, or immediately after, a clausal adverbial. **Alle** may refer back to the subject, which can be a noun phrase or a pronoun:

Eleverne bestod alle eksamen.	The pupils all passed the exam.
Har I alle set den nye film?	Have you all seen the new film?
Vi er alle i samme båd.	We are all in the same boat.

Alternatively, **alle** may specify the direct or indirect object, in which case the latter must be a pronoun:

Chefen roste os alle.	The boss praised all of us.
Karen gav dem alle en is.	Karen gave them all an ice-cream.

Alle may be replaced by **alle sammen** for greater emphasis. This can even be used independently to address people:

De gik alle sammen lige hjem.	They all went straight home.
Farvel, alle sammen!	Goodbye everybody!

3 **Alle** has the genitive form **alles**:

Alles øjne var rettet mod ham.	All eyes were directed at him.
alles kamp mod alle	everyone for himself

(c) Idiomatic expressions (see also (b)(i) above):

alt i alt	all in all
alt iberegnet	all inclusive
alt taget i betragtning	considering everything
alt vel	everything's fine
frem for alt	above all
Jeg er alt andet end stolt af det.	I'm anything but proud of it.
Når alt kommer til alt ...	When all is said and done ...
trods alt	after all, despite everything
alle og enhver	all and sundry, one and all
(Hun/Det er) alle tiders!	(She/It is) fantastic/super!
alle vegne	everywhere
én for alle og alle for én	one for all and all for one
én gang for alle	once and for all

439 Anden (andet, andre)

For **anden** as an ordinal number see 311(b).

(a) The forms **anden, andet, andre** represent common gender, neuter and plural, respectively. They are all used both attributively and nominally, corresponding to 'other(s)' in English, and they agree in gender and number with the noun to which they refer, whether it is present or implied:

Det skete en anden dag.	That happened on another day.
Dette æble er råddent. Har du et andet?	This apple is rotten. Have you got another?
Andre børn spiser pænt op.	Other children eat up their food.
Hvor er de andre?	Where are the others?

(b) The singular forms **anden/andet** appear very frequently in nominal use without a pro-form, whereas in English '(an)other' is often followed by a noun or the pro-form 'one':

Den anden er bedre.	The other (one) is better.
Hvad var det andet, du sagde?	What was the other thing you said?

(c) When used nominally about people, **anden** and **andre** have a genitive form in **-s**:

Det er en andens frakke.	That is another person's coat.
De andres pas var udløbet.	The others' passports had expired.

(d) After an interrogative or another indefinite pronoun, **anden (andet, andre)** often corresponds in meaning to 'else' in English:

Ingen anden har set det.	Nobody else has seen it.
Der er sket noget andet.	Something else has happened.
Hvem andre besøgte du?	Who else did you visit?

(e) '(The) one ... the other'

The Danish equivalent of English '(the) one ... the other' in nominal use is **den/det ene ... den anden/det andet**:

Den ene sagde ja, den anden nej.	One said yes, the other said no.
Den enes død er den andens brød.	One man's meat is another man's poison.
på den ene side ... på den anden side	on (the) one hand ... on the other (hand)

(f) 'Another'

The English pronoun 'another' has three main renderings in Danish, depending on its meaning:

(i) 'Another' = 'a different (one)': **en anden/et andet**. The gender is determined by the noun, whether present or implied:

Hun fortalte en anden historie.	She told a different story.
Han har fået et andet job.	He's got another job.
Det er noget helt andet.	That's another matter.

Note – There is a corresponding plural form **andre** (sometimes **nogle andre**):

Mine sokker er for gamle. Jeg køber nogle andre.
My socks are too old. I'll buy some others (i.e. different ones).

(ii) 'Another' = 'an additional (one)': **én/ét (...) til**. Again, the gender is determined by the noun, whether present or implied:

Vil du have en kop kaffe til?	Would you like another cup of coffee?
De har fået et barn til.	They have had another child.
Jeg vil have 1000 kr. til!	I want another 1000 kroner!
Jeg gi'r én til.	I'll buy another (drink).

(iii) 'One another': **hinanden** (see 411).

(g) Note the following idiomatic expressions:

en anden gang	another time
en eller anden	someone, somebody
af en eller anden grund	for some reason (or other)
på en eller anden måde	in some way, somehow (or other)
som en anden idiot	like a proper fool
et eller andet	something (or other)
blandt andet (bl.a.)	among other things
blandt andre (bl.a.)	among others (i.e. persons)

Note 1 – Colloquially, **en anden en** is sometimes used ironically for **jeg**, i.e. the speaker him/herself:

Og her går en anden en og sparer!	And here I'm trying to save!

Note 2 – English use of 'other' in vague time references is rendered in Danish as:

forleden dag/aften/uge	the other day/evening/week

440 Begge

Begge corresponds to 'both (of)' in English and is associated with the notion of 'two'. It is indeclinable.

(a) Attributive use

Begge is used attributively before a noun or a noun phrase. The noun in question must be in the plural form, but may be either definite or indefinite:

Begge huse(ne) er hvide.	Both (the) houses are white.
Jeg talte med begge brødre(ne).	I spoke to both (the) brothers.
Han har begge hænder(ne) i lommen.	He has both (his) hands in his pockets.

A noun phrase after **begge** may be introduced by a possessive pronoun, a genitive or the front article + an adjective:

begge mine børn	both my children
begge Johns forældre	both John's parents
begge de store skorstene	both (of) the big chimneys

(b) Nominal use

In nominal use **begge** is often followed by **to** (two) for greater emphasis. However, **begge** and **begge to** do not have quite the same distribution.

(i) Both **begge** and **begge to** may function as subject, though **begge** is the more common of the two:

Begge (to) mødte op på arbejdet.	Both turned up at work.
Er begge til stede?	Are both present?

(ii) When specifying the subject, both can appear in front of subject complements or what are termed 'other adverbials' (see 1007(e), 1009), but only **begge to** can follow these. Note that **begge (to)** cannot immediately follow the subject:

Vi blev begge (to) syge.	We both fell ill.
Vi blev syge begge to.	We fell ill, both of us.
I skriver begge (to) godt.	You both write well.
I skriver godt begge to.	You write well, both of you.
Vi skal begge (to) på ferie.	We are both going on holiday.
Vi skal på ferie begge to.	We are going on holiday, both of us.

(iii) When functioning as direct/indirect object or prepositional complement, both **begge** and **begge to** are usually preceded by a personal pronoun which they specify:

Jeg kender dem begge (to).	I know them both.
Hun gav dem begge (to) en is.	She gave them both an ice-cream.
Vi stoler på jer begge (to).	We trust both of you.

(iv) In nominal use, **begge** has the genitive form **begges** but **begge tos** is also found in the spoken language:

Begges helbred er godt.	The health of both of them is good.
for begges/begge tos vedkommende	as far as both are concerned

(c) Note the following expressions:

en ven af os begge	a friend of both of us
i begge tilfælde	in both cases

Note – Historically, **begge** is the genitive form of **både**. The latter is now only used in the copulative conjunction **både ... og**, both ... and (cf. 613(c), 905(c)).

441 Få (færre, færrest)

(a) Få

(i) **Få** is a quantifier which is used either attributively with a plural noun, corresponding to English 'few', or nominally, corresponding to English 'few (people)' (but *not* 'few things' = **få ting**). In itself, **få** carries the implication 'very few', and this is often emphasized by adding the adverb **kun** (only) or **meget** (very), i.e. **kun få** or **meget få**:

Der er (kun) få roser i haven.	There are few roses in the garden.
Hun lavede (meget) få fejl.	She made few mistakes.
Han er en mand af få ord.	He is a man of few words.
Der var (kun) få til stede.	There were few people present.
Han var en af de få, der rejste.	He was one of the few who left.

Note – Danish uses **for lidt**, not **for få**, corresponding to 'too few' in English, when it modifies a count noun in expressions like the following (cf. 444):

Vi købte en flaske for lidt.	We bought a bottle too few.
Holdet havde to points for lidt.	The team had two points too few.

(ii) The meaning 'a few' is often expressed by means of **nogle få (stykker)**:

Der er nogle få kager tilbage.	There are a few cakes left.
Giv mig nogle få stykker!	Give me a few!

Note – **Få** forms part of the compound noun **et fåtal**, a small minority:

Kun et fåtal af medlemmerne stemte for forslaget.
Only a small minority of the members voted in favour of the proposal.

(b) Færre, færrest

The comparative form **færre** and the superlative form **færrest** are also used either attributively with a plural noun or nominally, corresponding to English 'fewer/fewest'. In attributive use, they may modify or refer not only to words for people but also to those for any countable object, animate or inanimate. In nominal use, both forms occur more easily in Danish than in English.

(i) With **færre**, a comparative element is always either present (introduced by **end**, than) or implied:

Der er færre tigre end løver.	There are fewer tigers than lions.
Hun har færre problemer nu.	She has fewer problems now.
Der kom færre end ventet.	Fewer people turned up than expected.
Færre og færre går i kirke.	Fewer and fewer people go to church.

(ii) **Færrest** adds the adjective ending **-e** in the definite form:

Vi har haft færrest uheld.	We have had fewest accidents.
Kun de færreste forstod det.	Only a very few people understood it.

442 Hver

(a) Attributive use

(i) In this usage there are two gender forms: **hver** (common gender) and **hvert** (neuter). They both correspond to 'each' or 'every' in English and often occur with time expressions:

Hver deltager fik et nummer.	Each participant got a number.
På hvert bord stod der blomster.	There were flowers on every table.
hver time/dag/uge/måned, etc.	each/every hour/day/week/month, etc.
hvert minut/år/århundrede, etc.	each/every minute/year/century, etc.

Note especially the use of **hver(t)** before an ordinal number + a noun:

hver anden dag	every second day
hvert fjerde år	every fourth year

(ii) **Hver(t) enkelt** and **hver(t) eneste** + a count noun are used to stress that an action applies to each individual person, item, etc., corresponding in meaning to 'every single' + a count noun in English:

De undersøgte hver enkelt plan.	They examined every single plan.
Hvert enkelt offer blev behandlet.	Every single victim was treated.
Han mødte op hver eneste gang.	He turned up every single time.

Hvert eneste brev blev åbnet.	Every single letter was opened.

(iii) **Enhver/Ethvert** may be used for greater emphasis, corresponding to English 'any':

Det gælder til enhver tid.	That applies at any time.
Ethvert barn kan lære det.	Any child can learn that.

(iv) Sometimes **hver(t)** corresponds to English 'any':

Toget kan ankomme hvert øjeblik.	The train may arrive any moment.

For **hver sin (sit, sine)** see 417(j).

(b) Nominal use

(i) As subject, object or prepositional complement, corresponding to English 'everyone/everybody':

1 **Hver** does not usually occur independently as subject or object, but **enhver** (anyone, everyone) may do so, especially in well-established expressions. Furthermore, **enhver** has the genitive form **enhvers:**

Det kan enhver forstå.	Anyone can understand that.
Han gav enhver sit.	He gave every one their due.
Det er enhvers sag at ...	It is up to everyone to ...

2 Both **hver** and **enhver** can appear as prepositional complement:

Her er 10 kroner til hver.	Here's 10 kroner for each of you.
Jeg vil gerne have tre af hver.	I would like three of each.
Der var noget for enhver.	There was something for everyone.

(ii) As specifier, corresponding to English 'each':

1 **Hver** may occur on either side of a numerical expression:

Han gav os hver 100 kroner.	He gave each of us 100 kroner.
Han gav os 100 kroner hver.	He gave us 100 kroner each.
De fik hver to måneders fængsel.	They each got two months' prison.
De fik to måneders fængsel hver.	They got two months' prison each.

2 **Hver især** strongly emphasizes the individuals involved:

Hver især bidrog de en masse.	Each one contributed a lot.
De gjorde hver især deres bedste.	Each of them did their best.

For **hver for sig** see 410(g).

(c) Idiomatic expressions:

hver og én	absolutely everyone
Hver ting til sin tid.	There's a time for everything.
alle og enhver	all and sundry, one and all
Enhver sin lyst.	There is no accounting for taste. (*lit.*: Everyone his pleasure.)
Enhver er sin egen lykkes smed.	Everyone is the architect of his own fortune.

443 Ingen, intet

Ingen has both attributive and nominal function. In both uses **ingen** is often synonymous with **ikke nogen. Intet** is the neuter form; it too has attributive and nominal function and may alternate with **ikke noget**. Stylistically, however, use of **ikke nogen/noget** is often felt to be more natural than **ingen/intet**, which can have a rather formal and stilted ring to it. See 448.

(a) Ingen

(i) Attributive use

Ingen modifies common gender singular and all plural nouns. In this use, **ingen** corresponds to English 'no' or 'not any':

Ingen adgang!	No admittance!
Jeg har ingen bil.	I have no car.
Det var ingen spøg.	That was no fun/joke.
Der er ingen problemer.	There are no problems.
Han har ingen penge.	He has no money.
De har ingen børn.	They have no children.

Note the following idiomatic expressions:

Livet er ingen dans på roser.	Life is not a bed of roses.

Det var ingen sag at gøre det. It was no problem doing that.
Det var ingen anden end Jens! It was none other than Jens!
Ingen tvivl om det! No doubt about it!
ingen verdens ting nothing at all
på ingen måde in no way

(ii) Nominal use

This corresponds to English 'no one', 'nobody' or 'none':

Ingen er fuldkommen. Nobody is perfect.
Ingen vidste det. No one knew.
Ingen af eleverne svarede. None of the pupils answered.
Der kom ingen. Nobody came.
Der er ingen, der har set ham. Nobody has seen him.
Jeg kender ingen her i byen. I know no one in this town.

Ingen has the genitive form **ingens**:

Det var ingens skyld, at han døde. It was nobody's fault that he died.

(b) Intet

(i) Attributive use

Intet can only modify singular neuter nouns and corresponds to English 'no':

Der er intet tapet på væggene. There's no wallpaper on the walls.
Der var intet tøj i skabet. There were no clothes in the wardrobe.
De har intet sted at bo. They have nowhere to live.
Intet nyt er godt nyt. No news is good news.

(ii) Nominal use

This corresponds to English 'nothing':

Jeg har intet gjort. I've done nothing.
Jeg har intet at tilføje. I've got nothing to add.
Der var intet at gøre. There was nothing to be done.
Der er intet at være bange for. There is nothing to be afraid of.
Der er intet i vejen. There is nothing wrong.

Intet can often be replaced by **ingenting** (nothing):

Jeg fik den for ingenting. I got it for nothing.
Hvad er der sket? Ingenting. What's happened? Nothing.

Note the following idiomatic expressions:

alt eller intet
all or nothing

Det er intet mindre end bedrageri.
It is nothing short of fraud.

Hans mål var intet mindre end direktørstolen.
His aim was nothing less than the manager's chair.

Det gør ingenting.
It doesn't matter.

Hun lod som ingenting.
She pretended nothing had happened.

Note 1 – For greater emphasis the word **slet** (at all) may precede **ingen/intet** in all uses:

Der kom slet ingen (mennesker). Nobody at all turned up.
Han kunne slet intet stille op. He could do nothing at all.
Der skete slet ingenting. Nothing at all happened.

Note 2 – With even stronger emphasis, corresponding to 'not (a single) one', one of the phrases **ikke én/ét** or **ikke en/et eneste** is often found:

Ikke én af dem hjalp mig. Not a single one of them helped me.
Jeg har ikke en eneste plade. I haven't got a single record.
Ikke et eneste hus står tilbage. Not a single house remains.

444 Lidt

Lidt is a neuter singular form that can occur both attributively and nominally. It can only modify non-count nouns to specify quantity or degree and may be seen as the singular equivalent of **få** (see 441). **Lidt** in itself has positive connotations and corresponds to 'a little' or 'some' in English.

(a) Attributive use:

Må jeg låne lidt sukker? May I borrow some sugar?

Der er lidt vin i flasken.	There is a little wine in the bottle.
Hun har lidt vrøvl med chefen.	She has some trouble with the boss.

The negative connotation of English 'little' is rendered in Danish by adding a preceding modifier such as **for** (too), **kun** (only) or **meget** (very):

Han har for lidt energi.	He has got too little energy.
Det har de kun lidt glæde af.	They have little joy of that.
Der er meget lidt mad tilbage.	There is very little food left.

Note – Occasionally **lidt** can combine with a plural noun:

Jeg har lidt penge i banken.	I have a little money in the bank.
Han har lidt problemer med vægten.	He has some problems with his weight.

(b) Nominal use:

Han kender lidt til sagen.	He knows a little about the case.
Skal jeg spille lidt for dig?	Shall I play a little for you?
Du ved for lidt om det.	You know too little about it.
Det er lidt for meget.	It's a little too much.

Note the following idiomatic expressions:

Bliv lidt!	Stay a little!
Skynd dig lidt!	Hurry up!
Vent lidt!	Wait a little!
Det var så lidt!	Not at all! / You're welcome!
Det var ikke så lidt!	That was quite something!
lidt efter lidt	little by little
Lidt har også ret.	Even a little is not to be sneezed at.
lidt, men godt	not much but of high quality
om lidt	shortly, in a moment

Note 1 – **Lidt** may sometimes alternate with the noun phrase **en (lille) smule**:

Har du en (lille) smule mælk?	Have you got a little milk?
Bare en (lille) smule!	Just a little!

Note 2 – Formally, **lidt** is the neuter form of the adjective **liden**, meaning 'little'. However, the latter is now virtually obsolete and only appears in set expressions:

Han havde liden tro på fremtiden.	He had little faith in the future.

Note 3 – The earlier neuter form **lidet** is now only used as an adverb of degree in formal language:

en lidet tilfredsstillende løsning	a far from satisfactory solution
Det var lidet sandsynligt.	It was not very probable.

For **lidt** as an adverb see 615(a).

445 Man

Subject	*Object*	*Possessive*	*Reflexive*
man	**én**	**sin (sit, sine), ens**	**sig** (see 410)

(a) **Man** is a 3rd person singular pronoun that is used with general reference to human beings. **Man** is far more common in Danish than its most obvious equivalent, 'one', is in English. Thus in individual examples it may correspond to 'one', 'you', 'we', 'they', 'people' or a passive construction:

Man kan aldrig vide.	One/You never know(s).
Man ser mange cykler i Danmark.	You see a lot of bikes in Denmark.
Man skal ikke tro på alt.	You shouldn't believe everything.
Man lærer, så længe man lever.	We live and learn.
Man spiser med pinde i Kina.	They/People eat with chopsticks in China.
Man mente, at det var farligt.	It was thought to be dangerous.

(b) The form **én** can function as direct/indirect object or prepositional complement:

Han svigter aldrig én.	He never lets one down.
Det gav én chancen for at rejse.	It gave one the chance to travel.
De stoler ikke længere på én.	One is no longer trusted.

(c) **Man** has two possessive forms: **ens** and **sin (sit, sine)**, both corresponding to English 'one's'. However, the two forms are *not* interchangeable.

(i) **Ens** modifies a noun which may have any nominal function, but it can never refer to **man** as a subject:

Ens børn er dyrebare.	One's children are precious.

De kan fjerne ens ejendele.	They can remove one's possessions.
Ingen stoler på ens egne ord.	Nobody trusts one's own words.

(ii) When **man** occurs as subject, the possessive pronoun referring to it is **sin (sit, sine)**; the form is determined by the following noun (see 416-18):

Man betaler sin skat.	One pays one's taxes.
Man kan gøre sit bedste.	One can do one's best.
Man bør ikke opgive sine idealer.	One shouldn't give up one's ideals.

(d) **Man** is sometimes used in colloquial Danish instead of **jeg**:

Hvor længe skal man vente her?	How long does one have to wait here?
Må man begynde?	May I/one start?

Note – **Én** used as subject instead of **man/jeg** is now obsolete and only used jokingly:

Én får jo gøre sin pligt.	One has to do one's duty.

(e) Although **man** is formally singular, it often has plural association (cf. (a) above):

Det er sjovere, hvis man er flere.
It is more fun with several people.

Man løslod snart den anklagede.
The accused was soon set free (i.e. by the police).

Man/Folk siger, at Jeppe drikker.
People say that Jeppe is a drinker.

(f) Since **man** is often used in a general sense, a construction with **man** can sometimes come close in meaning to a corresponding passive construction with **der** as formal subject:

Man taler meget om det. / Der tales meget om det.
There is a lot of talk about it.

Man hørte pludselig et skud. / Der hørtes pludselig et skud.
A shot was suddenly heard.

Note 1 – **Man** (and its inflected forms) should be used consistently throughout a sentence:

Hvis nogen yder én og ens familie hjælp, bør man være taknemmelig.
If someone helps you and your family, you ought to be grateful.

Note 2 – With a preceding adjective or pronoun, **én** can also appear as subject or subject complement and refer to an animal or an object as well as to a person. This comes close to the use of **én** as a numeral (see 302):

Du er da en værre én!	You are really something!
Den kat er en sjov én.	That cat is a funny one.
Sådan én er tung at bære.	One like that is heavy to carry.

446 Mange (flere, flest)

Mange is a quantifier which is only used with plural meaning, corresponding to English 'many'. It has the comparative form **flere** and the superlative form **flest**, which correspond to English 'more' and 'most' (with plural meaning). All three forms occur in both attributive and nominal use.

(a) Mange

(i) **Mange** is used in much the same way as 'many' in English, i.e. either followed by the plural form of a noun or on its own, but **mange** may also correspond to English 'a lot (of)' or 'lots (of)' with plural meaning. Notice that without a specific referent **mange** in nominal use is almost exclusively used of people:

Mange arbejdere gik i strejke.	Many workers went on strike.
Vi ser ikke mange film.	We don't watch many films.
Han har mange gode idéer.	He has a lot of good ideas.
Var der mange til koncerten?	Were there many at the concert?
Det er der ikke mange, der ved.	Not many (people) know that.
Fem øl! Det er ikke (ret) mange.	Five bottles of beer! That's not very many.

(ii) When the attached plural noun in Danish corresponds to a singular noun in English, **mange** will normally be rendered in English as 'much' or 'lots/a lot' (with singular meaning) (see 128):

Han fortalte mig mange nyheder.	He told me a lot of news.
Vi har ikke (ret) mange penge.	We haven't got much money.
Hun gav mig mange gode råd.	She gave me a lot of good advice.

(iii) **Mange** has the genitive form **manges**:

Manges ejendele gik tabt.	Many people's possessions were lost.

Note – Historically, **mange** has two equivalent singular forms: **mangen** (common gender) and **mangt** (neuter). Both are now archaic, but when found they occur attributively, sometimes with the indefinite article in front of the following noun (obligatory with **mangt**), like 'many a' in English:

Mangen (en) sømand mistede livet.	Many a sailor lost his life.
Der faldt mangt et hårdt ord.	Many a harsh word was spoken.

Notice the idiomatic phrase **mangt og meget**:

Hun ligner ham i mangt og meget.	She is like him in many respects.

(b) Flere

Flere is used both in a comparative and in an absolute sense:

(i) Comparative sense

Flere in a comparative sense may appear with or without a following noun, but always with a notion of 'compared with someone or something else', whether this element of comparison is overtly expressed or not. Where this element does occur, it is introduced by the comparative item **end** (than):

Ulla har flere bøger end Lone.	Ulla has more books than Lone.
Der bor flere mennesker i Asien.	More people live in Asia.
Kommer der flere?	Are there more (people) coming?
Mange flere dukkede op end i går.	Many more turned up than yesterday.

Notice also:

Der er ikke flere tilbage.	There are no more left.

(ii) Absolute sense

Flere can be used in an absolute sense, with no implication of a comparison with something else. **Flere** in this use can only occur attributively. Its English equivalents here are 'several', 'quite a few', 'a number of ' and the like:

I flere dage skete der intet.	For several days nothing happened.
Han har været på flere rejser.	He has been on quite a few trips.

Det sker flere steder. That happens in a number of places.

Flere is also used as a plural marker:

en bog - flere bøger one book - several books

(c) **Flest**

The superlative form **flest** adds the definite adjective ending **-e** when preceded by the plural front article **de**:

Af alle børnene har Jens flest plader.
Of all the children Jens has got most records.

Der er flest roser i vores have.
There are most roses in our garden.

De skriver alle mange breve, men Bente skriver flest.
They all write many letters, but Bente writes the most.

De fleste af mine venner cykler.
Most of my friends ride a bike.

De fleste banegårde er kedelige.
Most railway stations are dreary.

Notice the following idiomatic phrase:

Han er, som folk er flest.
He is like most people.

447 Meget

Meget is a quantifier that is used both attributively and nominally of quantity. Though formally a neuter singular form, it can nowadays modify any gradable adjective/adverb and singular non-count noun. Depending on the context, **meget** corresponds on the one hand to 'very', and on the other hand to 'much', 'a good deal of', 'a lot (of)' and 'lots (of)' (with singular meaning).

(a) Attributive use

(i) **Meget** can modify adjectives or adverbs in the basic form and thus act as an uptoner (cf. 615). This corresponds to English 'very':

Der var meget mørkt i stuen. It was very dark in the room.
Hun er en meget smuk dame. She is a very beautiful woman.

Holdet spillede meget dårligt.	The team played very badly.

However, this is not possible with non-gradable adjectives/adverbs (i.e. those that have an absolute sense). Compare:

***Bygningen er meget firkantet.**	*The building is very quadrangular.
But: **Han er meget firkantet.**	He is very awkward to deal with.

Notice that with certain frequently used adjectives or adverbs with positive connotations (e.g. **god**, good; **pæn**, nice; **sjov**, funny, amusing; **sød**, nice, sweet, etc.), **meget** can lose some of its intensifying meaning and may have no more force than 'quite', 'reasonably' or 'all right' in English. In the spoken language, **meget** has main stress and the adjective secondary stress in such cases and the adjective/adverb is part of a rising intonation pattern, whereas normally **meget** and the adjective/adverb will have equal stress:

Han er meget god.	He is reasonably good. (But no more!)
Hun er meget sød.	She is quite nice. (But ...)
Det ser meget pænt ud.	It looks all right. (But ...)

(ii) If the adjective or adverb appears in the comparative form, the English equivalent of **meget** is 'much':

en meget mere interessant idé	a much more interesting idea
Det er et meget større hus.	It is a much bigger house.
Det gjorde han meget bedre.	He did that much better.

(iii) **Meget** is used as an uptoner with singular non-count (mass) nouns, irrespective of the gender of the noun. Here English uses 'much', 'a lot (of)', 'lots (of)', etc.:

Der er meget mad tilbage.	There is a lot of food left.
Hun fik ikke meget støtte.	She didn't get much support.
Der er for meget bly i benzinen.	There is too much lead in the petrol.

Note – **Meget** has a common gender parallel form **megen**, which is only used attributively with common gender non-count nouns. It now sounds rather stilted and archaic and has virtually been ousted by **meget**:

Hunden er hende til megen glæde.	The dog gives her much pleasure.
(Cf. **Hunden glæder hende meget.**	The dog pleases her a lot.)
al den megen tale om miljøet	all that talk about the environment
(Cf. **Der tales meget om ...**	There is a lot of talk about ...)

(b) Nominal use:

(i) **Meget** can be used as an equivalent to **mange ting** (many things). This corresponds to English 'much':

Der er meget at se på.	There is much to look at.
Vi kan ikke gøre meget ved det.	We can't do much about it.

(ii) **Meget** may also be used about 'degree' and can then be preceded by an interrogative or an intensifier:

Hvor meget skylder du ham?	How much do you owe him?
Så meget er det ikke værd.	It's not worth that much.

(iii) As well as corresponding to 'too much', **for meget** may also be the equivalent of 'too many' when it is the complement of a plural noun:

Det hele blev for meget for ham.	It all became too much for him.
Jeg kogte ti kartofler for meget.	I boiled ten potatoes too many.

(c) Idiomatic expressions:

Det er alt for meget!	It's far too much!
Det er for meget af det gode.	That's too much of a good thing.
Det er lige meget.	It doesn't matter.
Det er så meget sagt.	That's putting it a bit strong.
dobbelt så meget	twice as much
Hvor meget er klokken?	What's the time?
Jeg er ikke meget for likør.	I don't like liqueur very much.
mangt og meget (see 446(a)(iii)(Note))	a great many things
så meget som muligt	as much as possible
så meget mere som ...	the more so as ...
Sådan er der så meget.	That's life for you.

448 Nogen (noget, nogle)

The three forms **nogen** (common gender/plural), **noget** (neuter) and **nogle** (plural) can all occur both attributively and nominally and correspond to English 'some', 'any' or their compound forms (e.g. 'somebody', 'anyone', 'something', etc.). In English, the choice between 'some' and 'any' chiefly depends on whether the pronoun is *assertive* (like 'some' plus compounds), i.e. whether it postulates or implies the existence of a certain quantity/number of something, or *non-assertive* (like 'any' plus compounds), in which case it carries no such implication. This distinction is also important for the corresponding Danish pronouns.

(a) Nogen

(i) Attributive use

1 **Nogen** can combine with common gender nouns in the singular. It corresponds to English 'some', 'any' or (in some negative statements) 'a', 'any'. However, this use is most common in front of abstract nouns, since the idea of a certain 'quantity' of a substance is usually conveyed by **noget** (cf. (b)(i)(2) below):

Han har været her i nogen tid.	He has been here for some time.
Der opstod nogen uro i salen.	Some commotion broke out in the hall.
Har du nogen idé om hans planer?	Have you got any idea of his plans?
Jeg har ikke nogen bil/radio, etc.	I haven't got a car/radio, etc.

2 With plural nouns, the choice is between **nogen** and **nogle** (see (c) below). In the spoken language, **nogen** has completely replaced **nogle** before plural nouns, even when the pronoun has assertive meaning. In the written language, **nogen** is generally used with non-assertive meaning (equivalent to English 'any') and **nogle** with assertive meaning (equivalent to English 'some'), but the choice is not always clear-cut:

Spoken Danish

Giv mig nogen penge!	Give me some money!
Vi har kigget på nogen huse.	We have looked at some houses.

Written Danish

Giv mig nogle penge! / Vi har kigget på nogle huse.

In simple negations, whether spoken or written, the pronoun is always **nogen**:

Jeg fik ikke nogen julegaver.	I didn't get any Christmas presents.
Han har aldrig nogen penge.	He never has any money.

In written questions and conditional clauses, the plural form **nogle** is sometimes, though not always, found with plural nouns when the pronoun has assertive meaning. But there is good deal of uncertainty in this area, even among native speakers:

Vil I have nogen/nogle bolsjer?
Do you want any/some sweets?

Hvis hun ikke har nogen/nogle venner, der kan hjælpe hende ...
If she hasn't got any/some friends who can help her ...

(ii) Nominal use

1 With assertive meaning without a specific referent, **nogen** refers to people in the sense of 'somebody', 'someone':

Der står nogen uden for døren.	There is somebody outside the door.
Jeg tror, jeg så nogen i haven.	I think I saw someone in the garden.
Der er nogen, der har taget bogen.	Somebody has taken the book.

2 With non-assertive meaning, **nogen** is used in the sense of 'anybody', 'anyone' in questions, negations and conditional clauses:

Har nogen set min cykel?	Has anyone seen my bike?
Der er ikke nogen hjemme.	There isn't anybody at home.
Hvis nogen tror, det er sjovt ...	If anybody thinks it is funny ...

Notice that **ikke nogen** often replaces **ingen** (see 443):

A: **Hvem talte du med?** B: **Ikke nogen.**
A: Who did you talk to? B: Nobody.

3 **Nogen** has the genitive form **nogens**:

Er det nogens avis?	Is that anyone's newspaper?

(b) Noget

The neuter singular form **noget** corresponds to English 'some/something' with assertive meaning and to 'any/anything' with non-assertive meaning.

(i) Attributive use

1 **Noget** can precede a noun in the neuter singular form in the same way as 'some' (with assertive meaning) and 'any' (with non-assertive meaning) in English:

Der ligger noget papir på bordet.	Some paper is lying on the table.
Jeg har noget vrøvl med benene.	I have some trouble with my legs.
Han har ikke noget sted at være.	He hasn't got anywhere to stay.
Hvis du ikke giver mig noget vand ...	If you don't give me some water ...

Notice:

Sikke noget vrøvl!	What nonsense!

2 However, **noget** also combines with common gender non-count nouns to indicate 'a certain quantity of' (see 112(b)):

Der er ikke noget mad i huset.	There isn't any food in the house.
(Cf. **mad*en***, the food)	
Vi har brug for noget mere jord.	We need some more soil.
(Cf. **jord*en***, the soil)	
Du trænger til noget sol.	You could do with some sunshine.
(Cf. **sol*en***, the sun)	

3 **Noget** can precede an independent adjective, like 'something' or 'anything' in English. Notice that such an adjective has the neuter ending **-t**:

Vi fik noget godt at spise.	We had something nice to eat.
Er der noget sjovt i fjernsynet?	Is there anything funny on the telly?
Der sagde du noget klogt!	You said something wise there!

(ii) Nominal use

1 **Noget** is widely used independently, corresponding to English 'something' or 'anything':

Der er sket noget.	Something has happened.
Er der noget, jeg kan gøre?	Is there anything I can do?
Det er bare noget, man siger.	That's just something that one says.

2 **Ikke noget** is often used instead of **intet** (nothing):

Der er ikke noget i vejen.	There is nothing wrong.
A: **Hvad har du gjort?**	A: What have you done?
B: **Ikke noget!**	B: Nothing!

3 **Noget** appears in numerous idiomatic expressions of which the following are just a sample:

Det var noget værre noget!	Oh dear, that wasn't too good!
Der er noget, der hedder talent!	There is such a thing as talent!
Du siger noget!	That's true! / That's a good idea!
Han tror, han er noget.	He thinks he is somebody.
Han er noget af en hykler.	He's something of a hypocrite.
Hun er noget i en butik.	She's got some sort of job in a shop.
Hvad er nu det for noget?	What's that supposed to be?
noget for noget	*quid pro quo*
Vi morede os noget så godt.	We really enjoyed ourselves.

Note – **Noget** can also be used adverbially, corresponding to English 'rather', 'somewhat', etc.:

Du ser noget bleg ud!	You look rather pale!
Jeg blev noget overrasket.	I was somewhat surprised.

(c) Nogle

As indicated in (a) above, the use of the plural form **nogle** is decreasing and it has in practice disappeared from the spoken language. In the written language it is restricted to cases where it has clearly assertive meaning, corresponding to English 'some' or 'a few'. This is true in both attributive and nominal use:

(i) Attributive use

Jeg har stadig nogle problemer.	I still have some problems.
Nogle mennesker er født heldige.	Some people are born lucky.
Nogle dage senere kom han hjem.	A few days later he returned home.

(ii) Nominal use

1 If there is no specific referent, **nogle** on its own is used of people:

Nogle er store, andre er små.	Some are tall, others are short.
Nogle mener, at det er farligt.	Some think that it is dangerous.
Nogle af dem gik ud af skolen.	Some of them left school.

Der er ikke mange æbler på træet, men der er da nogle.
There aren't many apples on the tree, but there are some.

2 **Nogle** has the genitive form **nogles**, used mainly of people:

Efter nogles mening er det godt. In some people's opinion it is good.

Notice the expression:

Det er nogle underlige nogle. They are rather strange ones.

449 Vis (vist, visse)

Vis (common gender), **vist** (neuter) and **visse** (plural) are all used attributively and nominally. Functionally, the singular forms may be regarded as adjectives in the sense of '(a) certain', whereas the plural form **visse** is used in ways similar to other indefinite pronouns:

(a) Vis

Vis can combine with common gender singular nouns:

en vis person/hr. Smidt	a certain person/Mr Smith
efter en vis tid	after a certain time
i en vis forstand	in a certain sense
Det er til en vis grad rigtigt.	It's true to a certain extent.

Man bør holde en vis afstand.
One ought to keep a certain distance.

Han er oppe, før en vis mand får sko på.
He is up before a certain man [the devil] gets his shoes on (i.e. very early).

Note, however, that the definite form **visse** is not commonly used, except in idiomatic expressions like **den visse død**, certain death.

Vis on its own may alternate with **sikker** in the sense of '(quite) certain' or 'sure':

Er du vis på det?	Are you sure of that?
Sejren er os vis.	We are certain of victory.

(b) Vist

The neuter form **vist** can combine with neuter singular nouns:

Et vist antal personer mødte op.	A certain number of people turned up.
Jeg skal ud på et vist sted.	I'm off to a certain place (i.e. the WC).

Vist can also appear on its own:

Der er noget vist over hende.	There's a certain something about her.
Det er sikkert og vist.	It's absolutely certain.
Så meget er vist, vi tabte!	So much is certain, we lost!

For **vist** as a discourse particle, see 618.

(c) Visse

The plural form **visse** can combine with plural nouns. However, like singular **vis**, **visse** cannot be preceded by the front article and it has limited use as a nominal item. In these respects, it resembles indefinite pronouns such as **mange** (see 446(a)) and **nogle** (see 448(c)).

(i) Attributive use

i visse tilfælde	in certain cases
på visse betingelser	on certain conditions
på visse undtagelser nær	with certain exceptions

(ii) Nominal use

This use of **visse** is heavily constrained and only found about people as a now rather old-fashioned alternative to **nogle**:

Visse mener, at det bør gøres.	Some (people) think that it ought to be done.

Note 1 – The prepositional phrase **til visse** (certainly) is now obsolete:

Det er til visse en god bog.	It is certainly a good book.

Note 2 – The indefinite pronoun **somme** (etymologically identical with English 'some') only exists in the plural, but it is rarely used in modern Danish except in set expressions like **somme tider/sommetider**, sometimes. In other uses it has now been replaced by **nogle** or **visse**.

450 Constructions with **som helst** and **end**

In order to emphasize the meaning expressed by English 'at all' or '-ever', certain interrogative and indefinite pronouns can add the indeclinable phrase **som helst** or be followed by **end**.

(a) Som helst

(i) With nominal function only:

enhver som helst	anybody/anyone (at all, etc.)
hvem som helst	whoever, anybody/anyone (at all, etc.)
hvad som helst	whatever, anything (at all, etc.)
ingen som helst	none at all, not ... any at all
intet som helst	nothing at all, not ... anything at all
nogen som helst	anybody/anyone (at all, etc.)
noget som helst	anything (at all, etc.)

(ii) With attributive or nominal function:

hvilken som helst (common)	whatever, whichever
hvilket som helst (neuter)	whatever, whichever
hvilke som helst (plural)	whatever, whichever

(iii) With adverbial function:

hvor som helst	wherever, anywhere (at all, etc.)
(hvor)når som helst	whenever, at any time (at all, etc.)

(iv) When any of the expressions above (except for those involving **ingen/intet** and **nogen/noget**) is negated, the meaning is usually 'not just anyone/anything', etc:

Hun kysser ikke hvem som helst.	She doesn't kiss just anyone.
Jeg køber ikke hvad som helst.	I don't buy just anything.

(v) Instead of 'at all', English sometimes adds tag phrases such as 'you like', 'you want', etc. Similar tag phrases exist in Danish and may (dependent on style) either be added to **... som helst** or may replace **som helst**:

Du kan tage, hvad (som helst) du vil.	You may take whatever you like.
Vælg, hvilken (som helst) du ønsker.	Choose whichever one you want.

Note – **Ikke nogen/noget som helst** is often preferred to **ingen/intet som helst**. See 448.

(b) End

A similar meaning of '-ever' may be expressed when one of the pronouns mentioned above (except for **enhver, ingen/intet** and **nogen/noget**) introduces a concessive clause that includes **end**:

(i) Pronominal function

hvem du end er	whoever you are
hvad der end blev sagt	whatever was said
hvilken de end mener	whichever they mean

(ii) Adverbial function

hvor han end bor	wherever he lives
hvordan hun end gør det	however she does it
hvornår det end sker	whenever it happens

5 VERBS

A FORMS

501 The main forms of the verb and their endings

Most verbs have six forms: three *finite* forms (the *present tense*, the *past tense* and the *imperative*) and three *non-finite* forms (the *infinitive*, the *present participle* and the *past participle*). The *principal parts* of the verb, i.e. those from which the other forms are derived, are: the *infinitive*, the *past tense* and the *past participle*. These are also the forms which (sometimes together with the *present tense*) occur in most lists of verbs.

In addition, we should mention the *stem*, which is the part of the verb to which inflexional endings are added. Danish has both *consonant stems*, which make up the vast majority of verbs:

læs	read	conjugation II
sig	say	conjugation III

and *vowel stems*, which constitute a tiny minority of verbs:

tro	believe	conjugation I
stå	stand	conjugation IV

Note 1 – The vowel stems are all monosyllabic, except for compound verbs that are formed by adding a prefix to one of these verb stems, e.g. **betro**, entrust; **forstå**, understand. However, in some cases this is no longer obvious, e.g. **attrå**, desire; **formå**, manage, persuade. Vowel stems do not have a conjugation of their own; there are examples of both vowel stems and consonant stems in all four conjugations.

If we take the weak verb **vente**, wait (conjugation I), as our model, the paradigm looks as follows:

Infinitive	*Present*	*Past*	*Past participle*
vent*e*	**vent*er***	**vent*ede***	**vent*et***
Imperative	*Present participle*		
vent	**vent*ende***		

However, not all verbs follow this paradigm and hence they do not all have the same endings in the various forms. The main distinction is between weak and strong verbs, each of which can be further divided into subgroups, which in turn may have irregular members. Whether a verb is weak or strong is determined by its past tense form. Thus a *weak* verb is a verb that has a syllabic inflexional ending in the past tense, whereas a *strong* verb has a monosyllabic past tense form. Many strong verbs show vowel change (often referred to as 'Ablaut') between the infinitive and the past tense form (and sometimes the past participle), but this is not always the case.

Thus **tale** (talk) and **vente** (wait) are weak verbs because of their inflected past tense forms: **tal*te*** and **vent*ede***, whereas **drikke** (drink) and **finde** (find) are strong verbs, having monosyllabic past tense forms: **dr*a*k** and **f*a*ndt**, which also show vowel change (**i** - **a**).

Note 2 – There is often confusion between the terms 'strong' and 'irregular' verbs. Some grammars treat all verbs that do not follow a regular weak pattern as 'irregular'. In the present book, the term 'irregular' is only applied to those verbs, whether weak or strong, that deviate from the regular weak or strong patterns.

502 The six verbal forms and their inflexional endings

The regular inflexional endings of each of the six verbal forms mentioned in 501 are as follows:

(a) The infinitive

The infinitive marker in Danish is **at** (to).

(i) *Vowel stems* (see 501) are unchanged in the infinitive form, e.g. **at bo**, to live, stay; **at dø**, to die; **at få**, to get; **at glo**, to stare; **at gå**, to go, walk; **at le**, to laugh; **at se**, to see, look; **at slå**, to beat, hit; **at stå**, to stand; **at sy**, to sew; etc.

(ii) *Consonant stems* add an **-e** to form the infinitive, e.g. **at hent*e***, to fetch; **at lad*e***, to let; etc.

No verb stem ends in a double consonant, but monosyllabic consonant stems with a short stressed vowel double any single final consonant in the infinitive before the **-e** ending (the double consonant is preserved in the present tense and – in conjugation I – in the past tense and the past participle), e.g. **at glem*me***, to forget; **at hop*pe***, to hop, jump; etc.

But if the stem has a long vowel or two different consonants after the vowel, consonant doubling is not possible, e.g. **at led*e***, to search; **at vend*e***, to turn; etc.

For the use of the infinitive see 528.

(b) The present tense

Nearly all verbs add an **-r** to the infinitive to form the present tense. Danish has no person or number distinction in the present tense.

(i) The vowel stems thus add **-r** directly to the stem vowel (see (a)(i) above), e.g. **bo*r*, se*r*, slå*r***. However, those in **-i, -u** and **-y** can add **-(e)r**, e.g. **det du*(e)r* ikke**, it's no good; **jeg fri*(e)r***, I propose (to someone); **jeg si*(e)r***, I strain/filter; **jeg sy*(e)r***, I sew; etc.

(ii) The consonant stems add **-r** to the infinitive ending **-e**, e.g. **jeg finde*r***, I find; **jeg glemme*r***, I forget; **jeg synge*r***, I sing; etc.

(iii) Exceptions:

1 The central modal verbs have irregular present tense forms not ending in **-r**. Thus: **at kunne** but **jeg kan**, I can; **at måtte** but **jeg må**, I may/must; **at skulle** but **jeg skal**, I must/have to; **at ville** but **jeg vil**, I will/want (to). See 532.

But a few verbs that are usually included under the modals do have an **-r** ending: **jeg bør**, I ought to; **jeg tør**, I dare. Notice that, unlike the other modals, both have an **-r-** in the infinitive: **at burde/turde**.

2 A few verbs have a non-systematic **-r** ending:

Infinitive	*Present tense*	*Meaning*
gøre	**gør**	do(es)
have	**har**	have/has
være	**er**	am/are/is

3 Notice the completely irregular present tense form of **vide**:

vide	**ved**	know(s)

Note 1 – Contracted present tense forms in informal written Danish such as **be'r/ber** (for **beder**), request; **gi'r/gir** (for **giver**), give; **si'r/sir** (for **siger**), say; **ta'r/tar** (for **tager**), take; etc., are ignored here, as these can always be expanded to the full form, but they are becoming increasingly common.

Note 2 – Until 1900, written Danish officially observed number distinction in the present tense, with plural forms having the ending **-e**, as in: **jeg griber**, I catch; **vi gribe**, we catch. This has now long been obsolete.

For the use of the present tense see 515f.

(c) The past tense

Danish has no person or number distinction in the past tense. As mentioned in 501, the past tense form is the determining factor in distinguishing between weak and strong verbs.

(i) There are three main groups of weak verbs: those ending in **-ede** (conjugation I), those ending in **-te** (conjugation II) and those ending in **-de** (conjugation III) (for vowel change in weak verbs see 504(e)–(f) and 505):

Infinitive	*Past tense*		*Meaning*
svare	**svar*ede***	(conj. I)	answered
sende	**send*te***	(conj. II)	sent
have	**hav*de***	(conj. III)	had

(ii) Strong verbs (conjugation IV) have a monosyllabic past tense form either with no inflexional ending or with the ending **-t** (after consonant + **d**), and often with vowel change:

sidde	**s*a*d**	(conj. IV)	sat
vinde	**v*a*nd*t***	(conj. IV)	won

Note – Older Danish showed number distinction in the past tense of strong verbs, with plural forms having the ending **-e**, as in: **jeg greb**, I caught; **vi grebe**, we caught. But as with the present tense (see (b) Note 2 above), such plural forms have long been obsolete.

(iii) The past tense of modal verbs is identical with the infinitive, see 532. For the use of the past tense see 517f.

(d) The past participle

The past participle ending is **-(e)t**, but the four conjugations implement this in different ways. Notice that monosyllabic consonant stems with a short stressed vowel double a single final consonant before the **-et** ending (e.g. **drukket**, drunk):

(i) Weak verbs with the past tense ending **-ede** (conjugation I) have the past participle ending **-et**:

Infinitive	*Past tense*	*Past participle*	*Meaning*
love	**lovede**	**lov*et***	promised
svare	**svarede**	**svar*et***	answered

(ii) Weak verbs with the past tense ending **-te** (conjugation II) have the past participle ending **-t** (with no **-e-** before it):

høre	**hørte**	**hør*t***	heard
sende	**sendte**	**send*t***	sent

(iii) Weak verbs with the past tense ending **-de** (conjugation III) have the past participle ending **-t**:

gøre	**gjorde**	**gjor*t***	done
sige	**sagde**	**sag*t***	said

(iv) Most strong verbs end in **-et** in the past participle:

drikke	**drak**	**drukk*et***	drunk
finde	**fandt**	**fund*et***	found

But the majority of those whose stem ends in **-d**, without a preceding consonant, only add **-t**:

bide	**bed**	**bid*t***	bitten
snyde	**snød**	**snyd*t***	cheated

(v) Modal verbs end in **-et**:

kunne	**kunne**	**kunn*et***	been able to
ville	**ville**	**vill*et***	have wanted to

For more on the form and for the use of the past participle see 530.

(e) The imperative

The imperative is usually identical with the stem (and, in the case of vowel stems, with the infinitive):

Infinitive	*Stem*	*Imperative*	*Meaning*
køre	**kør**	**kør!**	drive!
læse	**læs**	**læs!**	read!
gå	**gå**	**gå!**	go!
se	**se**	**se!**	look!

For semantic reasons, not all verbs have an imperative form.

For more on the form and for the use of the imperative see 533.

(f) The present participle

The present participle is formed by adding **-ende** to the stem. Notice that a single final consonant is doubled after a short stressed vowel:

Stem	*Present participle*	*Meaning*
gå	**gå*ende***	going, walking
se	**se*ende***	seeing, looking

hop	**hop/p/*ende***	jumping
læs	**læs*ende***	reading

For semantic reasons, not all verbs have a present participle form.

For more on the form and for the use of the present participle see 529.

(g) A generalized pattern of inflexional endings of Danish verbs

Based on the forms shown in (a)–(f) above, the following generalized pattern of Danish verb endings can be established (v.st. = vowel stems; c.st. = consonant stems). Note that all endings are related to the stem of the verb:

Infinitive	*Present*	*Past*	*Past participle*	*Imperative*	*Present participle*
-zero (v.st.) **-e** (c.st.)	**-r** (v.st.) **-er** (c.st.) **(er/har/ gør/ved)** (modals)	**-ede** (I) **-te** (II) **-de** (III) **-zero,-t** (IV)	**-et** (I) **-t** (II) **-t** (III) **-(e)t** (IV)	**-zero**	**-ende**

Other forms dealt with in subsequent paragraphs are: the subjunctive (see 534) and the **-s** forms (see 538–42). The following paragraphs deal with each of the four conjugations.

503 First conjugation

Main paradigm:

Infinitive	*Present*	*Past*	*Past participle*	*Present participle*	*Meaning*
bo/	**bo/*r***	**bo/*ede***	**bo/*et***	**bo/*ende***	live, stay
vent/*e*	**vent/*er***	**vent/*ede***	**vent/*et***	**vent/*ende***	wait

(a) In vowel stems (like **bo**), the infinitive = the stem; consonant stems (like **vent**) add an **-e**. To the stem are added the endings **-er** (present), **-ede** (past), **-et** (past participle) and **-ende** (present participle).

(b) Verbs of the first conjugation never have vowel change.

(c) Approximately 85% of all weak verbs in Danish belong to the first conjugation, and this is the only conjugation that is still productive. This means that all new verbs that come into the language (e.g. foreign loans or those arising from new discoveries or technological inventions) conform to this paradigm. Thus: **faxe**, fax; **screene**, screen; **telefonere**, phone; etc.

(d) All verbs whose infinitives end in **-ere** (with the stress on the penultimate syllable) belong to this conjugation. They include nearly all verbs of foreign origin: **ekspandere**, expand; **ignorere**, ignore; **involvere**, involve; etc.

(e) Vowel stems belonging to the first conjugation constitute a small, non-productive group. The following stem vowels are involved:

-e: **sne**, snow; **te (sig)**, behave
-i: **fri**, free, propose (to); **si**, strain, filter
-o: **bo**, live, stay; **glo**, stare; **gro**, grow; **ro**, row (a boat); **sno**, twist; **tro**, believe
-u: **du**, be of use, be any good
-y: **fly**, flee; **forny**, renew; **gry**, dawn; **sky**, shun; **spy**, spew; **sy**, sew
-ø: **klø**, scratch; **strø**, scatter
-å: **attrå**, desire; **flå**, flay, fleece; **formå**, manage, persuade; **nå**, manage (in time), reach; **spå**, predict; **så**, sow

(f) Examples of frequently used verbs of the first conjugation:

arbejde, work; **betragte**, look at, consider; **bygge**, build; **danse**, dance; **elske**, love; **forklare**, explain; **hade**, hate; **handle**, act, shop; **hente**, fetch; **hoppe**, hop, jump; **koste**, cost; **lave**, do, make; **love**, promise; **lukke**, close, shut; **regne**, calculate, rain; **rette**, correct; **spille**, play; **stille**, place; **svare**, answer; **svømme**, swim; **vente**, wait; **virke**, work (of things); **øge**, increase; **åbne**, open

(g) Some verbs vacillate between the first and the second conjugation:

Infinitive		*Past*	*Past participle*	*Meaning*
gabe	(I)	**gabede**	**gabet**	yawn
	(II)	**gabte**	**gabt**	
hejse	(I)	**hejsede**	**hejst**	hoist
	(II)	**hejste**		
lede	(I)	**ledede**	**ledet**	lead (firm, etc.)
	(II)	**ledte**	**ledt**	lead or seek
låse	(I)	**låsede**	**låst**	lock
	(II)	**låste**		

Infinitive		*Past*	*Past participle*	*Meaning*
male	(I)	**malede**	**malet**	paint
	(II)	**malte**		paint (artistically)
nævne	(I)	**nævnede**	**nævnt**	mention
	(II)	**nævnte**		
skabe	(I)	**skabede**	**skabt**	act unnaturally
	(II)	**skabte**		create
smile	(I)	**smilede**	**smilet**	smile
	(II)	**smilte**		
suse	(I)	**susede**	**suset**	rush, whistle
	(II)	**suste**		
vække	(I)	**vækkede**	**vækket**	awake (trans.)
	(II)	**vakte**	**vakt**	arouse

Notice also the difference between **syne**, inspect (conj. I), and the deponent verb **synes** (past **syntes**, past part. **syntes**), think.

(h) A few verbs vacillate between the first and the fourth conjugation:

Infinitive		*Past*	*Past participle*	*Meaning*
briste	(I)	**bristede**	**bristet**	break, burst
	(IV)	**brast**		
fare	(I)	**farede**	**faret**	hurry
	(IV)	**for**		
jage	(I)	**jagede**	**jaget**	hunt, chase
	(IV)	**jog**		hurry, stick
klinge	(I)	**klingede**	**klinget**	ring, sound
	(IV)	**klang**		
lade	(I)	**ladede**	**ladet**	load
	(IV)	**lod**	**ladet/ladt**	let
skryde	(I)	**skrydede**	**skrydet**	brag, bray
	(IV)	**skrød**		
skælve	(I)	**skælvede**	**skælvet**	tremble
	(IV)	**skjalv**		
smyge	(I)	**smygede**	**smyget**	slide, slip
	(IV)	**smøg**	**smøget**	
sprække	(I)	**sprækkede**	**sprækket**	crack
	(IV)	**sprak**	**sprukket**	

Infinitive		*Past*	*Past participle*	*Meaning*
svinge	(I)	**svingede**	**svinget**	swing
	(IV)	**svang**	**svunget**	
sværge	(I)	**sværgede**	**sværget**	swear
	(IV)	**svor**	**svoret**	
tie	(I)	**tiede**	**tiet**	be silent
	(IV)	**tav**		

(i) Although compound verbs usually belong to the same conjugation as the uncompounded verb, there are a few exceptions, e.g.:

Infinitive	*Past*	*Past participle*		*Meaning*
stille	**stillede**	**stillet**	(conj. I)	place
bestille	**bestilte**	**bestilt**	(conj. II)	do, order
tyde	**tydede**	**tydet**	(conj. I)	interpret
betyde	**betød**	**betydet**	(conj. IV)	mean

504 Second conjugation

Main paradigm:

Infinitive	*Present*	*Past*	*Past participle*	*Present participle*	*Meaning*
tal/*e*	**tal/*er***	**tal/*te***	**tal/*t***	**tal/*ende***	talk

(a) To the stem are added the endings **-er** (present), **-te** (past), **-t** (past participle) and **-ende** (present participle).

(b) Only one genuine vowel stem follows this conjugation: **ske**, happen (present tense: **sker**).

(c) 10–15% of all weak verbs in Danish belong to this conjugation.

(d) There are certain formal characteristics of the verbs of the second conjugation. As a rough guide, we may set up the following subgroups:

(i) Many verbs with a long stem vowel (or diphthong) followed by **-b**, **-d**, **-g**, **-l**, **-n**, **-r** or **-s**. The long stem vowel is usually shortened in the past tense and the past participle:

-b: **købe**, buy; **råbe**, shout; **skabe**, create; **tabe**, drop, lose
-d: **bløde**, bleed; **føde**, give birth; **møde**, meet; **støde**, push
-g: **bruge**, use; **smage**, taste; **stege**, fry; **søge**, look for, seek
-l: **dele**, share; **føle**, feel; **kvæle**, strangle; **tale**, talk
-n: **låne**, borrow, lend; **mene**, mean; **pine**, torture; **tjene**, earn, serve
-r: **føre**, lead; **høre**, hear; **køre**, drive; **lære**, learn, teach
-s: **blæse**, blow; **læse**, read; **rejse**, travel; **spise**, eat; **vise**, show

(ii) Some verbs with a short stem vowel followed by **-ld**, **-l(l)**, **-m(m)**, **-nd**, **-ng** (all pronounced as a single consonant):

-ld: **hælde**, pour; **kalde**, call, name; **fylde**, fill; **volde**, cause
-l(l): **bestille**, do, order; **skille**, separate
-m(m): **drømme**, dream; **gemme**, hide; **glemme**, forget
-nd: **begynde**, begin; **brænde**, burn; **kende**, know; **sende**, send; **vende**, turn
-ng: **hænge**, hang; **slænge**, fling; **trænge**, need, push

(iii) A few verbs with a short stem vowel followed by **-ls** or **-nk**:

-ls: **frelse**, save; **hilse**, greet
-nk: **tænke**, think

(e) A number of verbs belonging to the second conjugation have vowel change (mostly **æ** ⇨ **a** or **ø** ⇨ **u**). Notice the dropping of **-n-** in **bragte/bragt** and the addition of **-s-** in **vidste/vidst**:

Infinitive	*Present*	*Past*	*Past participle*	*Meaning*
bringe	**bringer**	**bragte**	**bragt**	bring
dølge	**dølger**	**dulgte**	**dulgt**	hide
følge	**følger**	**fulgte**	**fulgt**	follow
kvæle	**kvæler**	**kvalte**	**kvalt**	strangle
række	**rækker**	**rakte**	**rakt**	reach, pass

Infinitive	*Present*	*Past*	*Past participle*	*Meaning*
smøre	**smører**	**smurte**	**smurt**	smear, butter
spørge	**spørger**	**spurgte**	**spurgt**	ask
strække	**strækker**	**strakte**	**strakt**	stretch
sælge	**sælger**	**solgte**	**solgt**	sell
sætte	**sætter**	**satte**	**sat**	set, place
træde	**træder**	**trådte**	**trådt**	tread
tælle	**tæller**	**talte**	**talt**	count
vide	**ved**	**vidste**	**vidst**	know
vælge	**vælger**	**valgte**	**valgt**	choose, elect

(f) A few verbs vacillate between the second and the fourth conjugation:

Infinitive	*Past*	*Past participle*	*Meaning*
fnyse	**fnyste** **fnøs**	**fnyst**	snort
gyse	**gyste** **gøs**	**gyst**	shudder
hænge	**hængte** (trans. or intrans.) **hang** (intrans.)	**hængt**	hang
nyse	**nyste** **nøs**	**nyst**	sneeze

For verbs vacillating between the first and the second conjugation see 503(g).

505 Third conjugation

(a) The third conjugation, as set out here, is not always acknowledged as a separate conjugation. However, a very small group of high frequency verbs form the past tense by means of the inflexional ending **-de**, which must be distinguished from both the **-ede** ending of conjugation I and the **-te** ending of conjugation II. The past participle ending is **-t** (except in **død**, died, but this form functions more as an adjective than as a verb), and most of the verbs have vowel change.

(b) This is the most irregular of the four conjugations, so we shall simply list the main forms of the verbs involved. The modals **burde** and **turde** have been included here:

Infinitive	*Present*	*Past*	*Past participle*	*Meaning*
burde	**bør**	**burde**	**burdet**	ought (to)
dø	**dør**	**døde**	**død**	die
gøre	**gør**	**gjorde**	**gjort**	do
have	**har**	**havde**	**haft**	have
lægge	**lægger**	**lagde**	**lagt**	place (horizontally)
sige	**siger**	**sagde**	**sagt**	say
turde	**tør**	**turde**	**turdet**	dare

Note – Until the spelling reform of 1948, the modals **kunne, skulle** and **ville** had the past tense forms **kunde, skulde** and **vilde,** respectively. These forms conformed to the third conjugation in the same way as **burde** and **turde.**

506 Fourth conjugation: introduction

(a) All strong verbs belong to the fourth conjugation. Our definition of a strong verb is a verb that has a monosyllabic past tense form, except for compound verbs. The past tense will either have a zero ending or a **-t** ending. The past participle of most strong verbs ends in **-et**, but usually in **-t** after **-id**, **-ud** and **-yd**. The group of strong verbs numbers some 120 in all.

(b) Most strong verbs have vowel change, and although this is not their defining characteristic (some verbs of conjugation II and III also have vowel change), we shall first divide the strong verbs into groups with the same stem vowel, and then subdivide these according to *vowel gradation series*, i.e. verbs that have the same vowels in the same principal parts. In the following paragraphs, each gradation series will show the three principal vowels (in alphabetical order), i.e. the vowels of the infinitive/present tense, of the past tense and of the past participle.

Alternative forms belonging to other conjugations will appear in brackets, but see also 503(h) and 504(f).

507 Fourth conjugation: verbs with the stem vowel **-a-**

There is only one gradation series for strong verbs that have -a- as their stem vowel.

Gradation series: **a-o-a**

Infinitive	*Present*	*Past*	*Past participle*	*Meaning*
drage	**drager**	**drog**	**draget**	draw, go
fare	**farer**	**for** (**farede**)	**faret**	hurry
jage	**jager**	**jog** (**jagede**)	**jaget**	hurry, stick hunt, chase
lade	**lader**	**lod** (**ladede**)	**ladet/ladt** (**ladet**)	let load
tage	**tager**	**tog**	**taget**	take

508 Fourth conjugation: verbs with the stem vowel **-e-**

Although there are three gradation series with the stem vowel **-e-**, each of them has only one member. Notice that two of the three verbs are vowel stems, and that **bede** rhymes with **le** and **se** in many people's pronunciation:

(a) Gradation series: **e-a-e**

Infinitive	*Present*	*Past*	*Past participle*	*Meaning*
bede	**beder**	**bad**	**bedt**	ask, pray

(b) Gradation series: **e-o-e**

Infinitive	*Present*	*Past*	*Past participle*	*Meaning*
le	**ler**	**lo**	**le(e)t**	laugh

(c) Gradation series: **e-å-e**

Infinitive	*Present*	*Past*	*Past participle*	*Meaning*
se	**ser**	**så**	**set**	see, look

509 Fourth conjugation: verbs with the stem vowel -i-

Strong verbs with the stem vowel **-i-** make up the largest group. They comprise five gradation series:

(a) Gradation series: **i-a-i**

Infinitive	*Present*	*Past*	*Past participle*	*Meaning*
briste	**brister**	**brast** (**bristede**)	**bristet**	break, burst
gide	**gider**	**gad**	**gidet**	feel like
give	**giver**	**gav**	**givet**	give
klinge	**klinger**	**klang** (**klingede**)	**klinget**	ring, sound
sidde	**sidder**	**sad**	**siddet**	sit
stinke	**stinker**	**stank**	**stinket**	stink
tie	**tier**	**tav** (**tiede**)	**tiet**	be silent

(b) Gradation series: **i-a-u**

Infinitive	*Present*	*Past*	*Past participle*	*Meaning*
binde	**binder**	**bandt**	**bundet**	bind, tie
drikke	**drikker**	**drak**	**drukket**	drink
finde	**finder**	**fandt**	**fundet**	find
rinde	**rinder**	**randt**	**rundet**	pass, roll by
slippe	**slipper**	**slap**	**sluppet**	give up, let go
spinde	**spinder**	**spandt**	**spundet**	spin, weave
springe	**springer**	**sprang**	**sprunget**	jump, spring
stikke	**stikker**	**stak**	**stukket**	prick, stick
svinde	**svinder**	**svandt**	**svundet**	decrease
svinge	**svinger**	**svang** (**svingede**)	**svunget** (**svinget**)	swing
tvinde	**tvinder**	**tvandt**	**tvundet**	twine, twist
tvinge	**tvinger**	**tvang**	**tvunget**	force
vinde	**vinder**	**vandt**	**vundet**	win

(c) Gradation series: **i-e-e**

Infinitive	*Present*	*Past*	*Past participle*	*Meaning*
blive	**bliver**	**blev**	**blevet**	be, become
drive	**driver**	**drev**	**drevet**	drive, idle
glide	**glider**	**gled**	**gledet**	glide, slide
gnide	**gnider**	**gned**	**gnedet**	rub
gribe	**griber**	**greb**	**grebet**	catch, seize
hive	**hiver**	**hev**	**hevet**	heave, pull
knibe	**kniber**	**kneb**	**knebet**	pinch
pibe	**piber**	**peb**	**pebet**	squeak
ride	**rider**	**red**	**redet**	ride
rive	**river**	**rev**	**revet**	scratch
skride	**skrider**	**skred**	**skredet**	slip, walk off
skrige	**skriger**	**skreg**	**skreget**	cry, shout
skrive	**skriver**	**skrev**	**skrevet**	write
slibe	**sliber**	**sleb**	**slebet**	grind
snige	**sniger**	**sneg**	**sneget**	sneak
stige	**stiger**	**steg**	**steget**	rise
svide	**svider**	**sved**	**svedet**	burn, singe
svige	**sviger**	**sveg**	**sveget**	betray
vige	**viger**	**veg**	**veget**	retreat
vride	**vrider**	**vred**	**vredet**	wring

(d) Gradation series: **i-e-i**

Infinitive	*Present*	*Past*	*Past participle*	*Meaning*
bide	**bider**	**bed**	**bidt**	bite
lide	**lider**	**led**	**lidt**	suffer
skide	**skider**	**sked**	**skidt**	shit
slide	**slider**	**sled**	**slidt**	tear, toil, wear
smide	**smider**	**smed**	**smidt**	throw
stride	**strider**	**stred**	**stridt**	struggle

(e) Gradation series: **i-å-i**

This gradation series has only one member. Notice that the stem consonant **-g-** is dropped in the past tense:

Infinitive	*Present*	*Past*	*Past participle*	*Meaning*
ligge	**ligger**	**lå**	**ligget**	lie (of position)

510 Fourth conjugation: verbs with the stem vowel **-y-**

Strong verbs with the stem vowel **-y-** make up the second largest group. They comprise five gradation series, four of which change the vowel to **-ø-** in the past tense:

(a) Gradation series: **y-a-u**

This gradation series has only two members:

Infinitive	*Present*	*Past*	*Past participle*	*Meaning*
synge	**synger**	**sang**	**sunget**	sing
synke	**synker**	**sank**	**sunket**	sink

(b) Gradation series: **y-ø-o**

This gradation series has only one member:

Infinitive	*Present*	*Past*	*Past participle*	*Meaning*
fryse	**fryser**	**frøs**	**frosset**	feel cold, freeze

(c) Gradation series: **y-ø-u**

Infinitive	*Present*	*Past*	*Past participle*	*Meaning*
bryde	**bryder**	**brød**	**brudt**	break
byde	**byder**	**bød**	**budt**	bid, offer
fortryde	**fortryder**	**fortrød**	**fortrudt**	regret
skyde	**skyder**	**skød**	**skudt**	shoot

(d) Gradation series: **y-ø-y**

Infinitive	*Present*	*Past*	*Past participle*	*Meaning*
betyde	**betyder**	**betød**	**betydet**	mean
flyde	**flyder**	**flød**	**flydt**	flow
gyde	**gyder**	**gød**	**gydt**	pour, spawn
gyse	**gyser**	**gøs (gyste)**	**gyst**	shiver
lyde	**lyder**	**lød**	**lydt**	sound
nyde	**nyder**	**nød**	**nydt**	enjoy
nyse	**nyser**	**nøs (nyste)**	**nyst**	sneeze
skryde	**skryder**	**skrød (skrydede)**	**skrydet**	brag, bray
snyde	**snyder**	**snød**	**snydt**	cheat

(e) Gradation series: **y-ø-ø**. Notice the change of consonant in **fløj/fløjet** and **løj/løjet**.

Infinitive	*Present*	*Past*	*Past participle*	*Meaning*
flyve	**flyver**	**fløj**	**fløjet**	fly
fyge	**fyger**	**føg**	**føget**	drift, sweep
krybe	**kryber**	**krøb**	**krøbet**	crawl, creep
lyve	**lyver**	**løj**	**løjet**	lie (i.e. deceive)
ryge	**ryger**	**røg**	**røget**	smoke
smyge	**smyger**	**smøg (smygede)**	**smøget (smyget)**	slide, slip
stryge	**stryger**	**strøg**	**strøget**	cancel, iron, stroke

511 Fourth conjugation: verbs with the stem vowel **-æ-**

Strong verbs with the stem vowel **-æ-** comprise six gradation series, but each series has very few members:

(a) Gradation series: **æ-a-a**

This gradation series has only one member, which has an alternative past participle form:

Infinitive	*Present*	*Past*	*Past participle*	*Meaning*
gælde	**gælder**	**gjaldt**	**gjaldt** **(gældt)**	apply, be valid

(b) Gradation series: **æ-a-u**

Infinitive	*Present*	*Past*	*Past participle*	*Meaning*
hjælpe	**hjælper**	**hjalp**	**hjulpet**	help
sprække	**sprækker**	**sprak** **(sprækkede)**	**sprukket** **(sprækket)**	crack
træffe	**træffer**	**traf**	**truffet**	meet, hit
trække	**trækker**	**trak**	**trukket**	draw, pull

(c) Gradation series: **æ-a-æ**

This gradation series has three members. **Hænge** has two past tense forms, of which the strong form is used intransitively (e.g. **frakken hang på knagen**, the coat hung on the peg), while the weak form is used both transitively and intransitively (e.g. **han hængte frakken på knagen**, he hung the coat on the peg; **frakken hængte på knagen**, the coat hung on the peg). **Kvæde** is now rather old-fashioned and really only occurs (jokingly) in the combination: **kvæde en vise**, chant/sing a ballad/ditty. **Være** has an irregular present tense form:

Infinitive	*Present*	*Past*	*Past participle*	*Meaning*
hænge	**hænger**	**hang** **(hængte)**	**hængt**	hang
kvæde	**kvæder**	**kvad**	**kvædet**	chant, sing
være	**er**	**var**	**været**	be, exist

(d) Gradation series: **æ-a-å**

Infinitive	*Present*	*Past*	*Past participle*	*Meaning*
bære	**bærer**	**bar**	**båret**	bear, carry
skære	**skærer**	**skar**	**skåret**	cut, slice
stjæle	**stjæler**	**stjal**	**stjålet**	steal

(e) Gradation series: **æ-o-æ**

This gradation series has only one member, which has alternative past tense and past participle forms. The weak forms are always used in the phrase: **sværge til (noget)**, swear by (something), i.e. strongly prefer:

Infinitive	*Present*	*Past*	*Past participle*	*Meaning*
sværge	**sværger**	**svor** **(sværgede)**	**svoret** **(sværget)**	swear

(f) Gradation series: **æ-å-æ**

This gradation series has only one member:

Infinitive	*Present*	*Past*	*Past participle*	*Meaning*
æde	**æder**	**åd**	**ædt**	eat, gobble

512 Fourth conjugation: verbs with the stem vowel -å-

Strong verbs with the stem vowel **-å-** comprise two gradation series, each with two members. All four verbs are vowel stems:

(a) Gradation series: **å-i-å**

Infinitive	*Present*	*Past*	*Past participle*	*Meaning*
gå	**går**	**gik**	**gået**	go, walk
få	**får**	**fik**	**fået**	get

(b) Gradation series: **å-o-å**

Infinitive	*Present*	*Past*	*Past participle*	*Meaning*
slå	**slår**	**slog**	**slået**	beat, hit
stå	**står**	**stod**	**stået**	stand

513 Fourth conjugation: verbs with the same stem vowel in all forms

Seven strong verbs have the same stem vowel in all their forms. However, they clearly belong to the fourth conjugation since they have a monosyllabic past tense form. There are five different stem vowels. Two of the verbs add **-t** in the past tense:

Infinitive	*Present*	*Past*	*Past participle*	*Meaning*
(a) Stem vowel **-a-**				
falde	**falder**	**faldt**	**faldet**	fall
(b) Stem vowel **-e-**				
hedde	**hedder**	**hed**	**heddet**	be called
(c) Stem vowel **-o-**				
holde	**holder**	**holdt**	**holdt**	hold
komme	**kommer**	**kom**	**kommet**	come
sove	**sover**	**sov**	**sovet**	sleep
(d) Stem vowel **-æ-**				
græde	**græder**	**græd**	**grædt**	cry, weep
(e) Stem vowel **-ø-**				
løbe	**løber**	**løb**	**løbet**	run

B THE USE OF THE TENSES

514 Definition of tense

By tense is meant the grammatical realization of time references through verbal forms. This may be done morphologically by means of inflexional endings, in which case we talk about a *synthetic* realization; or it may be done periphrastically by means of a sequence consisting of one or more auxiliaries + a main verb, in which case we talk about an *analytic* realization. The main function of tense is to locate a state of affairs, an action or an event in time, relative to some other temporal reference point.

The question of how many tenses there are in Danish (or in English) is largely a matter of definition. In view of our definition above, we shall operate with eight tenses: present (515f), past (517f), perfect (519f), past perfect (521), future (522), future perfect (523), future of the past (524), and future perfect of the past (525). Of these, the present and the past tense are realized synthetically by means of inflexional endings and/or vowel change, i.e. they consist of a finite verb form only, and are therefore known as 'simple tenses'. The other six are realized analytically by means of auxiliaries plus a main verb, i.e. they consist of a finite verb form plus one or more non-finite forms, and are known as 'composite tenses'. In the following paragraphs we shall examine the use of each of these tenses.

515 The present tense

For form see 502(b).

In most cases the present tense in Danish is used in much the same way as in English, but there are also differences.

The present tense has five main uses:

(a) Instantaneous present, with the emphasis on what is happening here and now:

Hvad laver Paul?	What is Paul doing?
Han sidder og ser fjernsyn.	He's (sitting) watching TV.

(b) State present, with the emphasis on the general and timeless:

Solen står op i øst.	The sun rises in the east.
Odense ligger på Fyn.	Odense is on the island of Funen.

(c) Habitual present, with the emphasis on regular repetition over a period of time. This meaning may be emphasized by use of **plejer at** + infinitive (cf. 517(c)):

Skolen begynder kl. 8.	School starts at 8 o'clock.
Vi rejser til Italien hvert år.	We go to Italy every year.

De plejer at gå ud om søndagen. They usually go out on Sundays.

(d) Future action, especially with **være**, **blive**, verbs of motion and expressions of future time:

På tirsdag er det min fødselsdag. It's my birthday on Tuesday.
I morgen bliver det regnvejr. There will be rain tomorrow.
Næste år rejser jeg til USA. Next year I'll go to the USA.

(e) The historic (dramatic) present is used:

(i) To create a dramatic illusion of 'now' in a narrative about the past. This is often seen in newspaper headings, reports of sports events, and historical accounts:

Tusinder demonstrerer for fred.
Thousands demonstrate for peace.

Efter en times spil løber Laudrup igennem og scorer.
After an hour's play Laudrup runs through and scores.

I 1807 angriber englænderne igen København.
In 1807 the British attack Copenhagen again.

(ii) To summarize or discuss the content of a book, film, etc.:

I *Den afrikanske Farm* beskriver Karen Blixen sit ophold i Kenya.
In *The African Farm* Karen Blixen describes her stay in Kenya.

516 The present tense in Danish – different realizations in English

(a) Although the use of the present tense is often similar in Danish and English, there are certain differences:

(i) Present tense in Danish – past tense in English

This is found in some passive constructions when an action is completed in the past, but the (tangible) result of the action remains:

Stykket er skrevet i 1723. The play was written in 1723.
Slottet er opført omkring 1450. The castle was built around 1450.

A typical example of this difference is the use of tense in connection with the passive form **være født** (be born), when used of people still alive:

Hvornår er du født?	When were you born?
Jeg er født i juni 1970.	I was born in June 1970.

But when referring to persons now dead, the past tense is normally used, as in English:

Kierkegaard blev født i 1813.	Kierkegaard was born in 1813.

(ii) Present tense in Danish – perfect tense in English

Det er første gang, jeg er her.	It's the first time I have been here.

(b) The English progressive forms (typically expressing a non-completed action of limited duration which is in progress at a given time) have no direct parallel in Danish, but there are other ways of expressing a similar notion:

(i) Simple present tense:

Hvad laver du?	What are you doing?
Jeg skriver et brev.	I'm writing a letter.

(ii) Two verbs in the present tense linked by **og** (and), the first being a verb of location/position (**ligge**, lie; **sidde**, sit; **stå**, stand; etc.), the second usually a verb of action:

Han ligger og hører musik.	He is (lying) listening to music.
Hun sidder og læser.	She is (sitting) reading.
De står og snakker.	They are (standing) chatting.

(iii) Such verbal constructions as **være ved at/være i færd med at** + infinitive:

De er ved at spise.	They are having their meal.
Han er i færd med at male.	He is painting.

Note, however, that **være ved at** + infinitive can also mean 'be about to/on the point of':

Jeg er ved at være færdig.	I'm about to finish.
Jeg er ved at dø af kulde.	I'm freezing to death.

517 The past tense

For forms see 502(c),(g), 506–13.

The past tense in Danish is used to express an action completed in the past. Use of the past tense is largely as in English.

(a) Reference to the past can be signalled by past tense alone:

Han standsede.	He stopped.
Vi løb hjem.	We ran home.

(b) In addition to the tense used, past time may be further underlined by other time markers, such as conjunctions (e.g. **da** (temporal), when) or temporal adverbs/adverbials (e.g. **dengang**, then; **i går/aftes/sidste uge** etc., yesterday/last night/last week etc.):

Da jeg vågnede, skinnede solen.	When I woke up, the sun was shining.
Alt så lysere ud dengang.	Everything looked brighter then.
I aftes kom vi sent hjem.	Last night we came home late.

(c) The past tense may express the habitual past. This interpretation depends either on the ability of the verb to be associated with a repeated action in the past or on other contextual pointers (e.g. **når**, when(ever); **hver gang**, every time; etc.

Han røg pibe tidligere.	He used to smoke a pipe.
Eva skreg, når hun så lægen.	Eva yelled whenever she saw the doctor.
Jeg tabte hver gang.	I lost every time.

In Danish, the habitual nature of an action may be emphasized by use of the verb form **plejede at** + infinitive (cf. 515(c)). The equivalent English verbs are 'used to/would':

Vi plejede at gå lange ture.	We used to go for long walks.
Mor plejede at synge for os.	Mother would sing to us.

(d) The past tense of modal verbs gives a present-time question or a request a higher degree of caution and politeness (cf. 532(c)):

Ville De række mig saltet? Would you pass the salt, please?
Kunne du lige hjælpe mig? Could you just help me, please?

(e) The past tense is used about unreal or counterfactual situations in the present. This is often expressed as a condition:

Gid jeg var på ferie! I wish I was on holiday!
Han taler, som om han var rig. He talks as if he was rich.
Jeg tog med, hvis jeg havde tid. I would come if I had the time.

518 The past tense in Danish – different realizations in English

(a) Past tense in Danish – present tense in English

Some constructions with **det var**, expressing the speaker's own, spontaneous feelings (emotive past tense), are found with the present tense in English:

Det var synd! That's a pity/shame!
Det var meget dyrt! That's very expensive!
Det var pænt af dig! That's nice of you!
Det var så alt for i dag! That's all for today!
Det var dog utroligt! That really is incredible!
Se, det var noget andet! Well, that's a different matter!

(b) An incomplete action in the past, which in English is expressed by the progressive past tense, can be rendered in Danish in ways similar to those corresponding to the progressive present tense (cf. 516(b)), only substituting past tense forms for present tense forms. Thus the following four sentences are all possible translations of the English sentence 'She was reading a book when the telephone rang':

Hun læste en bog, da telefonen ringede.
Hun sad (**lå**, etc.) **og læste en bog, da telefonen ringede.**
Hun var ved at læse en bog, da telefonen ringede.
Hun var i færd med at læse en bog, da telefonen ringede.

519 The perfect tense

(a) The perfect tense consists of the present tense of auxiliary **have/være** + a past participle (cf. 530). Generally speaking, the distribution of **have/være** is as follows:

(i) Transitive verbs, and intransitive verbs not expressing motion, use **have** as their auxiliary:

Jeg har læst bogen.	I have read the book.
Vi har brugt pengene.	We have spent the money.
Hun har ventet på dig.	She has waited for you.
Vasen har stået her.	The vase has stood here.

Notice that **have** and **være** both use **have** as their auxiliary:

Vi har haft en dejlig ferie.	We have had a lovely holiday.
Vi har været i Italien.	We have been to Italy.

(ii) Intransitive verbs expressing some kind of motion use **være** as their auxiliary (but see (iii) below):

Brevet er forsvundet.	The letter has disappeared.
De er kommet hjem.	They have come home.
Hun er allerede rejst.	She has already left.
Er han stukket af?	Has he run away?

Notice that **blive** (be, become) uses **være** as its auxiliary:

Han er blevet professor.	He has become a professor.
Det er blevet gjort.	It has been done.

For use in passive constructions see 543f.

(iii) Sometimes the same verb can combine with both auxiliaries. This is, for example, the case when a verb can be used both transitively and intransitively of motion:

Jeg har flyttet bordet. (trans.)	I have moved the table.
De er flyttet til Århus. (intrans.)	They have moved to Århus.
Han har fløjet en helikopter. (trans.)	He has flown a helicopter.
Han er fløjet til Japan. (intrans.)	He has flown to Japan.

In other cases, intransitive verbs of motion may express either an activity in the past (and use **have**) or a present state (and use **være**):

Han har gået 10 kilometer. He has walked 10 kilometres.
Nu er han gået. Now he has gone/left.

Hun har svømmet over Kanalen. She has swum the Channel.
Hun er svømmet væk. She has swum away.

Note – The verb **begynde** can be used with either **have** or **være**. **Have** occurs when it is used transitively, e.g.:

Jeg har begyndt oversættelsen. I have begun the translation.
Jeg er begyndt på oversættelsen.

(b) The perfect tense in Danish is primarily used to establish a link between a state or an action begun in the past and its relevance for the present. The length of time may be indeterminate or it may be specified by a time adverbial, but the point of reference is always the present moment:

Der har været mus i kælderen. There have been mice in the basement.
Det har regnet i nat. It has rained during the night.

(c) The perfect tense is used to indicate that a given action has taken place (and perhaps been repeated a certain number of times) before the present moment. The time span involved may or may not be expressed:

Vi har været i Paris to gange. We have visited Paris twice.
Jeg har ikke set ham siden jul. I haven't seen him since Christmas.

(d) The perfect tense is used to indicate that a state or an action begun in the past is still continuing. To express a non-completed action of this kind, a time adverbial is obligatory. In the following sentence pairs, the first sentence describes a state/action which is still going on, while the second carries no such implication:

Vi har boet her i ti år. We have lived here for ten years.
(Cf. **Vi har boet her.** We once lived here.)

De har været gift i lang tid. They have been married for ages.
(Cf. **De har været gift.** They used to be married.)

(e) The perfect tense may be used in a subordinate clause to refer to a future action which will be completed before the event mentioned in the main clause:

Når jeg har drukket min kaffe, går vi hjem.
When I have drunk my coffee, we'll leave.

520 The perfect tense in Danish – different realizations in English

(a) Perfect tense in Danish – present tense in English

A few English verbs ('forget', 'hear') are used idiomatically in the present tense to express a past action with present relevance. Here Danish uses the perfect tense:

Jeg har glemt, hvad hun hedder.	I forget her name.
Jeg har hørt, at han er i fængsel.	I hear that he is in prison.

(b) Perfect tense in Danish – past tense in English

When one or more actions carried out over a certain period of time in the past have left tangible results (e.g. in the shape of buildings, books, works of art, etc.), these actions may be viewed from two perspectives: either as actions completed in the past or as actions with relevance for the present. The former viewpoint is associated with the past tense (see 517), the latter with the perfect tense (see 519). In several cases of this type, Danish prefers the perfect tense (present relevance), where English employs the past tense (past completion):

The perfect tense	*The past tense*
Heiberg har skrevet *Elverhøj*.	Heiberg wrote *Elverhøj*.
Hvor har du hørt det?	Where did you hear that?
Din bror har ringet.	Your brother rang.
Hvornår har du lært fransk?	When did you learn French?

This difference is frequently found in connection with time adverbials that allow both perspectives (e.g. **aldrig**, never; **altid**, always; **nogensinde**, ever; and those denoting parts of the day). Although the perfect tense is sometimes possible in English, the past tense is often preferred:

Det har du aldrig fortalt mig!	You never told me that!
Hun har altid været venlig.	She was always kind.
Har du nogensinde hørt fra ham?	Did you ever hear from him?

Har I sovet godt i nat? Did you sleep well last night?

(c) Perfect tense in Danish – future perfect tense in English

The perfect tense may be used in a main clause to refer to a future action which will be completed (or a future state which will obtain) before an event mentioned in a subordinate clause. Here English normally uses the future perfect as the equivalent of the perfect tense in Danish (but see also 523):

Når det bliver jul, har jeg afsluttet arbejdet på min bog.
By Christmas, I will have completed the work on my book.

Når jeg går af til juli, har jeg tilbragt fyrre år i firmaet.
When I retire in July, I will have spent forty years in the firm.

521 The past perfect tense

(a) The past perfect tense consists of the past tense form of auxiliary **have/være** + a past participle (e.g. **de havde set nyhederne**, they had watched the news). For the choice between **have** and **være** see 519(a).

(b) As in English, the past perfect is used to indicate a state or an action in the past which takes place before another action in the past; this later action is usually expressed by means of another clause with the verb in the past tense. Thus where the perfect tense has its point of reference in the present, the past perfect has its point of reference in the past, although the latter may be implied rather than made explicit:

Da de havde spist, gik de en tur.
When they had eaten, they went for a walk.

(c) The past perfect may express the result of a completed action:

Da vi nåede stationen, var toget kørt.
When we got to the station, the train had left.

De havde dækket bordet, inden gæsterne kom.
They had set the table before the guests arrived.

(d) The past perfect may indicate that a state of affairs lasted up to the point of reference:

Hun havde arbejdet i firmaet i mange år, da hun tog sin afsked.
She had worked in the firm for many years when she handed in her notice.

(e) Like the past tense, the past perfect may be used about unreal or counterfactual situations, but seen in a past perspective:

Hvis du havde ladet bilen stå, var det ikke sket.
If you hadn't taken the car, it wouldn't have happened.

Jeg ville have gjort det, hvis jeg havde haft tid.
I would have done it if I had had the time.

(f) Notice that Danish always uses the past perfect in clauses introduced by **efter at** (after), whereas English can have either the past tense or the past perfect:

Efter at jeg havde set filmen, ringede jeg til ham.
After I (had) watched the film, I phoned him.

522 The future tense

It is not universally accepted that Danish (or English) has a future tense, but we shall say that '**vil** + infinitive' constitutes the future tense in Danish. However, other verbal forms too may be used to refer to future time:

(a) **Vil** + infinitive

This is the most neutral way of expressing future time in Danish; the point of reference is often the present. This 'future' use of **vil** should be distinguished from 'dynamic' **vil**, which expresses a will, a desire or an intention to do something. The equivalent future tense in English consists of 'will'/'shall' + infinitive.

(i) In simple sentences:

Hvad vil der ske med hende?	What will happen to her?
Det vil jeg ikke få at se.	I will/shall not get to see that.
De vil sikkert benåde ham.	They will probably pardon him.

(ii) In the main clause with an attached temporal or conditional clause. Note that the point of reference may be in the future:

Når semestret begynder, vil vi få travlt.
When the term starts, we'll be busy.

Hvis du ikke ringer inden søndag, vil det være for sent.
If you don't phone before Sunday, it will be too late.

For **ville** as a modal verb see 532(c)(vi).

(b) Skal + infinitive

Unlike **vil**, **skal** used with future time reference expresses modal meaning as well. **Skal** may imply an agreement/arrangement or (in the first person) a promise, and it does not only refer to the near future. English can express this in several ways ('will/shall', 'be going to', 'be to', etc.):

De skal giftes i morgen.	They are getting married tomorrow.
Jeg skal nok hjælpe dig.	I'll help you all right.
Hvad skal vi have til middag?	What are we having for dinner?
Hvad skal jeg gøre?	What am I going to do?

For other uses of **skulle** see 532(c)(iv).

(c) The present tense

(i) Present tense with future time reference is more common in Danish than in English. Though often used about the near future, it does not only refer to a short time span. In order to avoid confusion with present time reference, a time adverbial is often present to mark future meaning:

Jeg holder snart op.	I'll stop soon.
De kommer på søndag.	They are coming on Sunday.
Han går af næste år.	He retires next year.

However, the use of the present tense with future time reference is much more frequent with *telic* verbs (i.e. those whose action is directed towards a goal) than with *atelic* verbs. Thus it does not usually occur with such atelic verbs as: **arbejde**, work; **bo**, live; **læse**, read; **spise**, eat; **vente**, wait; etc. Here one would normally use future tense constructions like:

Skal han arbejde i ferien?	Will he be working in the holidays?
Vil du vente på mig?	Will you wait for me?

(ii) With certain telic verbs (e.g. **blive,** be; **få,** get; **komme**, come), the future time reference is clear even without a time marker:

Tror du, det bliver regnvejr?	Do you think it will rain?
Vi får se.	We shall see.
Kommer der mange mennesker?	Will there be a lot of people?

(iii) When the present tense is used about the future in temporal and conditional clauses (cf. (a)(ii) above), it may also appear in the attached main clause. Here English will nearly always use the future tense:

Når du kommer hjem, går vi ud og handler.
When you come home, we'll go shopping.

Jeg giver en omgang, hvis du vinder.
I'll buy a round if you win.

523 The future perfect

The future perfect tense is realized by the form: **vil have/være** + past participle (e.g. **jeg vil have/være rejst**, I will have travelled).

Like the perfect tense, the future perfect expresses a state or an action that lasts up to, or has relevance for, a certain point in time, but this point of reference is in the future rather than in the past:

Når dit tog ankommer, vil jeg være taget afsted.
When your train arrives, I will have left.

Når ferien begynder, vil han have afsluttet sin eksamen.
When the holidays start, he will have completed his exam.

524 The future of the past

(a) The future of the past is realized by the form: **ville** + infinitive (e.g. **jeg ville rejse,** I would travel).

It expresses a future state or action in relation to a point of reference in the past. Like future **vil**, **ville** here does not have the dynamic modal meaning of 'will' or 'desire'. The future of the past is mainly used in indirect speech with the reporting verb in the past tense:

> **Hun sagde, at hun ville vente på posten.**
> She said that she would wait for the post.

> **Han fortalte mig, at de ville vende tilbage det følgende år.**
> He told me that they would return the following year.

(b) **Skulle** + infinitive can also express future time meaning in such clauses, but with the same modal overtones as **skal** + infinitive in 522(b):

> **Hun sagde, at hun skulle skrive en stil.**
> She said that she had to write an essay.

> **Han spurgte, om jeg skulle rejse næste dag.**
> He asked if I was leaving the next day.

(c) Although the present tense can express future time (cf. 515(d), 522(c)), it cannot be used to express the future of the past. However, the past tense can be used in this way:

> **Han troede, at støjen snart hørte op, men det gjorde den ikke.**
> He thought that the noise would soon stop, but it didn't.

525 The future perfect of the past

The future perfect of the past is realized by the form: **ville have/være** + past participle (e.g. **jeg ville have/være rejst**, I would have travelled). It has two main functions.

(a) It resembles the future perfect in that it indicates a state or an action lasting up to a certain point in the past which is simultaneously a future point in relation to the point of reference (in the past). In this use, it usually appears in indirect speech with a declarative verb (e.g. **mene**, think; **sige**, say; **svare**, answer; etc.) in the main clause so that the state or action referred to (B) comes after the time represented by the declarative verb (A), but before another time reference (C), as in the following examples:

(A) (B) (C)
Han sagde, at han ville have læst bogen inden jul.
He said that he would have read the book before Christmas.

(A) (B) (C)
Jeg svarede, at jeg ville være rejst, når gæsterne ankom.
I answered that I would have left when the guests arrived.

(b) The second main function of the future perfect of the past is in a main clause which has an attached conditional clause with the verb in the past perfect tense, expressing a counterfactual situation in the past:

Hvis jeg havde hørt om din sygdom, ville jeg have besøgt dig.
If I had heard of your illness, I would have visited you.

Jeg ville være gået i operaen, hvis jeg havde haft tid.
I would have gone to the opera if I had had time.

Here the future perfect of the past has certain aspects in common with the past tense and the past perfect, which can also be used about hypothetical situations (cf. 517(e) and 521(e)).

(i) The future perfect of the past compared with the past tense

The future perfect of the past is distinguished from the past tense by the fact that the condition expressed relates to a situation in the past (counterfactual condition), whereas the past tense in this use relates to one in the present (unreal condition). Note also that in the latter case any conditional clause has the verb in the past tense:

Future perfect of the past in counterfactual condition

Hvis jeg havde været rask,	If I had been well,
ville jeg være gået med.	I would have gone.
(i.e. **Jeg var ikke rask.**	I was not well.)
Jeg ville have købt den,	I would have bought it
hvis jeg havde haft råd.	if I had had the money.
(i.e. **Jeg havde ikke råd.**	I didn't have the money.)

Past tense in unreal condition

Hvis jeg var rask, gik jeg med.	If I were well, I would go.
(i.e. **Jeg er ikke rask.**	I am not well.)

Jeg købte den, hvis jeg havde råd.	I would buy it if I had the money.
(i.e. **Jeg har ikke råd.**	I haven't got the money.)

(ii) The difference in use between the future perfect of the past and the past perfect is less clear-cut, as they both relate to an event in the past and in both cases the conditional clause has its verb in the past perfect tense. Thus it is often possible to substitute one for the other, even though the future perfect of the past emphasizes the counterfactual aspect more strongly:

Hvis du ikke havde ringet, havde jeg skrevet til dig.
Hvis du ikke havde ringet, ville jeg have skrevet til dig.
If you hadn't rung, I would have written to you.

526 Time planes

There are two time planes in Danish: a *now* plane and a *then* plane. The *now* plane includes the present, perfect, future and future perfect tenses, whilst the *then* plane includes the past, past perfect, future of the past and future perfect of the past tenses.

NOW plane

Before now	*Now*	*After now*
Perfect:	Present:	Future:
Jeg har skrevet.	**Jeg skriver.**	1 **Jeg vil skrive.** 2. **Jeg skriver (i morgen).**
		Future perfect: **Jeg vil have skrevet.**

THEN plane

Before then	*Then*	*After then*
Past perfect:	Past:	Future of the past:
Jeg havde skrevet.	**Jeg skrev.**	**Jeg ville skrive.**
		Future perfect of the past: **Jeg ville have skrevet.**

527 Compatibility of tenses

It is not usual to change time plane in mid-sentence. If a sentence begins in one plane, it is commonly completed in the same plane:

Now:	**Jeg siger,** I say/am saying	**at jeg har læst bogen.** that I have read the book.	Before *now*
	Jeg siger, I say/am saying	**at jeg læser bogen.** that I am reading the book.	*Now*
	Jeg siger, I say/am saying	**at jeg snart vil læse bogen.** **at jeg snart læser bogen.** that I will soon read the book.	After *now*
	Når du kommer, When you arrive,	**vil jeg have læst bogen.** I will have read the book.	After *now*
Then:	**Ole skrev,**	**at han havde læst bogen.** that he had read the book.	Before *then*
	Ole skrev, Ole wrote	**at han læste bogen.** that he was reading the book.	*Then*
	Ole skrev, Ole wrote	**at han ville læse bogen.** that he would read the book.	After *then*
	Ole skrev, Ole wrote	**at han ville have læst bogen inden jul.** that he would have read the book before Christmas.	After *then*

Tense does *not* express the time plane itself, but rather the speaker's relation to the time plane in terms of 'before', 'now/then' and 'after'.

There are occasions when a change of plane is possible, or even logically necessary, but it is then usually signalled by an adverbial expression of time:

Comparative

Vejret var (*then*) **bedre sidste søndag, end det har været** (*now*) **i dag.**
The weather was better last Sunday than it has been today.

Indirect speech

Ole skrev (*then*) **for en måned siden, at han kommer** (*now*) **i næste uge.**
Ole wrote a month ago that he is coming next week.

A change in mid-sentence is sometimes possible when a following clause has a different subject and offers a new type of information:

Turisterne besøgte (*then*) **Kronborg Slot, der ligger** (*now*) **i Helsingør.**
The tourists visited Kronborg Castle, which is situated in Elsinore.

C THE USE OF THE NON-FINITE VERB FORMS

528 The infinitive

For forms see 502(a),(g). The infinitive is used both as the dictionary form and the citation form of the verb. It is *not* identical with the stem of the verb, except in some monosyllabic vowel stems (e.g. **bo**, live/stay; **få**, get; **gå**, go/walk; **se**, see; etc.)

Like finite verb phrases, infinitives can show tense, as seen in the following types of infinitive: *present infinitive* (e.g. **at bruge**, to use), *perfect infinitive* (e.g. **at have brugt**, to have used), future infinitive (e.g. **at ville bruge**, to be going to use), future perfect infinitive (e.g. **at ville have brugt**, to be going to have used). Notice also that these forms may have passive equivalents (e.g. **at bruges / at blive brugt**, to be used). For the use of the passive see 541–43.

(a) Verbal use of infinitive without **at**

The following types of verbal construction require the infinitive without the infinitive marker **at**:

(i) After the following modal auxiliaries: **burde**, should/ought to; **kunne**, be able to; **måtte**, have to/be allowed to; **skulle**, have to; **ville**, want to. (See 532(c).)

Hun kan spille klaver.	She can play the piano.
Måtte du ikke gå ud?	Weren't you allowed to go out?

Note – In Danish, modal verbs can combine with a directional adverb instead of an infinitive, e.g. **Jeg skal ind nu,** I must go in now. If an infinitive expressing intention is added to such a verb phrase, it must be preceded by **at**. However, since both **at** as an infinitive marker and the coordinating conjunction **og** often have the same pronunciation /å/, some confusion can arise in informal language. This vacillation even extends to other occurrences of **at** + infinitive:

Vi skal ud at/og spise i aften. We are going out to dine tonight.
Jeg må ind at/og lave mad. I must go in and cook the dinner.
Skal du hen at/og stemme? Are you going round to vote?

(ii) Sometimes after **turde** (dare to) and the 'semi-auxiliaries' **behøve** (need), and **gide** (feel like). These three verbs can all combine with an infinitive with or without **at**, but they are currently undergoing contrasting developments in that **behøve** is increasingly found without **at**, whereas **gide** and **turde** are beginning to accept **at** before the infinitive (cf. 532(c)(v), 532(e)(iii)):

Du behøver ikke (at) skynde dig. You don't need to hurry.
Jeg gider ikke (at) lege. I don't feel like playing.
Tør du godt (at) klatre op i træet? Dare you climb the tree?

(iii) After **få** (in certain idiomatic uses):

Vi får se. We'll see.
Det får være. It'll have to be left as it is.

(iv) After **bede** (ask), **lade** (let) and some 'verbs of sensation': **føle** (feel); **høre** (hear); **se** (see). These verbs are often followed by a non-finite complement clause (an 'accusative + infinitive' construction; see 410(c) and 417(a)):

Hun bad ham rydde op. She asked him to clean up.
Han følte sit hjerte banke. He felt his heart beating.
Jeg hørte bilen køre bort. I heard the car drive away.

(v) When two infinitives are coordinated, the second one is usually without **at**:

At gavne og fornøje ... To improve and please ...
De begyndte at råbe og skrige. They started to shout and scream.

(vi) In non-finite clauses, an infinitive often occurs without **at**. There are two types of these, and both may be said to involve ellipsis:

1 Questions introduced by **hvorfor** (why), and usually followed by a subordinate clause beginning with **når** (when). The general nature of such questions can be seen from the fact that the expanded version would normally have a finite modal verb and the indefinite pronoun **man** (you, one, etc.) as its subject, e.g. **Hvorfor skal man ...** ,Why should one .... They often have a proverbial ring to them:

Hvorfor stå tidligt op, når man kan blive liggende i sengen?
Why get up early when it is possible to stay in bed?

Hvorfor løbe, når man kan gå?
Why run when it is possible to walk?

2 Prohibitions and warnings used jokingly or to children. This too involves ellipsis, e.g. **Du må ikke ...** ,You mustn't ...:

Ikke kigge/røre/snyde!	Don't look/touch/cheat!
Altid være opmærksom!	Always pay attention!
Aldrig sige aldrig!	Never say never!

(b) Verbal use of infinitive with **at**

(i) When **at** appears as an infinitive marker, nothing can intervene between **at** and the infinitive. In other words, there is no such thing as a split infinitive in Danish:

Jeg var besluttet på rigtigt at more mig.
I was determined to really enjoy myself.

(ii) A number of verbs (so-called *catenative* or 'linking' verbs) enter into two-verb constructions with **at** + the infinitive of another verb, e.g.:

begynde, begin; **beslutte**, decide; **formå**, be able to; **forstå**, know how to; **forsøge**, try; **håbe**, hope; **love**, promise; **lykkes**, succeed; **orke**, have the energy to; **pleje**, usually do; **synes**, seem; **vælge**, choose; **ønske**, want/wish

Det begyndte at regne.	It began to rain.
Du lovede at hjælpe mig.	You promised to help me.
De valgte at køre med toget.	They chose to go by train.

For other uses of infinitive with **at** see (c) below.

(c) Nominal use of infinitives

An infinitive (usually with **at**) can assume most of the clausal functions of a noun:

(i) Infinitive as subject:

At fejle er menneskeligt.	To err is human.
At skrive blev hans hobby.	Writing became his hobby.

A nominally used infinitive is treated as a neuter singular noun so that predicative adjectives must have the neuter singular ending **-t** in order to agree with it (cf. **menneskeligt** in the example above and see 105(d), 210(a)–(b)). However, it is more frequent to have the formal subject **det** (it) in initial position and the infinitive later in the clause (see 406(d)):

Det er dejligt at slappe af. It's lovely to relax.
Det er sundt at spise frugt. It's healthy to eat fruit.

(ii) Infinitive as subject complement:

Hans mål var at blive rig. His aim was to become rich.
Planen er at udbetale lånet. The plan is to pay off the loan.

Note that in such cases subject and subject complement can often be switched round with very little change of meaning. However, since the focus is on the subject rather than on the subject complement, this establishes at least a difference of emphasis:

At blive rig var hans mål. To become rich was his aim.

The position of a clausal adverbial can show which is the subject:

At blive rig var ikke hans mål. (Subject: **At blive rig**)
At blive rig var hans mål ikke. (Subject: **hans mål**)

(iii) Infinitive as object

An infinitive with **at** often functions as object after a catenative verb (cf. (b) above):

Jeg håber at komme til festen. I hope to come to the party.
Hun ønskede ikke at se ham igen. She didn't want to see him again.

(iv) Infinitive as prepositional complement

In Danish it is very common for a preposition to govern an infinitive. This is not possible in English, which normally uses a gerund (or verbal noun) ending in '-ing' instead of the infinitive (see 702(c)(iii)):

Han var bange for at falde ned. He was afraid of falling down.
Hun gik uden at sige noget. She left without saying anything.

Note especially the use of **for at** (in order to) to express intention:

Jeg gik ud for at hente en kop.	I went out to fetch a cup.
Jeg tog fri for at hjælpe dig.	I took time off in order to help you.

(v) Infinitive as complement of a noun or an adjective

Here too **at** is obligatory and the infinitive always follows the noun/adjective. The infinitive is often preceded by a preposition:

De har to børn at forsørge.	They have two children to support.
Har du tid til at gøre det?	Have you got time to do it?
Han er umulig at gøre tilpas.	He is impossible to please.
De har travlt med at lege.	They are busy playing.

(d) Infinitive in Danish – infinitive or gerund in English

As can be seen from the examples above, Danish and English often use the infinitive in the same environment and with similar functions. There are, however, situations where this is not the case or only partly so.

(i) Certain verbs in English can combine with either an infinitive or a gerund, but since Danish does not possess a gerund, an infinitive is often the only alternative:

Han begyndte at skrive.	He began to write/writing.
Jeg foretrækker at flyve.	I prefer to fly/flying.
At dyrke sport er sundt.	To do/Doing sport is healthy.

(ii) In other cases only the gerund is possible in English corresponding to an infinitive in Danish:

Vi kunne ikke undgå at se ham.	We couldn't avoid seeing him.
Er du holdt op med at ryge?	Have you stopped smoking?
Det nytter ikke at forsøge.	It's no use trying.

This is always the case after a preposition (cf. (c)(iv) above):

Jeg glæder mig til at møde dig.	I look forward to meeting you.
Efter at have betalt gik vi.	After having paid we left.

Note – The subject of the finite verb is also the subject of the infinitive. Examples of the following type are incorrect:

> ***Efter at have malet huset blev det solgt til en høj pris.**
> *After having painted the house it was sold at a high price.

(e) Finally, there are cases where an infinitive or a gerund in English corresponds not to an infinitive, but to a finite clause in Danish:

(i) Often when English has a non-finite complement clause (see 410(c) and 417(a)) and the subject of the infinitive is not identical with the subject of the main clause verb:

> **Jeg forventer, at de afslutter arbejdet inden fredag.**
> I expect them to finish the work before Friday.

> **Hvad vil du have, at jeg skal gøre?**
> What do you want me to do?

(ii) When English has a genitive/proper noun or a possessive/personal pronoun in the objective case followed by a gerund:

> **Det, at John studerede, gjorde mange ting vanskeligere.**
> John's/John being a student made many things more difficult.

> **Han rejste på falsk pas, uden at jeg vidste det.**
> He travelled on a false passport without my/me knowing it.

(iii) Danish often has preposition + **at**-clause where English has preposition + gerund:

> **Han takkede mig for, at jeg kom til tiden.**
> He thanked me for arriving on time.

529 The present participle

(a) Form (see also 502(f))

(i) The present participle is formed by adding **-ende** to the stem of the verb, whether this ends in a consonant or a vowel, corresponding to English forms in '-ing':

Stem/infinitive	*Present participle*	*Meaning*
Consonant stems:		
arbejd/*e*	**arbejd/*ende***	work
hop/p/*e*	**hop/p/*ende***	jump
skriv/*e*	**skriv/*ende***	write
Vowel stems:		
bo/	**bo/*ende***	live/stay
dø/	**dø/*ende***	die
gå/	**gå/*ende***	walk

When functioning as nouns (see (b)(ii) below), present participles can have the genitive ending **-s**:

den døendes sidste ønske	the dying person's last wish
de levendes land	the land of the living

(ii) Nearly all verbs can form a present participle, but there are a few groups that either do not possess one or very rarely make use of it:

1 Generally speaking, modal verbs do not possess a present participle form for semantic reasons (see 532), though one may occasionally come across **villende**.

2 Verbs which have **-s** form only (e.g. **lykkes**, succeed; **synes**, seem, think; **trives**, thrive; **væmmes**, feel disgust; etc.) do not possess a present participle (see 539ff.).

Note – Those verbs which have double forms with and without **-s** (e.g. **bryde(s)**, break, clash, wrestle; **læge(s)**, heal; **stride(s)**, fight, quarrel; etc.) do often have a present participle, e.g.:

de brydende	the wrestlers
de stridende parter	the contending parties

3 Reflexive verbs rarely make use of the present participle, but when they do (mainly in officialese), the reflexive pronoun precedes the participle:

de sig i Danmark opholdende flygtninge (cf. **opholde sig**)
the refugees who are staying in Denmark

Occasionally the reflexive pronoun can disappear from the present participle of a verb which otherwise does not occur without it, e.g.:

en nedladende bemærkning	a condescending remark
(cf. **nedlade sig til ...**	condescend to ...)

4 In a very few cases, a present participle has survived idiomatically, even though the verb itself has become obsolete:

en glubende appetit	a ravenous appetite
en standende strid	an unresolved conflict
(Also: **Striden er standende.**	The conflict is unresolved.)

(b) Use

(i) As a verb indicating position, movement or mood, after verbs like **blive**, remain; **gå**, walk; **komme**, come; **løbe**, run; etc.:

Jeg blev stående i døren.	I remained standing in the doorway.
Barnet kom kravlende ind i stuen.	The baby came crawling into the room.
Hun gik smilende ned ad gaden.	She walked smiling down the street.

After **finde** (find), present participles can make up the verbal element of a non-finite complement clause (see 410(c) and 417(a)):

Vi fandt liget liggende i en grøft.	We found the body lying in a ditch.

An idiomatic use of this type of construction is found in expressions like **få ... forærende/sendende**, have presented as a gift/have sent (from); **gøre ... gældende**, claim, maintain, bring to bear; **holde ... uvidende (om)**, keep ... in ignorance (of); etc.:

Hun fik bogen forærende.	She got the book as a present.
Jeg gjorde min indflydelse gældende.	I brought my influence to bear.

Notice also the special use of the present participle to denote a person's current means of transport. It is important to remember that this does *not* carry the implication of 'being in the process of ...' and should not be confused with the progressive tense in English (cf. 516(b)):

A: **Er du kørende eller gående?**	A: Are you driving or walking? (i.e. Have you come by car or ...)
B: **Jeg er faktisk cyklende.**	B: Actually, I'm cycling. (i.e. I have come on my bike.)

(ii) As a noun

Certain present participle forms are now treated as full nouns. This is especially the case when participles are used as common gender nouns denoting persons who are characterized by the verbal activity associated with the participle. Present participle forms of this kind cannot usually appear in the indefinite singular in English:

> **en boligsøgende**, a person looking for somewhere to live; **en døende**, a dying person; **en rejsende**, a traveller; **en studerende**, a student; **en troende**, a believer; **en uvedkommende**, an intruder; etc.

In the definite form (singular or plural) there are numerous examples, including words which may or may not occur with an indefinite article:

> **de(n) besøgende**, visitor(s); **de(n) spisende**, a person/people who is/are eating; **de(n) syngende**, a person/people who is/are singing; **de(n) talende**, the speaker(s); etc.

Vedkommende (the person(s) in question) normally occurs without article, unlike **de(n) pågældende** (with the same meaning).

There are also examples of neuter nouns:

> **et anliggende**, a business/matter; **et indestående**, a bank balance; etc.

as well as idiomatic phrases like:

> **efter pålydende**, at face value; **efter sigende**, reputedly; etc.

(iii) As an adjective

This is by far the most important function of present participles. They appear in both attributive and predicative position:

1 In attributive position

In this position present participles, like other adjectives, modify nouns:

en omfattende beretning	a comprehensive account
ovenstående paragraffer	the above paragraphs
i skrivende stund	at the moment of writing

2 In predicative position

Not all present participles can appear in this position, or appear with the same meaning as in the attributive position. Thus although the first of the three examples in (1) above could be transformed into **Beretningen er omfattende**, we could not have ***Paragrafferne er ovenstående** or ***Stunden er skrivende**. Other examples:

Du ser fortryllende ud!	You look enchanting!
Resultatet syntes overvældende.	The result seemed overwhelming.
Heden var trykkende.	The heat was oppressive.

(iv) As an adverb

Present participles with adverbial function can modify verbs, adjectives or other adverbs:

1 Modifying verbs:

Du skriver imponerende.	You write impressively.
Hun talte beroligende.	She spoke soothingly.
Han arbejdede tilfredsstillende.	He worked satisfactorily.

2 Modifying adjectives

Present participles here often have an intensifying effect:

blændende hvide tænder	dazzling white teeth
Vi har rasende travlt.	We are frightfully busy.
Maden var rygende varm.	The food was steaming hot.

3 Modifying adverbs:

De spillede bragende godt.	They played supremely well.

Hun løb overraskende hurtigt.	She ran surprisingly fast.
Han sang skingrende falsk.	He sang awfully out of tune.

530 The past participle

(a) Form (see also 502(d),(g))

The past participle always ends in **-(e)t**. This ending is not just added to the stem, but depends on the conjugation of the verb:

Infinitive	*Present*	*Past*	*Past participle*	*Meaning*
(i) Weak verbs of conjugation I end in **-et**:				
svare	**svarer**	**svarede**	**svaret**	answer
(ii) Weak verbs of conjugation II end in **-t**:				
høre	**hører**	**hørte**	**hørt**	hear
(iii) Weak verbs of conjugation III end in **-t** (with a few exceptions):				
sige	**siger**	**sagde**	**sagt**	say
(iv) Strong verbs (conjugation IV) end in **-(e)t**, mainly **-t** after **-d**:				
skyde	**skyder**	**skød**	**skudt**	shoot
synge	**synger**	**sang**	**sunget**	sing
(v) Modal verbs end in **-et**:				
kunne	**kan**	**kunne**	**kunnet**	can

As far as the stem vowel in the past participle of strong verbs is concerned, it can be related to the stem vowel in the other principal verb forms in four ways:

Infinitive	*Present*	*Past*	*Past participle*	*Meaning*
1 The same vowel as in the infinitive/present tense, but different from the past tense, e.g.:				
give	**giver**	**gav**	**givet**	give
2 The same vowel as in the past tense, e.g.:				
flyve	**flyver**	**fløj**	**fløjet**	fly
3 Different vowel from both the infinitive/present tense and the past tense, e.g.:				
drikke	**drikker**	**drak**	**drukket**	drink
4 The same vowel in all principal forms, e.g.:				
komme	**kommer**	**kom**	**kommet**	come

(vi) When used as attributive adjectives, the past participles that end in consonant + **-t** add an **-e** in the definite and/or plural form, while those that end in **-et** usually change **-t** to **-d** when adding **-e** (see 204(e)):

en indbudt gæst an invited guest	**den indbudte gæst** the invited guest	**(de) indbudte gæster** (the) invited guests
en lejet bil a rented car	**den lejede bil** the rented car	**(de) lejede biler** (the) rented cars

(vii) Some strong verbs have an adjectival indefinite common gender form in -**en** and a definite/plural form in **-ne**. Notice that the definite/plural **-ne** ending can also be used with neuter nouns:

en bunden opgave a compulsory paper	**den bundne opgave** the compulsory paper	**(de) bundne opgaver** (the) compulsory papers
et bundet snørebånd a tied shoelace	**det bundne snørebånd** the tied shoelace	**(de) bundne snørebånd** (the) tied shoelaces

(viii) When used predicatively of a state rather than an action, inflected and uninflected forms are often both possible:

Gæsterne er indbudt(e).	The guests are invited.
Bilerne er lejede/lejet.	The cars are rented.
Slipsene er bundne/bundet.	The ties are knotted.

(b) Use

(i) Verbal function

The past participle has verbal function when it combines with auxiliary **have/være** (have/be) to form the composite tenses (the perfect, the past perfect, etc.), or with auxiliary **blive** to form one of the passive constructions (see 543). In these uses, it normally expresses an action or activity:

Composite tenses

Jeg har/havde set den nye film.	I have/had seen the new film.
Han er/var rejst.	He has/had left.

Passive

Pakken bliver undersøgt.	The parcel is being examined.
Målmanden blev vist ud.	The goalkeeper was sent off.

(ii) Adjectival function

1 When a past participle expresses a completed action or a change of state rather than an action/activity, it often functions as an adjective, and like an adjective it can occur both attributively and predicatively:

det ventede resultat	the expected outcome
Resultatet var ventet.	The outcome was expected.

2 It is usually transitive verbs that are found with attributive adjectival function:

en strøget skjorte	(Cf. **Han har strøget skjorten.**)
an ironed shirt	(Cf. He has ironed the shirt.)
	obj.

But not:

***en ligget skjorte**	(Cf. **Skjorten har ligget der.**)
*a lain shirt	(Cf. The shirt has lain there.)
	adv.

3 However, the past participle of intransitive verbs is sometimes used as an attributive adjective:

en krympet skjorte a shrunken shirt	(Cf. **Skjorten er krympet.**) (Cf. The shirt has shrunk.)
et forsvundet billede a vanished painting	(Cf. **Billedet er forsvundet.**) (Cf. The painting has vanished.)

4 The past participle of compound verbs can often appear as an attributive adjective even when the corresponding simple verb has no equivalent form:

en afgjort sag (Cf. ***en gjort sag**)	a settled matter
et vedtaget forslag (Cf. ***et taget forslag**)	an adopted proposal

(c) Inflected or uninflected form?

As indicated in (a)(viii) above, there is often great uncertainty about when an adjectival past participle in predicative position should be inflected. There are two types of inflexion involved: (i) uninflected form or **-e/-ede**, and (ii) uninflected form or **-en/-ne**.

(i) **-e/-ede** or uninflected form

1 When the past participle expresses a state rather than an action, both the inflected **-e/-ede** form and the uninflected form can be found:

Stolene er solgt(e).	The chairs are sold.
Dørene er malet/malede.	The doors are painted.

Notice the difference between this static meaning and the emphasis on action in the corresponding passive construction, where the participle must be uninflected:

Stolene er (blevet) solgt af Ole.	The chairs have been sold by Ole.
Dørene er (blevet) malet af mig.	The doors have been painted by me.

The adjectival nature of such participles can also be seen from the fact that they can be coordinated with genuine adjectives:

de fattige og forsømte børn	the poor and neglected children

2 When a preposition follows the participle, the uninflected form is the more common one:

Vi er indstillet(/indstillede) på at møde op.
We intend to turn up.

De var irriteret(/irriterede) over hans opførsel.
They were annoyed at his behaviour.

3 When the participle is used as a complement, both forms occur, but the inflected form is increasingly preferred:

De løb forskrækkede/forskrækket ud.
They ran out, frightened.

De følte sig lettede/lettet.
They felt relieved.

4 If the participle can be associated with degree, the inflected form is the norm:

Skoene er meget slidte.	The shoes are very worn.
Hans planer var ret uventede.	His plans were rather unexpected.

(ii) **-en/-ne** or uninflected form

1 Some strong and irregular verbs have an inflected common gender form in **-en** and a definite/plural form in **-ne**:

en ankommen gæst	(def./plur. **ankomne**)	an arrived guest
(Cf. **de sidst ankomne**		the latest arrivals)
en forsvunden skat	(def./plur. **forsvundne**)	a lost treasure
en vunden kamp	(def./plur. **vundne**)	a win
en undsluppen fange	(def./plur. **undslupne**)	an escaped prisoner

But in most of these cases the uninflected form is also possible. Generally speaking, the **-en** form is on the decline and appears chiefly in long-established and fixed collocations, while the uninflected participle form is becoming more and more frequent:

en stjålen/stjålet bil	a stolen car
en beskåren/beskåret artikel	an abridged article

en indløben/indløbet meddelelse a newly arrived message

2 There are a few examples where a participle and a corresponding adjective differ in both form and meaning, so that the participle has literal and the adjective figurative meaning:

Participle	*Adjective*
slebet glas, cut glass	**et slebent væsen**, a polished manner
et stjålet ur, a stolen watch	**et stjålent blik**, a stealthy glance

See also 205.

D MOOD

531 Introduction

Mood as a verbal category usually signifies the speaker's or another person's attitude to a given utterance. Mood can be expressed in different ways, but the most important ones are the use of:

(a) Modal auxiliary verbs (see 532):

Det bør ikke ske.	It ought not to happen.
Han må ikke cykle.	He must not cycle.

(b) Finite forms of other verbs:

(i) The indicative

This is a finite verb form (in practice, a present or past tense form) of non-modal verbs that is neither imperative nor subjunctive. It presents a given utterance as a fact and is often referred to as the 'unmarked' mood form:

Jeg arbejder i Odense.	I work in Odense.
Han svømmer hver dag.	He swims every day.

For an extensive treatment of the indicative see Section B above.

(ii) The imperative (see 533):

Bliv lidt længere!	Stay a little longer!
Kom herop!	Come up here!

(iii) The subjunctive (see 534):

Michael længe leve!	Three cheers for Michael! (*lit.* Long live Michael!)
Gud være med dig!	God be with you!

Note – Mood can be expressed by other word classes than verbs, such as *adjectives* (e.g. **det er *nødvendigt*,** it is necessary), *participles* (e.g. **han kan *givet* klare det,** he can clearly manage it), *adverbs* (e.g. **det er *muligvis* rigtigt,** it is possibly true), *modal particles* such as **ja, nok, vel,** etc. (e.g. **han bliver *nok* læge,** he'll probably become a doctor).

532 Modal auxiliary verbs

(a) Form

Unlike English modals, Danish modals possess all four main forms, but the infinitive and the past tense forms are identical:

Infinitive	*Present*	*Past*	*Past participle*	*Meaning*
burde	**bør**	**burde**	**burdet**	should, ought to
kunne	**kan**	**kunne**	**kunnet**	can
måtte	**må**	**måtte**	**måttet**	may, must
skulle	**skal**	**skulle**	**skullet**	must, shall
turde	**tør**	**turde**	**turdet**	dare
ville	**vil**	**ville**	**villet**	will, want to

Note – A few other verbs resemble the modal auxiliaries in function but not in form, e.g. **behøve,** need; **få** (in some idiomatic uses); **gide,** feel like. See (e) below.

Both the present and the past tense forms are irregular, whereas the past participle adds the regular ending **-t** to the past tense form. See also 505 Note.

(b) Epistemic, deontic and dynamic modality

Most of the modal auxiliaries can express different modal meanings and thus be used in different kinds of situation. We shall distinguish between three types of modal usage (though further subdivisions are possible):

(i) Epistemic modality

This is concerned with the speaker's degree of knowledge of, and commitment to, his/her utterance. It covers such notions as 'possibility', 'probability' and 'logical necessity':

Det kan være en fejltagelse.	It may be a mistake.
Det må have været morsomt.	It must have been fun.

(ii) Deontic modality

This is concerned with the speaker's own decisions about the verbal action. It covers such notions as 'permission', 'command', 'necessity', etc.:

Du må gerne gå i biografen.	You may go to the cinema.
Du skal gøre, hvad jeg siger.	You must do as I tell you.

(iii) Dynamic modality

This is chiefly concerned with the notions of 'ability' and 'volition':

Han kan spille på klaver.	He can play the piano.
Hun vil ikke spille.	She won't play.

For more details see (c) below.

(c) Main uses

Syntactically, the modal auxiliaries combine with a bare infinitive (i.e. an infinitive without **at**) or with a directional adverbial (e.g. **du må vente her**, you must wait here; **jeg må på arbejde**, I must go to work). Semantically, the modal auxiliaries express the speaker's attitude, belief, insistence, etc., in relation to the activity of a following main verb or of the whole clause. The main uses of each of the modals are shown below (in alphabetical order):

(i) **Burde**

Epistemic use

1 Assumption, probability:

Hun bør/burde være nået hjem.	She should have reached home.

Det bør/burde stå i avisen. It ought to be in the newspaper.

Deontic use

2 Strong recommendation:

Du bør/burde læse hans nye bog. You should read his new book.
De bør/burde købe sig et hus. They ought to buy a house.

In the examples in (1) and (2) above, past tense **burde** is more polite or tentative than present tense **bør**.

3 Moral obligation:

Man bør gøre sin pligt. One ought to do one's duty.
I bør passe jeres barn. You ought to look after your child.

Past tense **burde** cannot easily replace **bør** in this sense.

(ii) **Kunne**

Epistemic use

1 Possibility:

Han kan have fået arbejde. He may have got a job.
Der kan komme nogen regn. There may be some rain.

Deontic use

2 Permission:

Du kan gå nu. You may go now.
Han kan ikke komme med. He can't come with us.

Dynamic use

3 Ability:

Hun kan tale dansk. She can speak Danish.
Jeg har engang kunnet løbe hurtigt. I could once run fast.

Note – When referring to ability, **kunne** can be used as a main verb in the sense of 'know'. In this sense, it can even occur in the passive infinitive:

De kan russisk. They know Russian.
Rollen skal kunnes i morgen. The part must be learnt by tomorrow.

In questions asking for information, help, etc., the past tense form **kunne** is considered more polite than the present tense form **kan**:

Kunne du hjælpe mig op? Could you help me up, please?
Kunne De række mig saltet? Would you pass the salt, please?

4 Theoretical possibility:

Broen kan bygges. The bridge can be built.
(NOT: ... may be built!)

Sometimes there is ambiguity between theoretical possibility ('can be ...') and epistemic possibility ('may be ...'):

Det kan være varmt i Rom. It can be hot in Rome (i.e. generally).
It may be hot in Rome (i.e. when we go).

(iii) **Måtte**

Epistemic use

1 Logical necessity:

Du må være tørstig. You must be thirsty.
Han må have taget nøglerne. He must have taken the keys.

2 Hopes and wishes for the future:

Må det gå dig godt! May you do well!
Måtte de bare blive lykkelige! May they only be happy!

3 Concession:

Hvor svært det end må være ... However difficult it may be ...
Hvad der end måtte hænde ... Whatever may happen ...

Deontic use

4 Permission:

Mor, må jeg få en is? Mother, may I have an ice-cream, please?
Ja, det må du godt. Yes, you may.
Nej, det må du ikke. No, you may not.

5 Command:

Du må være her kl. 7! You must be here at 7 o'clock!
Du må gøre noget ved det! You must do something about it!
Nu må du holde op! Stop that now!

6 Necessity (note that a directional adverbial can replace the infinitive):

Vi må arbejde hårdt. We have to work hard.
Jeg må videre. I have to move on.

(iv) **Skulle**

Epistemic use

1 Report:

Hun skal være meget venlig. She is said to be very kind.
De skal have købt bil. They are said to have bought a car.

2 Future of the past (**skulle** implying 'as fate would have it'):

Sådan skulle det ikke gå. That wasn't to be.

Det var en forudsigelse, der skulle vise sig at være forkert.
That was a prediction that would turn out to be wrong.

3 Weak possibility (only past tense):

Du skulle vel ikke have set Jens?
You wouldn't have seen Jens by any chance?

Han skulle vel ikke være gået?
He wouldn't have left, would he?

Deontic use

4 Arrangement (note that a directional adverbial can replace the infinitive):

De skal giftes.	They are getting married.
Vi skal i teatret.	We are going to the theatre.

5 Promise, threat:

Du skal nok få dine penge.	You shall have your money.
Det skal du få betalt!	You'll pay for this!

6 Command:

Du skal opføre dig pænt!	Behave properly!
Du skal se den film!	You must see that film!

7 Obligation:

Man skal gøre sit bedste.	One ought to do one's best.
Du skulle tage på ferie.	You ought to go on a holiday.

8 Uncertainty:

Hvad skal jeg gøre?	What am I to do?
Hvem skal man stole på?	Who are we to trust?

9 Unreal/counterfactual situations:

Man skulle være millionær.	One should be a millionaire.
Han skulle have været sagfører.	He should have been a lawyer.

10 Condition:

Hvis projektet skal lykkes ...	If the project is to succeed ...
Hvis det ikke skal gå galt ...	If it is not to go wrong ...

Other uses of **skulle**:

11 **Skulle til at ...** (be about to ...):

Vi skulle til at spise.	We were about to have our dinner.
Hun skal lige til at gå.	She is just about to leave.

12 Idiomatic expressions:

Hvad skal der blive af ham?	What's to become of him?
Hvad skal det betyde?	What's the meaning of that?
Hvad skal det gøre godt for?	What's the good of that?
Tak skal du have.	Thank you.
Hvad skulle det være?	What would you like? (e.g. in a shop)

(v) Turde

Epistemic use

1 A matter of course:

Det turde være en selvfølge.	It goes without saying.
Det turde være løgn.	I very much doubt that.

This use is now rather old-fashioned.

2 Idiomatic epistemic use:

Det tør nok siges!	It certainly is!
Det tør svagt antydes!	I dare say!

Deontic use

3 Bravery, courage:

In this use **turde** sometimes accepts **at** in front of the infinitive (see 528(a)(ii)):

Jeg tør ikke (at) springe ned.	I daren't jump down.
Tør du sige det igen?	Dare you say that again?

4 Permission:

Tør man spørge hvorfor?	Dare/May one ask why?

(vi) **Ville**

Epistemic use

1 Future tense marker (see 522(a)):

Han vil være her kl. 8.	He will be here at 8 o'clock.
Vejret vil klare op senere.	The weather will brighten up later.
Det vil vise sig.	Time will tell.

2 Marker of other tenses (future perfect, future of the past, future perfect of the past) (see 523–25):

Hun vil have skrevet det inden da.	She will have written it before then.
Han troede, at det ville høre op.	He thought that it would end.
De ville have givet mig pengene.	They would have given me the money.

3 Unreal/counterfactual situations:

En fridag ville være dejligt!	A day off would be nice!
Det ville have været sjovt at se det!	It would have been fun to see that!

Dynamic use

4 Volition:

Jeg vil have fred!	I want some peace!
Han vil også være med.	He wants to take part, too.

With a negation it amounts to a refusal:

Jeg vil ikke høre på det!	I won't listen to it!
Hun vil ikke mødes med mig.	She won't meet me.

Note that a directional adverbial can replace the infinitive:

Jeg vil hjem!	I want to go home!

De vil i byen i aften. They want to go out tonight.

5 Inherent power (of inanimate objects):

Bolden vil ikke ligge stille. The ball won't lie still.
Verden vil bedrages. The world wants to be fooled.

Idiomatic use

6 **Ville hellere/helst**:

Jeg vil hellere have en whisky. I'd rather have a whisky.
Hun ville helst være fri for det. She'd prefer not to do it.

7 Others:

Du skal, enten du vil eller ej! You must, whether you want to or not!
Gør, hvad du vil! Do as you like!
Man kan, hvad man vil. One can do what one wants to.
Vi vil et retfærdigere samfund. We want a more just society.

(d) The sequence of modals

Since Danish modals have infinitive and past participle forms, it is syntactically possible for two modals to occur in the same verb phrase. In practice, however, there are quite heavy restrictions. Thus only **skulle** (occasionally) and **kunne** can normally appear as the second modal element. (The usual order in such combinations is epistemic – deontic/dynamic.) The main combinations involving two modals are the following:

1 Modal (present/past tense) + modal (infinitive) + verb:

Hun ville kunne klare det. She would be able to manage it.
Han må skulle gå snart. He must be leaving soon.

2 **Have** + modal (past participle) + modal (infinitive) + verb:

Han har måttet kunne se det. He must have been able to see it.

3 Modal (present/past tense) + **have** + modal (past participle) + verb:

Hun ville have kunnet hjælpe.	She would have been able to help.
Han må have skullet skynde sig.	He must have had to hurry.

(e) Some semi-auxiliary verbs

(See 528(a)(ii)–(iii), 532(a)Note.)

(i) **Behøve**

Traditionally, **behøve** combines with **at** + infinitive, but it is beginning to appear with the bare infinitive (cf. 528(a)(ii)):

Det behøver ikke (at) være sandt.	It needn't be true.
Behøver jeg (at) gøre det?	Need I do it?

(ii) **Få**

Få occurs as a semi-auxiliary in a few idiomatic expressions (see 528(a)(iii)):

Det får være.	We'll have to leave it at that.
Vi får se.	We shall see.

Få can also combine with a past participle:

Får I gjort noget ved det?	Are you getting something done?
Jeg fik skrevet en masse.	I got a lot written.

(iii) **Gide**

Though traditionally **gide** combines with a bare infinitive, it is beginning to appear with **at** + infinitive (cf. 528(a)(ii)):

Gider du (at) hjælpe mig?	Would you help me?
Jeg gider ikke (at) lave noget.	I don't feel like doing anything.

533 The imperative

(a) Form

The imperative is identical with the verb stem (cf. 502(e)). This means that the imperative of vowel stems ends in that vowel, while consonant stems end in the consonant in question. Note that the imperative never ends in a double consonant, even when there is a double consonant before the **-e** ending in the infinitive:

	Infinitive	*Imperative*	*Meaning*
vowel stems:	**gå**	**gå!**	go!
	se	**se!**	look!
consonant stems:	**hjælpe**	**hjælp!**	help!
	løbe	**løb!**	run!
with double consonant:	**komme**	**kom!**	come
	sidde	**sid!**	sit

Note – Older Danish had a separate plural form in **-er** in the imperative. This is now completely obsolete:

Kommer til mig, alle, som ... Come to me all those who ...

Verbs whose infinitive has consonant + **-l**, **-m**, **-n**, **-r** in front of **-e** (e.g. **handle**, act; **rødme**, blush; **åbne**, open; **klatre**, climb) are felt to be a little awkward in the imperative (**handl, rødm, åbn, klatr**). This is due partly to the fact that words in Danish do not usually end in such consonant clusters and partly to the difficulties this creates for the pronunciation, where an **-e-** is often inserted before the last consonant.

(b) Use

Semantically, the imperative constitutes a directive addressed to one or more people. Verbs which cannot be used as a directive do not appear in the imperative. This is obviously true of the modals, but also of verbs with **-s** form (e.g. **mindes**, remember; **synes**, seem, think; etc.), as well as several other verbs (e.g. **forekomme**, seem; **gælde**, be valid; **hedde**, be called; etc.).

Note 1 – The verb **slås** (fight) can be used in the imperative together with a negation (cf. 540(a)):

Slås ikke, mens jeg er væk! Don't fight while I'm away!

Occasionally, the imperative appears with a subject:

Vær du glad for, at det er søndag!
(You) be glad that it's Sunday!

Bær du maden, så bærer jeg flaskerne.
You carry the food, then I'll carry the bottles.

The directives can be divided into various subgroups, of which the following are only a sample:

(i) Commands:

Gå ind og hent avisen! Go in and fetch the paper!
Kom her! Come here!

Note 2 – Many brusque or rude directives fall under this heading, e.g. **Hold mund/kæft!** Shut up!; **Skrup af!** Get lost!; **Slå ørene ud!** Open your ears properly!; etc.

(ii) Requests:

Giv mig fri i morgen! Give me tomorrow off!
Gør mig lige en tjeneste! Do me a favour, please!

(iii) Advice, warnings:

Kør hellere lige hjem! Better drive straight home!
Luk ikke døren op for nogen! Don't open the door to anyone!

(iv) Instructions:

Sæt anden i en opvarmet ovn. Put the duck in a heated oven.

(v) Permission:

Spis så meget, I vil. Eat as much as you want.

(vi) Prayer:

Led os ikke i fristelse ... Lead us not into temptation ...

The directness of an imperative may be softened by the addition of a phrase meaning 'please':

Vær venlig og tag/at tage plads.	Please take a seat.
Vær sød og tænd for fjernsynet.	Please turn the television on.

An imperative clause can function as a conditional clause:

Sig ét ord til, og du er fyret!	Say one more word and you are fired!
(Cf. **Hvis du siger ...**	If you say ...)

Note 3 – In certain idiomatic phrases the imperative may be merely implied, e.g. **Hold** (Keep) is implied in **Fingrene væk!**, Hands off!

534 The subjunctive

(a) Form

The present subjunctive does not exist as an independent form in Danish as it is formally identical with the infinitive. This means that consonant stems end in **-e**, while vowel stems end in the vowel in question (cf. 502(a)). The past subjunctive has now been replaced by constructions with modal verbs.

(b) Use

The present subjunctive has a very restricted use in modern Danish. It is found almost exclusively in fixed, formulaic expressions:

(i) Wishes, requests:

Gud velsigne dig!	God bless you!
Formanden længe leve!	Three cheers for the chairman!

(ii) Curses (functioning as expletives) (see 807):

Fanden tage ham!	(*lit.*) May the Devil take him!
Kræft æde mig!	(*lit.*) May cancer eat me!
Den onde lyne mig!	(*lit.*) May the Evil One strike me with lightning!

(iii) Concessions:

Forstå det, hvem der kan.	Whatever that means.
koste, hvad det vil	whatever the cost
... hun være sig rig eller fattig.	... be she rich or poor.

(c) Subjunctive meaning expressed by other means

(i) Unreal or counterfactual situations introduced by **bare/gid**:

These may refer to the present, the past or the future and may use a finite verb form or a modal auxiliary + infinitive. Notice that **bare/gid** functions as a verb in this type of construction:

Bare han ikke var så dum!	I wish he wasn't so stupid!
Bare der ikke er sket noget!	I hope nothing has happened!
Gid det må gå dig godt!	I hope you'll do well!

(ii) Subjunctive 'were' in English - **var** in Danish:

While English sometimes uses the subjunctive 'were' as an alternative to 'was', only **var** is possible in Danish:

Hvis jeg var dig ...	If I were you ...
Hvis det var tilfældet ...	If that was/were the case ...
Hvis hun var yngre ...	If she was/were younger ...

(iii) Other hypothetical conditional clauses

See also 525(b)(ii).

These are used to express an imagined situation in the present or the past. The hypothetical content is signalled by a shift in the tense of the verb, viz. present ⇨ past; past ⇨ past perfect. Note that the main clause often contains a modal auxiliary:

Hvis vi havde råd, ville vi købe nye møbler.
If we could afford it, we would buy new furniture.

Hvis du havde ringet, havde jeg ikke været urolig.
Hvis du havde ringet, ville jeg ikke have været urolig.
If you had phoned, I wouldn't have been worried.

E TRANSITIVE, INTRANSITIVE AND REFLEXIVE VERBS

535 Introduction

(a) *Transitive* verbs are verbs that take a direct object:

Vi dyrker grøntsager.	We grow vegetables.

Many transitive verbs can also be used intransitively. (See 536(b)(iv).)

(b) *Intransitive* verbs are verbs that do not take an object:

De ankom til hotellet.	They arrived at the hotel.

(c) *Reflexive* verbs (see 537) are verbs that consist of a verb + a reflexive pronoun (cf. 410). They are intransitive insofar as the reflexive pronoun replaces the object:

Transitive:	**Han vasker bilen.**	He washes the car.
Reflexive:	**Han vasker sig.**	He washes himself.

536 Transitive and intransive verbs

(a) Related pairs

Some transitive and intransitive verbs exist in pairs with related forms and meanings. Quite often the transitive verb is weak, while the intransitive verb is strong:

Transitive	*Intransitive*
fælde, fell	**falde**, fall
lægge, lay, place	**ligge**, lie
sprænge, blow up	**springe**, spring, jump
stille, place (upright)	**stå**, stand
sænke, sink (a ship, etc.)	**synke**, sink (into water)
sætte, set, place	**sidde**, sit

Very occasionally both verbs are weak:

vække, wake up (someone)	**vågne**, wake up (of one's own accord)

Note 1 – Even clearly intransitive verbs may be used transitively in fixed collocations, e.g.:

at springe soldat	to do national service
at stå distancen	to go the distance/stay the course
at stå brud	to be a bride
at sidde/stå model	to pose as a model

Note 2 – A transitive verb may be identical in form with an intransitive verb, e.g. **synke**, swallow (trans.)/sink (intrans.).

(b) Transitive verbs

(i) Some verbs are transitive only, i.e. they must have a direct object:

Vi fandt løsningen.	We found the solution.
Hun tømte askebægeret.	She emptied the ashtray.

Notice that the corresponding English verb is sometimes used intransitively:

Jeg forlod kontoret tidligt.	I left (the office) early.
De kyssede hinanden.	They kissed (each other).

(ii) Certain verbs are *ditransitive*, i.e. they take two objects, a direct object (DO) and an indirect object (IO):

Ulla	**gav**	**Brian**	**kagen.**
subj.	*verb*	*IO*	*DO*
Ulla	gave	Brian	the cake.

Some (potentially) ditransitive verbs:

berøve, deprive of; **betro**, entrust; **efterlade**, leave; **fortælle**, tell; **give**, give; **love**, promise; **låne**, lend; **meddele**, inform of; **misunde**, envy; **sende**, send; **sige**, say; **skænke**, donate, pour; **tiltro**, credit with; **unde**, not begrudge

Notice, however, that the indirect object can also be expressed by means of a prepositional phrase with **til**:

Ulla	**gav**	**kagen**	**til Brian.**
subj.	*verb*	*DO*	*IO*
Ulla	gave	the cake	to Brian.

(iii) Most transitive verbs can appear in passive constructions. The direct object in an active sentence becomes the subject in the corresponding passive sentence, leaving the latter without a direct object (see 541):

Claus ejer cyklen.	⇨	**Cyklen ejes af Claus.**
Claus owns the bike.		The bike is owned by Claus.

(iv) Many transitive verbs can also be used intransitively, but when this is the case, an object is generally 'understood'. Such verbs are therefore at least potentially transitive:

Ryger hun (cigaretter, etc.)**?**	Does she smoke (cigarettes, etc.)?
De sad og spiste (mad, etc.).	They were eating (food, etc.).
Vi vasker (tøj, etc.) **hver dag.**	We wash (clothes, etc.) every day.

However, in some cases the verb has acquired a slightly different meaning when used intransitively. Compare:

Han drikker te om morgenen.	He drinks tea in the morning.
Jeg tror, at han drikker.	I think that he drinks (i.e. alcohol).
Så skød jægeren haren.	Then the huntsman shot the hare.
Så skød jægeren.	Then the huntsman fired.

(c) Intransitive verbs

(i) Some verbs are intransitive only, i.e. they cannot take a direct object:

Du lyver!	You are lying!
Billedet forsvandt pludselig.	The picture suddenly disappeared.

(ii) A special group of intransitive verbs is made up of the so-called *copulas*. These are verbs which are functionally identical to the verb **være** (be) and which, instead of an object, can take a subject complement, usually in the form of a noun or an adjective (see 1006):

subj.	*copula*	*subject complement*	
Jens	**er**	**elektriker.**	Jens is an electrician.
Karin	**blev**	**meget vred.**	Karin became very angry.

Copulas may be divided into two groups: *current* copulas and *resulting* copulas:

1 Current copulas, indicating a state of affairs, include:

forblive, remain, stay; **forekomme**, appear, seem; **forholde sig**, remain, stay; **føle sig**, feel; **lyde**, sound; **se ... ud**, look; **synes**, appear, seem; **være**, be

Note – **Lugte** (smell) and **smage** (taste) are not treated as copulas in Danish, unlike their English equivalents. Thus in constructions where 'smell' and 'taste' combine with an adjective, **lugte** and **smage** are followed by an adverb (note the adverbial ending **-t**):

Vinen lugter godt.	The wine smells good.
(Cf. **Vinen er god.**	The wine is good.)
Maden smager lækkert.	The food tastes delicious.
(Cf. **Maden er lækker.**	The food is delicious.)

2 Resulting copulas, implying a change, include:

blive, become; **vise sig (at være)**, turn out (to be); **vokse sig**, grow; etc.

(iii) Some intransitive verbs can take a 'cognate' object, i.e. an object consisting of a noun which is etymologically related to the verb. This is more common in Danish than in English:

Hun lever livet.	She lives life to the full.
Han sov de retfærdiges søvn.	He slept the sleep of the just.

(iv) Some intransitive verbs are made transitive by adding the prefix **be-**:

sejre	⇨	**besejre**
win		defeat

Other examples:

bearbejde, adapt/process; **bebo**, inhabit; **begrænse**, limit; **belyse**, illuminate

537 Reflexive verbs

For the forms and use of reflexive pronouns see 410.

(a) Reflexive verbs consist of a verb + a reflexive pronoun. Since verb + pronoun forms a unit, reflexive verbs are by definition intransitive, the reflexive pronoun occupying the object position. The reflexive pronoun refers to the subject of the clause and must agree with it in person and number:

Jeg morede mig til festen.	I enjoyed myself at the party.
Vi stillede os ved døren.	We placed ourselves by the door.
De opførte sig pænt.	They behaved themselves.

(b) A number of Danish verbs can be used both transitively and reflexively:

Transitive	*Reflexive*
Hun satte vasen på bordet.	**Hun satte sig på bordet.**
She put the vase on the table.	She sat down on the table.
Han skar brødet i skiver.	**Han skar sig på kniven.**
He cut the bread in slices.	He cut himself on the knife.

Other examples:

bevæge/bevæge sig, move; **bøje/bøje sig**, bend; **føle/føle sig**, feel; **gemme/gemme sig**, hide; **lægge/lægge sig**, lay/lie down; **vende/vende sig**, turn (round); **vise/vise sig**, show/appear; etc.

(c) Some verbs occur only as reflexive verbs, e.g.:

begive sig, set off; **forivre sig**, get carried away; **forlove sig**, become engaged; **henvende sig**, address, turn to; **indfinde sig**, present oneself; **påtage sig**, take on; **skynde sig**, hurry; **vægre sig**, refuse; etc.

(d) A number of verbs which are reflexive in Danish are intransitive in English in the equivalent sense. Notice that many of these indicate movement:

beklage sig, complain; **bevæge sig**, move; **forandre sig**, change; **glæde sig**, rejoice; **klæde sig på/af**, dress/undress; **lægge sig**, lie down; **parre sig**, mate; **rejse sig**, get/stand up; **skynde sig**, hurry; **sætte sig**, sit down; **vise sig**, appear; **ærgre sig**, feel annoyed; etc.

F -S FORMS OF VERBS AND THE PASSIVE VOICE

538 Introduction

(a) Form

	Infinitive	*Present*	*Past*	*Past participle*	*Meaning*
I - cons.	**lykkes**	**lykkes**	**lykkedes**	**lykkedes**	succeed
I - vowel	**vies**	**vies**	**viedes**	**viedes**	marry (trans.)
II	**mødes**	**mødes**	**mødtes**	**mødtes**	meet
III	**lægges**	**lægges**	**lagdes**	**lagdes**	lay, place
IV	**slås**	**slås**	**sloges**	**sloges**	fight

(i) The infinitive adds **-s** to the active infinitive for both consonant and vowel stems. Deponent verbs and others with no active form have an identical form.

(ii) The present **-s** form is identical to the infinitive **-s** form.

(iii) The past tense of weak verbs adds **-s** to the active past tense form, while the past tense of strong verbs adds **-es** to the active past tense form. Deponent verbs and others with no active form have a similar form to weak verbs.

(iv) The past particle, in the rare cases where it occurs, is identical with the past tense **-s** form, but in nearly all cases a form with **blive** is used instead:

Bilen er blevet repareret. The car has been repaired.

(b) Use

There are three distinct uses of the **-s** form of verbs: deponent verbs, reciprocal verbs and the passive **-s** form.

(i) Deponent verbs (see 539):

Jeg mindes ikke noget lignende. I don't remember anything like it.

(ii) Reciprocal verbs (see 540):

Vi mødes i morgen aften. — We'll meet tomorrow evening.

(iii) The passive **-s** form (see 542):

De ventes på søndag. — They are expected on Sunday.

539 Deponent verbs

(a) Deponent verbs are verbs that have passive form (**-s** form) but active meaning. They may be transitive or intransitive:

Der findes mange dyrearter. — There exist many species of animals.
Hun mindedes sin ungdom. — She recalled her youth.
Jeg synes, at det er en god idé. — I think that it's a good idea.

Examples of deponent verbs:

dages, dawn; **fattes**, lack; **findes**, be, exist; **færdes**, move, travel; **grønnes**, become green; **kendes ved**, acknowledge; **længes**, long; **lykkes**, succeed; **mindes**, remember; **mislykkes**, fail; **omgås**, handle, mix with; **rygtes**, be rumoured; **synes**, seem, think; **trives**, thrive; **væmmes**, feel disgusted; **ældes**, become older; etc.

Note – In contrast to its English equivalent 'succeed', **lykkes** cannot have an animate subject in Danish:

Forsøget lykkedes. — The attempt was successful.
Det lykkedes ham at bestå eksamen. — He succeeded in passing the exam.
Det er lykkedes hende at få et job. — She has succeeded in getting a job.

(b) Whereas deponent verbs all appear in the infinitive, the present and the past tense, they do not all occur naturally in the composite tenses. Of the verbs mentioned in (a), this is certainly true of **fattes, grønnes, trives, væmmes, ældes**.

Der har fandtes bjørne i Danmark.
There have once been bears in Denmark.

Jeg har længtes efter foråret.
I have longed for spring.

Hun havde længe syntes, at arbejdet var kedeligt.
She had long thought that the work was boring.

(c) Deponent verbs cannot normally be used in the imperative, but note, e.g.:

Omgås skydevåben med forsigtighed!
Handle firearms with care!

(d) Deponent verbs do not possess a form without **-s**. Where a verb with such a form exists (e.g. **finde/findes, minde/mindes**, etc.), there will usually be a marked difference in meaning from the deponent verb, and they must be regarded as two separate verbs. Compare:

Han mindede mig om mødet. He reminded me of the meeting.
Jeg mindes ikke hans tale. I can't remember his speech.

540 Reciprocal verbs

(a) Some **-s** verbs are reciprocal in the sense that the individuals denoted by the subject carry out the action on a mutual basis, i.e. x (verb) y and y (verb) x. Reciprocal verbs are intransitive since the implied object is contained in the verb itself:

Vi enedes om at gå hjem. We agreed on going home.
De skiltes som gode venner. They parted as good friends.

Reciprocal verbs do not often occur in the imperative (cf. 533(b)), but note, e.g.:

Skændes/Slås nu ikke! Don't argue/fight!

Examples of reciprocal verbs:

brydes, clash, wrestle; **enes**, agree, get on; **forliges**, become reconciled; **følges (ad)**, accompany (each other); **hjælpes (ad)**, help (each other); **kappes**, compete; **kives**, bicker; **mødes**, meet; **samles**, gather; **ses**, meet; **skiftes**, take turns; **skilles**, part; **skændes**, quarrel; **slås**, fight; **tales ved**, talk; **træffes**, meet; **trættes**, quarrel; etc.

Only some of them occur naturally in the composite tenses:

Vi har ofte fulgtes på arbejde. We have often gone to work

(b) A few reciprocal verbs can even be used with a singular subject, although the activity involved presupposes at least two individuals. The notion of 'plurality' may in these cases be expressed by the preposition **med** (with) + complement:

Den dreng slås altid.	That boy is always fighting.
Jeg skal mødes med min ven.	I'm going to meet my friend.

(c) Reciprocal meaning can also be expressed by a transitive verb + the reciprocal pronoun **hinanden**, each other (see 411). Sometimes the same verb can appear in both constructions:

Vi hjælper hinanden. / Vi hjælpes ad.	We help each other.
De mødte hinanden. / De mødtes.	They met.

Note – Some verbs which until quite recently could appear as reciprocal **-s** verbs, such as **kysses**, kiss, now only occur with the reciprocal pronoun **hinanden**:

De kyssede hinanden lidenskabeligt.	They kissed (each other) passionately.

541 The passive voice – introduction

(a) The relationship between active and passive sentences

(i) Active and passive sentences are syntactically related. Under normal circumstances, when an active sentence is turned into the equivalent passive sentence, three things happen:

1 The *object* of the active sentence becomes the subject of the passive sentence.

2 The *subject* of the active sentence becomes a prepositional complement governed by the preposition **af** (by) in the passive sentence. However, this prepositional phrase can be, and often is, omitted.

3 The *verb* changes from an active to a passive form. Notice that the verb usually has to be transitive (but see (c) below).

These changes may be summed up as follows:

Active sentence		*Passive sentence*
object	⇨	subject
subject	⇨	(**af** +) prepositional complement
active verb form	⇨	passive verb form

Example:

Active:	**Løven**	**jager**	**zebraen.**
	subject	active verb	object
	The lion	chases	the zebra.
Passive:	**Zebraen**	**jages/bliver jaget**	**af løven.**
	subject	passive verb	prep. phrase
	The zebra	is chased	by the lion.

This change is sometimes called the *passive transformation*.

(ii) A change from an active to a passive sentence is a *syntactic* change, which does *not* change the basic *meaning* of the sentence. In the example above, it is the lion that does the chasing and the zebra that is being chased in both sentences. That means that the *semantic* roles of *agent* (the one that carries out the action, i.e. the 'doer') and *patient* (the one that the action is directed against, i.e. the 'sufferer') are unaffected by the change. This can be demonstrated as follows:

Active:	**Løven**	**jager**	**zebraen.**
syntactic level:	subject	active verb	object
semantic level:	agent		patient
	The lion	chases	the zebra.
Passive:	**Zebraen**	**jages/bliver jaget**	**af løven.**
syntactic level:	subject	passive verb	prep. phrase
semantic level:	patient		agent
	The zebra	is chased	by the lion.

However, one thing *has* changed in terms of meaning, viz. the *focus* of the sentence. In the active sentence, the focus is on the agent (i.e. the lion), while in the passive sentence the focus is on the patient (i.e. the zebra). The active sentence would therefore be appropriate in a 'story' about the lion, the passive sentence in one about the zebra.

(b) The agent in passive sentences

The agent in a passive sentence is frequently omitted if it is unknown, unimportant or obvious:

Han blev dræbt på slagmarken.	He was killed on the battlefield.
Middagen serveredes i salen.	The dinner was served in the hall.
Mødet blev holdt på kroen.	The meeting was held at the inn.

(c) Some 'impersonal' passive constructions do not have any agent at all. Notice that even intransitive verbs can have passive form when **der** or **her** is used as formal subject. This type of construction has no parallel in English:

Transitive verbs	
Der blev spist og drukket meget.	People ate and drank a lot.
Her må gøres noget.	Something must be done here.
Intransitive verbs	
Der festedes til kl. 2.	They went on partying till 2 a.m.
Der snakkes, men handles ikke.	There is talk but no action.

(d) If the indirect object becomes the subject in the passive sentence, the direct object may remain unchanged:

Han frakendtes kørekortet.	His driving licence was suspended.
Hun idømtes en bøde.	She was given a fine.

However, this is not always possible in Danish, e.g.:

***Jeg blev fortalt nyheden.**	I was told the news.
***Han blev givet et ur.**	He was given a watch.

(e) There are two main types of passive construction in Danish plus a third, somewhat different version:

(i) The **-s** passive (where the verb has the ending **-s**) (see 542):

Dørene lukkes kl. 7.	The doors are closed at 7 o'clock.

(ii) The **blive** passive constructed with a form of **blive** + past participle (see 543). (For the form of the past participle see 502(d),(g) and 530):

Dørene bliver lukket nu.	The doors are being closed now.

(iii) A form of **være** + past participle (see 544). Owing to the difference in meaning, this is not in competition with the two other forms:

Dørene er lukkede nu.	The doors are now closed.

These three forms will be dealt with in greater detail in 542–44.

542 The -s passive

(a) The **-s** passive is much less used than the **blive** passive. It is formed by adding the ending **-s** to the infinitive, the present tense (which drops its **-r** ending) or the past tense form of the verb. The composite tenses (the perfect, the past perfect, etc.) are rarely found with the **-s** passive:

Maleriet kan ses på museet.	The painting can be seen at the museum.
Slottet ejes af en fond.	The castle is owned by a foundation.
Hun forventedes at møde op.	She was expected to turn up.

Note – Vowel stems in **-i** and **-y** add **-(e)s** in the infinitive and the present tense, e.g. **befri(e)s**, be/are/is set free; **forny(e)s**, be/are/is renewed; etc.

(b) The infinitive of the **-s** passive most often occurs after a modal verb. In general, the non-epistemic modals require the **-s** passive, while the epistemic modals usually combine with the **blive** passive (see 543). (For the term 'epistemic' see 532(b)):

Brevet bør afsendes i dag.	The letter should be sent off today.
Græsset må ikke betrædes.	Do not walk on the grass.
Verden vil bedrages.	The world wants to be fooled.

(c) The vast majority of instances of the **-s** passive occur in the present tense. They may express the following verbal meanings (but see also 543):

(i) A habitual or repeated action:

Her arbejdes der altid hårdt.	Here people always work hard.
Varer udbringes om fredagen.	Goods are delivered on Fridays.

(ii) General requests or prohibitions:

Alle bedes møde op.	Everybody is requested to attend.
Rygning frabedes!	No smoking!
Uvedkommende forbydes adgang!	No admittance to unauthorized persons!

(iii) Certain verbs indicating 'possession', 'opinion', 'knowledge' or 'need' usually occur with the **-s** passive:

Statuen ejes af greven.	The statue is owned by the count.

Det menes at være sandt. It is thought to be true.
Der vides endnu intet. Nothing is known yet.
Der trænges til nye idéer. New ideas are needed.

(iv) Other verbs that frequently occur with the **-s** passive:

angre, repent; **behøve**, need; **besidde**, possess; **erfare**, learn; **få**, get; **have**, have; **håbe**, hope; **indse**, realize; **miste**, lose; **skylde**, owe; **tænke**, think

Note – The verbs **have** and **vide**, which have irregular active forms (**har** and **ved**, respectively) in the present tense, have regular corresponding passive forms: **haves** and **vides**.

(d) The **-s** passive is used far less in the past tense than in the present tense. With a few exceptions, it is confined to weak verbs (including some of those mentioned in (c) above) with the endings **-ede** or **-te**, which simply add an **-s** in the passive, but even among these the **-s** passive is not very common and is usually replaced by the **blive** passive:

Use of -s passive
Han pintes af anger. He was tormented by remorse.
Der spistes altid præcis kl. 20. Dinner was always at exactly 8 p.m.
Der ventedes nyt om ulykken. News was expected about the accident.

Use of either passive form
Billedet fjernedes/blev fjernet. The picture was removed.
Han sendtes/blev sendt i byen. He was sent shopping.
Vinderen udråbtes/blev udråbt. The winner was announced.

Few strong verbs with zero-ending accept the **-s** passive in the past tense, but **se** (see) does:

Hun sås ofte i teatret. She was often seen in the theatre.

In other cases, it often has an old-fashioned ring:

Der gaves ingen pardon. No quarter was given.

Some strong verbs with past tense **-t** ending allow a passive form:

Mødet afholdtes på hotellet. The meeting took place at the hotel.
Kampen vandtes af hjemmeholdet. The match was won by the home team.

543 The **blive** passive

The passive constructed by means of **blive** + past participle is by far the most widely used of the two main passive forms. Apart from those instances where the **-s** passive is obligatory or at least possible (see 542), the **blive** passive dominates the use of passive in Danish. Unlike the **-s** passive, it is commonly used in the composite tenses.

(a) The infinitive

(i) The infinitive of the **blive** passive is generally used after epistemic modals, i.e. those that express such notions as 'possibility', 'logical necessity' and 'future' (cf. 532(b)). Compare the different meanings of the following sentence pairs (the first example in each pair shows epistemic use):

Han kan blive afskediget. He may be sacked. (It may happen.)
Han kan afskediges. He can be sacked. (Nothing prevents it.)

Kampen må blive udsat. The match must be postponed.
(It seems necessary, but no decision has been taken.)
Kampen må udsættes. The match has to be postponed.
(It is necessary, the decision has been taken.)

De vil blive rost på mødet. They will be praised at the meeting.
De vil roses på mødet. They want to be praised at the meeting.

(ii) **Skal** + passive infinitive can only be non-epistemic, but there is nevertheless a clear difference in meaning between the two passive forms:

Sagen skal blive undersøgt. The matter shall be examined. (i.e. promise)
Sagen skal undersøges. The matter is to be examined. (i.e. necessity)

However, with past tense **skulle**, the distinction between epistemic and non-epistemic use (the first with non-past meaning) again becomes relevant:

Sagen skulle blive undersøgt. The matter will probably be examined.
Sagen skulle undersøges. The matter was to be examined.

Notice also the epistemic use ('report') of **skal** in connection with a past event:

Han skal være blevet overfaldet.
He is said to have been attacked.

(iii) **Bør/burde** (both with non-past meaning) can also combine with the two kinds of passive infinitive, but with little or no difference of meaning:

Han bør/burde blive straffet. He ought to be punished.
Han bør/burde straffes. He ought to be punished.

(b) The present tense

Apart from the types of verb mentioned in 542(c)(iii), which most naturally appear with the **-s** passive, the two passive constructions are sometimes in competition in the present tense, whereas at other times the **blive** passive is the only possibility. Some guidelines can be laid down for their various uses:

(i) Referring to a current activity or state of affairs

Here both possibilities may exist:

Han drilles i skolen. He is teased at school.
Han bliver drillet i skolen. He is teased at school.

There is a tendency to use the **-s** passive about a long-term or repeated action and the **blive** passive about a single event:

Posten udbringes hver dag. The post is delivered every day.
Posten bliver udbragt nu. The post is being delivered now.

Biler købes og sælges. Cars are bought and sold.
Min bil bliver solgt i dag. My car will be sold today.

But the **blive** passive can also be used about a repeated action:

Vi bliver kørt hjem hver dag. We are driven home every day.

(ii) Referring to a future activity or event

When the verb has obvious future time reference, the **blive** passive is nearly always preferred. Notice that in such cases the equivalent English sentence often uses the future tense:

Vi bliver hentet på stationen. We'll be met at the station.

But here too there may be vacillation. Thus it is hard to see any difference in meaning between the following two sentences:

Kampen spilles på Wembley.
The match will be played at Wembley.

Kampen bliver spillet på Wembley.
The match will be played at Wembley.

(iii) Some deponent and reciprocal verbs (see 539ff) have a parallel non-deponent/reciprocal transitive verb with a different meaning. Such verbs usually take the **blive** passive:

Nøglen bliver nok ikke fundet.	The key will probably not be found.
(Cf. **Nøglen findes nok ikke.**	The key probably doesn't exist.)
Børnene bliver slået i skolen.	The children are beaten at school.
(Cf. **Børnene slås i skolen.**	The children fight at school.)

(iv) In general, the **blive** passive is more common with a concrete (especially human) subject than with an abstract subject:

Vi bliver ofte påvirket af støj.	We are often affected by noise.
Vores helbred påvirkes af røg.	Our health is affected by smoke.

But this distinction is far from strictly observed. In the spoken language, in particular, the **blive** passive is completely dominant and in most cases the **-s** passive would not be possible at all.

(c) The past tense and the composite tenses

As pointed out in 542, the use of the **-s** passive in the past tense is extremely limited, and it is virtually absent in the composite tenses. Consequently, the vast majority of the verbs that can appear in the passive take the **blive** passive in these tenses:

Past tense

Hun blev væltet af cyklen.	She was knocked off her bike.
Idéen blev stjålet af firmaet.	The idea was stolen by the firm.
Patienten blev hjulpet af lægen.	The patient was helped by the doctor.

Composite tenses

Huset er blevet solgt.	The house has been sold.
Brevet var blevet skrevet.	The letter had been written.

544 Være + past participle

This construction can range from being closely related to the **blive** passive, in which case the participle has a clearly verbal function, to being a kind of 'copula + subject complement', in which case the participle has an adjectival function.

(a) Participle with verbal function

When the participle has verbal function, this construction usually describes the result of a completed action, i.e. it emphasizes a state rather than the action which brought it about. However, the semantic relationship between the participle and the subject remains that of verb and patient, as in the **blive** passive. Notice that English examples are often ambiguous since 'be' is used for both **blive** and **være**:

Bogen er oversat.	The book is translated.	*a state*
Bogen er blevet oversat.	The book has been translated.	*an action*

The two constructions thus represent cause and effect, which, using the example above, may be expressed in the following way:

Action	*Result/State*
Bogen er blevet oversat,	**så nu er den oversat.**
The book has been translated,	so now it is translated.

When the participle has verbal function, it is unchanged in the plural:

Sagen er afgjort.	The matter is decided.
Træerne er fældet.	The trees are cut down.
Flagene var hejst.	The flags were hoisted.

(b) Participle with adjectival function

When the notion of an action is vague or absent, the participle may take on the function of an adjective. This may have consequences not only for the meaning, but also for the form of the participle. Since past participles already have a **-t** ending, the adjectival gender distinction between the common gender zero-ending and the neuter **-t** ending cannot be exploited, but the plural adjectival ending **-e** (where formally possible) is often used in these cases (see 205, 530(c)):

Singular	
Hun er (u)gift.	She is (un)married.
Døren er lukket.	The door is closed.
Vandet er frosset.	The water is frozen.
Plural	
Mulighederne er begrænsede.	The possibilities are limited.
Vinduerne er lukkede.	The windows are closed.
Grøntsagerne er frosne.	The vegetables are frozen.

545 Alternative constructions to the passive

Certain active constructions may compete with passive ones:

(a) Man + an active verb (for the use of **man** in general see 445)

The indefinite pronoun **man** has such vague personal reference that it sometimes alternates with an impersonal passive construction with **det/der** + passive verb:

Man venter mange mennesker.	They expect many people.
Der ventes mange mennesker.	Many people are expected.
Man siger, at han er syg.	They say that he is ill.
Det/Der siges, at han er syg.	It is said that he is ill.
Man gør meget for de unge.	They do a lot for young people.
Der gøres meget for de unge.	A lot is done for young people.
Der bliver gjort meget for de unge.	A lot is done for young people.

(b) De or **folk** + an active verb

In both (i) and (ii) below, the range of verbs that can occur is rather limited:

(i) When **de** (they) is used without specific reference, it comes close in meaning to **man**:

De sender kampen i fjernsynet.	They'll show the match on the television.

(Cf. **Kampen sendes i fjernsynet.**	The match'll be shown on the television.)
De siger, at der kommer sne.	They say that there'll be snow.
(Cf. **Det siges, at der ...**)	

(ii) **Folk** (people) may be used with similarly vague reference:

Folk påstår, at det ikke passer.	People claim that it isn't true.
(Cf. **Det påstås, at det ...**)	
Folk siger, at han bliver valgt.	People say that he'll be elected.
(Cf. **Det siges, at han ...**)	

G COMPOUND VERBS

546 Introduction

A compound verb is a verb that has a prefix, a particle or another type of word attached to it. In some compound verbs, this prefix/particle, etc., is an integral part of the verb and cannot be separated from it. These are known as *inseparable* compounds and they generally inflect in the same way as the uncompounded form (but see 503(i)):

Infinitive	*Past*	*Past participle*	*Meaning*
stå	**stod**	**stået**	stand
forstå	**forstod**	**forstået**	understand

In other cases, a particle (i.e. an adverb or a preposition) is more loosely attached to the verb and may be separated from it. These verbs are known as *separable* compounds (see 548):

stå op, get up, rise; **tage til**, increase

Sometimes a verb may be either separable or inseparable without any real difference in meaning:

underskrive/skrive under, sign

or the two forms may have very different meanings and must be considered as completely separate verbs:

nedkomme, give birth; **komme ned**, get down

547 Inseparable compound verbs

The most important types of inseparable compound verb may be grouped as follows:

(a) Most verbs compounded with nouns:

bogføre, enter into a ledger; **brolægge**, pave; **håndhæve**, enforce; **landsætte**, land (e.g. troops); **pantsætte**, pawn; **planlægge**, plan; **rådgive**, advise; **støvsuge**, vacuum-clean; **vejlede**, guide; etc.

(b) Most verbs compounded with adjectives:

dybfryse, deep-freeze; **frikende**, acquit; **fuldende/fuldføre/færdiggøre**, complete; **godkende**, approve; **vildlede**, mislead; etc.

(c) Most verbs compounded with other verbs:

brændemærke, brand; **sultestrejke**, go on hungerstrike; **trøstespise**, eat between meals (to comfort oneself); etc.

Note – When a verb is used as the first part of a compound verb, it sometimes acts as an uptoner (cf. 615). Notice that in these examples the infinitive **-e** of the first part of the compound is dropped:

snorksove, sleep like a log; **spilkoge**, boil furiously; **tudbrøle**, blubber; **øsregne**, rain cats and dogs; etc.

(d) Verbs compounded with numerals (very few types of verb can enter into these compounds):

tredele, divide into three; **fir(e)doble**, quadruple; etc.

(e) Verbs compounded with **selv-** (very few in number):

selvangive, fill in one's tax return; **selvantænde**, self-ignite; etc.

(f) Verbs compounded with adverbs or prepositions

This is the most heterogenous group since some of them may be both inseparable and separable, with or without a difference in meaning, while others can only be one or the other.

Examples of inseparable verbs:

> **bortforklare**, explain away; **forbigå**, ignore, overlook; **gennemføre**, complete; **opnå**, achieve; **overdrive**, exaggerate; **tilstå**, confess; **udfordre**, challenge; **undervise**, teach; **vedrøre**, concern; etc.

Note – In compounds, the adverb **igen** always appears as **gen-**, **(i)gennem** as **gennem-** and **(i)mod** as **mod-**:

> **gengælde**, repay; **genkende**, recognize; **genlyde**, echo; **genoptage**, renew; **gennembore**, drill through; **gennemføre**, carry out; **gennemtvinge**, enforce; **modsige**, contradict; **modtage**, receive; **modvirke**, counteract; etc.

(g) Verbs compounded with prefixes:

(i) Unstressed prefixes:

be-	**bestemme**	decide
er-	**erhverve**	acquire
for-	**forstå**	understand

(ii) Stressed prefixes:

an-	**anvende**	use
bi-	**bidrage**	contribute
fore-	**foregribe**	anticipate
hen-	**henrykke**	delight
mis-	**mistænke**	suspect
sam-	**samtykke**	consent
und-	**undslippe**	escape
van-	**vanære**	disgrace

548 Separable verbs

These may be divided into two main groups: (a) those that always appear separated and (b) those that may appear both separated and compounded.

(a) Some Danish verbs, while constituting a semantic unit, are always separated into verb + particle. They are mostly intransitive and the stress is on the particle. English has far more separable verbs (known as 'phrasal verbs' or 'prepositional verbs') than Danish has:

bort	**løbe bort**	run away

fra	**sige fra**	back out
igen	**slå igen**	hit back
ned	**falde ned**	fall down
om	**vende om**	turn round
omkuld	**falde omkuld**	fall over
op	**holde op**	cease, stop
over	**gå over**	pass away
til	**køre til**	drive fast
ud	**se ud**	look

If the past participle of separable verbs can be used as an adjective, it will have a compounded form (cf. 547):

en bortløben hund	a runaway dog
nedfaldne æbler	windfall apples

(b) Some verbs can appear as both separated and compounded with little or no difference in meaning. They are transitive and, where a separated form is used, the object will be placed between the verb and the particle:

Han skrev brevet under.	He signed the letter.
Han underskrev brevet.	He signed the letter.

Other examples:

af	**spærre af**	**afspærre**	cordon off
fast	**gøre fast**	**fastgøre**	fasten
frem	**rykke frem**	**fremrykke**	advance
igennem	**læse igennem**	**gennemlæse**	read through
ind	**sætte ind**	**indsætte**	put in
ned	**kaste ned**	**nedkaste**	throw down
op	**tælle op**	**optælle**	count
over	**strege over**	**overstrege**	cross out
sammen	**bringe sammen**	**sammenbringe**	bring together
ud	**sende ud**	**udsende**	send out

(c) Some compounded verbs have no separated parallel, either (i) because of a gap in the system (e.g. **aflyse**, cancel; **underkende**, disallow; but *not* ***lyse af**; ***kende under**) or (ii) because the second part does not exist as an independent verb (e.g. **indlemme**, incorporate; **overnatte**, stay overnight; but there are no such verbs as ***lemme**; ***natte**).

549 Separated or compounded forms – stylistic differences

Even when both separated and compounded forms exist with little or no difference in meaning, there is usually at least a stylistic difference between them, i.e. they often display different degrees of formality. Generally speaking, the separated form is typically used in the spoken and informal written language, whereas the compounded form is found in more formal contexts such as official reports, documents, religious language, etc. This difference may be illustrated by the following sentence pairs:

Han lagde pakken ned på bordet. He put the parcel down on the table.	**Han nedlagde en krans på graven.** He laid a wreath on the grave.
Jeg sendte fem indbydelser ud. I sent out five invitations.	**Radioen udsendte koncerten.** The radio transmitted the concert.
John steg ned ad stigen. John climbed down the ladder.	**Kristus nedsteg til dødsriget.** Christ descended into hell.

However, participles used as adjectives always have a compounded form:

en opvartende tjener (cf. **varte op**), an attending waiter
vores udsendte medarbejder (cf. **sende ud**), our special correspondent

550 Separated or compounded forms – semantic differences

There is often a difference in meaning between the separated and the compounded form, but this too may be a matter of degree. Broadly speaking, we can distinguish between (a) the cases where the semantic difference between the two forms is somehow transparent, and (b) the cases where the two meanings are completely divorced from each other. Whereas separated forms usually have *concrete* or *literal* meaning, the compounded forms of type (a) above most often have *figurative* meaning and those of type (b) above *abstract* meaning. But it is sometimes difficult to decide where to draw the line between the two types.

(a) Literal vs. figurative meaning

The literal meaning of separated verbs may in compounded verb forms be 'extended' to become figurative, even though it is still possible to see a connection between the two meanings:

Literal meaning	*Figurative meaning*
De førte fangen ind. They brought the prisoner in.	**De indførte en ny regel.** They introduced a new rule.
Han tog flasken ud. He got out the bottle.	**Han udtog holdet.** He selected the team.
Hun stregede ordet under. She underlined the word.	**Hun understregede ordets betydning.** She emphasized the meaning of the word.

Other examples:

kaste ud, throw out/**udkaste**, outline; **lyse op**, illuminate/**oplyse**, enlighten; **stille frem**, put out/**fremstille**, produce

(b) Literal vs. abstract meaning

Sometimes it is difficult or impossible to see any semantic connection between the two forms:

Literal meaning	*Abstract meaning*
Han holdt hånden under. He held his hand under.	**Han underholdt publikum.** He entertained the audience.
Hun kom ned fra loftet. She came down from the attic.	**Hun nedkom med tvillinger.** She gave birth to twins.
Jeg satte over åen. I jumped across the stream.	**Jeg oversatte bogen.** I translated the book.

Other examples:

gå under, go down/**undergå**, undergo; **nå op**, reach/**opnå**, achieve

(c) Literal – figurative – abstract meaning

There are certain cases where a compounded form may have both a figurative and an abstract meaning:

Literal	*Figurative*	*Abstract*
Jeg gik over gaden. I crossed the street.	**Huset overgik til mig.** The house passed to me.	**Det overgik mine drømme.** It exceeded my dreams.

Vi satte kassen ned.	**Vi nedsatte prisen.**	**Vi nedsatte et udvalg.**
We put the box down.	We lowered the price.	We set up a committee.

(d) As before (see 548(a), 549), participles used as adjectives have compounded form only, but notice that participles of the verbs mentioned in (a)–(c) above usually appear with their figurative/abstract meaning. Thus we may find:

et nedsat udvalg, but *not* ***en nedsat kasse** (except when referring to price)
en oversat bog, but *not* ***en oversat å**
et underholdende foredrag (an entertaining talk) but *not* ***en underholdende hånd**

It is rare that such participles have a literal meaning, though it does occur:

et understreget ord, a word underlined ...

H SOME PROBLEM VERBS

This section lists some common English verbs with two or more different meanings and gives some of their realizations in Danish. Obviously, neither the list of verbs nor the number of their Danish translations is intended to be in any way complete.

551 Translation into Danish of some English problem verbs

(a) Ask = 1 **spørge** - enquire:
We asked him what he was called.
Vi spurgte ham, hvad han hed.
= 2 **bede** - beg, request:
She asked him to ring home.
Hun bad ham ringe hjem.
= 3 **stille (spørgsmål)** - ask (questions):
The teacher asked a lot of questions.
Læreren stillede en masse spørgsmål.

(b) Be = 1 **være** - indicating a fact or a state:
He is a teacher/kind, etc.
Han er lærer/venlig, etc.

= 2 **findes** - exist, be found:
There are no mountains in Denmark.
Der findes ikke bjerge i Danmark.

= 3 **blive** - become (indicating a change):
You mustn't be angry!
Du må ikke blive vred!

= 4 **blive** - with passive construction:
The postman was bitten by the dog.
Postbudet blev bidt af hunden.

= 5 **ligge** - of geographical position:
Where is Esbjerg/Tivoli?, etc.
Hvor ligger Esbjerg/Tivoli?, etc.

= 6 **koste** - cost:
How much is that bike?
Hvor meget koster den cykel?

(c) Change

= 1 **ændre** - alter:
I changed a few things in the letter.
Jeg ændrede et par ting i brevet.

= 2 **forandre sig** - of people (looks or manner):
She hasn't changed.
Hun har ikke forandret sig.

= 3 **bytte** - exchange:
They changed places.
De byttede plads.

= 4 **skifte** - change trains/one's clothes/gear (in car):
They changed trains in Nykøbing Falster.
De skiftede tog i Nykøbing Falster.
He changed clothes before going home.
Han skiftede tøj, inden han tog hjem.

= 5 **veksle** - change money:
They changed their pounds into kroner.
De vekslede deres pund til kroner.

(d) Feel

= 1 **føle** - transitive:
He felt a hand on his shoulder.
Han følte en hånd på sin skulder.

= 2 **føle sig** - reflexive:
She felt rich.
Hun følte sig rig.

= 3 **føles** - deponent:
It feels warm.
Det føles varmt.

(e) Go = 1 **rejse, tage** - travel:
They went to Spain.
De rejste/tog til Spanien.

= 2 **gå** - walk away, progress (of things):
They went home.
De gik hjem.
It's going very well.
Det går fint.

= 3 **køre** - by public transport, car, etc.:
We went by bus/train.
Vi kørte med bus(sen)/tog(et).

= 4 **blive** - turn (+ adjective):
He went bald/red/wild, etc.
Han blev skaldet/rød i hovedet/vild, etc.

(f) Grow = 1 **dyrke** - produce (in the soil); transitive:
We grow potatoes.
Vi dyrker kartofler.

= 2 **vokse** - in the soil; intransitive:
Roses are growing in the garden.
Der vokser roser i haven.

= 3 **vokse** - increase in size or number:
He/The tree has grown a lot.
Han/Træet er vokset meget.

= 4 **stige** - increase in degree or number:
The excitement grows.
Spændingen stiger.
The number of crimes is growing.
Antallet af forbrydelser stiger/er stigende.

= 5 **blive** - gradually become (+ adjective):
She grew old/pale/richer, etc.
Hun blev gammel/bleg/rigere, etc.

(g) Know = 1 **vide** - facts (object: **det** or a clause):
I don't know.
Det ved jeg ikke.
Do you know when the train leaves?
Ved du, hvornår toget går?

= 2 **kende** - acquaintance:
Do you know John/the tower?, etc.
Kender du John/tårnet?, etc.
= 3 **kunne** - languages, specialisms:
I know Italian/the list of monarchs.
Jeg kan italiensk/kongerækken.

(h) Live = 1 **bo** - dwell, reside:
She lives in Copenhagen.
Hun bor i København.
= 2 **leve** - be alive, conduct one's life:
Is he still alive?
Lever han endnu?
He has something to live up to!
Han har noget at leve op til!

(i) Put = 1 **lægge** - place (horizontally):
She put the letter on the desk.
Hun lagde brevet på skrivebordet.
= 2 **stille, sætte** - place (upright):
She put the vase on the table.
Hun stillede/satte vasen på bordet.
= 3 **sætte** - place (in general):
He put a stamp on the letter.
Han satte et frimærke på brevet.
= 4 **putte, stikke, stoppe** - insert:
He put his hand in his pocket.
Han puttede/stak/stoppede hånden i lommen.

(j) See = 1 **se** - of vision:
Can you see the red building?
Kan du se den røde bygning?
= 2 **møde/træffe** - meet (by chance):
I saw Jean in the library.
Jeg mødte/traf Jean på biblioteket.
= 3 **tale med** - meet (by arrangement):
I would like to see the manager.
Jeg vil gerne tale med direktøren.
= 4 *N.B.* I see! **Javel / Nå sådan! / Nu forstår jeg!**

(k) Stop = 1 **standse, stoppe** - bring to a halt (trans.):
She stopped the car.
Hun standsede bilen.
= 2 **standse, stoppe** - come to a halt (intrans.):
Suddenly the car stopped.
Pludselig standsede bilen.
= 3 **ophøre/holde op (med)** - cease:
He stopped smoking.
Han holdt op med at ryge.

(l) Think = 1 **tænke** - ponder (indicating brain activity):
Do you often think of me?
Tænker du tit på mig?
= 2 **tro** - believe (indicating uncertainty):
I think that Denmark will win.
Jeg tror, at Danmark vinder.
= 3 **synes** - be of the opinion (based on experience):
He thinks that the book is boring.
Han synes, at bogen er kedelig.
= 4 **mene** - like **synes**, but of strong conviction:
Do you really think that?
Mener du virkelig det?

(m) Want = 1 **ønske** - desire, wish:
We do not want to see it.
Vi ønsker ikke at se det.
= 2 **vil have** - insist on having:
I want a beer.
Jeg vil have en øl.

6 ADVERBS

A FORM

601 Introduction

The class of adverbs is the most heterogeneous of all the word classes, and many of the words that are traditionally included in this class have very little in common, either in terms of form or function, or of both.

From a formal point of view, the members of this class can be broadly divided into three main groups:

(a) those that are derived from other classes (usually adjectives) either through the addition of suffixes (e.g. **-t**, as in **langsomt**, slowly; **-vis**, as in **heldigvis**, fortunately) or through their use as adverbs in indeclinable form (e.g. **bedre**, better; **forbavsende**, surprisingly).

(b) those whose form is simple and invariable (e.g. **der**, there; **her**, here; **kun**, only; **nu**, now).

(c) those that are compounds, i.e. formed by combining two or more originally separate items (e.g. **derved**, thereby, from **der** (adv.) + **ved** (prep.); **undertiden**, at times, from **under** (prep.) + **tiden** (noun)).

602 Adverbs derived from adjectives

(a) The majority of adverbs are formed from adjectives, and *in principle* all adjectives except those which are indeclinable in the singular (see 207) may form an adverb through the addition of the ending **-t** to the common gender singular form (see 202ff):

smuk = beautiful (adjective)
smuk*t* = beautiful*ly* (adverb)

The adverb and the neuter singular form of the adjective are often identical. It is, therefore, important to distinguish between them, especially when translating into English. Compare:

Hun var meget smuk. *(= adj., common)*
She was very beautiful.

Huset var meget smuk*t*. *(=adj., neuter)*
The house was very beautiful.

Hun sang meget smuk*t*. *(= adverb)*
She sang very beautiful*ly*.

Huset ligger meget smuk*t*. *(= adverb)*
The house is beautiful*ly* situated.

These adverbs ending in **-t** are adjuncts (see 608), and have two main functions in a clause:

1 As adverbs of manner (see 609(b) and 611(b)):

Det gjorde du god*t*! You did that well!
Det var sød*t* sagt. That was sweetly put.

2 As uptoners qualifying adjectives or adverbs (see 615):

Det var hel*t* utroligt.
It was quite unbelievable.

Jens klarede opgaven lang*t* bedre end Jørgen.
Jens managed the task far better than Jørgen.

(b) Many adjectives, however, and especially those which end in **-ig/-lig**, may also form adverbs without the addition of the **-t** ending, depending on their precise function and/or meaning within a clause. The forms with **-t** are usually adverbs of manner, and are often used when the original, concrete sense of the adjective is being conveyed, whereas the forms *with optional* **-t** or *without* **-t** are usually clausal adverbs, whose meaning represents some shift away from the original concrete meaning of the adjective (see 611). For example:

Barnet kan ikke stave rigtig*t*. The child can't spell correctly.

But:

Barnet kan ikke rigtig*(t)* stave. The child can't really spell.
Hun synger dejlig*t*. She sings beautifully.

But:

Det er dejlig*(t)* nemt. It's delightfully easy.
Han var nær*t* knyttet til sin kone. He was very attached to his wife.

But:

Jeg var nær død af skræk. I nearly died of fear.

Note – There is a small group of words ending in **-ig/-lig** which only ever occur as adverbs and therefore never take the adverbial **-t** ending. The most important of these are **aldrig**, never; **navnlig**, particularly; **nemlig**, namely; **sandelig**, indeed, in truth; **temmelig**, rather. See 611(a) for a full list.

(c) Certain adjectives ending in **-ig/-lig** also form adverbs through the addition of **-vis** (= 'way, manner') to the common gender singular form and never take the adverbial **-t** ending (see 611(a)). For example:

> **almindelig*vis***, generally; **heldig*vis***, luckily; **mulig*vis***, possibly; **naturlig*vis***, of course; **rimelig*vis***, probably; **sandsynlig*vis***, probably; **sædvanlig*vis***, usually; **tilfældig*vis***, accidentally; **tydelig*vis***, evidently; **vanlig*vis***, usually

Similarly **nødvendig*vis*** (necessarily), which is the only adverbial form of the adjective **nødvendig** (necessary).

The same adjectival stem may, therefore, produce two different types of adverb. Those ending in **-t** are adverbs of manner, whereas those ending in **-vis** are clausal adverbials (see 611):

Han talte meget tydelig*t*.	He spoke very clearly.

But:

Han var tydelig*vis* meget nervøs.	He was obviously very nervous.
Han talte helt naturlig*t*.	He spoke completely naturally.

But:

Han var naturlig*vis* ikke hjemme.	He was of course not at home.

Note – **-vis** may also be added to some nouns to form both adjectives (see 207(c) note 2) and adverbs. As adverbs, they may or may not take the adverbial **-t** ending (see 611(d)(iv)):

> **delvis(t)**, partially, partly; **etapevis(t)**, in stages; **fortrinsvis(t)**, chiefly; **gradvis(t)**, gradually; **indledningsvis(t)**, by way of introduction; **månedsvis(t)**, monthly; **stedvis(t)**, locally, in places; **stykvis/stykkevis**, piece by piece; **stødvis(t)**, spasmodically, intermittently; **trinvis(t)**, step-by-step, in steps, gradually; **ugevis(t)**, weekly; **undtagelsevis(t)**, exceptionally; **årsvis(t)**, yearly

Henholdsvis (respectively) only occurs as an adverb, and does not take the adverbial **-t** ending.

(d) Present participles (see 529) may also be used as adverbs:

Han klarede det forbavsende hurtigt.	He managed it amazingly quickly.

(e) Past participles (see 530) are also used as adverbs:

Han klappede begejstret.	He clapped enthusiastically.

603 Other adverbs which are derivatives

(a) Forms in **-mæssig**:

-mæssig (= approximately 'as far as *x* is concerned') may be added to some nouns to form both adjectives (1107) and adverbs. As adverbs, these words will normally take the adverbial **-t** ending (see 611):

> **forholdsmæssig**, proportionally; **forretningsmæssig**, in a businesslike way; **hensigtsmæssig**, suitably, appropriately; **lovmæssig**, legally; **regelmæssig**, regularly; **samfundsmæssig**, socially; **standsmæssig**, in a manner befitting one's rank; **tidsmæssig**, as regards the period/time

The ending **-mæssig** is still productive in the formation of new adjectives and adverbs.

(b) Forms in **-s**, **-es** (old genitives):

> **dels (... dels)**, partly (... partly); **ellers**, otherwise; **indendørs**, indoors; **tværs**, across; **udenbords**, overboard; **udenbys**, out of town; **udendørs**, out of doors; **udenlands**, abroad

> **afsides**, secluded; **aldeles**, completely; **forgæves**, in vain; **hinsides**, beyond; **særdeles**, particularly

(c) Forms in **-e**:

> **alene**, only; **bare**, only; **ikke**, not; **ilde**, badly; **lige**, just; **længe**, long (of time); **ofte**, often; **sagte**, quietly; **stedse**, always; **stille**, calmly; **såre**, very

In this category are also the following adverbs of place (see 609(c)):

> **borte**, away; **fremme**, there (in front); **henne**, over; **hjemme**, at home; **inde**, inside; **nede**, down; **omme**, over; **oppe**, up; **ovre**, over; **ude**, outside

(d) Forms in **-steds** (expressing location (see 617)):

> **allesteds**, everywhere; **andetsteds**, elsewhere; **dersteds**, there; **etsteds**, somewhere; **hersteds**, here, locally; **ingensteds**, **intetsteds**, nowhere; **mangesteds**, in many places; **nogetsteds**, anywhere; **sammesteds**, in the same place

(e) Forms in **-ledes** and **-lunde**:

anderledes, otherwise, differently; **hvorledes**, how; **ligeledes**, also, too; **nogenledes**, fairly; **således**, so, thus

ingenlunde, by no means; **nogenlunde**, fairly; **sålunde**, so, thus

These express manner (see 609(b)).

(f) Forms in **-sinde**:

ingensinde, never; **nogensinde**, ever

These express time (see 609(a)).

604 Some simple adverbs which are not derivatives

(a) Adverbs of time:

da, then; **før**, previously; **nu**, now; **straks**, immediately; **så**, then; **tit**, often

(b) Adverbs of place:

bort, away; **der**, there; **frem**, forward; **hen**, over; **her**, here; **hid**, hither; **hjem**, home; **hvor**, where; **ind**, in, into; **ned**, down; **om**, over; **op**, up; **over**, over; **ud**, out (see 616 for precise meanings and usage)

(c) Modal adverbs:

da, **dog**, **jo**, **mon**, **nok**, **nu**, **sgu**, **skam**, **vel**, **vist** (see 618); **ej**, not; **gerne**, willingly

(d) Conjunctional adverbs:

dog, however; **så**, so

(e) Adverbs of degree:

lidt, somewhat, a little; **meget**, much, very; **næsten**, nearly

Note – Although strictly speaking these adverbs are derivatives (**lidt** being a contracted form of **lidet**, the neuter form of **liden**, **meget** being the neuter form of **megen**, and **næsten** being the old accusative masculine singular form of **næste**), they are now no longer perceived as such.

605 Compound adverbs

Of the compound adverbs to be found in Danish, the following are among the most common:

alligevel, nevertheless; **altid**, always; **dernæst**, next; **efterhånden**, gradually; **endnu**, still, yet; **forleden**, the other day; **fornylig**, recently; **hvordan**, how; **igen**, again; **måske**, perhaps; **omkring**, around; **rigtignok**, certainly; **sommetider**, sometimes; **undertiden**, at times; **vistnok**, probably

There are particularly many compound adverbs in Danish which are formed from a simple adverb (see 604) and a preposition or another adverb, the first element nearly always being an adverb. The following is by no means an exhaustive list:

(a) **-ad**

hjemad, homewards; **nedad**, downwards; **opad**, upwards; **udenad**, by heart

(b) **-af**

deraf, of that; **heraf**, from this, hence; **hvoraf**, of which

(c) **-efter**

bagefter, behind, afterwards; **derefter**, after that; **herefter**, after this; **hvorefter**, after which; **østefter**, east, towards the east

(d) **-for**

derfor, therefore; **hvorfor**, why; **nedenfor**, below; **ovenfor**, above; **overfor**, opposite

(e) **-fra**

bagfra, from behind; **derfra**, from there; **forfra**, from in front, from the beginning; **herfra**, from here; **hjemmefra**, from home; **hvorfra**, from where; **nede(n)fra**, from below; **oppefra**, **ovenfra**, from above; **sydfra**, from the south

(f) -hen

derhen, there; **herhen**, here; **hvorhen**, where, whither; **simpelthen**, simply

(g) -imod

derimod, on the other hand; **herimod**, against this; **hvorimod**, whereas; **tværtimod**, on the contrary

(h) -med

dermed, with that; **hermed**, with that; **hvormed**, with which; **tilmed**, moreover

(i) -om

bagom, behind; **derom**, about that; **herom**, about this; **hvorom**, about which; **udenom**, around

(j) -over

bagover, backwards; **derover**, over there; **fremover**, forward(s), in future; **herover**, over here

(k) -på

bagpå, behind; **derpå**, then, on that; **herpå**, then, on this; **hvorpå**, on which, whereupon; **vestpå**, westward

(l) -til

dertil, to that (place); **hertil**, here, to this (place); **hidtil**, hitherto, till now; **hvortil**, where to, for which

(m) -ud

bagud, to the rear; **forud**, beforehand, ahead; **herud**, out here; **østerud**, eastwards

(n) -ved

derved, thereby; **henved**, about, nearly; **herved**, by this, hereby; **hvorved**, at which

606 Other common adverbial phrases

The following types of adverbial are frequently used in Danish; some are prepositional phrases, while others are adverb + coordinating conjunction + adverb:

for det meste, generally; **fra nu af**, from now on; **i alle henseender**, in every respect; **i alle tilfælde**, at all events; **i bedste tilfælde**, at best; **i bedste/værste fald**, at best/worst; **i den/så henseende**, in that respect; **i det hele taget**, altogether, everything considered; **i det lange løb**, in the long run; **i hvert tilfælde/fald**, at any rate; **i og for sig**, actually; **oven i købet**, into the bargain; **under alle omstændigheder**, in/under any circumstances; **under ingen omstændigheder**, in/under no circumstances

af og til, now and again; **først og fremmest**, primarily; **hid og did**, to and fro; **hist og her**, here and there; **nu og da**, now and then

607 Comparison of adverbs

(a) Adverbs derived from adjectives possess the same comparative and superlative forms as their adjectival counterparts (cf. 225), i.e. the adverbial **-t** ending (where present) is dropped before the addition of the comparative and superlative endings **-(e)re, -(e)st**:

Basic	*Comparative*	*Superlative*
tidligt, early	**tidligere**	**tidligst**
sent, late	**senere**	**senest**
højt, high, loud	**højere**	**højest/højst**
langt, **længe**, far, long	**længere**	**længst**

Note 1 – **Høj** as an adverb has two superlative forms, **højest** and **højst**. The former is used when the original concrete meaning of **høj** is intended, the latter when the meaning has shifted to a more abstract concept. E.g.:

Han sang højest af alle.	He sang loudest of all.
Jeg sprang højest.	I jumped highest.

But:

Det er højst beklageligt.	It is extremely regrettable.
Det drejer sig højst om 20 kroner.	It's a question of 20 kroner at the most.

Note 2 – The adjective **lang**, long, has two basic adverbial forms: **langt**, far (of distance), and **længe**, long (of time); the comparative and superlative forms are the same for both:

Hun var langt borte.	She was far away.
Han har været her længe.	He's been here a long time.

(b) Adverbs derived from adjectives which have an irregular comparison compare in the same way as their adjectival counterparts. **Dårlig** may compare in the same way as **ilde** (but may also compare in the standard way), and **lidt** compares as **lille** (see 227(a)):

Basic	*Comparative*	*Superlative*
godt, well	**bedre**	**bedst**
dårligt, badly	**værre/ dårligere**	**værst/ dårligst**
ilde, badly	**værre**	**værst**
lidt, somewhat	**mindre**	**mindst**
meget, much	**mere**	**mest**
ondt, badly	**værre**	**værst**

(c) Some other adverbs which compare are:

Basic	*Comparative*	*Superlative*
gerne, willingly	**hellere**	**helst**
nær, closely	**nærmere**	**nærmest**
ofte, often	**oftere**	**oftest**
tit, often	**tiere**	**tiest**

(d) Adverbs which end in **-vis** and **-mæssig** do not usually compare.

(e) Adverbs formed from participles compare using **mere, mest** (cf. 228):

Per argumenterede mere overbevisende end Jørgen.
Per argued more convincingly than Jørgen.

(f) For the comparison of some adverbs (or prepositions) of place see 226(b). The comparative and superlative forms are usually, but not exclusively, regarded as adjectives:

Han stod forrest i køen.	He stood at the front of the queue.
Vi sad øverst på trappen.	We sat at the very top of the stairs.

B FUNCTION

608 Introduction to adverbial meaning and function

As regards *meaning*, adverbs can be divided into several categories. The traditional division is into the categories of adverbs of manner, time, place, degree, modal and clausal adverbs, etc.

It is, however, also possible to divide adverbs into three broad categories according to their basic *function*, namely adjuncts, conjuncts and disjuncts.

Adjuncts (typically adverbs of manner, time, place and degree) are, to some degree at least, an integral part of the clause structure, whereas conjuncts and disjuncts are peripheral elements and therefore outside the clause structure. Thus the adverbs **smukt** and **uhyre** are adjuncts in:

Hun synger smukt.	She sings beautifully.
Den bog er uhyre populær.	That book is extremely popular.

Conjuncts have a connective, or cohesive, function, in that they establish a connection between a clause or phrase and a previous part of the same utterance. In the following examples, **derfor** and **alligevel** are conjuncts since they refer back to the previous clause:

Han var rejst til Odense; derfor så jeg ham ikke den dag.
He had gone to Odense; consequently I did not see him that day.

Selvom han var meget træt, gik han alligevel på arbejde.
Even though he was very tired, he nevertheless went to work.

Disjuncts have no such connective function, but typically express the speaker's attitude or evaluation. Examples of this are **desværre** and **sandsynligvis** in:

Desværre kan jeg ikke komme.	Unfortunately I can't come.

Det var sandsynligvis hans skyld. It was probably his fault.

A useful way of distinguishing conjuncts from disjuncts is that conjuncts cannot serve as a response to a question, whereas disjuncts can. Thus in the following examples **derfor** can be seen to be a conjunct, whereas **sandsynligvis** is a disjunct:

A: **Så du ham den dag?** Did you see him that day?
B: ***Nej, derfor.** *No, consequently.

A: **Var det hans skyld?** Was it his fault?
B: **Ja, sandsynligvis.** Yes, probably.

A distinction should be made between adverbs and adverbials. *Adverbs*, as we have seen, can be defined formally and functionally, and with a few exceptions they are one-word units.

Adverbials on the other hand are purely functional units, whose internal syntactic structure may vary widely. The important point is that they can have the same function in the clause as adverbs can. Compare the different kinds of adverbial in the following examples, which all consist of subject + verb + adverbial:

1 **Han arbejder *hver dag.*** (noun phrase)
2 **Han arbejder *om morgenen.*** (prepositional phrase)
3 **Han arbejder *meget langsomt.*** (adverbial phrase)
4 **Han arbejder, *når han vil.*** (clause)

Translations: He works: 1 every day; 2 in the morning; 3 very slowly; 4 when he wants to.

In other words, the syntactic structure of adverbials is irrelevant to their function in the clause.

The distinction between adverbs (or adverb phrases) and adverbials, and between adjuncts, conjuncts and disjuncts, is of special importance for the question of word order in the clause (see 1014ff).

Traditionally, adverbs are said to modify a verb, an adjective, another adverb, or a whole clause. This may be seen from the following examples:

- a verb:
Han arbejder *hårdt.* He works hard.

- an adjective:

Hans arbejde er *utrolig(t)* hårdt.	His work is incredibly hard.

- an adverb:

Han arbejder *utrolig(t)* hårdt.	He works incredibly hard.

- an entire clause:

Hans arbejde er *ofte* hårdt.	His work is often hard.

An adverb can, however, also modify a noun phrase and a prepositional phrase:

- a noun phrase:

***Næsten* hele landsbyen mødte op.**	Almost the whole village turned up.

- a prepositional phrase:

De boede *næsten* i midten af byen.	They lived almost in the centre of town.

609 Adverbs classified by meaning

In the following, common examples are provided of the different types of adverbs/adverbials found in Danish, grouped together according to traditional classifications. The lists are by no means exhaustive:

(a) Time (answering the questions: ***Hvornår?*** *- When?*, ***Hvor længe?*** *- How long?*, ***Hvor ofte?*** *- How often?*, etc.):

af og til/nu og da, now and then, from time to time; **aldrig**, never; **allerede**, already; **altid**, always; **bagefter**, afterwards; **da**, then; **en gang imellem/lejlighedsvis**, occasionally; **endelig**, finally; **endnu**, still; **fornylig**, recently; **før**, previously; **først**, first; **i forvejen/tidligere**, previously; **i timevis**, for hours; **i årevis**, for years; **igen**, again; **længe**, for a long time; **nu**, now; **ofte/tit**, often; **oprindeligt**, originally; **siden**, since; **sjældent**, seldom; **snart**, soon; **sommetider**, sometimes; **straks**, immediately; **til sidst**, finally, at last

This group may be further subdivided, for example, into:

(i) Point in time: **da**, **før**, **nu**, etc.

(ii) Period of time: **i timevis**, **i årevis**, **længe**, etc.

(iii) Frequency: **aldrig**, **altid**, **ofte**, etc.

(b) Manner (answering the question: ***Hvordan?*** - *How?*):

> **dejligt**, delightfully; **dårligt**, badly; **forsigtigt**, carefully; **godt**, well; **hurtigt**, quickly; **ilde**, badly; **langsomt**, slowly; **sagte**, quietly; **smukt**, beautifully; **således**, thus (+ others in **-ledes**, **-lunde**; see 603(e))

(c) Place (answering the question: ***Hvor?/Hvorhen?*** - *Where?/Where to?*) (see also 616):

> **bort**, away; **borte**, away; **der**, there; **foran**, in front; **forbi**, past; **her**, here; **herfra**, from here; **hjem**, home; **hjemme**, at home; **igennem**, through; **ind**, in(to); **inde**, in(side); **indenfor**, inside; **omkring**, around; **overalt**, everywhere; **tilbage**, back; **ud**, out; **ude**, out; **udenfor**, outside; **udenlands**, abroad

(d) Degree (answering the question: ***Hvor meget?*** - *To what extent?*):

> **ganske**, absolutely, quite; **helt**, entirely; **højst**, extremely; **lidt**, a little; **meget**, a lot; **mest**, mostly; **næsten**, nearly, almost; **omtrent**, approximately; **ret**, rather; **særdeles**, especially; **særlig**, particularly; **temmelig**, rather; **yderst**, exceedingly

610 Adverbs classified by function

The heterogeneity of adverbs is most apparent when one considers their *function*. While some adverbs are semantically independent, for example the adverbs of manner (i.e. adjuncts) listed in 609(b), many others (e.g. conjuncts) need a context in order for their significance to be established. Cf.:

Han kørte langsomt.	He drove slowly.
Derfor så jeg ham ikke.	Consequently I didn't see him.

Langsomt modifies the action of the verb; it tells us *how* he drove. **Derfor** refers back to a previous statement, which would tell us the *reason* why the speaker did not see him.

In Danish, the semantic function of adverbs can have special significance not only for their form (the presence or absence of the adverbial **-t** ending) but also for their position within a clause. In 611 below the problem of the adverbial **-t** ending is dealt with, and in 612–17 the main types of adverb are classified by their function. (See 1014ff for the treatment of adverbial position within clauses.)

611 The adverbial -t ending

This is an aspect of Danish where there is still some uncertainty and confusion, even among native speakers. The problem of whether or not to use the adverbial **-t** ending is in many instances purely orthographical, in that the **-t** ending, especially when used with adverbs ending in **-ig/-lig**, is seldom pronounced. There is, however, a general trend towards an increased (and historically unjustified) use of the **-t** ending in modern written Danish, a trend which is 'legitimized' in *Retskrivningsordbogen*. What follows here, therefore, has taken account of the new and more liberal set of principles and guidelines governing the use of the adverbial **-t** ending as set out in that dictionary, though quite naturally some deviation from them may be encountered in written Danish from time to time.

(a) Adverbs which *never* take the **-t** ending

To this category belong all those words which only ever occur as adverbs:

> **aldrig**, never; **altid**, always; **desværre**, unfortunately; **ofte**, often; etc.

Adverbs ending in **-lig**:

> **følgelig**, consequently; **gladelig**, cheerfully; **klogelig**, wisely, prudently; **navnlig**, particularly; **nemlig**, namely; **rettelig**, rightfully; **sagtelig**, softly, gently; **sandelig**, indeed; **temmelig**, rather, fairly; **visselig**, assuredly

Adverbs ending in **-vis:**

> **almindeligvis**, generally; **anstændigvis**, in decency; **begribeligvis**, of course; **beklageligvis**, unfortunately; **fornuftigvis**, sensibly; **glædeligvis**, happily; **heldigvis**, fortunately; **henholdsvis**, respectively; **lykkeligvis**, fortunately; **muligvis**, possibly; **mærkværdigvis**, oddly enough; **naturligvis**, of course; **nødvendigvis**, necessarily; **ordentligvis**, normally, ordinarily; **retfærdigvis**, in fairness; **rimeligvis**, probably; **sandsynligvis**, probably; **sædvanligvis**, usually; **tilfældigvis**, accidentally; **tydeligvis**, evidently; **uheldigvis**, unfortunately; **ulykkeligvis**, unfortunately; **vanligvis**, usually

Han har *aldrig* været i Odense.	He has never been to Odense.
Det var en *temmelig* fjollet idé.	That was a rather silly idea.
Han var *naturligvis* ikke hjemme.	He wasn't home, of course.
Det har du *sandelig* ret i.	You're dead right about that.

(b) Adverbs which *always* take the **-t** ending

This category includes all adverbs – except those formed from adjectives ending in **-vis** – when they are used as adverbs of manner (see 609(b)) and whenever it is morphologically possible for them to take the **-t** ending (see 202, 203, 207):

Hun spiller *dejligt*.	She plays delightfully.
Han kørte meget *hurtigt*.	He drove very fast.
Han talte *langsomt* og *tydeligt*.	He spoke slowly and clearly.

De betragtede ham *sporgende* og *nysgerrigt*.
They looked at him inquiringly and inquisitively.

Note – The only exceptions to this are **bitterlig**, bitterly; **grangivelig**, exactly; **udtrykkelig**, expressly, where the **-t** ending is optional:

De har *udtrykkelig(t)* bedt om lov til at se ham.
They have expressly asked for permission to see him.

Hun ligner *grangivelig(t)* sin mor.
She is exactly like her mother.

(c) Adverbs which in certain cases take the **-t** ending

There are some Danish adverbs which, when used in the original, concrete sense of the adjective from which they are derived, take the adverbial **-t** ending. If, however, they are used in a sense which is either figurative or abstract, or which represents some shift away from the adjective's original meaning, they will not take the adverbial **-t** ending. In many instances, this shift of meaning represents a change in the function of the adverb from being an adjunct (here as adverbs of manner) to being either a disjunct or a conjunct. The most important examples of this are given below. It is worth noting, however, that in many instances other adverbs or adverbials with the same meaning as the **-t** form adverbs may also be used; where this is so, the alternatives are given in brackets:

Han udførte arbejdet *antageligt* (= tilfredsstillende, acceptabelt).
He did the job satisfactorily.

But:

Han har *antagelig* udført arbejdet.
He has presumably done the job.

***Egentlig(t)* talt kan jeg ikke fordrage ham.**
Actually, I cannot stand him.

But:

Jeg kan *egentlig* ikke fordrage ham.
I basically cannot stand him.

Nu er sagen blevet *endeligt* afgjort (= definitivt).
The matter has now been definitively settled.

But:

De afgjorde *endelig* sagen.
They settled the matter at last.

Han behersker dansk *fuldkomment* (= perfekt).
He commands Danish perfectly (i.e. He has a perfect command of Danish).

But:

Han havde *fuldkommen* glemt sit dansk.
He had completely forgotten his Danish.

Vores rationer var *knapt* afmålte (= sparsomt).
Our rations were apportioned sparsely.

But:

Vi havde *knap* tid til at afmåle vores rationer.
We scarcely had time to apportion our rations.

For at sige det *ligefremt* er han vanskelig at forstå (= på en ligefrem måde, ligeud).
To put it plainly, he's difficult to understand.

But:

Han er *ligefrem* vanskelig at forstå.
He's positively difficult to understand.

Nævningerne var *lovligt* undskyldt fra retten i går (= legalt, på en lovlig måde).
The members of the jury were legally excused from the trial yesterday.

But:

Men de var alligevel allesammen *lovlig* dovne.
But they all were rather lazy anyway.

Hun er *nært* knyttet til sin mand (= inderligt).
She's closely attached to her husband.

But:

Jeg havde *nær* sagt, at hun ikke elsker ham.
I was on the point of saying that she doesn't love him.

Hun havde forladt mig så *pludseligt* og så uventet.
She had left me so suddenly and so unexpectedly.

But:

Og så gik det *pludselig* op for mig, at jeg nu var helt alene.
And then it suddenly dawned on me that now I was completely alone.

Han udtrykte sig altid meget *præcist* (= med præcision).
He always expressed himself very precisely.

But:

Men en gang imellem var det svært at finde ud af, *præcis* hvad han mente.
But now and again it was hard to make out exactly what he meant.

And:

Du skal være her *præcis* kl. 12!
You must be here at 12 o'clock sharp!

Da hun kom ind i værelset, rejste alle herrerne sig *samtidigt* (= på én gang).
When she entered the room, all the gentlemen stood up simultaneously (i.e. at the same time, together).

But:

Hun gjorde dem *samtidig* opmærksom på, at sådan noget gjorde man ikke længere.
At the same time she pointed out to them that one didn't do such things any more.

Tyvens tilståelse kom helt *selvfølgeligt* (= naturligt, på en selvfølgelig måde).
The thief's confession was made completely as a matter of course.

But:

***Selvfølgelig* gjorde den det – han kunne ikke gøre andet.**
Of course it was – he couldn't do anything else.

Et *stadigt* tilbagevendende problem er, hvordan vi kan få vores grammatik færdig (= konstant).
A constantly recurring problem is how we can finish our grammar.

But:

Den er *stadig* ikke færdig.
It still isn't finished.

Olsen spillede rollen som skraldemanden i 'Pygmalion' meget *virkeligt* (= naturtro, realistisk).
Olsen played the dustman in 'Pygmalion' very realistically.

But:

Olsen? – Hedder han *virkelig* sådan?
Olsen? – Is he really called that?

Note – For the forms of **virkelig** when used as an adverb of degree see (d)(ii) below.

(d) Adverbs where the **-t** ending is *optional*

For the remainder of those adverbs *formed from adjectives and nouns*, and which end in **-ig/-lig** and **-vis**, the addition of the adverbial **-t** ending has become optional – *except* when they are used as adverbs of manner (see 609(b) above) – since the 1986 edition of *Retskrivningsordbogen*. (In texts written prior to that date, one may therefore expect to find some deviation from what follows here.) There are four categories under which these may be described:

(i) Adverbs with a shift of meaning

Unlike the examples in (c) above, where the **-t** ending is always *absent* when the adverbs are used in a different meaning from their original one, and as clausal adverbs, the use of the **-t** ending has become *optional* for *all* other adverbs formed from adjectives ending in **-ig/-lig** in the same circumstances. Adverbs in this category function as disjuncts:

> **Vi kan ikke *rigtig(t)* finde en løsning på problemet.**
> We can't really find a solution to the problem.
>
> (But:
> **Vi kunne ikke løse problemet *rigtigt.***
> We couldn't solve the problem correctly.)
>
> **Du kan *rolig(t)* blive hjemme.**
> You can safely stay at home.
>
> **Det kan du *magelig(t)* gøre.**
> You can easily do that.

(ii) Adverbs ending in **-ig/-lig** when used as adverbs of degree:

> **Det var et *ualmindelig(t)* godt måltid.**
> That was an exceptionally good meal.
>
> **Den frakke er *forfærdelig(t)* dyr.**
> That coat is terribly expensive.
>
> **Filmen var ikke *særlig(t)* spændende.**
> The film wasn't particularly exciting.
>
> **Jens klarede opgaven *virkelig(t)* godt.**
> Jens managed the task really well.

(iii) Adverbs ending in **-ig/-lig** when used as adverbs of time or place:

Foreløbig(t) **bliver jeg her i London.**
For the time being I'll stay in London.

Hvor meget tjener du ***årlig(t)*****?**
How much do you earn a year?

Michael kommer ***jævnlig(t)*** **for sent til timerne.**
Michael is regularly late for his classes.

Jeg plejer altid at vågne meget ***tidlig(t)*** **om morgenen.**
I usually wake up very early in the morning.

Udvendig(t) **er husene meget smukke, men** ***indvendig(t)*** **er de grimme.**
From the outside the houses are very pretty, but inside they're ugly.

(iv) Adverbs formed from adjectives ending in **-vis**:

OB nåede ***gradvis(t)*** **frem til pokalfinalen.**
OB (= **Odense Boldklub**, a Danish football team) gradually made their way to the cup final.

Betalingen sker ***månedsvis(t)*****.**
The payment is made on a monthly basis.

Vi spiser kun ***lejlighedsvis(t)*** **rejer.**
We eat prawns only occasionally.

612 Pronominal adverbs

As in the case of pronouns, the meaning of these adverbs is determined by their context. They may:

– point out:	**Den** ***dér*** **pige er høj.** That girl is tall.
– refer back:	**Vi spiste vores middag.** ***Bagefter*** **drak vi kaffe.** We ate dinner. Afterwards we drank coffee.
– refer forward:	***Fremover*** **vil der ske ændringer.** Henceforth there'll be changes.

See also 402(b). Whereas pronouns replace noun phrases, pronominal adverbs replace prepositional phrases:

Bilen	**standsede**	***foran huset.***
Noun phrase		*Prepositional phrase*
The car	stopped	in front of the house.

Den	**standsede**	***der.***
Pronoun		*Pronominal adverb*
It	stopped	there.

The main types of pronominal adverb are:

(a) Demonstrative:

Herefter **skal du virkelig passe på.**
From now on you must really be careful.

Han sad *der*, mens vi spiste.
He sat there while we ate.

Others are: **da, her, hid** and compounds in **her-**, **der-** (see 617).

(b) Relative:

Den by, *hvor* jeg er født, hedder Skive.
The town where I was born is called Skive.

Den måde, *hvorpå* han udtrykte sig, var imponerende.
The way in which he expressed himself was impressive.

Others are compounds of **hvor** + preposition, e.g. **hvorom, hvortil, hvorved**, etc. (For function as a subordinator see 919ff.)

(c) Interrogative:

Hvor **er mine bukser?**
Where are my trousers?

Jeg ved ikke, *hvor* dine bukser er.
I don't know where your trousers are.

Hvornår **kommer han tilbage?**
When's he coming back?

Jeg ved ikke, *hvornår* han kommer tilbage.
I don't know when he's coming back.

Hvordan **klarede han det?**
How did he manage it?

Jeg ved ikke, *hvordan* han klarede det.
I don't know how he managed it.

Jeg kan ikke forstå, *hvorledes* det er gået til.
I can't understand how it's come about.

Notice that interrogative adverbs introduce both direct and indirect questions, i.e. both main and subordinate clauses, and that as a result the word order varies (see Chapter 10).

(d) Indefinite:

Andetsteds **har man en helt anden opfattelse.**
Elsewhere they have a completely different view.

Det var det bedste, han *nogensinde* havde gjort.
That was the best thing he had ever done.

Mine forældre er *nogenlunde* lige gamle.
My parents are more or less the same age.

613 Clausal adverbials

These adverbs are either conjuncts or disjuncts (see 608), and they qualify the clause as a whole rather than one particular word or phrase within the clause. For their position in the clause see 1015ff.

Clausal adverbials include:

1 Adverbs formed by adding **-vis** to adjectives ending in **-ig/-lig** (see 602(c)):

heldigvis, fortunately; **muligvis**, possibly; **naturligvis**, naturally

***Heldigvis* var han hjemme.** **(Det var heldigt, at han var hjemme.)**	Fortunately he was at home.
***Muligvis* drikker han snaps.** **(Det er muligt, at han drikker snaps.)**	He possibly drinks akvavit.

2 Some other adverbs: **jo**, **nok**, **vel** (see 618); **altså**, therefore; **desværre**, unfortunately; **faktisk**, in fact; **gerne**, willingly; **måske**, perhaps

The main types of clausal adverbial are:

(a) Negations (and equivalents):

aldrig, never; **ikke**, **ej**, not; **ingenlunde**, by no means; **knap**, scarcely, hardly; **slet ikke**, not at all

Hun var *slet ikke* glad for at se os.	She wasn't at all glad to see us.
Enten du vil eller *ej*.	Whether you want to or not.

Negations are disjuncts and are sometimes regarded as a kind of modal adverb (see (b) below).

Note – **ikke** is also found in compounds. See 1104ff.

(b) Modal adverbs

These are disjuncts and show the speaker's attitude to the utterance, his/her involvement or reservation, degree of certainty, etc. They include:

da, **endda**, **jo**, **nok**, **nu**, **sgu**, **skam**, **vel**, **vist** (see also 618); **desværre**, unfortunately; **minsandten**, really, upon my word; **mon**, **monstro** (see 618); **sikkert**, surely, probably; **såmænd**, really, I am sure

Det er *sikkert* rigtigt.	That's probably correct.
Det er *minsandten* en alvorlig sag.	That's really a serious matter.
***Desværre* har jeg ikke set ham idag.**	Unfortunately I haven't seen him today.

(c) Conjunctional adverbs

These adverbs, which are conjuncts, link clauses in a similar way to coordinating and subordinating conjunctions (see also 903). However, a clause beginning with a conjunctional adverb has inverted word order (see also two-part constructions in (iv) below). Conjunctional adverbs also occur within a clause:

Hans er professor. Han er *altså* akademiker.
Hans is a professor. He is therefore an academic.

Else er bibliotekar. *Desuden* passer hun familiens gård ude på landet.
Else is a librarian. In addition she looks after the family farm out in the country.

The main relationships expressed in this way are the following:

(i) Opposition:

alligevel, still, yet, nevertheless; **derimod**, on the other hand; **dog**, however; **heller ikke**, not ... either; **imidlertid**, however

Han var ikke rask; men han passede *dog* sit arbejde.
He was unwell; but he still attended to his work.

Jeg forstår, hvad du siger, men *alligevel* er jeg uenig med dig.
I understand what you're saying, but I still disagree with you.

(ii) Consequence or inference:

altså, therefore, consequently; **derfor**, therefore, so; **følgelig**, consequently, so; **så**, so, then; **således**, thus

Min trofaste ven, gravhunden Bob, blev syg; *derfor* kunne jeg ikke tage på ferie.
My faithful friend, Bob the dachshund, became ill; consequently I couldn't go on holiday.

(iii) Explanation or motivation:

jo, nemlig (see 618)

Ja, jeg kender ham godt – jeg har *nemlig* besøgt ham mange gange før.
Yes, I know him well – I've visited him many times before, you see.

(iv) Sequel:

desuden, endvidere, besides, moreover, further(more); **sluttelig**, finally; **så**, so, then; **til sidst**, finally; **til slut**, in conclusion

Han var i Danmark. *Endvidere* besøgte han Tyskland.
He was in Denmark. Moreover he visited Germany.

In two-part constructions of the type **både ... og** (both ... and), **såvel ... som** (as well as), **enten ... eller** (either ... or), **hverken ... eller** (neither ... nor), the first element is a conjunctional adverb, while the second is a coordinating conjunction (see also 905ff). In the construction **dels ... dels** (partly ... partly) both elements are conjunctional adverbs:

I dag har jeg været både i Tivoli og på Nationalmuseet.
I have been both to Tivoli and the National Museum today.

Dels havde han ikke tid, dels havde han ikke lyst.
Partly he didn't have the time, partly he didn't have the desire.

Note also the use of the construction **det være sig ... eller**, whether ... or (cf. 534(b), 906(b)(iii)):

Ingen, det være sig rig eller fattig, får adgang her.
No one, whether rich or poor, will gain entry here.

614 Adverbs restricting a noun phrase

These adverbs restrict a particular noun phrase by specifying its meaning in the clause more precisely. They include:

allerede, already, as early as, even; **bare**, only, just; **heller ikke**, nor; **ikke engang**, not even; **især**, especially; **kun**, only, just; **mindst**, at least; **også**, also; **selv**, even

Kun få mennesker ved, hvor gammel Tom er.
Only a few people know how old Tom is.

Ikke engang den stærkeste færing ville kunne løfte den sten.
Not even the strongest Faroeman would be able to lift that stone.

Det var en meget bedre lejlighed; selv altanen var større.
It was a much better flat; even the balcony was bigger.

615 Uptoners and downtoners

(a) A number of adverbs, especially those denoting degree or kind, can function as *uptoners* and *downtoners*. Uptoners (sometimes called amplifiers) are used to amplify or strengthen the meaning of adjectives or other adverbs, e.g.:

absolut, absolutely; **aldeles**, entirely, completely; **alt for**, far too; **bestemt**, certainly, definitely; **enormt**, enormously; **for**, too; **frygtelig(t)**, dreadfully, terribly; **fuldkommen**, perfectly, quite; **fuldt**, completely; **ganske**, absolutely, perfectly, very, quite, fairly; **helt**, completely; **meget**, very; **ret**, very; **særdeles**, extremely; **totalt**, totally; **vældig(t)**, very

Det var den *absolut* bedste fodboldkamp, jeg nogensinde har set.
It was absolutely the best football match I've ever seen.

Det er *ganske* rigtigt.
That's perfectly correct.

Han kørte *frygtelig(t)* stærkt.
He drove terribly fast.

Downtoners (sometimes called 'diminishers') lessen or weaken the meaning of adjectives or other adverbs, e.g.:

dels, partly; **lidt**, (a) little; **nogenlunde**, reasonably, sort of, somewhat; **nok**, enough; **næsten**, almost; **slet ikke**, not at all; **temmelig**, rather

Hun var *slet ikke* glad for at se ham.	She wasn't at all happy to see him.
Han var *temmelig* beruset i går.	He was rather drunk yesterday.
Kan du tale *lidt* langsommere?	Can you speak a little more slowly?

(b) The prefix **aller-** (very, by far, of all) may be added to the superlative form of adjectives (see 232(e)) and adverbs to fulfil an uptoner function:

Allerhelst blev jeg hjemme i dag.
I'd most prefer to stay at home today.

Preben kom allersidst.
Preben came last of all.

Min købmand har de allerlaveste priser.
My grocer has the very lowest prices.

(c) In colloquial Danish, prefixes such as **død-, edder-, skide-, smadder-,** etc., are sometimes added to adjectives to fulfil an uptoner function (see also 1103(b)(ii) and 1107):

Jeg var dødtræt i går.	I was dead tired yesterday.
Det er eddersmart.	That's really smart.
Han er skidefuld.	He's really pissed.

(d) When qualifying an adjective or an adverb in the positive, **meget** = very (for the negative 'not very' see (f) below; see also 447):

Hun er *meget* dygtig.	She's very competent.
Han skrev *meget* langsomt.	He wrote very slowly.

(e) When qualifying an adjective or an adverb in the comparative, **meget** = (very) much, a lot (for the negative 'not much' see (g) below):

Hun synger *meget* bedre end sin bror.
She sings much better than her brother.

Nu er han blevet *meget* klogere.
Now he's become much wiser.

(f) 'Not very' is rendered by **ikke + ret/særlig/synderlig/videre** in Danish:

Her er *ikke særlig* varmt.
It's not very warm here.

Han gjorde det *ikke ret* godt.
He didn't do it very well.

Hun var *ikke videre* tilfreds med hans arbejde.
She wasn't very pleased with his work.

Han er *ikke synderlig* intelligent.
He's not very bright.

(g) 'Not much' is rendered by **ikke + (ret) meget** in Danish:

Vi ser ham *ikke ret meget.*
We don't see him very much.

Han var *ikke meget* højere end Jens.
He was not much taller than Jens.

(h) Langt is frequently used as an uptoner in conjunction with adjectives and adverbs in the comparative and superlative, meaning '(by) far, very, much, a lot':

For tiden er han *langt* den bedste fodboldspiller i Danmark.
He's by far the best football player in Denmark at the moment.

Det vil være *langt* bedre, hvis du kommer i morgen.
It'll be much better if you come tomorrow.

(i) Endnu is used with adjectives and adverbs in the comparative to convey the sense of 'even':

Det var *endnu* større, end jeg havde troet.
It was even bigger than I'd imagined.

Du kunne gøre det *endnu* hurtigere.
You could do it even faster.

(j) In colloquial Danish (as in colloquial English) adverbs formed from adjectives are frequently used as uptoners with a meaning which no longer reflects their original, concrete sense but merely indicates degree:

Det var *forfærdelig(t)* koldt i Bulgarien.
It was dreadfully cold in Bulgaria.

Det var *frygtelig(t)* pænt af dig.
It was awfully nice of you.

C LOCATION AND MOVEMENT

616 Location and motion towards

See also 619.

(a) Among those adverbs denoting place (see 609(c)) are some which have two distinct but parallel forms. The base form (without **-e**) is used to indicate motion, whether actual, imagined or implied, towards a place, whereas the expanded form (with **-e**) is used to indicate location or rest or movement within the area in question. The adverbs of this type are:

Motion towards		*Location*	
ind	in(to), in(side)	**inde**	in(side)
ud	out(side)	**ude**	out(side)
op	up	**oppe**	up
ned	down	**nede**	down
bort	away	**borte**	away
hjem	home	**hjemme**	at home
frem	forward(s)	**fremme**	there, in front
hen	over	**henne**	over
over	over	**ovre**	over
om	over	**omme**	over

Examples:

Simon tog *hjem*, da han var træt.	Simon went home as he was tired.
Simon er ikke *hjemme* i dag.	Simon's not at home today.
Han klatrede *op* i træet.	He climbed up the tree.
Fuglene sidder *oppe* i træet.	The birds are sitting up in the tree.
Jeg skal *ud* i aften.	I'm going out tonight.
I aften skal vi spise *ude* – og jeg giver!	Tonight we'll eat out – and it's on me!

Efter at han havde taget pengene, løb han *bort*.
After he had taken the money, he ran away.

Vi bliver *borte* i flere dage.
We'll be away for several days.

(b) Notes on use (for the specific uses of and differences between **hen/henne**, **over/ovre** and **om/omme**, see 619):

(i) The use of this type of adverb occurs most frequently in conjunction with a prepositional phrase:

Han gik *op ad* trapperne. He went up the stairs.
Han er *oppe på* sit værelse. He's up in his room.

Hun gik *ind i* huset. She went into the house.
Hun var *inde i* huset. She was inside the house.

(ii) The motion involved need not always denote actual movement:

Jeg ringede *hjem* i aftes.
I rang home last night.

Om vinteren går mine tanker *ned* til Australien.
In the winter my thoughts go down to Australia.

(iii) Movement within a specific area is regarded as location, and not as motion towards:

INTO AN AREA: **Han gik *ud* i haven.**
He went out into the garden.

INSIDE AN AREA: **Han går *ude* i haven.**
He's walking in the garden.

(iv) **Nede** can also mean 'depressed, in low spirits':

Han var langt *nede,* da jeg besøgte ham.
He was depressed when I visited him.

Similarly, **oppe** can also mean 'in high spirits'.

(v) **Fremme** often means 'at one's destination':

Hvornår er vi *fremme*? When do we get there?

617 Compounded forms indicating location/motion, etc.

By means of compounding and the addition of derivational suffixes, certain adverbs in 616 above can be given special locational, directional or temporal significance. (See also 605.)

(a) When the particle **-til** is added to **her** and **der**, the directional significance of the word is amplified:

hertil, here/to this place (towards the speaker)
dertil, there/to that place (away from the speaker)

(b) When the particle **-til** is added to **hid**, it assumes a temporal significance:

hidtil, so far, up till now, hitherto

There is no equivalent form with **did**, 'up to then'; instead it is rendered by phrases such as **indtil da**.

(c) Note also:

(i) When **-steds** is added to forms of **nogen**, **ingen** or **anden**, a locational significance is implied:

nogetsteds, anywhere
ingensteds/intetsteds, nowhere
andetsteds, elsewhere

(ii) When **-sinde** is added to **nogen** or **ingen**, a temporal significance is implied:

nogensinde, ever
ingensinde, never

D SOME IDIOMATIC USAGES

618 Discourse particles

Discourse particles are words which are used – most frequently in the spoken language – to convey some attitude or comment on the part of the speaker to what is being said. The most common discourse particles in Danish are the following:

da, dog, jo, mon (ikke), nok, nu, sgu, skam, vel, vist

It is not always possible to provide a literal translation for each of these words, since their precise English equivalent (when it exists) will vary according to usage, speaker and listener perception, and the context in which they appear. As a rough guide, however, the following translations may generally be used to convey their intended meaning:

da, 'surely'
dog, 'really'
jo, '(as) you know'
mon, 'I wonder'
mon ikke, 'I suppose', 'you bet!'
nok, 'probably', 'I suppose'
nu, 'as a matter of fact'
sgu, '(I'm) damned', 'you bet'
skam, 'to be sure', 'really'
vel, 'I think', 'you'll agree'
vist, 'I think', 'it appears'

Unlike the other words in this list, **skam** and **vist** are derived respectively from a noun **skam** (shame) and an adjective **vis** (certain). When any of the above words are used in their original, 'concrete' meaning, they are usually placed at the beginning or end of an utterance (the 'extra', 'F', 'N' [in the case of **skam** and **vist**] or 'A' positions), but when they are used as discourse particles, they are normally placed immediately after the finite verb in the main clause (i.e. the 'a' position; see 1009). For example:

Hun var syg, og *dog* passede hun sit arbejde.
She was ill, and yet she attended to her work.

***Jo*, jeg har forstået det.** — Yes, I've understood it.

***Nu* har jeg spist min morgenmad.** — Now I've eaten my breakfast.
Jeg har spist min morgenmad *nu*. — I've eaten my breakfast (now).

Det var en *skam*! — That was a shame!

But:

Det var *dog* uheldigt! — That was really unfortunate!
Tom er *jo* en flink fyr. — Tom's a nice chap, you know.
Det passer *nu* ikke. — That's not true, as a matter of fact.
Henrik er *skam* i København. — Henrik is in Copenhagen, to be sure.

Da, jo, nu and **skam** are often used to convey some conviction on the part of the speaker about what is being said:

Han er *da/jo/nu/skam* i London.	He's surely in London/ He's in London, you know/ As a matter of fact, he's in London/ He's in London, to be sure.

Nok, **vel** and **vist** may be used by the speaker to express some measure of probability or uncertainty and/or to seek some measure of confirmation from the listener of what is being said:

Han er *nok/vel/vist* i London.	He's probably in London/ I think he's in London/ I suppose he's in London.

Dog is frequently used to express surprise, doubt or irritation on the part of the speaker:

Hvad har du *dog* gjort?	What on earth have you done?
Lad ham *dog* være!	Leave him alone, will you!

Sgu is a mild swearword (see 807); it often conveys an expression of surprise or conviction on the part of the speaker:

Der har vi *sgu* Martin!	I'm damned if it isn't Martin!
Det ved jeg *sgu* ikke.	How the hell should I know!
Det var *sgu* dejligt.	That was bloody marvellous.

Mon is used to express doubt or uncertainty. Unlike the other discourse particles it frequently introduces a clause or appears directly after an interrogative, and can also stand as a response in its own right:

***Mon* han er hjemme i dag?**
I wonder if he's home today?

Han nægter at svare. – *Mon dog*?
He refuses to answer. – Does he really?

Hvem *mon* har tid til sådan noget?
I wonder who's got the time for that sort of thing?

When used with **ikke**, it can be used both as an affirmation and a contradiction:

Hun er virkelig smuk. – Ja, *mon ikke*!
She's really pretty. – I'll say!

Du kender vel ikke den slags piger? – Jo, *mon ikke*?
You don't know that kind of girl, do you? – Don't I?

Mon ikke det er på tide at stå op?
I suppose it's time to get up?

619 Directional/positional adverbs

The directional/positional adverbs **hen/henne**, **om/omme** and **over/ovre** are frequently used in Danish, usually in conjunction with prepositional phrases, to indicate movement or location respectively (see 616); at times, they are untranslatable, but they generally convey the sense of 'over (there)' in some way or other:

Han gik *hen* til købmanden.	He went over to the grocer's.
Hun er *ovre* i Jylland.	She's over in Jutland.
Han er *omme* i baghaven.	He's over in the back garden.

The use of these adverbs is idiomatic and can vary considerably, depending on geography and the individual perception and preconceptions of the speaker; there is also some regional and dialectical variation in their usage. What follows can, therefore, only be a rough guide to the use of these adverbs in Danish, and deviations from this will certainly be encountered.

(a) Hen/henne are frequently used to indicate some kind of implicit purpose (often in conjunction with a modal verb; see 532). As a rule only short distances will be involved:

Jeg skal *hen* til købmanden i morgen.
I'm going to the grocer's tomorrow (i.e. I need to buy something).

Hvor skal du *hen*?
Where are you going (i.e. with what purpose)?

Hvor har du været *henne*?
Where have you been?

In the spoken language **hen** is often used in conjunction with **lige** (just), and there is an added implication that the subject will shortly return:

Jeg skal *lige hen* at tale med Birgitte.
I'm just going over to talk to Birgitte.

(b) Om/omme are used when there is an obstacle of some kind (e.g. a building) which one has to go around or circumvent; there is no straight or direct route to the place or area in question:

Han gik *om* bag busken.
He went over behind the bush.

Børnene leger *omme* i forhaven.
The children are playing (over) in the front garden (i.e. round the other side of the house).

(c) Over/ovre are used when something (e.g. a street, a stretch of water, etc.) has to be crossed; the route will normally be in a straight line, and there is no general restriction on distance as with **hen/henne**:

Han gik *over* til bageren.
He went over to the baker's (e.g. on the other side of a street).

De er *ovre* hos Jørgen.
They're over at Jørgen's.

They are also used geographically to express a positional or directional relationship on a horizontal east–west axis as perceived by the speaker:

Jeg skal *over* til Århus i morgen.
I'm going over to Århus tomorrow (e.g. when said by someone in Copenhagen).

Helene er *ovre* i Irland.
Helene's over in Ireland (e.g. when said by someone in Denmark).

(d) If the axis is perceived as being north–south, however, **op/oppe** and **ned/nede** are used, as appropriate:

Preben bor *oppe* i Norge.
Preben lives (up) in Norway (e.g. when said by someone in Denmark).

Næste sommer skal vi *ned* til Italien.
Next summer we're going (down) to Italy (e.g. from Denmark).

Op/oppe and **ned/nede** are also used when the axis is perceived as being north-east/south-west or north-west/south-east, including the geographical relationship between Greenland/Iceland/the Faroe Islands and Denmark:

Jeg skal *op* til Kalundborg i morgen.
I'm going over to Kalundborg tomorrow (e.g. when said by someone in Copenhagen).

***Oppe* på Færøerne er der mange flere får end mennesker.**
In the Faroes there are many more sheep than people.

Sidste år søgte Jannie en stilling *oppe* i Grønland.
Last year Jannie applied for a job (up) in Greenland.

I næste uge tager vi *ned* til København.
Next week we're travelling to Copenhagen (e.g. when said by someone in Iceland or the Faroes).

7 PREPOSITIONS

A INTRODUCTION

701 Prepositional form

Prepositions are indeclinable. According to form, they may be divided into four types:

(a) Simple prepositions

A *simple* preposition consists of a single morpheme. This group includes the most common prepositions, some of which are among the most frequently used words in Danish, e.g. **af, efter, fra, før, i, med, på, til, ved.**

(b) Compound prepositions

A *compound* preposition is written as one word, but consists of two independent roots:

(i) Preposition + preposition

The preposition **i** is used as a prefix to form a few compound prepositions: **iblandt**, among(st); **igennem**, through; **imellem**, between; **imod**, against, towards. These are largely stylistic variants of the equivalent uncompounded prepositions: **blandt, gennem, mellem, mod;** the compounded version being chiefly used in formal language. The compounded forms can also function as adverbs.

(ii) Preposition + noun

Ifølge (according to) is the only compound preposition consisting of a preposition + a noun.

(c) Complex prepositions

A *complex* preposition consists of two or more words (including a preposition) which together form a semantic unit that has a function similar to that of a preposition:

(i) Adverb + preposition

This combination is extremely common and the group is theoretically open-ended. Its members mostly consist of a positional/directional adverb (e.g. **bag,**

foran, frem(me), hen(ne), inden, ind(e), ned(e), neden, om(me), op(pe), oven, over/ovre, ud(e), uden, etc.) + a preposition. (For the use of adverbs indicating direction/motion see 616f, 619.)

Hun stod inde i butikken.	She was standing in the shop.
Katten sprang ned på gulvet.	The cat jumped down on the floor.
Han gik op ad trappen.	He went up the stairs.
De bor ovre på Fyn.	They live over on Funen.

Some of these adverbs (**bag, foran, inden, om, over, uden**) can also function as prepositions, whereas the rest cannot. Notice that for those with double forms (**om/omme** and **over/ovre**), only the directional version can be used as a preposition:

Han stod bag døren.	He was standing behind the door.
Hun sidder foran mig.	She is sitting in front of me.
Vi gik rundt om huset.	We went behind the house.
De kiggede over muren.	They looked over the wall.

Note 1 – Whereas certain items mentioned above, such as **ind(e), ned(e), op(pe), ud(e)**, are adverbs only, some of their English counterparts can also function as prepositions, usually with directional meaning, e.g. 'down', 'off ', 'up' as in 'down the street', 'off the table', 'up the hill', etc. Notice also **ind i** = 'into'.

Note 2 – Written Danish formally distinguishes complex prepositions of the type mentioned above (written in two words) from the equivalent compound adverbs (written in one word), e.g. **ballonen fløj opad**, the balloon flew upwards; **vi bor i huset overfor**, we live in the house opposite; etc.

(ii) Preposition + noun + preposition

There are a large number of complex prepositions that consist of a preposition + a noun + another preposition, which together constitute a semantic unit. **Af** is the most common second preposition in such constructions (cf. 'of ' in English):

> **af hensyn til**, out of consideration for; **i mangel af**, for want of; **i overensstemmelse med**, in accordance with; **med henvisning til**, with reference to; **på grund af**, on account of; **til gavn for**, for the benefit of; **til trods for**, in spite of; **ved siden af**, next to; etc.

Note 3 – In a few cases, **som** can replace the first preposition, e.g. **som følge af**, as a result of; **som udtryk for**, as an expression of; etc.

(iii) Preposition + **og** + preposition

There are some coordinated phrases consisting of a preposition + **og** + another preposition that form an idiom, e.g. **(stå) af og på**, (get) on and off; **for og imod**, for and against; **fra og med**, from and including; **med og uden**, with and without; **til og fra**, to and from; **til og med**, up to and including; etc.

(iv) Discontinuous prepositions

There are a few examples of *discontinuous* prepositions, where the prepositional complement is positioned between the two prepositional elements, e.g. **ad ... til**, in the direction of; **for ... siden**, ago; **fra ... af**, from ... onwards; etc. See also 703(b).

(d) Prepositions derived from other word classes

(i) Some participle forms can be used as prepositions, e.g. **angående**, concerning; **fraregnet**, not counting; **undtagen**, except; **vedrørende**, relating to; etc.

(ii) Some words which function as adverbs and/or conjunctions can also occur as prepositions, e.g. **bag**, behind; **efter**, after; **indtil**, until; **langs**, along; **nær**, near; **siden**, since; etc.

(iii) The adjective **lig** (like) is sometimes used as a preposition.

702 Prepositional complements

(a) The prepositional phrase

The most important function of prepositions is to form a relation between two entities. One of these is represented by the prepositional complement, the other by a different clause constituent. A preposition + complement is called a *prepositional phrase*.

(b) Prepositions and case

A preposition is said to *govern* its complement. Where possible, the prepositional complement appears in the *objective* case, but of the different types of prepositional complement mentioned in (c) below, only (some) personal pronouns have distinct objective case forms in modern Danish.

Earlier stages of the language had far more case inflexions, and prepositions governed their complements in the accusative, the genitive or the dative case. A number of fossilized prepositional phrases retain some of the old case endings after certain prepositions, notably **til** and **i** (cf. 710(j), 716(a)(ii)):

(i) Old genitive endings **-s/-e** after **til**: **til bords**, at/to (the) table; **til lands**, on land; **til låns**, on loan; **til søs**, at/to sea; **til vejrs**, up in the air; **(gå) til hånde**, lend a hand; **(komme) til orde**, be heard; **(være) til stede**, (be) present; **(komme) til syne**, (come) into sight; etc.

(ii) Old dative ending **-e** after prepositions such as **ad, for, fra, i, på**, etc., e.g. **ad åre**, in years (to come); **for fode**, at one's feet; **fra borde**, (go) ashore; **i hænde**, to hand; **i live**, alive; **på tinge**, in Parliament; etc.

(iii) After the preposition **i**, words denoting the days of the week or certain sections of a day often have an **-s** ending when used of the near past. Historically, **-s** is here an adverbial ending (cf. German: 'abends/nachts', in the evening/at night), while use of the preposition **i** is a later addition analogous with e.g. **i går**, yesterday; **i morgen**, tomorrow. Examples: **i morges**, this morning (already gone); **i aftes**, last night; **i forgårs**, the day before yesterday; **i søndags**, last Sunday; etc. The **-s** form is not acceptable in combinations like **i sommer(s)/vinter(s)** (last summer/winter) in more formal style, but such constructions are often found in colloquial language.

Note – A few prepositional phrases are loan translations from German, e.g. **til dels**, partly; **til mode**, at ease; **i sinde**, in mind; etc.

(c) Types of prepositional complement

The prepositional complement may be a noun/pronoun, an adverbial (including a prepositional phrase), an infinitive or a subordinate clause.

(i) Preposition + noun/pronoun

In the vast majority of cases, the prepositional complement is either a noun or a pronoun:

for min onkel / for ham	for my uncle / for him
fra Ulla / fra hende	from Ulla / from her
i Danmark	in Denmark
med glæde	with pleasure
under bordet / under det	under the table / under it
ved søerne / ved dem	at the lakes / at them

(ii) Preposition + adverbial

Adverbials such as adverbs and prepositional phrases can occur as prepositional complement:

1 Adverbs:

for altid	for ever
Tak for sidst!	Thank you for your recent hospitality!
Hvor kommer han fra?	Where does he come from?
indtil nu	until now
Tænk bare på dengang!	Just think of that time/those times!

2 Prepositional phrases:

Efter i morgen er det for sent.	After tomorrow it will be too late.
Fra på mandag stiger priserne.	From next Monday prices go up.
Har du set ham siden i vinter?	Have you seen him since last winter?
Tak for i dag/i går! etc.	Thank you for today/yesterday! etc.

(iii) Preposition + infinitive

In Danish, it is very common for an infinitive to function as prepositional complement. This is not possible in English, where often the preposition does not appear or a gerund is used instead of the infinitive (see 528(c)(iv)). The subject of the finite verb must also be the subject of the infinitive:

Hun har travlt med at lave mad.	She is busy cooking.
Jeg tænker på at holde op.	I'm thinking of stopping.
Det er for godt til at være sandt.	It's too good to be true.
Han gjorde det uden at blinke.	He did it without batting an eyelid.

Note 1 – **For at** (in order to) followed by an infinitive (or a subordinate clause) expresses intention:

Han kom for at hjælpe mig.	He came (in order) to help me.

Note 2 – The preposition **efter** (used of time) often governs a perfect infinitive:

Efter at have slukket lyset gik han i seng.
After having turned the light off, he went to bed.

(iv) Preposition + subordinate clause

1 **At**-clauses

In English, a preposition cannot govern a 'that'-clause. In Danish, there is no such restriction concerning **at**-clauses:

Hun sørgede for, at jeg kom hjem. She saw to it that I got home.
Det endte med, at han blev fyret. It ended with him being fired.
Jeg tror på, at hun består. I believe that she will pass.
Det lader til, at vi må flytte. It seems as if we have to move.

When the subjects of the two clauses are identical, it is often possible to have either a subordinate clause or the equivalent infinitive construction with no difference in meaning (see (c)(iii) above):

Han standsede maskinen ved at trykke på en knap.
Han standsede maskinen ved, at han trykkede på en knap.
He stopped the machine by pressing a button.

However, when there are two distinct subjects, only a subordinate clause is possible:

Ulykken skete ved, at han kørte for hurtigt.
The accident happened because he drove too fast.

A preposition is obligatory between certain verbs and a following subordinate clause or an infinitive. In each case, the relationship between verb and preposition is so close that no other preposition would be possible without changing the meaning, e.g. **bede om (at)**, ask, request; **lade til (at)**, seem; **protestere mod (at)**, protest about; **regne med (at)**, expect; **tvivle på (at)**, doubt; etc.:

Hun bad om, at hun måtte gå. She asked if she could go.
Jeg tvivler på, at han husker det. I doubt that he'll remember it.

On the other hand, there are also cases where the preposition is optional, e.g. **håbe (på) at**, hope that; **tro (på) at**, believe that; etc.

Jeg håber (på), at maden er klar. I hope that the food is ready.

Similarly, a particular preposition may be attached to a noun, e.g. **give udtryk for**, express; **føre regnskab med**, keep account of; **føle sorg over**, feel grief at; **have troen på**, believe; **have tillid til**, have confidence in; **føle glæde ved**, feel pleasure at; etc.:

Han gav udtryk for, at han var træt. He indicated that he was tired.
Hun har troen på, at det vil gå godt. She believes that it will go well.

Or a preposition may be attached to an adjective, e.g. **bange for (at)**, afraid; **glad for (at)**, glad; **ked af (at)**, sorry; **sikker på (at)**, certain, sure; etc.

Han er glad for, at han gik med.	He is glad that he went along.
Jeg er ked af, at du ikke vandt.	I'm sorry that you didn't win.

2 Other types of subordinate clause

In Danish, a preposition can govern an interrogative clause introduced either by **om** (whether) or by an interrogative **hv**-word. This construction is also possible in English:

Det afhænger af, om vi kan få støtte til projektet.
It depends on whether we can get support for the project.

Jeg er bange for, hvad der kan være sket.
I'm afraid of what may have happened.

Han er ikke sikker på, hvor de bor.
He is not sure where they live.

703 The place of prepositions

Prepositions in Danish can be divided into three groups according to their position in relation to the prepositional complement:

Preposed prepositions precede the prepositional complement.
Discontinuous prepositions surround the prepositional complement.
Postposed prepositions follow the prepositional complement.

(a) Preposed prepositions

The vast majority of prepositions precede their complement, e.g. **foran huset**, in front of the house; **fra byen**, from the town; **i spisestuen**, in the dining-room; **til hans søster**, to his sister; **uden hjælp**, without help; **ved stranden**, at the seaside; etc. But see also (c)(iii).

(b) Discontinuous prepositions

(i) A small number of prepositions consist of two parts with the complement placed between them:

ad ... til	**ad byen til**	towards the town
for ... siden	**for fem år siden**	five years ago

fra ... af	**fra valget af**	from the election on
på ... nær	**på ham nær**	apart from him
	(Also: **på nær ham**)	

(ii) A subgroup of these have a noun as their second element. The complement is usually a genitive or a possessive pronoun:

for ... skyld	**for hendes skyld**	for her sake
i ... sted	**i dit sted**	(if I were) in your place
på ... vegne	**på firmaets vegne**	on behalf of the company

But with a 'heavy' complement:

På vegne af hele det skandinaviske institut i Hull ...
On behalf of the entire Scandinavian Studies Department at Hull ...

(c) Postposed prepositions

(i) In certain idiomatic phrases, some prepositions may also be placed after the complement:

dem foruden	apart from them
mange år igennem	for many years
hele landet over	throughout the country

(ii) Some prepositions form the second element in compounded adverbs. These are characteristic of formal written Danish, and most of them have the locative adverbs **der-** or **her-** as their first element:

deriblandt, among which; **derefter**, thereafter; **derfor**, therefore; **derigennem**, through which; **desuden**, in addition; **herover**, over here, at which; **herpå**, on which; **hertil**, to which; **herved**, at which; **hidtil**, hitherto; etc.

(iii) In three types of construction, the preposition is often found in clause-final position:

1 When the complement is moved to front (topic) position in the clause, in order to give it greater emphasis. This is especially common with personal pronoun complements, though it is rarely found in English:

Jeg kan godt lide Karen, men Jens synes jeg ikke om.
I like Karen, but Jens I don't care for.

Ham er der fut i.	There are no flies on him.
Hende kan man regne med.	You can count on her.
Det tror jeg ikke på.	I don't believe that.
Dem har Peter ringet til.	Peter has phoned them.

2 Often in interrogative and relative clauses, when the interrogative/relative pronoun is a prepositional complement (or part of it). Notice that the relative pronoun may be omitted:

Interrogative pronoun

Hvem synes du bedst om?	Whom do you like best?
Hvilket hus bor du i?	Which house do you live in?
Hvad tænker du på?	What are you thinking of?

Relative pronoun

Landet, (som) vi bor i ...	The country (that) we live in ...
Pigen, (som) han talte med ...	The girl (whom) he talked to ...
Træet, (som) jeg sidder under ...	The tree (that) I'm sitting under ...

Notice also the following related type which may be expanded to include a relative clause:

en kop til at drikke af	a cup to drink from
(en kop, (som) man kan drikke af ...	a cup (that) one can drink from ...)
en blok til at skrive på	a pad to write on
Er det en måde at opføre sig på?	Is that a way to behave?
et lys til at læse ved	a light to read by

3 In some set expressions, especially when the preposition forms a semantic unit with the verb, a 'prepositional verb', Danish allows the preposition to appear without an overt complement where this is often not possible in English:

Han skal sidde efter.	He's got a detention.
Jeg skal nok stå for.	I'll shield you.
Vil du med?	Are you coming along?
Du må sige til.	You must tell me/us/them, etc.

704 Prepositions and related word classes

Prepositions are closely related to adverbs, in particular, and to conjunctions. In fact, many words that function as prepositions can also function as adverbs or as conjunctions. In this paragraph, we shall look briefly at these two word classes and their respective relationship to prepositions. For adverbs see Chapter 6; for conjunctions see Chapter 9.

(a) Prepositions and adverbs

A number of prepositions can also function as adverbs, e.g. **af, efter, for, i, med, på, til, ved,** etc. Traditionally the difference between these two word classes is that those items that have a complement are said to be prepositions, while those that do not are adverbs. In a number of cases, this is a reasonably clear distinction, but for various reasons it is not always entirely satisfactory. Alternatives include conflating the two classes into one (often called 'particles') and expanding the notion of prepositions to encompass those items that can *potentially* combine with a complement, i.e. those traditionally termed adverbs.

Even though, from a theoretical point of view, both these 'solutions' have some merits, we shall in general follow the traditional distinction between prepositions and adverbs, but for practical purposes some of the examples of the use of individual prepositions in Sections B and C below will feature items which strictly speaking fall under adverbs.

To exemplify: in the sentence, **du skal stå af bussen nu** (you must get off the bus now), **af** is a preposition because it has the complement **bussen**. However, in the sentence, **du skal stå af nu** (you must get off now), **af** is an adverb because it does not have a complement. The combination 'verb + preposition', which can potentially take a complement, is known as a *prepositional verb*.

By contrast, in the sentence, **du skal slappe af nu** (you must relax now), **af** could not possibly take a complement and is therefore defined as an adverb. In such cases, the combination 'verb + adverb', which tends to constitute both a syntactic and a semantic unit, is known as a *phrasal verb*. In phrasal verbs the adverb is usually stressed (see 705).

A verb may also have both an adverb and a preposition attached to it, in which case we have a *phrasal-prepositional verb*, e.g. **blive ved med**, keep on (doing); **slippe af med**, get rid of; compare English 'look down on', 'put up with', etc.

Unlike prepositional verbs, some phrasal verbs allow a direct object. The difference between this and a prepositional complement is that an object occurs *between* the verb and the adverb, whereas a prepositional complement (in these cases) *follows* the preposition. The following examples are all phrasal verbs with an object:

Han tog frakken af.	He took his coat off.
Jeg skar stegen for.	I carved the roast.
Hun klædte barnet på.	She dressed the child.

Note – English allows a noun object of a phrasal verb to appear both before and after the adverb, e.g. 'he took his coat off/he took off his coat', but with a pronominal object only the former possibility exists: 'he took it off'.

(b) Prepositions and conjunctions

Certain prepositions can also function as conjunctions, e.g. **efter, for, om, til.** The distinction between these two word classes is much more clear-cut than that between prepositions and adverbs (see (a) above). A conjunction introduces a clause, whereas a preposition can govern different types of complement, including a clause headed by a conjunction (see 702(c)(iv)). Even though the same item can occur both as preposition and conjunction, there is little risk of confusion:

Preposition

Vi læste efter mørkets frembrud.	We read after dusk.
Det er et spørgsmål om penge.	It's a question of money.
Har du set ham siden i går?	Have you seen him since yesterday?
Jeg ventede til klokken 4.	I waited until 4 o'clock.

Conjunction

Vi læste, efter (at) det blev mørkt.
We read after it got dark.

Det er et spørgsmål, om han har nogen penge.
It's doubtful whether he has any money.

Har du set ham, siden han kom hjem?
Have you seen him since he came home?

Jeg ventede, til klokken var 4.
I waited until it was 4 o'clock.

705 Prepositions and stress

(a) As one of the minor word classes, prepositions are usually unstressed in their primary function, viz. that of forming a relation between two entities (see 702(a)). However, prepositions may receive stress under certain circumstances.

(b) As far as prepositional stress is concerned, the interaction between the preposition and its complement is of vital importance. Personal pronouns are usually unstressed when they function as prepositional complements, unless they receive contrastive stress. Generally speaking, prepositions are stressed when their complement is unstressed. Otherwise, prepositions fall into two groups:

(i) Group I consists of the following prepositions: **ad, af, for, fra, hos, i, med, om, på, til, ved**. These are *unstressed* when their complement is stressed:

Stressed complement	*Unstressed complement*	
fra ´fyrtårnet	**´fra det**	from the lighthouse
i ´lommen	**´i den**	in the pocket
med ´børnene	**´med dem**	with the children
på ´bordet	**´på det**	on the table
til ´dig	**´til dig**	to you

(ii) Group II consists of the following prepositions: **bag, efter, foran, forbi, før, (i)gennem, (i)mod, (i)mellem, inden, indtil, langs, omkring, over (for), siden, uden, under**. These are either *stressed* or *unstressed* when their complement is stressed:

Stressed complement	*Unstressed complement*	
(´)efter ´valget	**´efter det**	after the election
(´)før ´krigen	**´før den**	before the war
(´)langs ´vejen	**´langs den**	along the road
(´)over ´døren	**´over den**	over the door
(´)uden ´dem	**´uden dem**	without them

(c) The distance of the complement from the preposition also plays a role for prepositional stress, insofar as a preposition will have at least secondary stress if it is not immediately followed by the complement. The preposition may be separated from its complement in two ways:

(i) Something may intervene between the preposition and the complement, e.g. a coordinated verb phrase whose object is also the prepositional complement:

Jeg ledte ˈefter og fandt også et egetræsbord.
I looked for and found an oak table.

Vi håber ˈpå og forventer et hurtigt svar.
We hope for and expect a speedy reply.

(ii) The prepositional complement may be fronted, leaving the preposition 'stranded' in final position. This is particularly common when the complement is a pronoun:

ˈDen bog har jeg ikke hørt om.	I haven't heard of that book.
ˈHam kan vi ikke regne med.	We can't count on him.
ˈHvad lytter du til?	What are you listening to?
Det er ˈhende, som jeg ser på.	She is the one I'm looking at.

(d) Postposed prepositions (see 703(c)) are always stressed:

livet iˈgennem	throughout life
mand og mand iˈmellem	among people in general
hele verden ˈover	throughout the whole world

(e) Coordinated prepositions are always stressed:

ˈfra og ˈmed i morgen	starting tomorrow
ˈi og ˈmed deres opfattelse	given their views
togene ˈtil og ˈfra Jylland	the trains to and from Jutland

This is also the case in less idiomatic constructions:

Jeg er spændt ˈpå, men bange ˈfor hans reaktion.
I am anxious about, but afraid of, his reaction.

(f) Prepositions are stressed when the complement is omitted. In such cases they have adverbial function and are often part of a 'prepositional verb' (see 704(a)), e.g. **stå ˈaf**, get off; **holde ˈmed**, support (in sport); **se ˈpå**, watch; **slå ˈtil**, hit hard, accept; etc.

Hvor står du ˈaf?	Where do you get off?
But: **Hun stod af ˈbussen.**	She got off the bus.
Hvem holder du ˈmed?	Whom do you support?

But: **Jeg holder med ´Danmark.**	I support Denmark.
Du skal slå ´til!	You must hit hard!
But: **Du må ikke ´slå til bal´lonen.**	You mustn't hit the balloon.

(g) Prepositions may be attached to verbs with strong or weak stress. Contrast e.g. **´regne med** (count on) and **holde ´med** (support); **´vente på,** (wait for) and **se ´på** (watch), etc. This difference will be further exemplified under the individual prepositions in Section B.

B THE USE OF SOME COMMON PREPOSITIONS

706 Introduction

In this section, we shall look at the use of twelve common prepositions in Danish. The number of distinctions relevant for translation into English varies from preposition to preposition, but a few fundamental ones will be mentioned here.

Nearly all the prepositions dealt with below can appear with both *spatial* and *temporal* meaning (i.e. location in space and location in time). Spatial meaning can be further subdivided into *literal/physical* and (by extension) *figurative* meaning; 'figurative' implies that the 'original' literal meaning is still more or less 'transparent'. Thus, for example, **på** has literal spatial meaning in **bogen ligger på bordet** (the book is lying on the table); it has figurative meaning in **vi er på randen af en katastrofe** (we are on the verge of a catastrophe); and it has temporal meaning in **vi kommer på søndag** (we are coming on Sunday). If, however, the meaning of the preposition or the prepositional phrase becomes so far removed from the original literal meaning that it is no longer transparent, i.e. it has become 'opaque', it is said to have *abstract* meaning. This is, for instance, the case in some idiomatic expressions, such as **på må og få** (at random). Other types of meaning will be distinguished under the individual prepositions.

Using prepositions correctly is one of the most difficult tasks facing learners of a foreign language, and the correct use of Danish prepositions is no exception. Nevertheless, when comparing Danish and English there are a number of correspondences in the basic meanings of many prepositions. Generally speaking, it is much easier to predict or 'guess' the right preposition when it has spatial (and, to some extent, temporal) meaning than it is when it has abstract meaning. This is not surprising since abstract meaning is furthest removed from notions of time and space and therefore not subject to the same restrictions of use. This fact is most clearly demonstrated by idiomatic expressions because, by definition, they cannot be broken down into the meanings of their individual parts, but must be understood – and learnt – as whole phrases.

It is, of course, impossible to provide an exhaustive treatment of prepositional usage and meanings within the scope of this chapter, but it is hoped that the following guidelines will be of some use to readers. For more specific exemplification of the use and meanings of individual prepositions, readers are advised to consult *Dansk Sprogbrug*, *Nudansk Ordbog* or a good Danish–English/English–Danish dictionary. The most comprehensive treatment is to be found in the monumental *Ordbog over det danske Sprog*, but that is decidedly not for beginners.

The following prepositions are examined in some detail below: **af** (707); **efter** (708); **for** (709); **i** (710); **med** (711); **mod** (712); **om** (713); **over** (714); **på** (715); **til** (716); **under** (717); **ved** (718).

707 Af

The preposition **af** often implies a source, an origin or a starting-point for something, whether material or not, but it also has other uses, including the important one of introducing the agent in a passive clause.

(a) Introducing the agent in a passive clause

When the agent appears in a passive clause, it is introduced by the preposition **af** (by) (see 541):

Billedet blev taget af min søn.	The photo was taken by my son.
(Cf. **Min søn tog billedet.**	My son took the photo.)
Han blev kørt over af en bil.	He was run over by a car.
Kødbenet blev spist af hunden.	The bone was eaten by the dog.

Note – **Af** also indicates the agent in constructions of the following type, where the verb of action has been omitted:

Det var dumt/pænt/sødt af dig.	That was stupid/nice/sweet of you.

(b) Direction – 'out of'

In this sense, **af** is usually preceded by a directional adverb, e.g. **frem, op, ud,** etc.:

out of

komme frem af sit skjul	come out of hiding
tage gaven op af æsken	take the present out of the box
gå ud af huset	go out of the house

(c) Source – material

(i) of

et hus af træ	a house of wood
en statue af marmor	a statue of marble

(ii) from

lave vin af hyldebær	make wine from elderberries

(d) Source – cause

(i) from, of

(physical)	
lide af gigt	suffer from rheumatism
(abstract)	
dø af sorg	die of grief
Hun vidste det af erfaring.	She knew it from experience.

(ii) with

(emotion)	
De græd af glæde.	They cried with joy.
Han blev grøn af misundelse.	He became green with envy.

(iii) for

af frygt for følgerne	for fear of the consequences
af mangel på penge	for lack of money

(e) Source – person

from/off

Man kan få/købe/låne det af ham.
One can get/buy/borrow it from/off him.

(f) Partitive

of

ingen/nogle/en del/halvdelen af ...	none/some/part/half of ...
i fire af fem tilfælde	in four out of five cases

Note – **Af** in this sense indicates an incomplete part of a 'whole'. Pronouns denoting a complete total cannot combine with **af**, unlike their English equivalents which can take an optional 'of ', e.g. **alle lærerne**, all (of) the teachers; **begge deltagerne**, both (of the) participants; **hele holdet**, the whole (of the) team. Equally, expressions of measure in Danish do not take **af**, e.g. **en kop kaffe**, a cup of coffee; **et glas vin**, a glass of wine; **en skefuld sukker**, a spoonful of sugar; etc.

(g) Possession, 'belonging to'

of

dronningen af Danmark	the Queen of Denmark
ejeren af hunden	the owner of the dog
et medlem af familien	a member of the family
en mand af få ord	a man of few words
på hjørnet af gaden	on the corner of the street
en bog af stor værdi	a book of great value
være af den opfattelse, at ...	be of the opinion that ...

Note – Some of these examples correspond to a genitive construction or a compound noun, e.g. **Danmarks dronning, hundens ejer, et familiemedlem, et gadehjørne**, etc.

(h) Attached to nouns

When attached to a noun, **af** often implies a result or trace of a past action:

i egenskab af, in the capacity of; **forekomsten af**, the existence of; **frugten af**, the fruits of; **gøre nar af**, make fun of; **resultatet/udfaldet af**, the result of; etc.

(i) Attached to verbs with strong stress (see 705(g))

bestå af, consist of; **komme af**, be due to; **leve af**, live off; etc.

(j) Attached to verbs with weak stress (see 705(g))

Several of these are 'phrasal verbs', in which **af** has adverbial function (see 704(a)):

børste af, brush off; **holde af**, be fond of; **klæde (sig) af**, undress (oneself); **runde af**, round off; **ryste af**, shake off; **skrubbe af**, clear off, disappear; **slappe af**, relax; **stige/stå af**, get off (e.g. the bus); **tørre af**, dry, wipe; etc.

(k) Attached to adjectives/participles

fuld af, full of; **ked af**, sorry about; **stolt af**, proud of; **træt af**, tired of; etc.

(l) Idiomatic expressions with **af**

Hvad blev der af ham?	What became of him?
Det blev der ikke noget af.	Nothing came of it.
Hvor bliver du af?	Are you coming then?
Hvad er den af?	What's going on?
Hvad går der af dig?	What's the matter with you?
Det har du (rigtig) godt af!	It serves you right!

708 Efter

The preposition **efter** is used of both space and time to indicate notions such as 'after', 'following', etc., as well as covering other senses.

(a) Space

(i) behind

Vi fulgte efter taxaen.	We followed the taxi.
Luk døren efter dig!	Shut the door behind you!

(ii) after

Han løb efter mig.	He ran after me.
B kommer efter A.	B comes after A.

(b) Time

after

efter kl. to, efter en time	after two o'clock, after an hour
efter arbejde, efter ferien	after work, after the holidays

(c) Succession

after/by

kilometer efter kilometer	kilometre after kilometre (mile after mile)

den ene efter den anden	one after the other
Efter Ole er Lise den ældste.	After Ole Lise is the oldest.
én efter én	one by one

(d) Source

from/of

Der er spor efter et dyr.	There are tracks from/of an animal.

(e) Reference

(i) according to/in accordance with

klæde sig efter årstiden	dress according to the season
stille op efter størrelse	line up according to size
sælge noget efter vægt	sell something by weight
Efter hvad han fortalte mig ...	According to what he told me ...
efter bedste evne	to the best of one's ability

(ii) by

sejle efter stjernerne	sail by the stars
spille efter gehør/reglerne	play by ear/the rules

(f) Attached to nouns

When attached to a noun, **efter** often implies a longing or desire for something. However, these are usually formed by analogy with the corresponding verb (see (g) below):

> **længsel efter**, longing for; **sende bud efter**, send for; **stræben efter**, striving for; **søgen efter**, search for; **holde udkig efter**, be on the lookout for; etc.

(g) Attached to verbs with strong stress (see 705(g))

In most of these cases, English uses 'for':

> **lede/søge efter**, look/search for; **længes efter**, long for; **løbe efter**, run for; **rette sig efter**, conform to, follow; **ringe efter**, phone for; **snappe efter (vejret)**, gasp for (breath); **spørge efter**, ask for; **stræbe efter**, strive for; **tørste efter**, thirst for; **være (ude) efter (noget)**, be after (something); etc.

(h) Attached to verbs with weak stress (see 705(g))

Several of these are 'phrasal verbs', in which **efter** has adverbial function (see 704(a)):

abe efter, imitate; **give efter**, give in; **høre efter**, listen; **sidde efter**, be in detention; etc.

Note – In many adverbial expressions of time, **efter** follows its complement, e.g. **kort/lidt efter,** shortly after; **længe efter,** long after; **snart efter,** soon after; **et øjeblik efter,** a moment later; **året efter,** the following year; etc.

709 For

The preposition **for** is used with a wide range of meanings in Danish, only some of which correspond to 'for' in English.

(a) Space

(i) **For** is not often used in a literal spatial sense; here **foran** is usually preferred:

in front of

Hold dig for munden!	Put your hand in front of your mouth!
sætte skodder for vinduerne	put shutters in front of the windows

(ii) Notice the following complex prepositions (see 701(c)) consisting of a positional adverb (expressing non-motion) + **for**:

inden for døren	inside the door
uden for huset	outside the house
oven for landsbyen	above the village
neden for kirken	below the church

(b) Time

(i) at

for nærværende, for øjeblikket	at present, at the moment

(ii) for

for altid/evigt, for livet, for tiden	for ever, for life, for the moment
et værelse for natten	a room for the night
vejrudsigten for weekenden	the weather forecast for the weekend

for første/sidste gang — for the first/last time

Note – Notice the discontinuous preposition **for ... siden** (ago):

for to uger siden, two weeks ago; **for længe siden**, a long time ago; etc.

(c) Means

with

købe noget for ens egne penge
buy something with one's own money

(d) Beneficiary, 'intended for'

(i) for

fjernsyn for børn — TV for children
boliger for ældre — homes for elderly people

transportmidler for handicappede
means of transport for disabled people

(ii) **for** + complement (usually animate) as indirect object:

to

beskrive/forklare/læse noget for nogen
describe/explain/read something to someone

præsentere nogen/noget for nogen
introduce someone/something to someone

være til hindring/hjælp/nytte for nogen
be a hindrance/of help/of use to someone

være fremmed/nyt for nogen
be strange/new to someone

Note 1 – The notion of 'beneficiary', including the role as indirect object, is often expressed by **til** rather than **for** (see 716).

Note 2 – **For at** + infinitive is used to express intention (see 528(c)(iv), 702(c) note 1).

(e) Concealment

from

gemme/skjule noget for nogen — hide something from someone

have hemmeligheder for nogen	have secrets from someone

(f) Genitive

of

chefen for firmaet	the manager of the company
tidspunktet for afrejsen	the time of the departure

(g) Replacement

(i) (in exchange) for

Vi købte en bil for 100.000 kroner.
We bought a car for 100,000 kroner.

Jeg betalte 20 kroner for en øl.
I paid 20 kroner for a beer.

noget for noget
something for something (quid pro quo)

øje for øje og tand for tand
an eye for an eye, a tooth for a tooth

i stedet for en ferie
instead of a holiday

Hvad er det engelske ord for 'hygge'?
What is the English word for 'hygge'?

(ii) for, on behalf of

Hun arbejder/spiser for to.	She works/eats for two.
Han taler for alle dem, som ...	He speaks for all those who ...
én gang for alle	once and for all
én for alle og alle for én	one for all and all for one

Note –The verb **betale** (pay) is often followed by a direct object rather than a prepositional phrase with **for** when a sum is not specified, e.g. **Jeg betalte avisen/frakken,** etc., I paid for the newspaper/the coat, etc.

(h) Response

for

rose/straffe/takke nogen for noget
praise/punish/thank someone for something

Han skældte mig ud for min næsvished.
He told me off for my impertinence.

Hun modtog et legat for sin indsats.
She received a scholarship for her achievement.

(i) Distributive

by

skridt for skridt, stykke for stykke, år for år
step by step, bit by bit, year by year

for

mand for mand, ord for ord man for man, word for word

(j) Enumeration

no prep.

for det første/andet, etc. first(ly)/second(ly), etc.

(k) Attached to nouns

have brug for, have a need for; **et emne for**, a subject for; **have/vise interesse for**, take/show an interest in; **et mål for**, a target for; etc.

(l) Attached to verbs with strong stress (see 705(g))

anklage for, accuse of; **anse for**, regard as; **dø for**, die for; **interessere sig for**, take an interest in; **kæmpe/slås for**, fight for; **mistænke for**, suspect of; **servere for**, serve; **spærre for**, obstruct; **sørge for**, see to; **takke for**, thank for; **tænde for**, switch/turn on; **vogte sig for**, be on guard against; etc.

(m) Attached to verbs with weak stress (see 705(g))

Some of these are 'phrasal verbs', in which **for** has adverbial function (see 704(a)):

have (lektier) for, have homework to do; **(ikke) kunne gøre for det**, (not) be able to help it; **holde for**, hold something up as cover, be a target; **se sig for**, look out; **stå for**, shield; **sætte sig for at**, resolve to; **synge for**, lead the singing; **tage for sig**, help oneself; **trække for**, draw the curtains; etc.

(n) Attached to adjectives/participles

bange for, afraid of; **berømt for,** famous for; **dårlig/god for,** bad/good for; **glad for,** (be) happy about, like; **kendt for,** renowned for; **urolig for,** worried about; **typisk for,** typical of; etc.

(o) Idiomatic expressions with **for**

for eksempel	for example/instance
for min skyld	for my sake
bo for sig selv	live on one's own
dø for egen hånd	die by one's own hand
Er det noget for dig?	Is that something for you?
være noget for sig (selv)	be rather special/peculiar
Hvad er det for én/noget?	What is that?

710 I

The preposition **i** is the most common of all Danish prepositions and (after **og,** and) the most frequently used word in the Danish language. In addition to its appearance in many prepositional phrases indicating space and time, it has a wide range of idiomatic uses.

(a) Space

(i) Of towns, areas, countries, etc. (but *not* islands, see **på,** 715)

in/at

i London/Jylland/Danmark	in London/Jutland/Denmark
Toget standsede i Odense.	The train stopped at Odense.

(ii) Of objects with the notion of 'inside'

in

i bilen/bogen/bygningen	in the car/book/building
i huset/slottet/toget	in the house/castle/train
i glasset/kassen/koppen/pakken	in the glass/box/cup/parcel
komme fløde i kaffen/salt i maden	put cream in the coffee/salt in the food

(iii) Of places or institutions in terms of function

at

være i kirke/skole	be at church/school

(iv) Possession

of

borgmesteren i Roskilde	the mayor of Roskilde
gulvet i huset	the floor of the house

(v) Of electronic media

on

tale i telefon	speak on the (tele)phone
høre i radioen, se i fjernsynet	hear on the radio, watch on TV

(vi) After verbs of motion in connection with institutions

to

gå i biografen/kirke/seng/skole/teatret
go to the cinema/church/bed/school/the theatre

(vii) Generally with verbs of motion

into

Han stak hænderne i lommen.	He put his hands into his pockets.
Han blev smidt i fængsel.	He was thrown into prison.

But usually **i** is preceded by a directional adverb (**ind, ned, op, ud**, etc.) when following a verb of motion and indicating movement 'into' something (cf. 619):

Jeg gik ind i stuen.	I went into the living-room.
Katten faldt ned i hullet.	The cat fell into the hole.
Hun løb ud i haven.	She ran into the garden.

(viii) Parts of the body

Here Danish often uses **i** (especially with reflexive verbs), while English typically has the relevant part of the body as direct object (i.e. without a preposition):

vaske sig i ansigtet, wash one's face; **skære sig i fingeren/tåen**, cut one's finger/toe; **holde/tage én i hånden**, hold/take someone's hand; **trække én i håret**, pull someone's hair; **have ondt i maven**, have stomach ache; **klø sig i nakken**, scratch one's head; **slå én i øjet**, hit someone in the eye; etc.

Also:

Det gør ondt i foden/hovedet, etc. — My foot/head, etc., is hurting.

(b) Time

(i) at

i begyndelsen/starten/slutningen af året
at the beginning/start/end of the year

(ii) for

Vi har boet her i fem år. — We have lived here for five years.

(iii) in

i april, i 1948, aldrig i livet — in April, in 1948, never in my life

(iv) of

den tiende i måneden — (on) the tenth of the month

(v) per/a(n)

to gange i minuttet/timen, 100 km i timen
twice a minute/an hour, 100 km per hour

(vi) (clock time) to

ti minutter/et kvarter i tolv — ten (minutes)/a quarter to twelve

(vii) no prep.

i går, i dag, i morgen, i år
yesterday, today, tomorrow, this year

i mandags, i aftes, i påsken
last Monday, last night, last/this Easter

(c) Material

in

støbe i bronze/jern — cast in bronze/iron
klædt i hvidt/pelsværk — dressed in white/fur
skåle i snaps — drink a toast in akvavit

(d) Condition, state

(i) **at**

være i krig, være i vildrede	be at war, be all at sea

(ii) in

i knibe, i syv sind, i tvivl	in a pickle, in two minds, in doubt
i form, i god tilstand	in shape, in good condition
i fyrrene, i sin bedste alder	in one's forties, in one's prime
leve i fattigdom/luksus	live in poverty/luxury

(e) Means

at

i fuld fart	at full speed

in

udtrykke noget i ord/tal	express something in words/figures

(f) In the form of

få for lidt i drikkepenge/løn/understøttelse
get too little in tips/wages/benefits

få noget i fødselsdagsgave/julegave
get something as a birthday/Christmas present

betale i kontanter
pay cash

blive trukket i skat
be deducted as tax

(g) Attached to nouns

have del i, have a share in; **tage del i**, take part in; **ekspert i**, expert in; **kundskaber i**, knowledge of; **professor i**, professor of; **have ret i**, be right about; etc.

(h) Attached to verbs with weak stress (see 705(g))

Some of these are 'phrasal verbs', in which **i** has adverbial function (see 704(a)):

falde i, fall in (e.g. into the water), slam to (e.g. a door), strike up (music); **hænge i**, get caught (e.g. clothes), keep at it; **plumpe i**, put one's foot in it; etc.

(i) Attached to adjectives/participles

ansat i, employed in; **forelsket/skudt i**, in love with; **forgabet i**, infatuated with; **holde/sidde fast i**, hold on to, be stuck in; **interesseret i**, interested in; etc.

(j) Idiomatic expressions with **i**

i og for sig	as such, in itself
i og med (at)	given/seeing (that)
få fat i	get hold of
hånd i hånd	hand in hand

Some of these retain the old dative case ending **-e** after **i** (see 702(b)), e.g.:

i drømme	in one's dreams
få i hænde	come to hand
have i sinde (at)	intend (to)

711 Med

The preposition **med** covers many of the ordinary meanings of English 'with', but in some cases English uses other prepositions.

(a) Concomitant/accompanying

with

Vi rejste på ferie med vores børn.
We went on holiday with our children.

kaffe med sukker og fløde
coffee with sugar and cream

Note – The combination **sammen med** is more frequent in Danish than is 'together with' in English:

Han var sammen med sin veninde.	He was with his girlfriend.
Hun ankom sammen med sin mand.	She arrived with her husband.

(b) Manner/accompanying gesture

(i) with

med et glimt i øjet, med et smil
with a twinkle in one's eye, with a smile

med beklagelse, med glæde, med sorg
with regret, with pleasure, with sadness

(ii) no prep.

Han stod der med hatten i hånden.
He stood there, cap in hand.

Hun løb af sted med håret flagrende i vinden.
She ran along, her hair flowing in the wind.

(c) Means

(i) by

rejse med bus/båd/fly/tog(et)	travel by bus/boat/plane/train
sende noget med posten	send something by post
betale med check	pay by cheque

Hun har to børn med sin første mand.
She has two children by her first husband.

(ii) Mode of expression

in

skrive med blyant, tale med høj stemme
write in pencil, speak in a loud voice

skrive med små/store bogstaver
write in small/capital letters

med andre ord
in other words

(iii) with

spise med kniv og gaffel, med fingrene
eat with a knife and fork, with one's fingers

se noget med det blotte øje

see something with the naked eye

fylde spanden med vand
fill the bucket with water

(d) Possession

(i) 'dressed in'

in

en mand med sort frakke, en dame med blå hat
a man in a black coat, a lady in a blue hat

en mand med brune sko, en dame med høje hæle
a man in brown shoes, a lady in high heels

(ii) 'containing'

of

en mand med evner/idéer	a man of ability/ideas
en kasse med champagne	a case of champagne
en kurv med blomster	a basket of flowers

(iii) 'having'

with

en kone med fire børn
a woman with (i.e. who has) four children

en pige med lyst hår, en mand med træben
a girl with blond hair, a man with a wooden leg

et stykke (smørrebrød) med sild
a piece of bread with herring

Note – When a major and a minor thing are felt to 'belong together', they are sometimes connected by **med** in Danish, but by 'and' in English, e.g.:

bøf med løg	steak and onions
pølser med brød	sausages and breadrolls

(e) Measure

by

forlænge med ti meter/fire uger	extend by ten metres/four weeks

Prisen faldt/steg (med) 10%.	The price fell/rose by 10%.
dele/gange med 5	divide/multiply by 5

Danmark vandt over Tyskland med 2–0.
Denmark beat Germany 2–0 (by two goals to nil).

(f) Elliptical expressions

with

Af med tøjet!
Off with your clothes!

Ned med regeringen/tyrannerne!
Down with the government/the tyrants!

Ud med ham! Ud med sproget!
Out with him! Out with it!

Ud med dommeren!
Get the referee off!

Note – Such emotional expressions are very colloquial and often idiomatic and can therefore vary widely from language to language, e.g.:

Op med humøret!	Cheer up!
Han måtte op med 100 kroner.	He had to fork out 100 kroner.

(g) Attached to nouns

i familie med, related to; **i forbindelse med**, in connection with; **i lighed med**, like; **medlidenhed med**, pity for; **sammenligning med**, comparison with; **have tålmodighed med**, have patience with; etc.

(h) Attached to verbs with strong stress (see 705(g))

begynde med, begin with; **beskæftige sig med**, do, be occupied with; **blive af med**, get rid of; **forlove sig med**, become engaged to; **gifte sig med**, marry; **handle med**, deal/trade with; **komme sammen med**, go out with; **lege med**, play with; **nøjes med**, make do with; **regne med**, count on; **skændes med**, quarrel with; **slutte med**, end/finish with; **sløse med**, be careless with; **tale med**, talk to; **vente med**, delay (doing something); etc.

(i) Attached to verbs with weak stress (see 705(g))

Some of these are 'phrasal verbs', in which **med** has adverbial function (see 704(a)):

følge med, keep up; **holde med**, support (in sport); **komme med**, come along; **køre med**, have a lift; **spille med**, join in a game; **spise med**, join someone for a meal; **synge med**, join in the singing; **tælle med**, count; **være med**, attend, participate; etc.

(j) Attached to adjectives/participles

(i) to

forlovet med, engaged to; **gift med**, married to; **identisk med**, identical to; **ligeglad med**, indifferent to; **sammenlignet med**, compared to/with; etc.

(ii) with

(be)kendt med, acquainted with; **(u)enig med**, in (dis)agreement with; **forsigtig med**, careful with; **færdig med**, finished with; **sammen/tillige med**, together with; **(u)tilfreds med**, (dis)satisfied with; etc.

(k) Idiomatic expressions with **med**

med fornøjelse	with pleasure
med henblik på	with a view to
med hensyn til (m.h.t.)	regarding
med mere (m.m.), med videre (m.v.)	and so on, etc.
med vilje	on purpose
lige med ét/det samme	suddenly
fra og med	as from
til og med	up to and including
være Des med	be on formal terms with
være dus med	be on familiar terms/familiar with
Hvad med børnene?	What about the children?
Hvad med en øl?	How about a beer?
Hvad er der i vejen med dig?	What's wrong with you?
Hvordan går det med dig?	How are you?

712 Mod

The preposition **mod** can correspond to both 'against' and 'towards' in English. It has an alternative form **imod**, which can also function as an adverb.

(a) Direction

(i) In motion

towards

Vi cyklede mod Helsingør.
We cycled towards Elsinore.

Kør først mod Århus og så mod Ålborg.
First drive towards Århus and then towards Ålborg.

mod nord/syd/øst/vest
towards the north/the south/the east/the west

mod fjerne strande
towards distant shores

(ii) Not in motion, bound for

for/to

Toget mod München afgår fra perron 5.
The train for/to Munich departs from platform 5.

Færgesejladsen mod Harwich er indstillet.
The ferry service to Harwich has been suspended.

(b) Space

(i) At rest, 'leaning'

against

Hun lænede sig mod træet.	She leaned against the tree.
Han havde ryggen mod muren.	He had his back against the wall.

(ii) Impact, 'crashing'

into

Jeg stødte mod en lygtepæl. I bumped into a lamp post.
Lastbilen kørte mod et træ. The lorry crashed into a tree.

(iii) Shared commodity

with

grænsen mod Tyskland the border with Germany

(c) Time

towards

Det bliver ofte koldere op mod jul.
It often gets colder towards Christmas.

mod slutningen af ugen/april/året
towards the end of the week/April/the year

mod bedre tider
towards better times

Note – Two now rather archaic verbs combine with **mod** + a time expression in set phrases:

Det lakker mod enden. The end is drawing near.
Det lider mod aften. Night is falling.

(d) Opposition to

against

tre mod én
three against one

Jeg er/stemmer (i)mod forslaget.
I am/am voting/ against the resolution.

Den, som ikke er med mig, er imod mig.
He that is not with me is against me.

mod ens principper against one's principles
mod mit ønske, mod min vilje against my wish/will
mod bedre vidende against one's better judgement

(e) Comparison

(compared) to

Inflationen er på 2% i år mod 3% sidste år.
Inflation is 2% this year compared to 3% last year.

Det er ikke noget (i)mod, hvad der skete i går.
That's nothing compared to what happened yesterday.

Forslaget blev vedtaget med otte stemmer mod to.
The resolution was passed by eight votes to two.

(f) Replacement, 'in exchange for'

on

købe noget mod kontant betaling	buy something on cash payment
mod legitimation	on (production of) proof of identity

(g) Attached to nouns

angreb/anslag mod, attack against; **forbrydelse mod**, crime against; **indvending mod**, objection to; **kampen mod**, the fight against; **middel mod**, remedy for; **modstand mod**, opposition to; **modvilje mod**, dislike of; **protest mod**, protest against; **retning mod**, direction towards; **trussel mod**, threat against; etc.

(h) Attached to verbs with strong stress (see 705(g))

beskytte sig mod, protect oneself against; **demonstrere mod**, demonstrate against; **forsvare sig mod**, defend oneself against; **indvende mod**, object to; **kæmpe mod**, fight against; **opponere mod**, oppose; **protestere mod**, protest against; **reagere mod**, react against; **spille mod**, play against; **vaccinere mod**, vaccinate against; **vende sig mod**, turn against/to; etc.

(i) Attached to verbs with weak stress (see 705(g))

Here **imod** is normally used. Some of these cases are 'phrasal verbs', in which **imod** is stressed and has adverbial function (see 704(a)):

gå imod, oppose; **sige én imod**, contradict someone; **stemme imod**, vote against; **stå imod**, resist; **tage imod**, accept, receive; **tale imod**, speak against; etc.

(j) Attached to adjectives/participles

gavmild mod, generous towards; **god mod**, nice to; **ond mod**, cruel to; **(u)retfærdig mod**, (un)fair to; **rettet/vendt mod**, directed towards; **sød/venlig mod**, nice/friendly to; **tro mod**, faithful/true to; etc.

(k) Idiomatic expressions with **(i)mod**

for og/eller (i)mod dødsstraf	for and/or against the death penalty
Det er mig meget imod.	I'm strongly opposed to that.
Har du noget (i)mod det?	Have you got anything against it?
Hele verden gik ham imod.	The whole world was against him.

713 Om

The preposition **om** can be used of both space and time, but it also has a wide range of other uses.

(a) Space

When used of physical space, **om** is often virtually synonymous with **omkring**, meaning '(a)round', 'surrounding', 'enveloping', etc.

(i) Location

(a)round

dreje om hjørnet	turn round the corner
gå bag om huset	go round the house (at the back)
sidde rundt om bordet	sit round the table
med et reb om halsen	with a rope round one's neck

Vi kørte nord/syd om slottet.
We drove round the north/south of the castle.

(ii) Physical objects

(a)round

et bælte om livet, et tørklæde om halsen
a belt round the waist, a scarf round the neck

holde om en pakke/person
hold (round) a parcel/person

lægge armen om livet på én
put one's arm round someone's waist

Note – **Om** is used colloquially (especially to children) after certain adjectives (e.g. **beskidt/snavset**, dirty; **kold**, cold; **varm**, hot, warm; **våd**, wet; etc.) to indicate the 'state' of parts of the body:

være kold om hænderne/snavset om fingrene/våd om fødderne, etc.
have cold hands/dirty fingers/wet feet, etc.

(b) Time

(i) When

1 'Day/night' as periods

by

De rejste om dagen og sov om natten.
They travelled by day and slept by night.

Paris om natten/ved nat(tetid)
Paris by night

2 Times of the day, seasons of the year

in

om morgenen/eftermiddagen/aftenen/natten
in the morning/afternoon/evening/night

om foråret/sommeren/efteråret/vinteren
in spring/summer/autumn/winter

3 Days of the week

In general:

on

om søndagen/mandagen/tirsdagen, etc.
on Sundays/Mondays/Tuesdays, etc.

In the past:

on (habitual)

Om lørdagen gik vi altid ud.
On Saturdays we always went out.

on/no prep (non-habitual)

Om søndagen besøgte vi mine forældre, og om mandagen tog vi hjem.
(On) that Sunday we went to see my parents, and on Monday we went home.

4 In the future

in

om to minutter/tre timer/en uge/et år, etc.
in two minutes/three hours/a week/a year, etc.

om lidt, om et øjeblik
in a short while, in a moment

(ii) Frequency

no prep.

to gange om ugen, ti gange om året twice a week, ten times a year
(But: **ti gange i minuttet/timen** ten times a minute/an hour)

Note – Notice also the idiomatic expressions:

langt om længe at long last
Det var du længe om. That took you a long time.

(c) Subject matter, 'concerning'

(i) Informal

about

en historie om hans barndom a story about his childhood
fortælle/læse/skrive om noget tell/read/write about something
Romanen handler om en skolelærer. The novel is about a teacher.

(ii) Formal

on

en afhandling om Holberg a dissertation on Holberg
en forelæsning om kernefysik a lecture on nuclear physics

(d) Distribution, competition

no prep.

De var tre om jobbet.
There were three of them doing the job.

Der var mange om buddet/pladserne.
There were many candidates (for the seats, etc.).

(e) Attached to nouns

Here **om** is usually followed by a complement indicating a 'subject matter':

anmodning om, request for; **ansøgning om**, application for; **beslutning om**, decision on; **bøn om**, prayer/request for; **drøm om**, dream of; **håb om**, hope of; **kamp om**, fight about; **løfte om**, promise of; **meddelelse om**, message about/report of; **spørgsmål om**, question of; **tvivl om**, doubt(s) about; **vision om**, vision of; **væddemål om**, bet on; etc.

(f) Attached to verbs with strong stress (see 705(g))

As in (e) above, **om** is usually followed by a complement indicating a 'subject matter':

anmode om, request; **ansøge om**, apply for; **bede om**, ask for, request; **binde (noget) om**, tie (something) round; **drømme om**, dream of; **handle om**, be about, concern; **holde om**, grasp; **kæmpe om**, fight about; **overbevise om**, convince of; **spørge om**, ask about; **tage om**, put one's arms/hands round; **tale om**, talk about; **vædde om**, bet on; etc.

(g) Attached to verbs with weak stress (see 705(g))

In most cases, unstressed verb + **om** constitutes a 'phrasal verb', in which **om** has adverbial function (see 704(a)):

(i) With the meaning 'afresh', 'again', 're-'

gøre om, undo, try again; **køre om**, drive a race again; **klæde sig om**, change clothes; **lave om**, change; **tage om**, retake; **tælle om**, re-count; etc.

(ii) With the meaning 'round', 'over' (cf. **omkring**)

dreje/vende (sig) om, turn round/over; **dratte/falde om**, collapse; **drive/drysse om**, drift about; etc.

(iii) Followed by a complement indicating a 'subject matter'

bryde sig om, care about, like; **synes om**, like, think of; etc.

(h) Attached to adjectives/participles

(med)vidende om, aware/conscious of; **overbevist om**, convinced of; etc.

(i) Idiomatic expressions with **om**

Om igen!	Do it again!
om og om igen	over and over again
Ham om det!	That's his business/headache!
være om sig	be active/busy
Det må du selv om!	That's up to you! / Please yourself!
Det var du selv ude om!	That was your own fault!
Nu er det om at skynde sig!	We've got to hurry!
Der er noget om det/snakken.	There is something in what you say.

714 Over

Used of space, the preposition **over** means both 'above' and 'over', but it also has a number of other meanings such as 'past', 'concerning', 'because of', etc.

(a) Space

(i) Level

above

10 meter over jorden	10 metres above the ground
500 meter over havets overflade	500 metres above sea level
nogle få centimeter over knæet	a few centimetres above the knee

(ii) From one side to the other

across

gå over broen/gaden/græsplænen
walk across the bridge/street/lawn

bred over skuldrene, smal over hofterne
broad-shouldered, with narrow hips

(iii) Obstacle, 'covering'

over

over hele landet	throughout the country
trække dynen over sig	pull the quilt over oneself
springe over hegnet	jump over the fence

(iv) Others

upon

Pludselig var de over os.	Suddenly they were upon us.

via

Toget til Næstved kører over Roskilde.
The train to Næstved goes via Roskilde.

Note – **Over** (not **ovre**) forms part of the complex preposition **over for** (opposite) as in:

Over for vores hus ligger der en bagerforretning.
Opposite our house there is a baker's shop.

Notice that as a preposition **over for** is written as two words. Cf. the adverb **overfor,** as in: **Der bor en gammel dame overfor,** An old woman lives opposite.

(b) Time

(i) Period

over

over en treårs periode	over a three-year period
blive julen/weekenden over	stay over Christmas/the weekend
blive natten over	stay overnight/the night

Notice the word order in the last two examples.

(ii) The clock

past

Klokken er fem minutter/et kvarter over syv.
It's five (minutes)/a quarter past seven.

Klokken er over ti/midnat.
It's past ten (o'clock)/midnight.

(c) Measure

(i) Age, number, price, size, etc.

over

Der var over 200 til stede.
There were over 200 present.

Uret kostede over 500 kroner.
The watch cost over 500 kroner.

Han er over 2 meter høj/40 år gammel.
He is over 2 metres tall/40 years old.

Hun har over 39 grader i feber.
She has a temperature of over 39 degrees.

(ii) Exceeding

beyond

Det lykkedes over al forventning.
It succeeded beyond all expectation.

Det går over min forstand.
It's (completely) beyond me.

(d) Cause

In the following examples, the prepositional complement represents the reason for the feeling expressed by the adjective or verb. This is a good illustration of the point made in 706 that the more abstract the meaning of a preposition is, the more unpredictable it is and the more equivalents it may have in another language. The number of English equivalents below could easily be extended:

about

Han er bekymret over min indstilling.
He's concerned about my attitude.

at

Hun var overrasket over hans opførsel.
She was surprised at his behaviour.

of

Vi er stolte over vores børn.
We are proud of our children.

over

De sørgede over barnets død.
They mourned over the child's death.

with

Jeg er skuffet over dig.
I'm disappointed with you.

(e) Superior in rank or quality

above

Hans præstation lå over min.
His achievement was above mine.

Hendes navn står over mit på listen.
Her name appears above mine on the list.

En general rangerer over en oberst.
A general is ranked above a colonel.

(f) Attached to nouns

(i) Space

storm over, storm over; **udsigt/udsyn over**, view of/over; etc.

(ii) Cause

bekymring over, concern/worry about; **forbløffelse/forundring over**, astonishment at; **glæde over**, happiness at; **klage over**, complaint about; **overraskelse over**, surprise at; **skuffelse over**, disappointment at; **sorg over**, grief at; etc.

(iii) Power, superiority

kontrol over, control over; **magt over**, power over; **overblik over**, overview of; **sejr over**, victory/win over; etc.

(iv) 'Containing', 'showing'

et kort over, a map of; **en liste over**, a list of; **et mindesmærke over**, a monument to; **en oversigt over**, a survey of; **gøre status over**, take stock of; etc.

(g) Attached to verbs with strong stress (see 705(g))

(i) Cause

gruble/grunde over; ponder; **klage over**, complain about; **skamme sig over**, be ashamed of; **undre sig over**, wonder at; etc.

(ii) Power, superiority

bestemme over, decide over; **disponere/råde over**, have at one's disposal; **herske over**, rule over; **vinde over**, beat, win against; etc.

(h) Attached to verbs with weak stress (see 705(g))

In most cases, verb + **over** constitutes a 'phrasal verb', in which **over** is stressed and has adverbial function (see 704(a)):

arbejde over, work overtime; **bære over (med én)**, be indulgent; **gå over**, cross, pass (intr.); **hoppe over**, jump over; **klippe over**, cut in two; **koge over**, boil over; **komme over**, get over; **krænge over**, capsize; **sove over (sig)**, oversleep; **springe (én) over**, jump over, pass over, skip; **tale over sig**, say too much; etc.

(i) Attached to adjectives/participles

The adjectives/participles generally express an emotion or state of mind:

bekymret over, worried about; **forbløffet/forundret over**, astonished at; **glad over**, glad at; **(u)lykkelig over**, (un)happy about; **overrasket over**, surprised at; **skuffet over**, disappointed at; **stolt over**, proud of; **sur over**, annoyed at; **vred over**, angry at; etc.

(j) Idiomatic expressions with **over**

over det hele (cf. **overalt**)	everywhere
sætte kedlen/vand over	put the kettle on
tværs over	across

ikke noget ud over det sædvanlige	nothing out of the ordinary
Ud over det kender jeg ham ikke.	Beyond that I don't know him.
Kom over og besøg os.	Come over and visit us.
Vi er over det værste.	The worst is over.

715 På

After **i** and **til**, **på** is the most commonly used preposition in Danish. As well as being used of time and space, **på** has a wide range of other uses.

(a) Space

The spatial meanings of **på** range from 'on top of ' something, whether horizontal or vertical, to 'at' or 'in' areas, buildings, institutions, etc.:

(i) Institutions and places in terms of function

at

på apoteket/biblioteket/hotellet/universitetet
at the chemist's/library/hotel/university

på banegården/stationen, på posthuset
at the (railway) station, at the post office

på bunden/hjørnet/stedet/toppen
at the bottom/corner/spot/top

Note 1 – The main difference between **i** and **på** when used about buildings, institutions, etc., is that **på** (like English 'at') emphasizes the address or function, while **i** (like English 'in') is associated with the interior. Thus, in many cases, **på** has two-dimensional meaning, whereas **i** has three-dimensional meaning. See also 710.

(ii) Areas

in

på gaden/himlen/landet/marken in the street/sky/country/field

(iii) Islands

on

på Falster/Sjælland/Grønland/Cypern/Mallorca
on Falster/Zeeland/Greenland/Cyprus/Majorca

Note 2 – When an island is also an independent (or partly independent) nation, usage can vary between **i** and **på**, e.g. **i/på Grønland/Island**, in/on Greenland/Iceland, **i/på Sri Lanka**, in Sri Lanka; but always **i Australien/Irland/Storbritannien**, in Australia/Ireland/Great Britain.

(iv) Surfaces

on

på bordet/græsplænen/gulvet/hylden/jorden
on the table/lawn/floor/shelf/ground

på muren/plankeværket/væggen
on the wall (exterior)/fence/wall (interior)

på bilen/huset/tøjet/side 222
on the car/house/clothes/page 222

på højre/venstre side
on the right/left

N.B. **Jeg har ingen penge på mig.**
I have no money on me.

(b) Time

(i) A point in time

1 at

på den tid, på samme tid	at that time, at the same time

2 Days of the week (forthcoming)

on

på lørdag/søndag, etc.	on Saturday/Sunday, etc.

Note – Notice a few idiomatic temporal phrases:

på forhånd	in advance
Det var på tide!	And about time too!
Det er på høje tid, du går!	It's (high) time you left!

(ii) Duration

På indicates how long a given action takes:

in

gøre noget på meget kort tid
do something in a very short time

Man kan sejle fra Danmark til Tyskland på en time.
You can sail from Denmark to Germany in an hour.

Man kan nå meget på to timer.
You can get a lot done in two hours.

(c) Measure

(i) of

et barn på tre år	a child of three
et ord på ni bogstaver	a word of nine letters
en rabat på 50 kroner	a discount of 50 kroner
et skib på 20.000 ton	a ship of 20,000 tonnes

(ii) with

en lejlighed på fire værelser	a flat with four rooms

(d) Genitive

In some cases, a prepositional phrase with **på** can replace an **-s** genitive:

of

farven på huset	the colour of the house
navnet på byen	the name of the town
prisen på kaffe	the price of coffee
begyndelsen/slutningen på krigen	the beginning/end of the war
den varmeste tid på året	the warmest time of the year

Note – In this kind of construction, the complement may have the function of an objective genitive, as in:

mordet på Kennedy	the murder of Kennedy
(Cf. **Nogen myrdede Kennedy.**	Someone murdered Kennedy.)
løsningen på problemet	the solution to the problem

(e) Manner

På is here mainly found in idiomatic expressions:

på dansk/engelsk, etc.	in Danish/English, etc.
gøre noget på skrømt	pretend to do something
Det er én måde at gøre det på.	That's one way of doing it.
på denne/min/samme måde	in this/my/the same way
på må og få	at random
på ny	anew, again

(f) Attached to nouns

abonnement på, subscription to; **angreb på**, attack on; **bevis på**, proof of; **eksempel på**, example of; **forklaring på**, explanation of; **jagt på**, chase/hunt for; **løsning på**, solution to; **mord på**, murder of; **prøve på**, sample/test of; **en stemme på**, a vote for; **svar på**, answer to; **tanke på**, thought of; etc.

(g) Attached to verbs with strong stress (see 705(g))

(i) **På** is used with verbs denoting four of the five senses:

føle på, feel; **høre på**, hear, listen to; **kigge/se på**, look at; **smage på**, taste; **tage på**, touch (with one's hands). But: **lugte til**, smell

(ii) **På** is sometimes used with verbs denoting movement of parts of the body:

falde på enden/halen, fall on one's bottom; **rynke på næsen**, turn up one's nose; **ryste på hovedet**, shake one's head; **ryste på hånden**, have shaking hands; **trække på det ene ben**, limp; **trække på skuldrene**, shrug one's shoulders; etc.

(iii) Others

bero på, be due to, depend on; **hilse på**, greet, shake hands with; **hvile på**, rest on; **hævne sig på**, take revenge on; **håbe på**, hope for; **kalde på**, call; **reagere på**, react to; **råbe på**, shout out for; **sigte på**, aim at; **skyde på**, shoot at; **stemme på**, vote; **stole på**, rely on, trust; **tro på**, believe (in); **tvivle på**, doubt; **tænke på**, think of; **vente på**, wait for; etc.

(h) Attached to verbs with weak stress (see 705(g))

In some cases, verb + **på** constitutes a 'phrasal verb', in which **på** is stressed and has adverbial function (see 704(a)):

> **finde/hitte på**, think up; **gå på**, go for it; **lade sig gå på (af noget)**, let something get one down; **hilse på**, say hello; **høre på**, listen; **komme på**, remember; **mase/mose på**, push on; **se på**, watch; **skrive sig på**, sign up; **tage på**, put on (weight); **tage tøj på**, put clothes on; etc.

(i) Attached to adjectives/participles

> **gal/vred på**, angry with; **jaloux på**, jealous of; **misundelig på**, envious of; **sikker/vis på**, certain/sure of; **spændt på**, anxious (e.g. to know); **sur på**, annoyed with; etc.

(j) Idiomatic expressions with **på**

På gensyn!	See you soon!
På ære!	On my honour!
På med ...	On with ... (i.e. put ... on)
På med vanten!	Get going!
På den igen!	Have another go!
på nær (to)	except for (two)
være på den	be in trouble
være sent på den	be late (for something)
Den hopper jeg ikke på.	I'm not falling for that one.

716 Til

Til is the second most common preposition in Danish after **i**. It usually indicates a movement in time or space towards or up to something, but it also has a number of other uses including that of marking an indirect object.

(a) Space

(i) To a specific place

to

> **Jeg rejser til England/Kina** (etc.) **i morgen.**
> I'm going to England/China (etc.) tomorrow.

bussen/flyet/toget til Stockholm
the coach/plane/train to Stockholm

Gå hen til nærmeste hjørne.
Go to the nearest corner.

Se til højre/venstre.
Look to the right/left.

Note – Notice the expression: **rejse til udlandet**, go abroad.

(ii) Idiomatic phrases with old case endings

In older Danish, the preposition **til** governed its complement in the genitive case, which (according to the gender and/or number of the noun) had the ending **-s** or **-e** (see 702(b)), e.g.:

With the ending ***-s***
til bords, at/to the table; **til fods**, on foot; **til lands**, on land; **til låns**, on loan; **til sengs**, to bed; **til søs/vands**, at/to sea; **til vejrs**, up in the air; etc.

With the ending ***-e***
(gå) til hånde, lend a hand; **(komme) til orde**, be heard; **(være) til stede**, (be) present; **(komme) til syne**, (come) into sight; etc.

(b) Time

(i) Up to a point in time

In this use, **til** has an alternative form **indtil**:

until, till

Bliv her til i morgen!	Stay here till tomorrow!
Jeg ventede (ind)til kl. 5.	I waited until 5 o'clock.
indtil videre	until further notice

(ii) 'In time for'

before

natten til fredag	the night before Friday

for

Kom ikke for sent til mødet!	Don't be late for the meeting!
Han tager hjem til jul.	He's going home for Christmas.

in

Hun skal på universitetet til september.
She is going to university in September.

De flytter til foråret.
They'll be moving in spring.

Notice the phrase **til sidst/slut**, at last, in the end, finally.

(c) Introducing an indirect object

(i) for

Han købte blomster til hende.	He bought flowers for her.
Hun bestilte også en billet til mig.	She also booked a ticket for me.

(ii) to / no prep.

Hun skrev et brev til mig.	She wrote me a letter/a letter to me.
Jeg ringede til ham i går.	I phoned him yesterday.
Hvad sagde hun til dig?	What did she say to you?

(d) End point of number or time

to

10 til 15 elever (*usually written:* **10–15**)
10 to 15 pupils

Der er reception på fredag kl. 16–18. (*Spoken:* **til**)
There is a reception on Friday from 4 to 6 p.m.

fra mandag til lørdag
from Monday to Saturday

åben fra maj til september
open from May to September

(e) Costing, priced at

at, costing

et hus til en million kroner	a house costing one million kroner
Prisen var sat til 500 kroner.	The price was fixed at 500 kroner.
fire flasker til 30 kroner hver	four bottles at 30 kroner each
til en pris af 100 kroner	at a price of 100 kroner

(f) Genitive

Some genitive relationships are expressed by means of a prepositional phrase with **til**:

of

en forstad til København	a suburb of Copenhagen
forfatteren til romanen	the author of the novel
døren til huset	the door of the house
nøglen til skabet	the key of/to the cupboard/ wardrobe

(g) Intended for

for

en gave til min kone	a present for my wife
en bil til fem personer	a car for five people
en ny skærm til lampen	a new shade for the lamp
en dug til bordet	a cloth for the table
et tæppe til entréen	a carpet for the hall
til leje, til salg, til udlejning	to let, for sale, to rent
Hvad skal vi have til middag?	What's for dinner?

Notice also the construction: **for** + adj. + **til (at** + infinitive), too + adj. + for/ to (+ infinitive):

for stor til dig	too big for you
for gammel til at bruge	too old to use

(h) Attached to nouns

alternativ til, alternative to; **anledning til**, occasion of/to, reason for; **begyndelse til**, beginning of; **forbindelse til**, connection to; **forslag til**, suggestion for; **grund/årsag til**, reason for; **had til**, hatred of; **hensyn til**, consideration/regard for; **idé til**, idea for; **indledning til**, introduction to; **initiativ til**, initiative to; **kilde til**, source of; **kærlighed til**, love of; **lejlighed til**, chance/occasion of/to; **lov til**, permission to; **(have) lyst til**, feel like; **modsætning til**, contrast to; **motiv til**, motive for; **nedrykning til**, relegation to (sport); **oprykning til**, promotion to (sport); **plads til**, room for; **(have) råd til**, be able to afford; **tid til**, time for; **udsigt til**, prospect of; **udsættelse til**, postponement until; **vilje til**, will to; etc.

(i) Attached to verbs with strong stress (see 705(g))

(i) In many cases, **til** establishes a close connection between the object and the prepositional complement:

anvende til, use as/for; **binde (sig) til**, tie (oneself) to; **du til**, be of use as/for; **føre til**, lead to; **glæde sig til**, look forward to; **henvise til**, refer to; **holde til**, endure; **holde sig til**, confine/restrict oneself to; **knytte (sig) til**, attach (oneself) to; **tvinge til**, force to; **udsætte til**, postpone till; **udvikle sig til**, develop into; **vænne sig til**, get used to; etc.

(ii) With certain verbs, **til** indicates a change in status (often a kind of promotion):

ansætte til, employ to; **forandre/forvandle til**, change (in)to; **forfremme til**, promote to; **oversætte til**, translate into; **udnævne til**, appoint to; **udpege til**, nominate to; **vælge til**, elect to; etc.

(j) Attached to verbs with weak stress (see 705(g))

In many cases, verb + **til** constitutes a 'phrasal verb', in which **til** is stressed and has adverbial function (see 704(a)):

blive til, come into being; **falde til**, get used to (being somewhere); **føje til**, add; **få til (at)**, get/persuade to; **gå til**, be bored stiff, come about, walk fast; **hjælpe til**, lend a hand; **kende til**, be familiar with; **komme til (at)**, do by accident; **lægge til**, add, dock (e.g. ship); **løbe til**, run fast, run up (to); **se til**, watch; **sige til**, say so; **slå til**, accept, hit hard; **(lade) stå til**, be inactive, not care; **stå til** (as in: **Hvordan står det til?** How are you?); **være til**, exist; etc.

(k) Attached to adjectives/participles

anvendelig til, usable as/for; **bundet til**, bound by, tied to; **knyttet til**, attached to; **parat/rede til**, ready for/to; **skabt til**, created/made for; **udset til**, chosen to; **vant til**, used to; etc.

(l) Idiomatic expressions with **til**

til fulde	fully
til fods/hest	on foot/horseback
til gavn/glæde for	for the benefit/pleasure of
til min overraskelse/skuffelse	to my surprise/disappointment

have til gode	be owed
være til gene/hinder	be in the way/a hindrance
være til hjælp/nytte	be of help/use
være til stede	be present
nu til morgen	this morning
én til, to til, etc.	another one, two more, etc.

717 Under

Used of space, the preposition **under** covers the English prepositions 'below', 'under' and 'underneath', but it also has a number of other meanings.

(a) Space

(i) Level

below

skrive over eller under linjen	write above or below the line
et stød under bæltestedet	a blow below the belt

(ii) Directly below/under

under

under bordet/jorden/lampen/taget
under the table/ground/lamp/roof

feje noget ind under gulvtæppet
sweep something under the carpet

tunnelen under Kanalen
the tunnel under the Channel

(iii) Covered by

beneath, in, under, underneath

Cyklen blev fundet under buskene.
The bike was found under the bushes.

Han lå begravet under en snedrive.
He lay buried in a snowdrift.

Hun havde ikke noget på under badekåben.
She had nothing on underneath her bathrobe.

(b) Time

(i) at the time of

Han var i London under den store brand.
He was in London at the time of the Great Fire.

(ii) during

under eksamen/krigen/hans sygdom
during the exam/the war/his illness

under en pause i forhandlingerne
during a break in the negotiations

Rosenborg Slot blev opført under Christian IV.
Rosenborg Castle was built during the reign of Christian IV.

(iii) towards

hen under aften/morgenen towards evening/morning

Note – **Under** on its own can only be used of time with the association of a certain activity. Thus it is not possible to use it about a simple period of time with no such association, e.g. ***under dagen/sommeren/året**, etc., during the day/summer/year, etc., but e.g. **under middagen**, during the dinner. Where **under** is not possible, Danish often uses **i løbet af** ...

(c) Measure – age, number, price, size, etc.

below

under frysepunktet/10 grader below freezing-point/10 degrees
under middel below average

fewer than

Der var under tyve personer til stede.
There were fewer than twenty people present.

less than

Han tjener under 100.000 kroner om året.
He earns less than 100,000 kroner a year.

under

Børn under 16 betaler halv pris. Children under 16 pay half price.
Huset er under 2 meter højt. The house is under two metres high.

(d) Inferior in dignity or rank, subjected to

(i) Rank

below

En lektor rangerer under en professor.
A lecturer is ranked below a professor.

(ii) Dignity

beneath

Det er under min værdighed at handle sådan.
It's beneath me to act like that.

Hun giftede sig under sin stand.
She married beneath her.

(iii) Subjected to

under

England under dronning Elizabeth I
England under Queen Elizabeth I

under general Pattons kommando
under the command of General Patton

under politibeskyttelse/regeringens kontrol
under police protection/government control

(e) Subject to current treatment

under

under behandling/reparation — under treatment/repair
være under bedøvelse — be under anaesthetic

(f) Circumstantial

amid(st)

Han holdt en tale under almindelig morskab.
He made a speech amid(st) general merriment.

among

under hurraråb fra tilhørerne — among cheers from the audience by

Han var kendt under navnet 'Pelikanen'.
He was known by the name 'the Pelican'.

on

under forudsætning af at ...	on condition that ...

under

rejse under falsk navn	travel under a false name
under disse/ingen omstændigheder	under these/no circumstances

(g) Attached to verbs with strong stress (see 705(g))

arbejde under, work under; **lide under**, suffer from/because of; **tjene under**, serve under; etc.

(h) Attached to verbs with weak stress (see 705(g))

In many cases, verb + **under** constitutes a 'phrasal verb', in which **under** is stressed and has adverbial function (see 704(a)):

feje under, sweep under; **gå under**, go down, sink; **holde under**, hold one's hand under something; **høre under**, belong to/under; **stikke under**, more than meets the eye; etc.

(i) Idiomatic expressions with **under**

under al kritik	deplorable
være under mistanke	be under suspicion
drikke én under bordet	drink someone under the table
komme under vejr med noget	get wind of something

718 Ved

The preposition **ved** often denotes adjacency or proximity to some point in time or space, but it also has a number of other uses.

(a) Space

This meaning is chiefly covered in English by 'at' or 'by', which sometimes overlap, but other prepositions are used in translation as well:

(i) at, by

ved døren/huset/vinduet — at/by the door/house/window
sidde ved bordet — sit at the table
et hotel ved kysten/søbredden — a hotel by the coast/lakeside

(ii) in

Det blev afgjort ved retten. — It was decided in court.

(iii) near

Herlufsholm ligger ved Næstved. — Herlufsholm is near Næstved.
De bor ved rådhuset. — They live near the town hall.

(iv) of

slaget ved Trafalgar — the battle of Trafalgar

(b) Time

(i) about, around

Lad os mødes ved syvtiden. — Let us meet around seven o'clock.
i morgen ved denne/samme tid — about this/the same time tomorrow

(ii) at

ved daggry/solopgang/solnedgang/midnat
at dawn/sunrise/sunset/midnight

(iii) by

ved dag/nat — by day/night

Note – The construction **være ved at** + infinitive, be in the process of, is often used as a Danish equivalent of the continuous tense in English, e.g. **Jeg er ved at skrive et brev**, I'm writing a letter. However, it can also mean 'be (just) about to', e.g. **Jeg er (lige) ved at være færdig/Han er (lige) ved at blive smidt ud**, I'm just about to finish/He's about to be thrown out. See 516(b)(iii) and 518(b).

(c) Occasion

(i) at

ved begravelsen/brylluppet/festen/middagen
at the funeral/wedding/party/dinner

ved ankomsten/afgangen
at the arrival/departure

kærlighed ved første blik
love at first sight

(ii) during

Varerne blev beskadiget ved transporten.
The goods were damaged during transportation.

Han brækkede benet ved aflæsningen.
He broke his leg during the unloading.

(iii) on

ved den lejlighed	on that occasion
ved nærmere eftertanke	on closer consideration

(d) Attachment to an institution

(i) at

en lærer/professor ved Handelshøjskolen
a teacher/professor at the Business School

en studerende ved University College London
a student at University College London

(ii) in

Hun er ved fjernsynet/radioen/teatret.
She is in television/radio/the theatre.

(iii) on

en journalist ved den lokale avis	a journalist on the local newspaper
en stilling ved jernbanen	a job on the railway

(e) Means

(i) A specific means

In this sense, **ved** may alternate with the complex preposition **ved hjælp af**, by means of:

by

læse ved stearinlys	read by candlelight
finde vej ved hjælp af et kort	find one's way by means of a map

(ii) **Ved + at +** infinitive

by + '-ing'

tabe sig ved at spise fornuftigt
lose weight by eating sensibly

redde sig ved at springe ud ad vinduet
save oneself by jumping out of the window

(f) Inherent characteristic

about

Der er noget mærkeligt/uærligt ved ham.
There is something strange/dishonest about him.

Der er noget ved hende, som jeg kan lide.
There is something about her that I like.

Note – Notice the expression: **Der er ikke noget ved det,** There is nothing interesting about it./It's boring.

(g) Oaths

Ved occurs as part of a number of oaths as a shortened form of: **jeg sværger ved ...,** I swear by ... Although most of the examples here are fixed expressions, these is some scope for innovation:

ved Gud! etc.	by God! etc.
ved den søde grød!	by golly! (*lit.* by the sweet porridge)
ved alt, hvad jeg har kært!	by all that I hold dear!

(h) Idiomatic expressions with **ved**

ved siden af	beside, next to
være ved bevidsthed	be conscious
være ved sine fulde fem	be in one's right mind
Ved brand bedes De ...	In case of fire you are requested ...
Vi tales ved.	We'll talk later.
Han ville ikke være ved det.	He wouldn't admit it.
Mens vi er ved det ...	While we're about it/ on the subject ...

C A BRIEF SURVEY OF SOME OTHER DANISH PREPOSITIONS

This section aims to provide a brief survey of a few other frequently used prepositions in Danish. The following prepositions are examined (the paragraph in question is given in brackets): **bag** (719), **blandt** (720), **forbi** (721), **fra** (722), **gennem** (723), **hos** (724), **ifølge** (725), **inden** (726), **langs** (727), **mellem** (728), **omkring** (729), **siden** (730), **uden** (731). For other prepositions and further exemplification see the references mentioned in 706.

719 Bag

Bag is used as a preposition corresponding to English 'behind' and appears with both literal and figurative spatial meaning. It can express both motion and non-motion:

gå om bag døren/huset/hækken	go behind the door/house/hedge
Stil dig bag stolen!	Go and stand behind the chair!
stå bag døren/huset/hækken	stand behind the door/house/hedge
bag hans barske ydre	behind his stern appearance
Bag ordene var der optimisme.	Behind the words there was optimism.

720 Blandt

The preposition **blandt**, which has the rather formal alternative form **iblandt**, is usually translated as 'among(st)' and is chiefly used of groups of people:

uenighed blandt kandidaterne	disagreement among the candidates
uro blandt arbejderne	unrest among the workers
komme ud blandt folk	get out among people
Han er (i)blandt de få udvalgte.	He is amongst the selected few.
Han faldt iblandt røvere.	He fell among thieves.

Notice the following expressions:

blandt andet (bl.a.)	among other things
blandt andre (bl.a.)	among others

721 Forbi

(a) The preposition **forbi** corresponds in meaning to English 'past', used of motion in space:

Vi kørte forbi hospitalet.	We drove past the hospital.
Jeg gik forbi Tivoli i går.	I walked past Tivoli yesterday.

(b) In a few fixed expressions, which are now rather archaic, **forbi** is positioned after its complement (i.e. postposed):

gå ens dør/hus forbi	not call in on someone
gå ram forbi	escape, get off scot-free
Det gik min næse forbi.	I missed out/didn't get it.

722 Fra

(a) The preposition **fra** is used of time and space in approximately the same way as English 'from':

(i) Space

toget fra Rødby	the train from Rødby
fra Esbjerg til Harwich	from Esbjerg to Harwich
Vi bor 1 km fra stationen.	We live one kilometre from the station.
Hvor kommer du fra?	Where do you come from?

(ii) Time

en roman fra det 19. århundrede	a novel from the 19th century
Hun er ansat der fra 1. juni.	She is employed there from 1st June.
fra 10.–20. august	from the 10th to the 20th August
Jeg har kendt ham fra barn (af).	I've known him since childhood.

(iii) Source

Er den gave fra dig?	Is that present from you?
Jeg har det fra avisen.	I know it from the newspaper.

(b) Notice the following expressions:

bortset fra	apart from, except for

fra nu af	from now on
fra og med	from ... up to (and including)
fra tid til anden	from time to time
sige fra	reject something
springe fra	back out, cry off

723 Gennem

The preposition **gennem** usually corresponds in meaning to English 'through', but has other equivalents too. It has the alternative form **igennem**, which may be found in slightly more formal style. Only **igennem** can also function as an adverb:

(a) Space

(i) through

gennem døren/isen/vinduet	through the door/ice/window
Han gik gennem stuen.	He walked through the living-room.

(ii) across, via

De rejste gennem Amerika.	They travelled across America.
Vi kørte hjem gennem Holland.	We drove home via Holland.

Note the expression: **gennem tykt og tyndt**, through thick and thin.

(b) Time

through

musikken gennem tiderne	music through the ages
gennem årene	through the years

(c) Source

through, via

Vi hørte om aflysningen gennem radioen.
We heard of the cancellation through the radio.

Jeg erfarede det gennem en bekendt.
I learnt about it through a friend.

De modtog det gennem Røde Kors.
They received it through/via the Red Cross.

724 Hos

In most cases, **hos** has no direct parallel in English, but it may be compared with German 'bei' and French 'chez'. It is used of people in the role of friends, hosts, shopkeepers, etc., to refer to the works of writers, composers, etc., and about an inherent characteristic in someone:

(a) In someone's home, with someone

bo hos sin familie	live with one's family
bo hos en ven	stay with a friend
Bliv hos mig!	Stay with me!
hjemme hos os	in our home
hos bageren/slagteren, etc.	at the baker's/butcher's, etc.

Note the expression: **Kom og sid hos mig**, Come and sit by me.

(b) In the works of ...

Der er mange tjenere hos Holberg.
There are many servants in Holberg.

Det tema finder man også hos Carl Nielsen.
That theme is also found in Carl Nielsen.

(c) Inherent characteristic

Det er et uheldigt træk hos ham.
That's an unfortunate trait in him.

Jeg kan se styrken hos hende.
I can see the strength in her.

725 Ifølge

The compound preposition (see 701(b)) **ifølge** corresponds in meaning to English 'according to':

ifølge bestemmelserne/loven	according to the regulations/law
ifølge hans eget udsagn	according to his own statement
ifølge den seneste undersøgelse	according to the latest study

726 Inden

As a preposition, **inden** is used of time, corresponding to English 'before':

inden jul/min fødselsdag	before Christmas/my birthday
betale inden den første	pay before the first of the month
inden længe	before long

Inden also forms part of the complex preposition **inden for** (inside, within) used of time and space (cf. the adverb **indenfor** as in: **Kom indenfor!** Come in(side)!):

inden for murene	inside the walls
inden for rækkevidde	within reach
inden for tidsfristen	within the time limit

Note 1 – **Inden** is used as a spatial preposition in the fixed phrase: **inden døre** (= **indendørs**), indoors; especially in the expression: **holde sig inden døre**, stay indoors.

Note 2 – Used of time, **inden** competes with **før**: **før middagen**, before dinner

727 Langs

The preposition **langs** corresponds in meaning to English 'along':

Der er mange butikker langs vejen.
There are many shops along the road.

Der er badestrande langs kysten.
There are beaches along the coast.

With verbs of motion, **langs med** is often used:

Jeg gik langs med kanalen.	I walked along the canal.
Han løb langs med cykelstien.	He ran along the cycle path.

728 Mellem

(a) The preposition **mellem** usually corresponds in meaning to English 'between', but can also equate to 'among'. It has the alternative form **imellem**, which may be found in slightly more formal style. Only **imellem** can also function as an adverb (see (b) below):

Floden løber mellem bjergene.
The river runs between the mountains.

afstanden mellem husene	the distance between the houses
Valget stod imellem de to.	The choice was between those two.
mellem 30 og 40	between 30 and 40
være mellem venner	be among friends
mellem os sagt	just between us
mellem år og dag	in the course of time

(b) Notice the adverbial use in the following expressions:

en gang imellem	once in a while
indimellem	from time to time
lægge sig imellem	intervene
Det siges mand og mand imellem ...	It is rumoured that ...

729 Omkring

The preposition **omkring** denotes a circular position or movement more precisely than does **om** (see 713). The English equivalents are '(a)round' and 'about':

(a) Circular position or movement

Vi sad omkring bordet.	We sat around the table.
Jeg gik hele vejen omkring byen.	I walked all the way round the town.
danse omkring juletræet	dance round the Christmas tree

(b) Approximately (= **cirka/ca.**)

Der var omkring 40 mennesker.
There were about 40 people.

Temperaturen er omkring 30 grader.
The temperature is about 30 degrees.

730 Siden

The preposition **siden** is only used of time and corresponds to English 'since':

siden foråret/jul/krigen	since the spring/Christmas/the war
Jeg har ventet siden kl. 3.	I've been waiting since 3 o'clock.
Hun har ikke været her siden maj.	She hasn't been here since May.
ikke siden i torsdags/sidste år	not since last Thursday/last year

Note that **siden** forms part of the discontinuous preposition **for ... siden**, ... ago (see 701(c)(iv)):

for fyrre år siden	forty years ago
for længe siden	a long time ago

731 Uden

(a) The preposition **uden** is the equivalent of English 'without'. It is used with both concrete and abstract nouns and can refer to both time and space:

en kjole uden ærmer	a dress without sleeves
kaffe uden sukker og fløde	coffee without sugar and cream
Jeg gjorde det uden din hjælp.	I did it without your help.
Vi kørte til Paris uden ophold.	We drove to Paris without a stop.

(b) Uden also forms part of a few complex prepositions: **uden for**, outside; **uden om**, (a)round; **uden på**, on (the outside of):

Der står træer uden for huset.	There are trees outside the house.
Uden om haven er der et hegn.	There is a fence round the garden.
Navnet står uden på døren.	The name is on the door.

Note – These three complex prepositions all have a corresponding adverb (written as one word), e.g. **træerne udenfor**, the trees outside; **hegnet udenom**, the surrounding fence; **navnet udenpå**, the name on the outside; etc.

(c) Notice the following expressions:

uden at blinke	without batting an eyelid
uden sammenligning	without comparison
uden tvivl	without doubt
uden tøven	without hesitation
uden videre	at once, without further discussion

D DANISH EQUIVALENTS OF ENGLISH 'OF'

732 English 'of' in Danish

'Of' is the most widely used preposition in English, often occurring as a grammatical marker with little or no content. No Danish preposition functions in quite the same way, so Danish must make use of a number of prepositions (and some other devices) to translate the English 'of'.

Needless to say, the present survey is far from complete, but it does at least provide a list of some of the most important Danish equivalents of the preposition 'of'.

(a) Genitive 'of' in English – **-s** genitive in Danish

The extensive use of 'of' as a genitive marker in English (chiefly with non-personal complements) is rendered in various ways in Danish.

Many English 'of' genitive constructions correspond to **-s** genitives in Danish (see 133):

the wings of the bird	**fuglens vinger**
the roof of the house	**husets tag**
the surface of the table	**bordets overflade**
the mystery of life	**livets mysterium**
the grapes of wrath	**vredens druer**

(b) Genitive 'of' in English – compound noun in Danish

Danish makes much more use of compound nouns (in one word) than English does. In many cases, these are alternatives to **-s** genitives. For instance, the first four examples above can appear as compound nouns as well: **fuglevingerne, hustaget, bordoverfladen, livsmysteriet**. Consequently, many English 'of' genitives (some of which can also be expressed as compound nouns) are translated into Danish as compound nouns:

the owner of the house	**husejeren**
the topic of conversation	**samtaleemnet**

(c) Genitive 'of' in English – preposition in Danish

'Of' genitives and related 'of' constructions often correspond to constructions with a preposition in Danish. Some of these may have alternative constructions with **-s** genitive and/or compound noun (see (a) and (b) above), but in such cases the prepositional construction is usually felt to be more informal and colloquial than the other two.

(i) **Af**

son of a miner	**søn af en minearbejder**
the owner of the house	**ejeren af huset**
the sound of water	**lyden af vand**
the top of the tree	**toppen af træet**

Also with 'objective genitive' (cf. 715(d) note):

the discovery of America	**opdagelsen af Amerika**
the sack of Rome	**plyndringen af Rom**
the presentation of the evidence	**fremlæggelsen af bevismaterialet**

(ii) **For**

For often denotes 'in charge of' or 'on someone's behalf':

the manager of the company	**chefen for firmaet**
the chairman of the club	**formanden for klubben**
a representative of the school	**en repræsentant for skolen**
the time of departure	**tidspunktet for afrejsen**

(iii) **I**

a professor of physics	**en professor i fysik**
the villain of the piece	**skurken i stykket**
knowledge of runes	**kundskaber i runer**

(iv) **Over**

a list of new publications	**en liste over nye publikationer**
an outline of Danish literature	**en oversigt over dansk litteratur**
a map of France	**et kort over Frankrig**

(v) **På**

the crew of the ship	**mandskabet på skibet**

the beginning/end of the story — **begyndelsen/slutningen på historien**
the price of oil — **prisen på olie**
the title of the book — **titlen på bogen**

Also with 'objective genitive' (cf. 715(d) note):

the murder of Duncan — **mordet på Duncan**

(vi) **Til**

the author of the article — **forfatteren til artiklen**
the instigator of the riot — **ophavsmanden til urolighederne**
a father of four children — **en far til fire børn**
the lid of the jam — **låget til marmeladen**
the outline of a plan — **skitsen til en plan**

Also with 'objective genitive':

the cause of the fire — **årsagen til branden**
hatred of violence — **hadet til vold**

(vii) **Ved**

Mainly used of a battle plus geographical position:

the battle of Waterloo — **slaget ved Waterloo**

(d) Appositive 'of' in English – direct attachment in Danish

In English, a proper noun is linked to a noun phrase by means of 'of'; Danish uses no preposition in such cases:

the town of Kolding — **byen Kolding**
the kingdom of Denmark — **kongeriget Danmark**
the republic of Iceland — **republikken Island**
a man by the name of Beck — **en mand ved navn Beck**
the Christmas/summer of 1968 — **julen/sommeren 1968**

(e) Partitive 'of' in English

(i) Measure, shape, etc. – direct attachment in Danish

a cup of coffee/tea	**en kop kaffe/te**
a bottle of wine	**en flaske vin**
five kilos of potatoes	**fem kilo kartofler**
two litres of milk	**to liter mælk**
a pair of glasses/trousers	**et par briller/bukser**
a great number of mistakes	**et stort antal fejl**
a kind/sort of headache	**en slags hovedpine**
a game of chess	**et spil skak**

(ii) 'All/both/the whole of' – direct attachment in Danish

all of the inhabitants	**alle indbyggerne**
both of the parents	**begge forældrene**
the whole of the town	**hele byen**
all of it, the whole of it	**det hele**

(iii) Part of a 'whole': **af**

half/some/any of the students	**halvdelen/nogle/nogen af de studerende**
many/none/ten of the spectators	**mange/ingen/ti af tilskuerne**
much/a lot/a little of it	**meget/en masse/lidt af det**
part of the book	**en del af bogen**
one tenth of the expenses	**en tiendedel af udgifterne**
the majority of the voters	**flertallet af vælgerne**
Which of you has done it?	**Hvem af jer har gjort det?**

Note also:

The bucket is full of water.	**Spanden er fuld af vand.**
She is full of energy.	**Hun er fuld af energi.**

For examples like 'a friend of mine' see 419.

(f) Material: English 'of' – Danish **af**

a heart of gold	**et hjerte af guld**
a statue of bronze	**en statue af bronze**
a chest of oak	**en kommode af egetræ**

But Danish may also use a compound noun:

a house of cards	**et korthus**

a block of wood — **en træstub**

Or direct attachment (cf. (e)(i) above):

a piece of paper/wood — **et stykke papir/træ**
a slice of bread — **en skive brød**

(g) Origin

Af

of humble origin — **af ringe herkomst**
born of Danish parents — **født af danske forældre**

Fra

the Wizard of Oz — **Troldmanden fra Oz**
Mr Olsen of our Maribo office — **Hr. Olsen fra vores Mariboafdeling**

(h) Title + place name

I

the mayor of Birkerød — **borgmesteren i Birkerød**
the Vicar of Wakefield — **Præsten i Wakefield**
the Merchant of Venice — **Købmanden i Venedig**

(i) Geographical position

(i) Motion: **om**

drive north/south (etc.) of Sorø — **køre nord/syd (etc.) om Sorø**
sail south of Africa — **sejle syd om Afrika**

(ii) Position: **for**

live north/south (etc.) of Sorø — **bo nord/syd (etc.) for Sorø**
a town south of Roskilde — **en by syd for Roskilde**

(iii) Area: compound noun

the north of England — **Nordengland**
the south of France — **Sydfrankrig**

(j) Dates, months, etc.

(i) Dates

the first of April — **den første april**
the twenty-fifth of December — **den femogtyvende december**

But:
the fifth of the sixth — **den femte i sjette**

(ii) Months, seasons

the month of May — **maj måned**
the summer of 1945 — **sommeren 1945**

(k) Numerical amount/number: **på**

a sum of 50 pounds — **et beløb på 50 pund**
a salary of 200,000 kroner — **en løn på 200.000 kroner**
a flat of four rooms — **en lejlighed på fire værelser**
a man of fifty — **en mand på halvtreds (år)**
a rent/interest/tax of ... — **en husleje/rente/skat på ...**

(l) 'Of' attached to verbs

accuse of, **anklage for**; assure of, **forsikre om**; boast of, **prale af**; complain of, **klage over**; consist of, **bestå af**; convict of, **dømme for**; cure of, **helbrede for**; despair of, **fortvivle over**; dream of, **drømme om**; remind of, **minde om**; speak/talk of, **snakke/tale om**; suspect of, **mistænke for**; think of, **tænke på**; etc.

(m) 'Of' attached to adjectives/participles

afraid of, **bange for**; ashamed of, **flov over**; aware of, **vidende om**; certain/sure of, **sikker på**; characteristic of, **karakteristisk for**; composed of, **sammensat af**; conscious of, **bevidst om**; contemptuous of, **hånlig over for**; convinced of, **overbevist om**; critical of, **kritisk over for**; devoid of, **blottet for**; envious of, **misundelig på**; fond of, **glad for**; full of, **fuld af**; guilty of, **skyldig i**; innocent of, **uskyldig i;** jealous of, **jaloux på**; proud of, **stolt af/over**; suspicious of, **mistænksom over for**; tired of, **træt af**; typical of, **typisk for**; etc.

8 INTERJECTIONS

801 Introduction

(a) Interjections are emotive words which above all belong to the spoken language. Many interjections are completely spontaneous exclamations and as such they represent a type of word that goes right back to the earliest stages of language as we know it. They are indeclinable and peripheral in the language in the sense that they are independent of the clause structure. For this reason they are often marked off from the rest of the sentence by a comma:

Av, det gør ondt!	Ow, that hurts!

(b) Some interjections function as a minimal type of expression, the meaning of which can be restated more explicitly. Compare:

Av!	Ow!
with	
Jeg slog mit hoved.	I hurt my head.
Det gør ondt i maven, etc.	My stomach hurts, etc.

(c) It is possible to make a distinction between *primary* and *secondary* interjections. The former are purely spontaneous exclamations and often contain sounds which do not otherwise occur in the language, while the latter are derived from other word classes and used as interjections. Such derived interjections are often greetings: **davs** (hello), or expletives: **satans også!** (oh damn!).

802 Affirmations, denials, responses

For **ja** and **nej** as nouns see 105(d). For **jo** as a discourse particle see 618.

(a) Ja, nej

These are the Danish equivalents of English 'yes' and 'no' whose main function is to be a response to a yes/no question (but see (b) below). As such they have anaphoric reference (cf. 402(b)) and can occur alone or with a following clause:

A: **Har du været i London?**	B: **Ja. / Ja, det har jeg.**
	B: **Nej. / Nej, det har jeg ikke.**
A: Have you been to London?	B: Yes. / Yes, I have.
	B: No. / No, I haven't.
A: **Kender du Ebbe Hansen?**	B: **Ja. / Ja, det gør jeg.**
	B: **Nej. / Nej, det gør jeg ikke.**
A: Do you know Ebbe Hansen?	B: Yes. / Yes, I do.
	B: No. / No, I don't.

(b) Ja, jo

(i) The affirmative answer ('yes') has two realizations in Danish: **ja** and **jo**. In general, **jo** is used when the question contains a negation (**aldrig**, never; **ikke**, not; etc.), while **ja** is used when this is not the case.

A: **Har du læst "Den grimme ælling"?**	B: **Ja, det har jeg.**
A: Have you read 'The Ugly Duckling'?	B: Yes, I have.
A: **Har du ikke læst "Den grimme ælling"?**	B: **Jo, det har jeg.**
A: Haven't you read 'The Ugly Duckling'?	B: Yes, I have.
A: **Slapper du aldrig af?**	B: **Jo, det gør jeg.**
A: Do you never relax?	B: Yes, I do.

(ii) **Jo(h)** is often used when there is a degree of hesitation in the answer, even if the question or statement contains no negation. This corresponds most closely to 'well' in English:

A: **Vil du have en øl?**	B: **Jo, måske, men så kun en enkelt!**
A: Would you like a beer?	B: Well, perhaps, but just one then!

A: **Han er da helt umulig!** B: **Joh, men ...**
A: He is quite impossible! B: Well, yes, but ...

A: **Jeg synes, at vi skulle plante et par træer i haven.**
B: **Joh, det kan du have ret i, men jeg synes nu alligevel, at ...**
A: I think we should plant a couple of trees in the garden.
B: Well, you may be right, but I still think that ...

(iii) **Jo** may introduce ironic exclamations or expressions of annoyance:

Om det er et livligt barn? Jo tak, det skal jeg love for!
Is it a lively baby? You bet it is!

Og han ville være her kl. 8? Jo, god morgen!
And he was going to be here at 8 o'clock? Oh yes, pull the other one!

(c) Nej, næ(h)

Whereas **nej** expresses a clear denial or refusal, **næ(h)** implies some doubt or hesitation:

A: **Tvivler du på, hvad jeg siger?** B: **Næh, men måske tager du fejl!**
A: Do you doubt what I'm saying? B: Well, no, but you may be wrong!

(d) Tja(h)

Tja(h) can indicate uncertainty, indifference, apprehension or a reluctance to disagree with the speaker:

A: **Hvad vil du gerne studere?** B: **Tja(h), jeg ved det ikke rigtigt.**
A: What do you want to study? B: Well, I'm not really sure.

A: **Skal vi invitere Søren?** B: **Tja(h), det må vi vel hellere.**
A: Shall we invite Søren? B: Well, I suppose we'd better.

(e) Nå

The interjection **nå** may indicate a wide range of reactions, including impatience, surprise, resignation, a sudden realization, disagreement or a change of subject. When some hesitation is involved, the form **nåh** is sometimes used:

Nå, er du snart klar? Well, are you almost ready?

A: **Peter har fået nyt job.** B: **Nå, har han det?**
A: Peter has got a new job. B: Oh, has he?

A: **Jeg kom for sent til toget.** B: **Nå, skidt med det.**
A: I missed the train. B: Oh well, never mind.

A: **Vores telefon var i uorden.** B: **Nå, sådan!**
A: Our telephone was out of order. B: Oh, that's why!

A: **Du var temmelig fuld i aftes!** B: **Nåh, det ved jeg nu ikke!**
A: You were rather drunk last night! B: Oh, I don't know about that!

Nå, vi må se at komme videre! Well, we had better move on!

Nå(h) can combine with **ja/jo** and **nej**, in both cases implying agreement with the speaker:

A: **Hun er da voksen nu!** B: **Nå ja, det ved jeg da godt.**
A: She is an adult now! B: Well yes, I realize that.

A: **Du kan ikke forvente andet!** B: **Nåh nej, jeg klager ikke.**
A: You can't expect anything else! B: Oh well, I'm not complaining.

(f) Jamen, jaså, javel, javist/jovist

Some compounds with **ja-/jo-** as prefix function as interjections with different shades of meaning.

(i) **Jamen** can signal mild protest or contradiction:

En dårlig taber? Jamen, det kan du da ikke mene!
A bad loser? But surely you can't mean that!

(ii) **Jaså** can indicate anything from a neutral response to information via aloofness to surprise or disapproval:

A: **Vi kan ikke komme på søndag.** B: **Jaså, det var jo en skam.**
A: We can't come on Sunday. B: Oh, that's a pity.

A: **Pia er gravid.** B: **Jaså, og hvem er så faderen?**
A: Pia is pregnant. B: I see, and who is the father?

(iii) **Javel** is used to indicate acceptance or acknowledgement, particularly by someone in a subordinate position (e.g. receiving orders), or to register a mild objection:

A: **Er det forstået?** B: **Javel!**
A: Is that understood? B: Yes, sir!

Du siger, at han har gjort sin pligt. Javel, men er det nu nok?
You say that he has done his duty. All right, but is that enough?

(iv) **Javist/jovist**

These express a stronger form of agreement than plain **ja/jo**. They can be used to comfort or reassure someone. The choice of **javist** or **jovist** is the same as that between **ja** and **jo** (see (b)(i) above):

A: **Er du sikker på, at jeg kan blive her?** B: **Javist så!**
A: Are you sure that I can stay here? B: Yes, certainly!

Note – A number of other variants are found in the spoken language, e.g. **ja da, jaja, jo da, jojo, nja(h)** (⇦ **nej** + **ja**), etc.

803 Expressions of feelings, exclamations

Interjections often signal a spontaneous reaction to a situation.

(a) Positive feelings

Delight or surprise: **ih, nej, å(h), hov(sa)**

Ih, hvor jeg glæder mig! Oh, I'm so looking forward to it!
Nej, hvor er den sød! Oh, isn't it sweet!
Hovsa, hvor blev den af? Whoops, where did it go?

Joy: **bravo, hurra**

(b) Negative feelings

Annoyance: **årh**

Disappointment: **øv**

Disapproval or disgust: **fy, føj**

Fy dog!	Shame on you!
Føj, hvor ulækkert!	Ugh, how disgusting!

Discomfort: **puh, puha**

Puh, hvor er det varmt!	Phew, it's hot!
Puha, det lugter!	Phew, it smells!

Fear: **ih, nej, uh(a)**

Ih, hvor var jeg bange!	Oh, how scared I was!
Nej, hvor uhyggeligt!	Oh, how spooky!
Uha, det tør jeg ikke!	Oh no, I daren't do that!

Pain: **av, å(h)**

Av, min tå!	Ow, my toe!
Åh, mit hoved!	Oh, my head!

(c) Others

Attracting attention: **pst**

Doubt: **ah, hm, tja(h)**

Hesitation: **øh**

Religious expressions: **amen, halleluja**

804 Commands

These often overlap with imperatives (see 533) and may be classified according to the individual(s) to whom they are directed:

To animals: **Dæk** (to dogs: Down!), **Hyp, Prr** (to horses: Gee up! Whoah!)
To children: **Hys, Ssh** (Hush! Ssh!)
To soldiers: **Holdt** (Halt!), **Giv agt** (Ready!), **Ret** (Attention!)

805 Imitations

These interjections are onomatopoetic, i.e. they imitate sounds of various kinds. Note, however, that such sounds may be perceived and represented differently from language to language:

(a) Sounds made by animals:

vov(vov)	(dog)	**kvivit**	(bird)
miav	(cat)	**pip**	(bird)
muh	(cow)	**kukkuk**	(cuckoo)
pruh	(horse)	**kykliky**	(cockerel)
mæh	(sheep)	**rap(rap)**	(duck)
øf	(pig)	**uhu**	(owl)

(b) Sounds made by man-made objects: **bang**; **ding-dong**; **plaf**, pop; **tik-tak**, tick tock

(c) Other sounds: **plask**, splash; **plump**, plop

(d) Some verbs are formed from interjections of this type, e.g.:

> **klukke**, gurgle; **knirke**, creak; **kukke**, call (like a cuckoo); **kvidre**, twitter; **mjave**, miaow; **pippe**, chirp; **plaffe**, pop; **plaske**, splash; **risle**, purl; **suse**, whistle (of the wind); etc.

(e) Nouns too may be formed from interjections of this type, e.g.:

> **et pip**, a chirp; **et plask**, a splash

806 Greetings, exhortations

These are often derived from other word classes:

(a) On meeting and parting: **dav(s)**, hello; **farvel**, goodbye; **goddag**, how do you do; **goddav(s)**, hello; **hej**, hi; **på gensyn**, see you again

(b) At mealtimes: **skål**, cheers; **tak for mad**, thank you for the meal; **velbekomme**, bon appétit/hope you liked it

(c) Seasonal greetings: **glædelig jul**, Happy Christmas; **godt nytår**, Happy

New Year; **god påske**, Happy Easter

(d) Thanks, apologies and responses: **selv tak/tak i lige måde**, thank ˈyou (in return); **(mange) tak**, thank you (very much); **tak for sidst**, thank you for the last time we met; **undskyld**, excuse me/sorry; **åh, jeg be'r/ingen årsag/det var så lidt**, not at all/don't mention it

(e) Others: **gud ske lov/gudskelov**, thank God; **hvad?/hvadbehager/hvabehar?** what?/pardon?; **herregud**, oh dear me; **til lykke/tillykke**, congratulations; **til lykke/tillykke med fødselsdagen**, happy birthday; **prosit**, bless you; **værsgo**, here you are

807 Expletives

Expletives are never compulsory, but are typically used to intensify a speaker's strong and spontaneous feelings. However, for many people they are now almost devoid of meaning and have become little more than formulas. They are often frowned on and are not considered part of polite conversation.

(a) Swear-words and coarse exclamations

These mainly comprise names for God, the Devil, diseases and excrement (the list is not exhaustive).

(i) Independent exclamations:

fandens (også), gud, lort, pis, satans (også)

(ii) With adverbial function:

faneme, for fanden, gudhjælpemig, ved gud, for helvede, kraftedeme, sateme, for satan, sgu

Note – The intensifying adjective prefix **skide-** (shit) is becoming more and more widespread and acceptable: **skidegod, skidehyggelig, skidelækker**, etc. (cf. 615(c), 1103(b)(ii)).

(b) A number of euphemisms have been created, which are used as mild swear-words. They are often derived from or modelled on the swear-words proper:

for hulen, for katten, pokkers, for pokker, skam, søreme, for søren, ved den søde grød

9 CONJUNCTIONS

A COORDINATION AND SUBORDINATION

901 Introduction

For main clause, subordinate clause, see 1008ff, 1012f; for the form, function and position of subordinate clauses see 1026ff.

(a) *Coordination* involves the linking together of two clauses or elements of a similar kind. The link used is often a *coordinating conjunction* placed between the elements to be linked (see 904–09):

Hans *og* Else bor på landet. Hans and Else live in the country.	*Subjects coordinated*
De sidder *og* læser. They are sitting reading.	*Verbs coordinated*
Hans kan lide øl, *og* Else kan lide vin. Hans likes beer and Else likes wine.	*Main clauses coordinated*
Han sagde, at han var træt, ***og* at han snart ville gå i seng.** He said that he was tired and that he would soon go to bed.	*Subordinate clauses coordinated*

(b) *Subordination* involves the incorporation of a subordinate clause into a main clause. The link word used is often a *subordinating conjunction* or other *subordinator* placed at the beginning of the subordinate clause (see 910–21).

<Jeg holder meget af hende,	**(*fordi* hun holder meget af mig.)>**
I like her a lot	because she likes me a lot.
main clause	*subordinate clause*
independent	*dependent*

In this example the subordinating conjunction is **fordi**. Notice how the subordinate clause here is subordinated to the main clause, i.e. dependent on it, and part of the larger sentence (see 1008(a), 1012ff, 1026ff).

Compare coordination:

<Jeg holder meget af hende,>	*og*	**<hun holder meget af mig.>**
I like her a lot		and she likes me a lot.
main clause		*main clause*
independent		*independent*

There is often a hierarchy of clauses, one within another, by which clauses are subordinated:

<Jeg tror,	**(at vi kan nå toget,**	**/hvis vi skynder os./)>**	
I think	that we can make the train	if we hurry.	
<A	(B	/C	C/B)A>

In this example the subordinate clause marked C–C is subordinated to the subordinate clause B–B which in turn is subordinated to (actually the object of) the whole sentence A–A (see 1008(a)).

902 Position of conjunctions

(a) *Coordinating conjunctions* (see 901) are found:

1 Usually between the two sentence elements, phrases or clauses to be coordinated. See 901(a) above, 1009(e) and 1012(e).

2 At the beginning of an independent sentence:

Og **jeg som stolede på ham!**	And I who trusted him!

Note – Certain conjunctions never appear at the beginning of the sentence; these include explanative, conclusive and comparative conjunctions (see 908ff., 918).

The use of a coordinating conjunction does not usually affect the word order in a following clause. For double conjunctions, see 905(c), 906(b).

(b) *Subordinating conjunctions* (see 901) are found at the beginning of the subordinate clause, either:

1 Between the main and subordinate clauses when the order is MC + SC (main clause + subordinate clause)

or

2 At the beginning of the sentence when the order is SC + MC.

Vi kan nå toget,	**hvis**	**vi skynder os.**
We can make the train	if	we hurry.
MC	*sub conj*	*SC*

Hvis	**vi skynder os,**	**kan vi nå toget.**
If	we hurry	we can make the train.
sub conj	*SC*	*MC*

This applies to most adverbial clauses but not to attributive clauses, some consecutive clauses or indirect questions when the subordinate clause cannot precede the main clause, and the conjunction or other subordinator therefore cannot begin the sentence.

Han spiste så meget, ***at*** **han blev syg af det.**
He ate so much that he became ill from it.
sub conj — *consecutive clause*

Han spurgte mig, ***om*** **jeg havde lyst til et glas vand.**
He asked me if I wanted a glass of water.
sub conj — *indirect question*

Hans kæreste, ***som er englænder,*** **hedder Kitty.**
His girlfriend, who is English, is called Kitty.
other subordinator — *attributive clause*

903 Conjunctions, conjunctional adverbs, and other subordinators

(a) Conjunctions are elements which are outside the actual clause and have a linking function. Coordinating conjunctions normally consist of a single word, e.g. **og** (and), **men** (but), **eller** (or), whereas subordinating conjunctions frequently consist of several, often a combination of adverb or preposition + subordinating conjunction, e.g. **efter at** (after); **selvom** (although).

(b) Clauses may also be linked by a *conjunctional adverb* (613(c)) in a separate clause. Compare:

Jeg går nu, ***for*** **det er meget sent.**
coord. conj.
I'm going now because it's very late.

Jeg går nu. Det er ***nemlig*** **meget sent.**
conjunct. adverb
I'm going now. It's very late, you see.

The function of **for** and **nemlig** is the same in both cases.

(c) The conjunctional adverb frequently occurs first in the clause, thereby causing inversion: finite verb – subject (FV–S) (cf. 1009ff), whereas subordinating conjunctions are found with subordinate clause (i.e. straight) word order: subject – finite verb (S–FV) (cf. 1012). Compare:

Jørgen kom ikke til min fødselsdagsfest i går.
***Alligevel* sendte han mig et kort.**
conjunct. FV S
adverb
Jørgen didn't come to my birthday party yesterday.
He still sent me a card.

Jørgen kom ikke til min fødselsdagsfest i går,
***selvom* han sendte mig et kort.**
conj. S FV
Jørgen didn't come to my birthday party yesterday,
even though he sent me a card.

(d) Other subordinators include interrogative pronouns and interrogative adverbs and relative pronouns and relative adverbs. These differ from conjunctions in that they introduce a subordinate clause and constitute a sentence element in that clause at the same time:

Ib vidste ikke, ***hvem der*** **havde arrangeret festen.**
subordinator FV
+ subject
Ib didn't know who had arranged the party.

Ib vidste ikke, ***hvad*** **gæsterne skulle have at spise.**
subordinator
+ object
Ib didn't know what the guests were going to eat.

Ib vidste ikke, ***hvor*** **de skulle sidde.**
subordinator
+ adverbial
Ib didn't know where they were to sit.

B COORDINATING CONJUNCTIONS

904 Introduction

There are very few coordinating conjunctions, but the conjunctional adverbs (903(b), 613(c)) fulfil almost the same function. Coordinating conjunctions are classified according to their function into: copulative, disjunctive, adversative, explanative and conclusive.

Paragraph	*Term*	
905	Copulative	**og, samt** (and)
906	Disjunctive	**eller** (or)
907	Adversative	**men** (but), neg. + **uden** (not ... but)
908	Explanative	**for** (for), **thi** (for)
909	Conclusive	**så** (so)

Conjunctional adverbs, see 905–09, 613(c).
Double conjunctions, see 905–09, 613(c)(iv).

905 Copulative conjunctions

Copulative means 'connecting'.

(a) **Og** (and) is the most frequently used word in Danish. As in English, in lists **og** is often only inserted before the last item:

Han har været i Grækenland, Tyrkiet *og* Albanien.
He has been to Greece, Turkey and Albania.

(b) **Samt** (and) is only found in formal written Danish and is used as a variant of **og**. It is often found after a series of phrases or clauses linked by **og**, and cannot link two clauses with different subjects:

Han er meget berejst i Grækenland, Tyrkiet *samt* Albanien.
He has travelled widely in Greece, Turkey and Albania.

(c) **Både ... og**, both ... and. Coordination of two elements may be strengthened by the addition of the conjunctional adverb **både** to form **både ... og**, which emphasizes that both elements have equal weight:

Jeg kan lide *både* øl *og* vin.
I like *both* beer *and* wine.

Vi skal ringe hjem, *både* inden vi kører, *og* når vi er kommet frem.
We must ring home *both* before we leave *and* when we arrive.

It is possible in Danish, unlike English, to link more than two elements using **både ... og ... og**, though frequently only one **og** will be used in such constructions:

Dinah er *både* smuk *og* charmerende *og* intelligent.
Dinah is pretty, charming and intelligent.

***Både* Kasper, Signe *og* Poul var med til festen.**
Kasper, Signe and Poul were all at the party.

Note 1 – **Både ... og** is used to express 'either . . . or' in constructions such as:

Han er større end *både* dig *og* mig.	He's bigger than either you or I.

Note 2 – **Både og** can be used in colloquial Danish to express 'yes and no, I do and I don't, etc.' in response to questions:

Synes du om det? – *Både og*.	Do you like it? – Yes and no.

Some other similar constructions are:

såvel ... som, both ... and (more formal than **både ... og**)
ikke bare/blot ... men også, not only ... but also
dels ... dels, partly ... partly
snart ... snart, now ... now

For other conjunctional adverbs which have a copulative function see 613(c).

906 Disjunctive conjunctions

Disjunctive means 'alternative'.

(a) **Eller**:

Vil du have te *eller* kaffe?
Would you like tea or coffee?

(b) A number of 'double conjunctions' consist of a conjunctional adverb + **eller**. These strengthen the element of choice:

(i) **Enten ... eller**:

Du kan få *enten* te *eller* kaffe.
You can have either tea or coffee.

When this construction is used to link clauses, the word **også** is almost invariably inserted after **eller**:

***Enten* vasker vi op i aften, *eller også* lader vi det stå til i morgen.**
Either we do the washing up tonight or we leave it until tomorrow.

***Enten* er han syg, *eller også* pjækker han igen.**
Either he's ill or he's playing truant again.

Note that **enten ... eller også** causes inversion in both clauses; when there is a change of subject, **også** may be omitted and consequently there is no inversion in the second clause:

***Enten* må du fjerne den gulerod fra blomsterdekorationen, *eller* jeg rødmer.**
Either you remove that carrot from the flower arrangement or I'll blush.

Note – For the use of **(hvad) enten ... eller (ej)** as a concessive conjunction to express 'whether ... or (not)', see 915(c).

As with **både ... og (... og)** (905(c)), it is possible to link more than two elements together with this construction:

Alt, hvad der er rart i livet, er *enten* ulovligt *eller* umoralsk *eller* fedende.
Everything that's nice in life is illegal, immoral or fattening.

(ii) **Hverken ... eller**:

Han kan *hverken* læse *eller* skrive.
He can neither read nor write.

This construction may also be used to link more than two elements together:

Han har *hverken* tid *eller* lyst *eller* kræfter til det mere.
He hasn't the time, desire or energy for it any more.

Note that **hverken** may be idiomatically placed in front of a past participle in order to express 'neither ... nor' + objects:

De har *hverken* set Ida *eller* Birthe i dag.
They have seen neither Ida nor Birthe today.

(iii) **Det være sig ... eller**

Det være sig ... eller (whether ... or) is usually only found in negative sentences in formal language:

Ingen, det *være sig* rig *eller* fattig, får adgang her.
No one, whether rich or poor, will gain entry here.

See also 532, 534(b), 613(c)(iv).

907 Adversative conjunctions

Adversative means 'opposite' and expresses a contrast, restriction or correction.

(a) **Men** (but) links words, phrases or clauses:

Det var trist, *men* sandt.
It was sad but true.

Han ville betale for maden, *men* han havde ikke penge nok.
He wanted to pay for the meal but he didn't have enough money.

Note 1 – **Men** can be strengthened in different ways by the addition of the conjunctional adverbs **alligevel** or **vist**:

Vejret var dårligt, *men alligevel* havde vi det skønt.
The weather was bad, but nevertheless we had a good time.

Vist var du syg, *men* du kunne *alligevel* godt have ringet til mig.
You were ill admittedly, but you still could have rung me.

Note 2 – **Men** can also be used to express surprise or disapproval:

***Men* dog! Hvad har du da gjort!**	Dear me! What have you done!
***Men* så hold dog op!**	Stop that now!

(b) **Uden** is used to convey the sense of 'but' when following a negative (**ikke, ingen, intet**) (see also 915(e)):

Ingen *uden* jeg vidste det.	Nobody but me knew it.

Opposition can also be expressed by, amongst other expressions, the conjunctional adverbs: **alligevel**, yet; **dog**, yet; **endnu**, still, yet; **imidlertid**, however, nevertheless.

908 Explanative conjunctions

Explanative means 'explaining'. **For, thi** (for, as) always link complete clauses:

Du skal skynde dig, *for* ellers når du ikke bussen.
You must hurry up, as you'll miss the bus otherwise.

Thi is only used in old-fashioned written Danish:

Denne sag var vanskelig at afgøre, *thi* begge parter var skyldige.
This matter was difficult to settle as both parties were to blame.

Note - The conjunctional adverbs **jo, nemlig** may also be used to express explanation (see 618):

Han kommer ikke. Han er *nemlig* syg.	He isn't coming. He's ill, you see.
Han kommer ikke. Han er *jo* syg.	He isn't coming. He's ill, you know.

909 Conclusive conjunctions

Conclusive indicates 'conclusion, result'. **Så** (so) links only clauses and expresses a conclusion or result:

Min bil var til reparation, *så* jeg måtte tage bussen.
My car was being repaired so I had to take the bus.

Klokken er mange nu, *så* du må se at komme hjem.
It's late now so you'd better be going home.

Note – Conclusion may also be expressed by means of the following conjunctional adverbs: **altså**, therefore; **derfor**, consequently; **følgelig**, consequently (see 613(c)):

Min bil var til reparation. *Derfor* måtte jeg tage bussen.
My car was being repaired. That is why I had to take the bus.

C SUBORDINATING CONJUNCTIONS

910 Introduction

See also 1012, 1026ff.

---

911 I General subordinators

Explicative	– indirect statement **at** (that) – indirect question **om** (whether)

II Semantically differentiated subordinators

912	Temporal	**da** (when), **efter at** (after), **før** (before), **førend** (before), **idet** (as), **imens** (while), **indtil** (until), **inden** (before), **lige siden** (ever since), **mens/medens** (while), **når** (when), **når som helst** (whenever), **siden** (since), **som** (as), **så længe som** (as long as), **så ofte som** (as often as), **så snart som** (as soon as), **til** (until)
913	Causal	**da** (as, since), **eftersom** (as, since), **fordi** (because), **idet** (as), **på grund af at** (owing to the fact that), **siden** (since)
914	Conditional	**dersom** (if), **forudsat at** (provided that), **hvis** (if), **(hvis) bare/blot** (if only), **ifald** (in case), **medmindre** (unless), **når** (if), **såfremt** (provided), **undtagen (hvis)**, unless
915	Concessive	**endskønt** (although, though), **hvad enten ... eller** (whether ... or), **hvor ... end** (however), **hvorimod** (whereas), **ihvorvel** (although, though), **om** ((even) if), **om end** (even though), **selvom** (even though), **skønt** (although, though), **til trods for at/trods det at** (in spite of (the fact that)), **uagtet** (even though), **uden at** (without ...-ing)

916	Final	**for at** (in order that), **for at ... ikke** (lest), **så at** (so that)
917	Consecutive	**så** (so that), **så at** (so that), **så ... at** (so that)
918	Comparative	**end** (than), **jo ... jo/des/desto** (the ... the), **lige ... som** ((just) as ... as), **lige som om** (as if), **ligesom** (as if), **som** (as), **som om** (as if), **så ... som** (as ... as)

Subordinating conjunctions are more complex than coordinating conjunctions as they often comprise a compound or word group, in many cases a combination of an adverb or preposition + **at** or **som**. In this way they are able to express many subtle semantic distinctions.

Simple subordinating conjunctions are, for example: **at, da, før, inden, mens, når, om, siden, som**.

Compound subordinating conjunctions are, for example: **dersom, eftersom, førend, imens, indtil, ligesom, selvom, såfremt**.

Word groups as subordinating conjunctions are, for example: **efterhånden som, for at, forudsat at, så længe som, til trods for at**.

911 General subordinators

The general subordinators are **at** (that) and **om** (whether). These merely indicate that the clause they introduce is a subordinate clause.

(a) **At** (that) is as important among subordinating conjunctions as **og** is among coordinating conjunctions. It is pronounced /at/ unlike the infinitive marker (see 528), which is normally pronounced /å/. **At** is used most often to introduce a statement in indirect speech, and follows a verb of saying or reporting; just as in English, it may often be omitted (1028(a)):

> **Han sagde, (*at*) han arbejdede hårdt.**
> He said (that) he was working hard.
> (Cf. direct speech: **Han sagde: "Jeg arbejder hårdt."**)

If, however, another sentence element occurs between it and the verb of the main clause, it will not normally be dropped:

De sagde til ham, *at* han arbejdede hårdt.
They told him (that) he was working hard.

If the **at**–clause introduces the sentence, **at** is never dropped:

***At* han arbejder hårdt, er der ingen tvivl om.**
That he works hard there is no doubt.

See also 1029 for the occurrence of main clause word order in **at**–clauses.

(b) Om corresponds to **at** but is used to introduce indirect questions formed from yes/no questions as an indicator of possibility and/or doubt (see also 1026(b)). Unlike **at, om** is never omitted:

Vi spurgte, *om* han arbejdede hårdt.
We asked whether he was working hard.
(Cf. direct question: **Vi spurgte: "Arbejder du hårdt?"**)

***Om* han er hjemme, tør jeg ikke sige.**
Whether he's at home I daren't say.

Hun spurgte mig, *om* han var hjemme.
She asked me if he was at home.

Om is also used elliptically in response to real or presumed questions:

***Om* jeg kan lide øl!**
Do I like beer!

Om is also used as a concessive conjunction (see 915(c)).

(c) At and **om** may introduce subject and object clauses and clauses constituting the predicative complement, attribute or adverbial in the sentence, while the semantically differentiated subordinators (see 912–19) may only introduce adverbial clauses.

912 Temporal conjunctions

Temporal means 'expressing a time'.

(a) Når as a temporal conjunction is used to convey 'when' in clauses describing present and (implied) future events, and for *repeated* actions in the past, present, and future:

Jeg skal nok hjælpe dig, *når* jeg har tid.
I'll help you when I've got the time.

***Når* han kommer hjem, skal jeg fortælle ham det.**
When he comes home I'll tell him.

***Når* jeg spiser rejer, bliver jeg syg.**
When I eat prawns I get ill.

***Når* de kom til byen, drak de sig altid fulde.**
When they came to town they always got drunk.

Når som helst may be used to express 'whenever':

Du kan gøre det, *når som helst* du vil.
You can do it whenever you want.

Nu når = now that (temporal):

***Nu når* du siger det, kan jeg godt høre det.**
Now that you say it, I can hear it.

The **når** may at times be omitted from this construction:

***Nu* du siger det, kan jeg godt høre det.**

Note – **Da** (see (b) below) can also be used instead of **nu** in this type of construction:

Nu da du siger det ...

Når ... nu is used to express circumstance or modality (see also 531):

***Når* du *nu* er i Odense, må du endelig besøge H.C. Andersens hus.**
Since you're now in Odense, you really must visit Hans Christian Andersen's house.

(b) **Da** as a temporal conjunction is used to convey 'when' for a single event or occasion which has taken place in the past:

***Da* jeg så ham, blev jeg pludselig meget vred.**
When I saw him I suddenly became very angry.

Note 1 – **Da** may also be used to convey the historic present, for example in the retelling of the plot of a novel or a play:

> ***Da*** **den grimme ælling forlader andegården, er hans mor slet ikke ked af det.**
> When the ugly duckling leaves the farm, his mother is not at all sad.

Note 2 – **Da** is also a causal conjunction (= as) in both written and spoken Danish (see 618, 913) and an adverb (= then) (see 604, 613(b)).

(c) **Siden** as a temporal conjunction is normally used to convey 'since':

> **Jeg har ikke spist frikadeller, *siden* jeg var i Skive.**
> I haven't eaten meatballs since I was in Skive.

Lige siden is used to express 'ever since':

> ***Lige siden*** **jeg var barn, har jeg altid kunnet lide frikadeller.**
> Ever since I was a child I've always liked meatballs.

Note 1 – **Siden** is also an adverb (see 609(a)):

> **Han ringede i går, men *siden* har jeg ikke hørt fra ham.**
> He rang yesterday, but I haven't heard from him since.

Note 2 – **Siden** is also a preposition (see 730):

> **Jeg har ikke hørt fra ham *siden* i går.** I haven't heard from him since yesterday.

Note 3 – **Siden** is also a causal conjunction, meaning 'since, as, seeing that':

> ***Siden*** **du nu har penge nok, kan du købe mig den kjole.**
> Since you've now got enough money you can buy me that dress.

(d) **Idet** and **mens (medens)** are both used in a temporal sense to express 'as, while'. **Idet** is now more or less restricted to the written language, and is used when describing events which are momentary or of very short duration; it is often preceded by **lige**:

> **(*Lige*) *idet* jeg så ham, gik det op for mig, at han var syg.**
> (Just) as I saw him, I realized he was ill.

Mens (or the longer form **medens**, which is now restricted to more formal written language) is used when the action or event being described is sustained or durative:

> **Vi kan ikke høre noget, *mens* du snakker.**
> We can't hear anything while you're talking.

***Mens* vi venter, kan vi lige så godt drikke en kop te til.**
While we're waiting we may just as well drink another cup of tea.

Note 1 – **Idet** is often used in Danish to render clauses which are expressed with the present participle in English:

***Idet* han trådte ind i stuen, fik han øje på sin kæreste.**
Entering the room, he caught sight of his sweetheart.

Note 2 – **Mens**, just as 'while' in English, can be used to indicate a contrast which is not temporal:

***Mens* han var høj, var hans bror lille.**	While he was tall, his brother was short.

(e) **Før, inden** (before):

These two conjunctions are generally interchangeable:

***Før* du kommer, vil jeg gerne have besked.**
Before you come I'd like to be told.

Han døde, *inden* der var gået et år.
He died before a year had passed.

Note 1 – **Før** has the alternative (and less frequently used) form **førend**.

Note 2– The English phrase 'not until' is usually rendered by **ikke før** or the adverb **først**, though **ikke inden** is also used:

Han kom ikke, *før* klokken var halv to.	He didn't come until it was half past one.
Han kom *først* i går.	He didn't come until yesterday.
Han ville helst ikke gøre det, *inden* han fik lov.	He'd rather not do it until he got permission.

Note 3 – **Næppe ... før** is used to express 'hardly ... before/when, no sooner ... than':

***Næppe* havde han forladt huset, *før* politiet kom.**
Hardly had he left the house when the police arrived/
No sooner had he left the house than the police arrived.

Note 4 – Both **før** and **inden** are also prepositions (see 726):

Det var *før* min tid.	That was before my time.
***Inden* længe er det sommer.**	Before long it will be summer.

(f) **Indtil, til** (until):

These are generally interchangeable, though in spoken Danish **til** is usually preferred:

***Indtil* du finder din paraply, kan du godt låne min.**
Until you find your umbrella you can borrow mine.

Hun blev med at råbe, *til* han hørte det.
She shouted until he heard it.

Notice: 'not until' = **ikke før/inden, først** (see (e) above).

Note – Both **indtil** and **til** are also prepositions (see 716).

(g) Efter at (after):

Han kom, *efter at* vi var gået. He came after we had left.

Efter is increasingly being used as a conjunction in modern Danish.

(h) Som (as, while) can be used in a temporal sense; in such cases, it is frequently used in conjunction with adverbs such as **netop** and **efterhånden**:

***Netop som* jeg ankom, forlod hun huset.**
As soon I arrived she left the house.

***Efterhånden som* jeg bliver ældre, kan jeg ikke tåle at drikke snaps mere.**
As I get older, I can't tolerate drinking akvavit any more.

(i) Notice also: **så længe som**, as long as; **så ofte som**, as often as; **så snart som**, as soon as.

913 Causal conjunctions

Causal means 'expressing reason, cause'.

(a) Fordi (because, as) is most often used to introduce a subordinate clause following a main clause, whereas subordinate clauses introduced by **eftersom** (because, as, since) may either precede or follow the main clause. Compare:

Vi tog til Odense, *fordi* vi ville besøge jernbanemuseet.
We went to Odense because we wanted to visit the railway museum.

***Eftersom* vi ville besøge jernbanemuseet, tog vi til Odense.**
As we wanted to visit the railway museum we went to Odense.

Vi tog til Odense, *eftersom* vi ville besøge jernbanemuseet.
We went to Odense as we wanted to visit the railway museum.

Eftersom is now very rarely used in the spoken language.

Fordi is the most commonly used causal conjunction in the spoken language, and there is also a certain tendency for the construction **fordi at** to be used as an alternative:

Vi tog straks hjem igen, *fordi at* museet var lukket.
We went home again straight away because the museum was closed.

(b) **Da** (see 912(b) above) is also frequently used as a causal conjunction, especially in the written language:

***Da* jeg ikke selv kan komme til mødet, sender jeg min sekretær i stedet.**
As I cannot come to the meeting myself, I shall send my secretary instead.

(c) The use of **idet** (see 912(d) above) as a causal conjunction is less common, and tends to be found in more formal language:

De fandt stedet, *idet* de spurgte sig for.
They found the place by asking the way.

(d) **Siden** (see 912(c) above) may also be used as a causal conjunction:

***Siden* du nu er her, kunne du hjælpe mig med at rydde op.**
Since you're here now you could help me tidy up.

(e) **På grund af at** (because of/on account of/owing to the fact that):

***På grund af at* han var syg, kunne han ikke komme til mødet i går.**
Owing to the fact that he was ill, he couldn't come to the meeting yesterday.

914 Conditional conjunctions

Conditional means 'expressing a condition'. See 1030 for different kinds of conditional clause.

(a) **Hvis** (if) is only used in Danish to introduce direct conditional clauses; it cannot be used instead of **om** in the sense of 'whether' (unlike 'if ' in

English):

Hvis **han gør det igen, bliver jeg vred på ham.**
If he does it again I'll be angry with him.

Så may often be inserted, especially in the spoken language, at the beginning of a main clause following a conditional clause introduced by **hvis**; this is much more common in Danish than the equivalent insertion of 'then' in English:

Hvis **han ikke kommer i morgen,** ***så*** **får han ingen penge.**
If he doesn't come tomorrow he'll get no money.

Inverted word order can be used to convey the sense of a conditional clause and replace **hvis**; this type of construction is used much more widely than in English:

Kommer han **ikke i morgen, bliver jeg vred.**
If he doesn't come tomorrow I'll be angry.

Hvis may be used in conjunction with **blot** or **bare** to express a condition or wish:

Hvis **jeg** *blot/bare* **havde tid, ville jeg gøre det bedre.**
Hvis blot/bare **jeg havde tid, ville jeg gøre det bedre.**
If I only had time I would do it better.

Notice the possible variation in the position of **blot** and **bare** in the sentences above.

Blot and **bare** are also used as conjunctions on their own to express the same:

Bare **Simon ser en pige, bliver han dybt forelsket.**
If Simon just sees a girl he falls madly in love.

Bare **han får pengene, er han tilfreds.**
If he just gets his money he'll be content.

Blot **jeg kunne få sandheden at vide!**
If only I could get to know the truth.

Bare tends to be used more frequently than **blot** in these types of construction.

Note – **Dersom** is used to convey exactly the same meaning as **hvis**, but its use is now restricted to formal and/or official language.

(b) Når (see 912(a)) can also be used to convey the sense of 'if (only)'; it often occurs in conjunction with **bare** (or **blot**):

> ***Når* du *bare* passer på, sker der nok ingenting.**
> If only you are careful, nothing will happen.
>
> ***Når bare* jeg havde vidst det, ville jeg have hjulpet dig.**
> If only I had known that I would have helped you.

Notice the possible variation in the position of **bare** after **når** in the above two sentences.

(c) Medmindre (unless):

> **Peter kommer ikke, *medmindre* du forlanger det.**
> Peter's not coming unless you demand it.

'Unless' may also be conveyed by **hvis (...) ikke** and **undtagen (hvis)**:

> **Gør det ikke, *undtagen* (*hvis*) du har lyst.**
> Don't do it unless you want to.

(d) Notice also: **forudsat at**, provided that, assuming that; **ifald**, if; **såfremt**, in case, provided

915 Concessive conjunctions

Concessive means 'expressing a concession'.

(a) Selvom, skønt (even though, (al)though) are in common usage in modern Danish, whereas the concessive conjunctions **endskønt, ihvorvel, om end, uagtet** (although, even though) are rarely used in the spoken language and have now essentially been relegated to formal/official language.

Both **selvom** and **skønt** mean 'even though, although', and in many instances they are entirely interchangeable, but of the two **skønt** is at times slightly stronger in its expression of contrast:

> ***Selvom* Janet er englænder, taler hun flydende dansk.**
> Although she's English, Janet speaks fluent Danish.

Scrooge sparede altid, *skønt* han havde penge nok.
Scrooge always saved, even though he had enough money.

Note – In the first sentence above, the actual name of the subject is given in the introductory subordinate clause in Danish, whereas English prefers to place the name in the main clause. The general rule in Danish is to place the name of the subject in whichever clause comes first (unlike English, where the subject's name is usually placed in the main clause).

Both **selvom** and **skønt** can be used for factual statements about the past, but for utterances referring to the future, **selvom** is generally used:

Vi var i skoven i søndags, *selvom/skønt* det regnede.
We were in the woods last Sunday, although it was raining.

Vi kommer i morgen, *selvom/*skønt* det regner.
We'll come tomorrow, even if it rains.

(b) **Til trods for at/trods det at** (though, in spite of the fact that):

***Trods det at* han var meget træt, gik han alligevel ikke i seng.**
In spite of the fact that he was very tired he nevertheless didn't go to bed.

(c) **Om** (see 911(b)) is used in conjunction with **så** to express 'even if':

***Om* det *så* skal koste mig en formue, vil jeg se den kamp.**
Even if it costs me a fortune, I want to see that match.

Om is also used with **eller** to express 'whether/if ... or' when the subordinate clause constitutes a noun clause:

Gad vide, *om* han tager med *eller* ej.
I wonder if he's coming along or not.

If the subordinate clause constitutes an adverbial clause, **hvad enten ... eller** is used:

Han tager med, *hvad enten* du kan lide det *eller* ej.
He's coming along whether you like it or not.

(d) **Hvor ... end** (however):

***Hvor* rig han *end* er, har han ikke råd til det.**
However rich he is he can't afford it.

Other intransitive verbs may also be used as copulas, e.g. **gå, ligge, sidde, stå**:

> **Han gik *bedrøvet* bort.**
> He went away full of sorrow.

> **Han lå *syg* hjemme.**
> He lay at home ill.

Copulas can also appear in the passive:

> **Stockholm kaldes *Nordens Venedig.***
> Stockholm is called the Venice of the North.

(b) Complements are of three kinds and agree in gender and number with either subject or object:

Subject complement:

Pigen er *køn.*	The girl is pretty.
Værelset er *rent.*	The room is clean.
Træerne er *høje.*	The trees are tall.
Preben er *dansker.*	Preben is a Dane.
Glyn er *waliser.*	Glyn's a Welshman.
De er begge *professorer.*	They are both professors.

Object complement:

De malede byen *rød* i aftes.	They painted the town red last night.
Det gjorde mig *vred.*	It made me angry.
De udnævnte Peter til *direktør.*	They appointed Peter director.

Free complement:

***Træt og nervøs* tog hun på ferie.** **Hun tog *træt og nervøs* på ferie.**	Tired and nervous she went on holiday.

(c) Complements may be:

A noun (phrase):

Festen var *en stor skandale.*	The party was a great scandal.

A pronoun:

Hvem er *det*? Det er *ham.*	Who is it? It's him.

(e) **Uden at** (without):

Ida sendte os bogen, *uden at* vi bad hende om at gøre det.
Ida sent us the book without us asking her to do it.

(f) **Hvorimod** (whereas):

Peter var fattig, *hvorimod* hans bror var rig.
Peter was poor whereas his brother was rich.

916 Final conjunctions

Final in this sense means 'expressing an intention'.

(a) **For at** (in order that):

De gjorde meget, *for at* han skulle føle sig hjemme.
They did a lot to make him feel at home.

When this construction is used with **ikke**, the meaning is 'lest, so that ... not':

Vi tog børnene med på Frihedsmuseet, *for at* de *ikke* skulle glemme, hvad der skete i Danmark under anden verdenskrig.
We took the children along to the Resistance Museum so that they would not forget what happened in Denmark during World War Two.

For at is much more common when followed by an infinitive (see 528(c)(iv)).

(b) **Så (at)** (so that):

Helene skjulte sig i haven, *så (at)* hun kunne blive lidt længere.
Helene hid in the garden, so that she could stay a bit longer.

917 Consecutive conjunctions

Consecutive means 'expressing a result, consequence'.

(a) **Så at, så ... at/så** (so that, so ... that). These particles are sometimes used together, and are sometimes separated:

Han spiste *så* meget, *at* han blev syg af det.
He ate so much he became ill from it.

Han spiste *så* meget, *så (at)* han blev syg af det.
He ate so much that he became ill from it.

(b) When the conjunction **så** is used to express a result there are two common word order patterns:

(i) **Så**: 'in order that, then'

Så (at) is used as a subordinating conjunction. Subordinate clause order (subject – finite verb, see 1012) (*N.B.* the position of the adverb **ikke**):

Spis det, *så* (*at*) det ikke går til spilde.
Eat it, then it's not wasted.

(ii) **Så**: 'so'

Så is used as a coordinating conjunction (cf. 909). Main clause statement order (subject – finite verb, see 1009) (*N.B.* the position of the adverb **ikke**):

Jeg blev bedt om at spise blodpølsen, *så* jeg vidste ikke, hvad jeg skulle stille op.
I was asked to eat the black pudding, so I didn't know what to do.

918 Comparative conjunctions

Comparative means 'expressing a comparison' (see also 232).

(a) **(Lige) så ... som** ((just) as ... as):

Jeg er *(lige) så* stor *som* min bror.
I'm (just) as big as my brother.

Michael er ikke *så* gammel *som* Peter.
Michael is not as old as Peter.

Som may sometimes be omitted from this type of construction:

Hun spiste *så* hurtigt, hun kunne.
She ate as fast as she could.

(b) **(Sådan) som** (as = in the way that, in accordance with):

> ***Som*** **jeg allerede har sagt, var Jens ikke med til festen.**
> As I've already said, Jens wasn't at the party.
>
> **Du må gøre, *som* jeg siger.**
> You must do as I say.
>
> ***Sådan som*** **han taler, skulle man tro, han var professor.**
> The way he speaks you would think he was a professor.

(c) **Ligesom/som om** (as if = in the same way that):

> **Hun ser ud, *som om* hun ikke har sovet i en uge.**
> She looks as if she hasn't slept for a week.
>
> **Han slog på sit glas, (*lige)som om* han ville holde en tale.**
> He tapped his glass, as if he wanted to make a speech.

In everyday speech, **som om** is the more commonly used.

(d) **End** (than):

> **Opgaven var sværere, *end* jeg havde regnet med.**
> The task was more difficult than I had anticipated.

(e) **Jo ... desto/des/jo** (the + comparative ... the + comparative):

> ***Jo*** **mere du læser, *jo/desto* klogere bliver du.**
> The more you read the wiser you become.
>
> ***Jo*** **mere han tjente, *jo/des/desto* mere brugte han.**
> The more he earned the more he spent.

Notice the word order in clauses with **jo ... desto/des/jo**; the subordinate clause introduced by **jo** must come first, and the main clause with **desto** has inversion. **Jo ... jo** is the most commonly used construction.

D OTHER SUBORDINATORS

919 Introduction

920	Interrogative pronouns	**hvem** (who), **hvad** (what), **hvilken** (which), **hvilket** (which), **hvilke** (which, who), **hvad for en/nogen/noget/nogle** (which)
920	Interrogative adverbs	**hvornår** (when), **hvor** (where), **hvorhen/hvortil** (where ... to), **hvordan** (how), **hvorfor** (why), **hvorfra** (where ... from)
921	Relative pronouns	**der/som** (who, which), **hvad (der)** (what, which), **hvis** (whose), **hvilken** (which), **hvilket** (which), **hvilke** (which, who)
921	Relative adverbs	**hvor** (where)

Pronouns and adverbs used to introduce a subordinate clause also function as subordinators.

920 Interrogative pronouns and adverbs

These include the pronouns: **hvem, hvad, hvilken, hvilket, hvilke, hvad for en/nogen/noget/nogle**, and the adverbs: **hvornår, hvor, hvorhen/hvortil, hvordan, hvorfor, hvorfra**. See 425ff, 612(c).

These words introduce **hv**-questions (see questions 1010(b) and also general subordinators 911(b)), and when they are used to form subordinate clauses, i.e. indirect questions, no other conjunction is required before them:

> **Jeg spurgte, *hvad* han hed.**
> I asked what he was called.

(Cf. direct question: **Jeg spurgte: "Hvad hedder han?"**)

When **hvad** and **hvem** are the subject of a subordinate clause, the word **der** is introduced as a subject marker; see 433ff:

> **Jeg vidste ikke, *hvem der* havde gjort det.**
> I didn't know who had done it.

Hun vidste ikke, *hvad der* var sket.
She didn't know what had happened.

921 Relative pronouns and adverbs

These include the pronouns **der, som, hvis, hvilken, hvilket, hvilke, hvad,** and the adverb **hvor**. See also 429–36, 612(b).

(a) **Der** and **som** are the most frequent of all subordinators, and form relative clauses:

Brevet, *som* jeg sendte ham, var skrevet på maskine.
The letter that/which I sent him was typewritten.

Han er en fyr, *der* ved, hvad han vil.
He's a man who knows what he wants.

See also 431f.

(b) **Hvilken**, etc.:

Hun gav ham et stort kys, *hvilket* var meget sødt af hende.
She gave him a big kiss, which was very sweet of her.

See also 436(a).

(c) **Hvis** can be regarded as supplying the genitive form of **som** (see 435):

En mand, *hvis* navn jeg ikke kender, bad mig om 100 kr.
A man whose name I don't know asked me for 100 kroner.

(d) **Hvor**:

Han fortalte hende, at han havde fundet et sted, *hvor* de kunne være helt alene.
He told her he had found a place where they could be completely alone.

10 SENTENCE STRUCTURE AND WORD ORDER

A CLAUSE ELEMENTS

1001 Word classes and clause elements

Previous chapters of this book have been concerned with *word classes*, that is classification of words according to their form, use and meaning. In this chapter the functions of words and word groups in the clause, i.e. *clause elements*, are examined. A comparison of the two viewpoints can be made from the following analysis:

Du	**har**	**ikke**	**vasket**	**bilen**	**i dag.**	
You	have	not	washed	the car	today.	
pronoun	*verb*	*adverb*	*verb*	*noun*	*adverb*	= *WORD CLASS*
subject	*verb*	*adverbial*	*verb*	*object*	*adverbial*	= *CLAUSE ELEMENT*

In Section A (1002–07) the different clause elements (or 'building blocks') are each examined in some detail, whilst in 1009 these are located in a schema in order to show their relative positions within the clause. This schema, with its seven basic positions, is explained for the main clause in Section B, and for the subordinate clause in Section C. The seven positions are then analysed in greater depth in Sections D and E.

1002 Subjects

(a) In a Danish clause, as in English, the subject is usually explicit, and its function may be fulfilled by several word classes or groups. It can, for example, be:

A noun (phrase):

***Drengen* sidder i stolen.**
The boy is sitting in the chair.

***Karen* laver middagsmaden i dag.**
Karen is cooking the dinner today.

***Den grimme ælling med det store næb* blev smidt ud af andegården.**
The ugly duckling with the big beak was thrown out of the duck farm.

A pronoun:

***De* dansede hele natten igennem.**
They danced all night long.

An adjective:

***Blå* er min yndlingsfarve.**
Blue is my favourite colour.

An infinitive phrase:

***At flyve til Billund* er det bedste, jeg ved.**
Flying to Billund is the best thing I know.

A subordinate clause:

***At han ikke besøgte os i går,* overraskede mig.**
That he didn't visit us yesterday surprised me.

(b) The subject (S) is usually placed next to the finite verb (FV) in the main clause, and its position relative to the verb often helps to indicate sentence type:

***Jens* vandt.**	S – FV = Statement	Jens won.
Vandt *Jens*?	FV – S = Question	Did Jens win?

But notice that Danish can also have inversion in statements:

I fjor vandt *Jens* to gange. Last year Jens won twice.
FV – S = Statement

Imperative clauses often have no formal subject:

Gå væk!	Go away!
Vær glad!	Be happy!

1003 **Det** and **der** as impersonal and formal (place-holder) subject

(a) As a subject in many descriptions of weather and some other constructions **det** (= it) lacks any real meaning. Its function is by means of its position to indicate sentence type, i.e. statement or question:

Det regner/sner/hagler.	It's raining/snowing/hailing.
Det bliver mørkt.	It's getting dark.
Det larmer.	It's noisy.
Regner det?	Is it raining?

Det used in this way is often known as the *impersonal subject*.

(b) The subject of a clause may be postponed, i.e. moved to the right in the clause, and an anticipatory **der** (= there) inserted (cf. 407). This additional subject is known as the *formal subject* (FS), and the postponed subject is known as the *real subject* (RS):

Der **sidder** ***to rødkælke*** **på hegnet.**
FS RS
There are two robins sitting on the fence.

Compare:

To rødkælke **sidder på hegnet.**
S

This kind of construction in English is known as an *existential sentence* as it is often found with the verb 'to be', thus expressing existence. Its use in Danish is less restricted in that many different intransitive verbs are used. The real subject may be of two kinds:

TYPE 1
Real subject = Noun phrase; Formal subject = 'there'

Der **ligger** ***ingen bøger*** **på dit skrivebord.**
FS RS
There are no books on your desk.

TYPE 2
Real subject = Infinitive phrase; Formal subject = 'it'

Det **er interessant** ***at læse om Kierkegaards opdragelse.***
FS RS
It's interesting to read about Kierkegaard's upbringing.

Type 1 is used to avoid beginning a sentence with an indefinite noun phrase, i.e. a new idea. In Type 2 **det** is used to anticipate a postponed 'heavy' (i.e. long or stressed) subject. Compare: ***At læse om Kierkegaards opdragelse* er interessant.**

1004 Finite and non-finite verbs

(a) A Danish clause usually contains a finite verb, i.e. a verb showing tense. Finite forms include:

Present tense:	**Han *kører* langsomt.**	He drives slowly.
Past tense:	**Han *kørte* langsomt.**	He drove slowly.
Imperative:	***Kør* langsomt!**	Drive slowly!

(b) There may be more than one finite verb in the clause:

Børnene *ligger* og *sover*.	The children are asleep.
Mor *sidder* og *læser*.	Mum is (sitting) reading.
***Gå* ud og *vask* bilen!**	Go out and wash the car.

When there is more than one finite verb, the subject is placed either immediately *before* or immediately *after* the first verb:

Børnene ligger og sover.	The children are asleep.
Ligger børnene og sover?	Are the children asleep?

(c) If there are both finite and non-finite verbs in the clause, the finite verb is often an auxiliary verb and, just as in English, it comes first in the verb group. The finite verb may be a temporal auxiliary, indicating tense:

De *er/var* rejst.	They have/had left.
Han *har/havde* gjort det.	He has/had done it.

The finite verb may be a modal auxiliary:

De *ville* have gjort det.	They would have done it.

(d) Non-finite verb forms usually occur together with a finite verb and include:

Infinitive:

Jeg vil *gøre* det.	I want to do it.

Jeg tænker på *at gøre* det. — I'm thinking of doing it.

Present participle:
Han kom *løbende.* — He came running.

Past participle:
Han har *gjort* det. — He's done it.

(e) Two infinitives may occur together:

Det var sjovt *at kunne gøre* det. — It was fun to be able to do it.

(f) In some cases after a modal auxiliary both an infinitive and a past participle may be found; the order in which these appear is identical to English:

Han burde *have gjort* det. — He should have done that.
Han burde *have kunnet gøre* det. — He should have been able to do that.

1005 Direct and indirect objects

(a) Direct objects are found with transitive verbs (see 536):

Jens spiste *kagen.* — Jens ate the cake.
Jeg har læst *bogen.* — I have read the book.

(b) Both direct and indirect objects are found with ditransitive verbs (see 536). The direct object (DO) is often an inanimate object affected by the action of the verb, while the indirect object (IO) is usually an animate being that is the recipient of the action:

De sendte *mig et brev.* — They sent me a letter.
IO DO

As in English, the indirect object in Danish precedes the direct object, regardless of whether they are nouns or pronouns, unless the indirect object is governed by a preposition. Compare:

Jeg lånte *Tom min bil.* — I lent Tom my car.
IO DO

Jeg lånte *ham den.* IO DO	I lent him it.
Jeg lånte *min bil til Tom.* DO IO	I lent my car to Tom.

Note – In English, it is sometimes possible for the direct object to precede the indirect object when they are both pronouns, such as 'Give it me!'; this type of construction is, however, impossible in Danish, and will always be rendered as **Giv mig den!**

(c) The prepositional object consists of a prepositional phrase, i.e. a preposition + complement:

Han bød mig *på en cigar.*	He offered me a cigar.

(d) Objects, whether direct or indirect, normally follow the finite and non-finite verb(s):

Jeg ryger *for mange cigarer.*	I smoke too many cigars.
Jeg har røget *mange cigarer.*	I have smoked many cigars.
Han har givet *mig en cigar.*	He has given me a cigar.

A direct or an indirect object may, however, introduce the clause:

***Den slags cigar* har jeg aldrig røget.**	I've never smoked that type of cigar.
***Mig* gav de ingenting.**	They gave nothing to me.

Object clauses generally come at the end of the sentence but may introduce the clause:

Han har ikke spurgt, *om vi har tid til det.*
He hasn't asked whether we've got the time for it.

***At vi har tid til det,* har jeg altid taget for givet.**
lit. That I have time fit I've always taken for granted.

For the position of unstressed object pronouns and the reflexive object pronoun see 1017, 1023.

(e) The form of the object varies. It may be:

A noun (phrase):

De købte *en brugt bil.*
They bought a second-hand car.

De vaskede *deres bil* i går.
They washed their car yesterday.

A pronoun:

De vaskede *den* i går.
They washed it yesterday.

An infinitive phrase:

Hun begyndte *at synge*.
She began singing.

A phrase/clause in direct speech:

Han sagde: *"Jeg er træt."*
He said, 'I'm tired.'

A subordinate clause:

De spurgte, *om han var træt*.
They asked whether he was tired.

De vidste, *at han havde arbejdet længe*.
They knew he had been working for a long time.

1006 Complements

(a) The predicative complement is usually found in the same position in a clause as the object. It is found with a copula verb. Copulas fulfil two main functions (see 536(c)(ii)):

1 They describe a state: **være**, be; **hedde**, be called; **synes**, seem; **se ... ud**, look (like); **virke**, look, seem

Englænderen derovre hedder *Phil*.
The Englishman over there is called Phil.

Han ser *meget glad* ud.
He looks very happy.

2 They denote a change: **blive**, be, become; **gøre ... til**, make into; **udnævne ... til**, appoint

Vejret bliver *koldere* i morgen.
The weather will be colder tomorrow.

Regeringen udnævnte ham til *ambassadør*.
The government appointed him ambassador.

An adjective (phrase):

Talen var *lang og kedelig.*	The speech was long and boring.

A subordinate clause:

Det er, *hvad jeg mener.*	That's what I think.

1007 Adverbials

(a) The various ways in which adverbials may be classified are dealt with in 608 where the concepts of *adjuncts, disjuncts* and *conjuncts* are introduced together with the more traditional type of adverbial classification. For the purposes of this particular section, and for the sake of transparency, the more traditional terminology is adopted, however. Adjuncts, disjuncts and conjuncts will be considered in more detail in Sections D onwards.

Adverbials can be said to be of two kinds: *clausal adverbials* (sometimes called *sentence adverbials*) and *other adverbials* (sometimes called *content adverbials*). Clausal adverbials usually modify the sense of the clause as a whole:

Vi plejer *ikke* at sejle til Færøerne om vinteren.
We don't usually sail to the Faroes in winter.

Other adverbials generally answer the questions: how? where? when? why?:

Vi plejer ikke at sejle	**til Færøerne**	**om vinteren.**
	where?	*when?*

(b) Clausal adverbials are often adverbs:

Er han *virkelig* så intelligent, som han tror?
Is he really as intelligent as he believes?

Du har *måske* snakket med ham i dag?
You have perhaps spoken to him today?

(c) Other adverbials are of the following kinds:

adverb phrase:	**Han arbejder *utrolig langsomt.*** He works incredibly slowly.
prepositional phrase:	**Han arbejder *i Viborg.*** He works in Viborg.

noun phrase: **Han arbejder *hele natten.***
He works all night.

subordinate clause: **Han arbejder, *når han kan.***
He works when he can.

(d) Clausal adverbials are usually classified into the following types:

modal adverbs: **Han er *sikkert* meget dum.**
He is probably very stupid.

conjunctional adverbs: **Jeg var syg. *Derfor* kunne jeg ikke komme.**
I was ill. That's why I couldn't come.

prepositional phrases: **Han er *trods alt* vores bedste målmand.**
He is after all our best goalkeeper.

negations: **De har *ikke* været her.**
They haven't been here.

(e) Other adverbials are often classified as:

manner adverbial: **Han arbejder *hårdt.***
He works hard.

place adverbial: **Han arbejder *hjemme.***
He works at home.

time adverbial: **Han arbejder *i næste uge.***
He works next week.

condition adverbial: **Han arbejder, *hvis han får tid.***
He works if he has time.

cause adverbial: **Han arbejder, *fordi han kan lide det.***
He works because he likes to.

instrument: **Han åbnede flasken *med en skruetrækker.***
He opened the bottle with a screwdriver.

comparison: **Han er så tynd *som en bønnestage.***
He's as thin as a rake (*lit.* as a beanstalk).

(f) Clausal adverbials usually come immediately after the finite verb (or after the subject in inverted word order) in main clauses, and immediately before the finite verb in subordinate clauses (for definitions see 1008):

Han havde *ikke* vasket sig.
He hadn't had a wash.

Havde han *ikke* vasket sig?
Hadn't he had a wash?

Det irriterede hans kone, at han *ikke* havde vasket sig.
It irritated his wife that he hadn't had a wash.

(g) Other adverbials usually come at either the beginning or the end of main clauses, or at the end of subordinate clauses:

Han havde ikke vasket sig *i mange uger*.
***I mange uger* havde han ikke vasket sig.**
He hadn't had a wash for many weeks.

Hun sagde, at han ikke havde vasket sig *i mange uger*.
She said that he hadn't had a wash for many weeks.

Note – It is also possible in some instances for such other adverbials to be moved to the position usually occupied by the clausal adverbial (see 1014–16, 1019):

Han har *af flere grunde* ikke vasket sig for nylig.
He hasn't had a wash recently for several reasons.

Han har *som tidligere nævnt* ikke vasket sig i lang tid.
He hasn't as mentioned earlier had a wash for a long time.

For further guidance on the position of adverbials in Danish clauses see 1014ff.

B MAIN CLAUSE WORD ORDER – BASIC POSITIONS

1008 Main clauses and subordinate clauses

(a) A clause is a sentence or part of a sentence usually including a subject and a finite verb. While a main clause (MC) can occur on its own, a subordinate clause (SC) usually occurs together with a main clause and may be regarded as forming part of that clause. Compare:

De besøger os i morgen. Det glæder mig.
MC MC
They're visiting us tomorrow. This pleases me.

At de besøger os i morgen, **glæder mig.**
SC = subject FV O
That they're visiting us tomorrow pleases me.

Jeg ved ikke, ***om jeg kan gøre det.***
SC = object
I don't know whether I can do it.

Some subordinate clauses, however, occur as sentences without a main clause (see 1031):

Om jeg kan lide øl! **Det kan du tro!**
Do I like beer! You bet!

(b) Most subordinate clauses begin with a subordinating conjunction (see 910ff, 1012, 1028):

Jeg ved ikke, ***om*** **han kommer i dag.**
I don't know whether he's coming today.

Jeg tror, (*at*) han kommer i dag.
I think (that) he's coming today.

1009 The order of clause elements in main clauses

In order to explain and analyse the order of the various elements within a clause, it is helpful to use the positional schema developed by the Danish grammarian Paul Diderichsen. Whilst most systems for learning word order are based on rules indicating the relative location of only two elements at a time, Diderichsen's sentence schema is a topographical one which maps the whole clause, indicating the relative positions of all the elements within it simultaneously, and especially in relation to the finite verb.

What follows here is essentially a description of *unmarked* word order; exceptions to the basic patterns are dealt with from Section F onwards. The basic positions of main clause elements are as follows (for definition of clause see 1008):

Main clause (MC):

Front position	Finite verb	(Subject)	Clausal adverbial	Non-finite verb	Object/ Complement/ Real subject	Other adverbial
F	v	n	a	V	N	A

To illustrate the type(s) of clause element which can occur in each of these seven basic positions, consider the following clauses placed in the schema under the abbreviated designations F/vna/VNA:

	F	v	n	a	V	N	A
1	**Jens**	**købte**	–	–	–	**en bil**	**i går**
2	**Jens**	**købte**	–	**ikke**	–	**en bil**	**i går**
3	**Han**	**har**	–	**ikke**	**købt**	**en bil**	**i år**
4	**I går**	**købte**	**Jens**	–	–	**en bil**	–
5	**Han**	**køber**	–	**altid**	–	**biler**	**i Odense**
6	**Bilen**	**købte**	**han**	–	–	–	**i går**
7	**I dag**	**kører**	**han**	–	–	**sin bil**	**på værksted**
8	**Desværre**	**kører**	**han**	**aldrig**	–	–	**hurtigt nok**
9	**I går**	**kunne**	**Peter**	**ikke**	**finde**	**vej**	**hjem**
10	**Peter**	**var**	–	–	–	**fuld**	**i går**
11	**Fuld**	**har**	**han**	**jo ofte**	**været**	–	–
12	**Om vinteren**	**drikker**	**han**	**altid**	–	**for meget**	–
13	**I aften**	**skal**	**han**	–	**male**	**byen rød**	**med sine venner**
14	**Drikke**	**kan**	**han**	**i alt fald!**	–	–	–
15	**Tom**	**er**	–	–	–	**læge**	–
16	**Det**	**har**	**han**	–	**været**	–	**i mange år**
17	**Der**	**sidder**	–	–	–	**to patienter**	**uden for hans kontor**
18	–	**Vil**	**du**	**ikke**	**sætte**	**dig**	**ned?**
19	–	**Har**	**du**	**aldrig**	**villet møde**	**hende**	**før?**
20	**Hvornår**	**kommer**	**de**	–	–	–	**hjem fra biografen?**
21	–	**Læg**	–	–	–	**avisen**	**på bordet!**

Translation of examples:

1 Jens bought a car yesterday. 2 Jens didn't buy a car yesterday. 3 He hasn't bought a car this year. 4 Yesterday Jens bought a car. 5 He always buys cars in Odense. 6 He bought the car yesterday. 7 Today he's driving his car to the garage. 8 Unfortunately he never drives fast enough. 9 Yesterday Peter couldn't find the way home. 10 Peter was drunk yesterday. 11 He's often been drunk, you know. 12 In the winter he always drinks too much. 13 Tonight he's going to paint the town red with his friends. 14 He certainly can drink! 15 Tom is a doctor. 16 He's been one for many years. 17 Two patients are sitting outside his office. 18 Won't you sit down? 19 Have you never wanted to meet her before? 20 When are they coming home from the cinema? 21 Put the newspaper on the table!

(a) Capital letters are used to indicate the verbals (i.e. non-finite verbs), nominals (i.e. nouns and pronouns) and adverbials in the last three positions to distinguish them from the verbals, nominals and adverbials in the centre of the schema. The following is a summary of the different elements to be found in each of the seven positions:

In the 'F' position, we find a variety of word classes: nominals (both as subject and object), adverbials, non-finite verbs, and adjectives. Normally, this position only contains **one** of these elements (1–17, 20).

In the 'v' position, we only ever find the finite verb (1–21).

The 'n' position contains nominals; if the subject of a clause does not appear under 'F', it will usually be placed here (e.g. 4 and 6).

In the 'a' position, we find certain types of adverbials (see 1014ff). This is where negations are consistently placed in the clause (e.g. 8 and 9). There may be more than one adverbial here (11).

In the 'V' position are non-finite verbs (infinitives (e.g. 13) and participles (e.g. 11). Sometimes both of these will occur simultaneously (e.g. 19)).

In the 'N' position are nominals (nouns and pronouns as objects (e.g. 1 and 19), subject and object complements (e.g. 10 and 13) and real subjects in **der**-clauses (17)).

In the 'A' position are adverbs and adverbials (see Section D). There may be more than one (20).

The 'v' position (= finite verb) is the only position in the schema that must be filled (see also 1011).

(b) Main clauses may in principle begin with any type of clause element (see 1022). Inverted word order (verb – subject) is much more common in Danish than in English:

Main clause

F	v	n	a	V	N	A
I morgen	**skal**	**jeg**	–	**arbejde**	–	–

(Tomorrow I have to work.)

(c) In main clauses the clausal adverbial is usually placed directly after the finite verb:

Han kan *ikke* danse.
F v a V
He can't dance.

(d) Danish main clauses can be divided into two main types according to the position of the finite verb (v) in the clause (see 1002): in v1 clauses the finite verb comes first in the clause, and in v2 clauses it comes second. Notice, however, that in v1 clauses the Front position (F, see also 1022) remains unfilled.

Type	F	v	n	a	V	N	A
v1							
1	–	**Læser**	**du**	–	–	**dansk?**	–
2	–	**Læs**	–	–	–	**dine lektier!**	–
v2							
3	**Han**	**læser**	–	–	–	**dansk**	–
4	**I år**	**læser**	**han**	–	–	**dansk**	–
5	**Hvorfor**	**læser**	**han**	–	–	**dansk?**	–

Translation of examples:

1. Are you studying Danish? 2. Do your homework! 3. He studies Danish. 4. This year he's studying Danish. 5. Why is he studying Danish?

As can be seen from these examples, v1/v2 represent different sentence types (see 1010):

– v1 clauses (with an unfilled F position) are either yes/no questions (1) or commands (2).

– v2 clauses are either statements (3, 4) or **hv**-questions ((5), see 428, 1022(a)).

While v1 clauses have inverted word order (finite verb – subject), v2 clauses may have either straight (subject – finite verb) or inverted (finite verb – subject) order.

(e) When two main clauses are linked by a conjunction, its position is as in English. In the schema it precedes 'F' and the position is given the designation ‘k’ (see also 901(a)):

k	F	v	n	a	V	N	A
–	**Hans**	**spiser**	–	–	–	**rundstykker**	–
men	**Else**	**spiser**	–	–	–	**rugbrød**	

(Hans eats rolls but Else eats rye bread.)

1010 Types of main clause

See 1009(d) for a definition of v1/v2.

The chief types of main clause in Danish are as follows:

(a) Statement

v2 straight:
Han kommer hjem i morgen.
He’s coming home tomorrow.

v2 inverted:
I morgen kommer han hjem.
Tomorrow he’s coming home.

(b) Question

(i) Yes/no question

v1 inverted:
Kommer han hjem i morgen?
Is he coming home tomorrow?

(ii) **hv**-question

v2 inverted:
Hvornår kommer han hjem?
When is he coming home?

(c) Command

v1 usually no subject:
Kom hjem nu!
Come home now!

1011 Summary of main clause word order

(a) Main clause statements and questions always have a finite verb and usually a subject. The other positions may be left vacant. The subject may occupy the front position (F). Alternatively, the subject may occupy the position immediately following the finite verb (v). When there are both a formal subject and a real subject the latter is postponed to the object position (N).

(b) The front position (F) is always occupied in statements and **hv**-questions, but is vacant in yes/no questions and commands, i.e. in v1 clauses. Normally, only one element may occupy the front position at any one time.

(c) There may be more than one adverbial in the 'a' position.

(d) There may be more than one non-finite verb in the 'V' position.

(e) There may be more than one object or complement in the 'N' position.

(f) There may be more than one adverbial in the 'A' position.

(g) There may be an extra position inserted before the front position but after any link, or after the 'A' position or both (see 1025).

(h) There may be a conjunction position ('k') before the extra position and/or 'F' position (see 1009(e)).

C SUBORDINATE CLAUSE WORD ORDER – BASIC POSITIONS

1012 Subordinate clause positions

The following schema describes the main features of unmarked subordinate clause word order in Danish: the designations v, n, a, etc., are used for exactly the same types of element as in the main clause schema; and k is used to indicate a subordinating conjunction (see 902ff, 910–18). Notice that there is no 'F' position.

Subordinate clause (SC):

Matrix	Conj.	Subj.	Clausal Adv.	Finite verb	Non-finite verb	Object/ Comp./ Real subj.	Other adv.
	k	n	a	v	V	N	A
1 **Vi spurgte,**	**om**	**han**	**ikke**	**havde**	–	**tid**	**til det**
2 **Han vidste,**	**(at)**	**hun**	**ikke**	**kunne**	**lide**	**ham**	–
3 **Han svarede,**	**at**	**han**	**altid**	**går**	–	–	**tidligt i seng**
4 **Jeg rejser nu,**	**selv om**	**det**	**ikke**	**passer**	–	–	**ind i mine planer**
5 **Det er det værste,**	–	**jeg**	**nogen-sinde**	**har**	**hørt**	–	–
6 **Han sagde,**	**(at)**	**han**	–	**var**	–	**træt,**	–
	og at	**han**	–	**trængte**	–	–	**til en ferie.**

Translation of examples:

1 We asked whether he hadn't got the time for it. 2 He knew that she didn't like him. 3 He replied that he always goes to bed early. 4 I'm going now even though it doesn't suit my plans. 5 That is the worst thing I've ever heard. 6 He said that he was tired and that he needed a holiday.

Notes on subordinate clause positions:

(a) The subject position is always occupied. If there is both a formal and a real subject the latter is postponed to the object position (6).

(b) The subordinating conjunction **at** may sometimes be omitted (2,6) (see 1028(a)).

(c) For independent clauses (with subordinate clause word order) see 1031.

(d) An extra position may be inserted after the 'A' position (see 1025).

(e) If there are two subordinate clauses, these, just as in English, can be linked by a coordinating conjunction which precedes any subordinating conjunction in the 'k' position (6).

1013 Differences between main clause and subordinate clause positions

The following is a summary of the major differences between the position of elements in main and subordinate clauses:

(a) Whereas main clauses may begin with almost any clause element (which is placed in the 'F' position), subordinate clauses almost invariably begin with a conjunction (k) followed by the subject (n). Occasionally, however, the conjunction **at** and relative pronouns when they do not function as the subject may be omitted in the subordinate clause. Thus, while main clause word order may be either subject – verb (straight) or verb – subject (inverted), subordinate clause order is usually subject – verb (straight).

(b) In main clauses the clausal adverbial comes *after* the finite verb. In subordinate clauses the clausal adverbial comes *before* the finite verb.

(c) These differences are illustrated by a comparison of the different schemas for main and subordinate clauses:

Main clause:	**k**	**F**	**v**	**n**	**a**	**V**	**N**	**A**
Subordinate clause:	**k**			**n**	**a**	**v V**	**N**	**A**

D THE POSITION OF ADVERBIALS

The correct placement of adverbials within Danish main and subordinate clauses (which can vary considerably) is an aspect of the language which frequently causes difficulties for foreign learners, and precise rules are difficult to formulate. Danish grammarians who have treated the subject typically put adverbs into three basic classes: final adverbial (Danish: *slutadverbial*), central adverbial (Danish: *centraladverbial*) and free adverbial (Danish: *frit adverbial*). These terms relate to Diderichsen's schema outlined above and refer to the possibilities of adverbial placement within it. Final adverbials are those which typically occupy the final 'A' position: they are the adverbials which are (almost) always placed here, the so-called fixed final adverbials (Danish *fast slutadverbial*); and those which may also occur in the front ('F') position, the so-called loose final adverbials (Danish *løst slutadverbial*). Both types of final adverbial form a semantic unit with the verb (e.g. **blive hjemme**, stay at home; **flyve bort**, fly away; **gå i seng**, go to bed; **gå væk**, go away; **stå op**, get up). Central adverbials are those which are typically placed in the 'a' position and are clausal adverbials. And free adverbials are those which can be found in the 'F', 'a' and 'A' positions, and usually indicate time, manner, place or some other circumstance which is not a necessary or integral part of the verbal construction; their precise placement, however, will often depend on the stress and rhythm of the utterance, as well as on the presence or absence of other adverbials (see 1007).

It is possible to predict at least a grammatically, if not stylistically, correct placement for adverbials in the vast majority of clauses by considering whether they are *adjuncts, conjuncts* or *disjuncts* (see 608), and if they are adjuncts, precisely what semantic function they perform in the clause.

1014 Adjuncts

(a) If an adjunct functions as an *adverbial expression of manner*, it will normally occur in the 'A' position in both main and subordinate clauses. Notice that this is the position where adverbs formed from adjectives ending in **-ig/-lig** through the addition of the adverbial **-t** morpheme (see 611) appear:

Main Clause:

F	v	n	a	V	N	A
Lasse	**dansede**	–	–	–	–	***med stor elegance***
Lasse danced with great elegance.						
Palle	**skar**	–	–	–	**brødet**	***med omhu***
Palle cut the bread carefully.						
Det	**kan**	**du**	–	**klare**	–	***hurtigt!***
You can do that quickly!						
(Cf.						
Det	**kan**	**du**	***hurtig***	**klare!**	–	–
You can easily do that!)						

Subordinate Clause:

k	n	a	v	V	N	A
, selvom	**Lasse**	–	**dansede**	–	–	***med stor elegance***
even though Lasse was dancing with great elegance.						
, selvom	**Palle**	–	**skar**	–	**brødet**	***med omhu***
even though Palle cut the bread carefully.						

k	n	a	v	V	N	A
, selvom	**du**	–	**kan**	**klare**	**det**	***hurtigt***
even though you can do it quickly.						
(Cf.						
, selvom	**du**	***hurtig***	**kan**	**klare**	**det**	–
even though you can easily do it.)						

(b) If an adjunct functions as an *adverbial expression of place* (and especially if it is a prepositional phrase), it can always be placed in the 'A' position if it is *directional*, but it may be placed in either the 'F' or 'A' position if it is *locational*:

Main Clause:

F	v	n	a	V	N	A
Jeg	**rejser**	–	**ikke**	–	–	***til Mexico***
I'm not going to Mexico.						
Du	**skal**	–	–	**stille**	**dem**	***på bordet***
You must put them on the table.						
Jens	**er**	–	–	**gået**	–	***hjem***
Jens has gone home.						
I søen	**svømmer**	**der**	–	–	**mange ænder**	–
A lot of ducks are swimming in the lake.						
Der	**er**	–	–	–	**mange biler**	***i London***
There are a lot of cars in London.						

Subordinate Clause:

k	n	a	v	V	N	A
, selvom	**jeg**	**ikke**	**rejser**	–	–	***til Mexico***
even though I'm not going to Mexico.						
, selvom	**du**	–	**skal**	**stille**	**dem**	***på bordet***
even though you must put them on the table.						

, selvom	**Jens**	–	**er**	**gået**	–	***hjem***
even though Jens has gone home.						
, selvom	**der**	–	**svømmer**	–	**mange ænder**	***i søen***
even though a lot of ducks are swimming in the lake.						
, selvom	**der**	–	**er**	–	**mange biler**	***i London***
even though there are a lot of cars in London.						

(c) If an adjunct is an *adverbial expression of time*, there are several possibilities for its placement, depending on the nature of the time being expressed, i.e. time *'when'*, time *'duration'* or time *'frequency'*:

'When', 'duration' and ***'definite*** *frequency' adverbials* appear in the 'F', 'a' or 'A' positions in main clauses, and in the 'a' or 'A' positions in subordinate clauses. However, in both main and subordinate clauses, they will normally appear in the 'A' position if it would otherwise be vacant:

Main Clause:

F	v	n	a	V	N	A
Jeg	**rejste**	–	–	–	–	**til Danmark** ***i fredags***
I fredags	**rejste**	**jeg**	–	–	–	**til Danmark**
I travelled to Denmark last Friday.						
Hele sit liv	**har**	**Viggo**	–	**boet**	–	**i Svendborg**
Viggo	**har**	–	–	**boet**	–	**i Svendborg** ***hele sit liv***
Viggo	**har**	–	***hele sit liv***	**boet**	–	**i Svendborg**
Viggo has lived in Svendborg all of his life.						
Viggo	**har**	–	–	**arbejdet**	–	***hele sit liv***
Viggo has worked all of his life.						
Lise	**har**	–	–	**ventet**	–	***længe*** **på Anders**
Længe	**har**	**Lise**	–	**ventet**	–	**på Anders**
Lise	**har**	–	***længe***	**ventet**	–	**på Anders**
Lise has waited a long time for Anders.						
Lise	**har**	–	–	**ventet**	–	***længe***
Lise has waited a long time.						
Hver dag	**kom**	**hun**	–	–	–	**for sent**
Every day she came too late.						
Hun	**er**	–	***hver dag***	**kommet**	–	**for sent**
She's come too late every day.						
Hun	**er**	–	–	**kommet**	–	***hver dag***
She's come every day.						

Subordinate Clause:

k	n	a	v	V	N	A
, selvom	**jeg**	***i fredags***	**rejste**	–	–	**til Danmark**

even though I travelled to Denmark last Friday.

k	n	a	v	V	N	A
, selvom	**jeg**	–	**rejste**	–	–	**til Danmark *i fredags***

even though I travelled to Denmark last Friday.

k	n	a	v	V	N	A
, selvom	**han**	***hele sit liv***	**boede**	–	–	**i Svendborg**

even though he lived all his life in Svendborg.

k	n	a	v	V	N	A
, selvom	**hun**	–	**kommer**	–	–	***hver dag***

even though she comes every day.

'Indefinite *frequency' adverbials* normally occur in the 'a' position:

Main Clause:

F	v	n	a	V	N	A
Hans	**har**	–	***ofte***	**været**	–	**i London**

Hans has often been in London.

F	v	n	a	V	N	A
Jeg	**ser**	–	***sjældent***	–	**mine forældre**	–

I rarely see my parents.

Subordinate Clause:

k	n	a	v	V	N	A
, selvom	**han**	***ofte***	**har**	**været**	–	**i London**

even though he has often been in London.

k	n	a	v	V	N	A
, selvom	**jeg**	***sjældent***	**ser**	–	**mine forældre**	–

even though I rarely see my parents.

Aldrig (never) is an exception to the above and may on occasion occur in the 'F' position, but it is more usually found in the 'a' position in both main and subordinate clauses:

Main Clause:

F	v	n	a	V	N	A
Aldrig	**har**	**jeg**	–	**set**	**noget lignende**	–
Jeg	**har**	–	***aldrig***	**set**	**noget lignende**	–

I have never seen anything like it.

Subordinate Clause:

k	n	a	v	V	N	A
, selvom	**jeg**	***aldrig***	**har**	**set**	**noget lignende**	–

even though I've never seen anything like it.

1015 Conjuncts

Conjuncts typically appear in either the 'F' or the 'a' position in main clauses and the 'a' position in subordinate clauses:

Main Clause:

F	v	n	a	V	N	A
Derfor	**kommer**	**hun**	–	–	–	**til mødet**
Hun	**kommer**	–	***derfor***	–	–	**til mødet**

Therefore she's coming to the meeting.

F	v	n	a	V	N	A
Hun	**ville**	–	***ellers***	**være kommet**	–	–
Ellers	**ville**	**hun**	–	**være kommet**	–	–

She would have come otherwise.

Subordinate Clause:

k	n	a	v	V	N	A
, selvom	**hun**	***ellers***	**havde**	–	**tid**	**til det**

even though she did have time for it.

1016 Disjuncts

Disjuncts can always be placed in the 'a' position, though many may also occur in the 'F' position in main clauses:

Main Clause:

F	v	n	a	V	N	A
Lise	**kan**	–	***desværre*** **ikke**	**komme**	–	**til mødet**
Unfortunately Lise can't come to the meeting.						
Heldigvis	**kan**	**Jens**	**ikke**	**komme**	–	**til mødet**
Luckily Jens can't come to the meeting.						

Subordinate clause:

k	n	a	v	V	N	A
, selvom	**han**	***sikkert***	**har**	–	**tid**	**til det**
even though he's probably got time for it.						

E ORDER WITHIN POSITIONS

It is often the case that there is more than one element present in the 'a', 'V', 'N' and 'A' positions. The relative order of elements within these positions is examined in this section.

1017 Order of objects and complements

See 1005ff.

(a) The order of objects is usually the same as in English, i.e. a prepositionless object precedes an object with a preposition:

Han gav bogen til Åse.
-prep +prep
He gave the book to Åse.

If neither object is preceded by a preposition, then the indirect object precedes the direct object:

Han gav	**Åse**	**bogen.**
	IO	DO

He gave Åse the book.

This is also the case for pronominal objects:

Han gav	**hende**	**den.**
	IO	DO

He gave her it.

Note – When the direct object is a subordinate clause, the prepositional object precedes the prepositionless object:

Michael sagde	**til alle,**	**at han var chefen.**
	IO	DO = SC

Michael told everyone that he was the boss.

(b) The direct object precedes the object complement (OC):

De malede	**bordet**	**grønt.**
	DO	OC

They painted the table green.

Hold	**bajerne**	**kolde!**
	DO	OC

Keep the beers cold!

(c) The subject complement (SC) is not found together with a direct object. When it is found with an indirect object, the subject complement immediately follows it:

Han var	**sin mor**	**en god støtte.**
	IO	SC

He was a good support for his mother.

Børnene var	**deres forældre**	**taknemmelige.**
	IO	SC

The children were grateful to their parents.

Jørgen var	**opgaven**	**voksen.**
	IO	SC

Jørgen was equal to the task.

Note – If the object is preceded by a preposition, the above order is reversed: **Han var en god støtte for sin mor**, etc.

(d) In main clauses where the 'V' position is empty, reflexive pronouns and unstressed object pronouns are placed in the subject position (n) immediately after the finite verb in subject – verb clauses and after the subject in verb – subject clauses (see also 1023):

F	v	n	a	V	N	A
Lise	**tog**	**sig**	**ikke**	–	–	**af sine børn**
Lise neglected her children.						
I går	**vaskede**	**John sig**	**ikke**	–	–	–
Yesterday John didn't wash.						
Jeg	**giver**	**dig den**	**aldrig**	–	–	–
I'll never give you it.						

1018 Order of clausal adverbials

See also 613, 1007, 1014–16.

The order is usually:

1 Short modal adverbs (613(b)): **da, jo, nok, vel**

2 Conjunctional adverbs (613(c)): **altså, derfor, desuden, dog**

3 Longer modal adverbs (613(b)) or prepositional phrases: **antagelig, egentlig, faktisk, i det hele taget, oven i købet, trods alt, virkelig**

4 Negations (613(a)): **aldrig, ikke**

The relative order when all of these are present in a clause (a rare occurrence, however!) is shown by the following:

	1	2	3	4	
Han har	***vel***	***derfor***	***faktisk***	***aldrig***	**drukket øl.**

He has therefore actually never drunk beer, I suppose.

But:

When **ikke** is used to modify another adverb and not the clause as a whole, thereby forming a negative adverb phrase, it is the modified adverb which will assume the last position, immediately preceded by **ikke**:

	1	2	3	4	
Han har	***nu***	***måske***	***ikke***	***altid***	**drukket vin.**

He hasn't perhaps always drunk wine.

1019 Order of other adverbials and the passive agent

See also 1007.

(a) The relative order of other adverbials within a clause is rather flexible. Two basic rules of thumb seem to apply:

– Adverbials of manner usually precede those of place and time (manner–place–time = MPT);

– Long adverbials usually follow the MPT group.

The order is, therefore, usually (but see (b) below):

1 Adverbial expressions of manner (609(b)):

forsigtigt, carefully; **godt**, well; **hurtigt**, quickly; **langsomt**, slowly; **smukt**, beautifully; etc.

2 Adverbial expressions of place (609(c)):

der, there; **her**, here; **hjemme**, at home; **i Odense**, in Odense; **på Færøerne**, in the Faroes; **tilbage**, back; etc.

3 Adverbial expressions of time (609(a)):

altid, always; **dagen derpå**, on the following day; **i går**, yesterday; **næste uge**, next week; **om eftermiddagen**, in the afternoon; **år 2000**, in 2000; etc.

4 Long adverbial expressions denoting cause, condition, manner, etc.:

af gode grunde, for good reasons; **hvis du er enig**, if you agree; **på en**

eller anden måde, somehow or other; etc.

Notice the alternatives in the table below (and see 1022):

	1 Manner	2 Place	3 Time	4 Long adverbials
Han rejste	**pludselig**	**bort**	**i går**	**af forskellige grunde**
He suddenly left yesterday for various reasons.				
(Cf. **Han rejste af forskellige grunde pludselig bort i går.**)				
Hun blev født	–	**i London**	**i 1941**	**under anden verdenskrig**
She was born in London in 1941 during the Second World War.				
(Cf. **Hun blev født under anden verdenskrig i London i 1941.**)				

The alternative order here is the result of a desire to emphasize the final element in the sentence.

(b) Adverbial expressions of frequency that can occupy the 'a' position (see 1014(c)) form an exception to the guidelines concerning the order of adverbials, in that, regardless of their semantic function within the clause, they may be positioned differently in any given series of adverbials. For example:

Han er *sjældent/ofte/altid/aldrig* hjemme om søndagen.
He is rarely/often/always/never at home on Sundays.
(Cf. **Han har *sjældent/ofte/altid/aldrig* været hjemme om søndagen.**)

Many adverbial expressions may also introduce a clause and therefore occupy the 'F' position (see 1014–16):

***Om søndagen* er han ofte hjemme.**
***Om søndagen* har han sjældent været hjemme.**

(c) Adverbial expressions of degree precede the adjective or adverbial they are modifying:

Det hele skete *usædvanligt* hurtigt.
It all happened unusually quickly.

Han blev *temmelig* beruset i aftes.
He got rather tipsy last night.

(d) The passive agent (see 541(a)–(b)) usually comes immediately before other adverbial expressions:

Jeg blev hentet	***af Hans og Else***	**på banegården**	**i går.**
	agent	place	time

I was met by Hans and Else at the railway station yesterday.

1020 Order within positions – summary

1 Front position (F)	any element from 3–7 below
2 Finite verb (v)	present or past tense or imperative
3 (Subject) (n)	subject – reflexive pronoun – unstressed pronominal object
4 Clausal adverbial (a)	short modal adverb – short conjunctional/ pronominal adverb – longer modal adverb – negation
5 Non-finite verb (V)	infinitive(s) or present/past participle + infinitive
6 Object/Complement/ Real subject (N)	reflexive pronoun – real subject – subject complement – indirect object – direct object – object complement
7 Other adverbial (A)	verb particle – passive agent – manner adverbial – place adverbial – time adverbial – long adverbials

F MAIN CLAUSE TRANSFORMATIONS AND EXCEPTIONS

This section deals in detail with the movement of words and phrases within the (very flexible) Danish main clause. These transformations are often made for different stylistic and at times grammatical reasons.

1021 The base clause

The basic main clause structure for Danish set out in previous sections is repeated here for convenience:

1 *Front position* F	2 *Finite verb* v	3 *Subject* n	4 *Clausal adverbial* a	5 *Non-finite verb* V	6 *Object/ Complement* N	7 *Other adverbials* A
Han	**vil**	–	**måske**	**sælge**	**bilen**	**i morgen**

(He will perhaps sell the car tomorrow.)

This base clause begins with the subject, i.e. has straight word order, and all other positions, with the exception of the 'n' are filled. In the paragraphs below possible variations of this order are examined. In paragraphs 1022–24 these variations largely involve changes for stylistic effect or grammatical reasons, whereas in paragraph 1025 the changes involve a more radical rearrangement of elements.

1022 Topicalization and emphasis

For the base clause, see 1021 above.

(a) Topicalization involves placing one of the clause elements from positions 4 to 7 in the base clause in the front position, thus displacing the subject to position 3. The most frequent topicalization is of adverbial expressions indicating when or where the action of the clause is taking place, but others are possible. This is normally done when one wishes to emphasize a particular clause element, or for stylistic reasons.

	1 F	2 v	3 n	4 a	5 V	6 N	7 A
Base clause:	**Han**	**vil**	–	**måske**	**sælge**	**bilen**	**i morgen**
1 A to F:	**I morgen**	**vil**	**han**	**måske**	**sælge**	**bilen**	–
2 N to F:	**Bilen**	**vil**	**han**	**måske**	**sælge**	–	**i morgen**
3 a to F:	**Måske**	**vil**	**han**	–	**sælge**	**bilen**	**i morgen**

When the non-finite verb is moved to the front position, the elements governed by it will normally also be moved with it:

	1 F	2 v	3 n	4 a	5 V	6 N	7 A
4 V + N to F:							
	Sælge bilen	**vil**	**han**	**måske**	–	–	**i morgen**
and:							
5 V + N + A to F:							
	Sælge bilen i morgen	**vil**	**han**	**måske**	–	–	–

It is possible to topicalize direct speech (which grammatically functions as the object of the clause):

6	**"For helvede!"**	**sagde**	**han**	–	–	–	–
('Blast!', he said.)							

The subject complement may also be topicalized, though this may at times sound affected:

7	**Syg**	**var**	**hun**	**ikke**	–	–	–
(Ill she was not.)							

The verb in the 'v' position may also be topicalized, and if it has an object this will also be moved with it (cf. 4 and 5 above):

8	**Læse aviser**	**gør**	**han**	**aldrig**	–	–	–
(= **Han læser aldrig aviser.**) He never reads newspapers.							

When (as in example (8) above) the verb is topicalized, it appears in its base (infinitive) form, and the finite verb **gør/gjorde/har gjort** replaces it as the 'place-holder' in the 'v' position. This place-holder indicates sentence type. Compare:

Læser han ikke? = yes/no question
Læse gør han ikke. = statement

Note – In colloquial Danish one also comes across this type of construction with a finite verb in the 'F' position followed by the place-holder **gøre** in the same tense. Notice that this is an exception to the general rule that a clause only contains one finite verb (cf. 1004, 1009(a)). This particular construction appears to occur more frequently in conjunction with the past tense than with the present tense:

Kyssede hinanden gjorde de aldrig, men skændtes gjorde de heller ikke.
They never kissed each other, but they didn't have rows either.

Jeg har lige talt med ham, så sover gør han i hvert fald ikke.
I've just spoken to him, so he's certainly not asleep.

In questions with **hv**-words (**hvad**, **hvem**, etc.) the interrogative will always occupy the front position, even when preceded by a preposition:

Hvem snakker du med?	Who are you talking to?
Hvad for en bog kunne du tænke dig?	Which book would you like?
I hvilket hus bor du?	In which house do you live?

(b) In the front position it is common to find a subordinate clause which would otherwise be a final adverbial:

1 F	2 v	3 n	4 a	5 V	6 N	7 A
Når vi kom hjem,	**drak**	**vi**	**altid**	–	**kaffe**	–
(When we got home we always drank coffee.)						
(Cf. **Vi**	**drak**	–	**altid**	–	**kaffe**	**, når vi kom hjem**)

(c) Notice that (with the exception of 4, 5 and 8 above) only one clause element usually occupies the front position at any one time. This means, for example, that only one adverbial may normally be topicalized (see also Section D for the possible placements of adverbials):

Der var fest	**i Århus**	**i går**	⇨	**I går**	**var der fest**	**i Århus**
	A-place	A-time		A-time		A-place

(There was a party in Århus yesterday.)

But:

I Århus	**var der fest**	**i går**
A-place		A-time

(d) In spoken Danish it is possible to use stress to emphasize any element in the clause without altering the word order:

***Kirsten* købte blomster i går.**
Kirsten bought flowers yesterday. (i.e. not Karen)

Kirsten *købte* blomster i går. (i.e. not free)
Kirsten købte *blomster* i går. (i.e. not fruit)
Kirsten købte blomster *i går*. (i.e. not today)

(e) In written Danish, in order to achieve a varied style and the desired emphasis, writers naturally exercise care in where they decide to position the various clause elements. To this end, they may choose to 'weight' their clauses with long elements either in the 'F' position or the 'A' position; either of these positions may be used to emphasize particular clause elements to give the desired stylistic or emphatic effect.

1023 'Light' elements

'Light' elements are short, unstressed clause elements, which may appear as e.g. direct/indirect object/reflexive pronouns. In clauses *without a non-finite verb* (i.e. the 'V' position is empty) these always move leftwards to occupy the 'n' position after the finite verb, thus preceding the clausal adverbial ('a' position). Note that the indirect object (IO) nevertheless will always precede the direct object (DO) (see 1005). In the following table, stressed elements are indicated by italics:

	F	v	n	a	V	N	A
1	**Jeg**	**kender**	–	**ikke**	–	***ham*** (stressed DO)	–
I don't know *him*.							
2	**Jeg**	**kender**	**ham** (light DO)	**ikke**	–	–	–
I don't know him.							
3	**Jeg**	**gav**	**ham** (light IO)	**ikke**	–	**bogen** (DO)	–
I didn't give him the book.							
4	**Jeg**	**gav**	–	**ikke**	–	***ham*** **bogen** (stressed IO)	–
I didn't give *him* the book.							
5	**Jeg**	**gav**	**ham** (light IO)	**ikke**	–	***den*** (stressed DO)	–
I didn't give him *that one*.							

	F	v	n	a	V	N	A
6	**Jeg**	**gav**	–	**ikke**	–	***ham* den** (stressed IO)	–
I didn't give *him* that one.							
7	**Jeg**	**gav**	**ham den** (light IO + DO)	**ikke**	–	–	–
I didn't give him it.							
8	**Jeg**	**har**	–	**ikke**	**givet**	**ham den** (IO – DO)	–
I haven't given him it.							
9	**I dag**	**har**	**han**	**ikke**	**vasket**	**sig**	–
Today he hasn't had a wash.							
10	**I dag**	**vaskede**	**han sig**	**ikke**	–	–	–
Today he didn't have a wash.							

Only when the pronoun is at least partly stressed (as in 1, 4, 5, 6) does it occupy the 'N' position:

Jeg kender ikke *ham*, men jeg kender *hende*.

Compare this with the emphatic (i.e. heavily stressed) topic:

***Ham* kender jeg ikke, men *hende* kender jeg.**

Similarly, the adverbs **her** (here) and **der** (there) move leftwards to occupy the 'n' position immediately after the finite verb when they are unstressed and when the 'V' position is vacant:

Han er her/der ikke. (= unstressed)
Han er ikke her/der. (= stressed)
Her/Der er han ikke. (= heavily stressed)
He is not here/there.

But:

Han har ikke været her/der. He has not been here/there.
Her/Der har han ikke været.

1024 Negative elements

(a) The main forms of negation in Danish are the clausal adverbs **ikke, aldrig, næppe**, etc. (see also 613). When these negate the entire clause they occupy the clausal adverbial ('a') position. Consider the following examples of negative clauses with different forms of the verb:

Present tense: **Jeg spiser ikke ost.**
I don't eat cheese.

Past tense: **De sagde aldrig noget.**
They never said anything.

Future: **Han vil næppe gøre det.**
He'll hardly do that.

Perfect, past perfect: **Jeg har/havde aldrig set ham.**
I have/had never seen him.

Imperative: **Gør det ikke!**
Don't do it!

Infinitive: **Vi bad dem om ikke at tale så højt.**
We asked them not to talk so loudly.

Notice that Danish cannot have a split infinitive (cf. 528(b)).

(b) On occasion the negative may come between the finite verb and the subject in inverted statements:

I dag kommer Jens ikke.
Jens is not coming today.

But:

I dag kommer ikke *Jens*, men Erik.
Jens isn't coming today, but Erik is.

(c) Negating pronouns and the negated object

Just as negative adverbials will normally occupy the 'a' position, so pronominal or noun phrase objects containing a negation are attracted to this position. Consider the following pairs of sentences:

F	v	n	a	V	N	A
Jeg	**havde**	–	**ikke**	**sagt**	**noget**	–
I hadn't said anything.						
But:						
Jeg	**havde**	–	**ingenting**	**sagt**	–	–
Han	**har**	–	**ikke**	**set**	**noget**	–
He hasn't seen anything.						
But:						
Han	**har**	–	**intet**	**set**	–	–
Vi	**har**	–	**ikke**	**fået**	**nogen penge**	–
We've received no money.						
But:						
Vi	**har**	–	**ingen penge**	**fået**	–	–

1025 Extra positions

Extra positions are occasionally necessary in the word order schema in order to accommodate clauses as real subject or object clauses or free elements which occur outside the clause. They can be located either at the beginning or the end of the normal schema:

X_1	F	v	n	a	V	N	A	X_2
1 **Olaf,**	**han**	**er**	–	–	–	**syg**	–	–
Olaf, he is ill.								
2 **I Ålborg,**	**der**	**fester**	**de**	–	–	–	–	–
In Ålborg, there they have a party.								
3 –	**Det**	**er**	–	–	–	**dejligt**	–	**at spille tennis**
It's nice playing tennis.								
4 –	**De**	**spurgte**	–	–	–	**ham**	**i går,**	**om Per var hjemme**
They asked him yesterday whether Per was at home.								

The extra position(s) may be added to the schema in order to accommodate duplicates; this is the case in examples 1 and 2 above, where **han** and **der** respectively appear in the main schema as 'substitutes' for the phrases in the extra position. Also found in the extra position are heavy elements such as subordinate clauses and infinitive phrases, in the case of example 3 as represented in the main clause by the formal subject **det**. The 'k' position precedes the 'X_1' position. See 1009(e), 1011(h).

G SUBORDINATE CLAUSES

This section comprises a brief introduction to the form of subordinate clauses, and an account of some problem areas as regards their word order and structure.

1026 Form of the subordinate clause

Some characteristics of subordinate clauses and basic positions within the subordinate clause are given in Section C above. As can be seen from that initial account, most subordinate clauses have an introductory 'subordinating' conjunction. Subordinate clauses are usually classified according to the type of 'conjunction' used. The main types are:

(a) Relative clauses introduced by a relative pronoun or relative adverb:

> **Den pige, *som* jeg traf i går, var meget smuk.**
> The girl that I met yesterday was very beautiful.
>
> **Det er et sted, *hvor* han kommer meget.**
> It's a place where he goes a lot.

(b) Indirect questions introduced by an interrogative pronoun, interrogative adverb or interrogative conjunction:

> **Jeg vil vide, *hvad* han gør.**
> I want to know what he's doing.
>
> **De forklarede, *hvorfor* de ikke kom til festen.**
> They explained why they didn't come to the party.
>
> **Han spurgte, *om* vi ville have te eller kaffe.**
> He asked if we wanted tea or coffee.

(c) Conjunctional clauses introduced by a subordinating conjunction:

Anna sagde, *at* hun ikke ønskede at danse.
Anna said that she didn't want to dance.

***Selvom* han var syg, tog han på ferie.**
Although he was ill, he went on holiday.

1027 Main and subordinate clause word order

The guidelines and rules concerning main clause word order outlined in previous sections apply equally to subordinate clauses, with the exception of the following:

(a) 'Light' or unstressed pronouns, whether as direct or indirect objects, do *not* move leftwards to the 'n' position in subordinate clauses but remain in the 'N' position:

... , selvom jeg ikke sendte ham det.
... although I didn't send him it.

(b) The subject will usually appear first in subordinate clauses, i.e. topicalization of other elements and consequent inversion of subject – verb *cannot* normally happen (but see 1029):

... , selvom Preben var ked af det.
... , even though Preben was unhappy about it.

(***selvom det var Preben ked af** and ***selvom ked var Preben af det** are ungrammatical.)

(c) There is *no* initial extra position in subordinate clauses; any other elements will appear at the end of the clause in the same way as in main clauses:

... , fordi han var meget klog, den fyr.
... , because he was very clever, that chap.

1028 Clauses with no indicator of subordination

Some subordinate clauses may have neither an introductory word which marks them as subordinate, nor any clausal adverbials whose position would show that they were subordinate. These clauses are of two main types:

(a) Clauses where **at** is omitted

These often contain verbs of saying, thinking and perceiving, e.g. **sige**, say; **tro, mene**, think; **se**, see:

	MC base:
Jeg tror, det bliver kedeligt. I think it'll be boring.	**Det bliver kedeligt.** It'll be boring.
Hun sagde, hun havde læst brevet. She said she had read the letter.	**Hun havde læst brevet.** She had read the letter.

(b) Clauses where the relative **som** is omitted

It is possible to omit **som** in a restrictive relative clause if it is not the subject, i.e. when **som** is the direct or indirect object or a prepositional complement (cf. 432(b)):

Bogen, (som) du lånte mig, var meget spændende.
The book you lent me was very exciting.

Her er en bog, (som) jeg har skrevet i.
Here's a book I've written in.

The relative **der**, which always functions as the subject of the subordinate clause it introduces, can never be omitted (cf. 431).

1029 Main clause word order in subordinate clauses

(a) Subordinate clauses which are reported speech usually have subordinate clause word order (1012f), i.e. the clausal adverbial precedes the finite verb:

Hun forklarede, at der ikke er mange hjemløse børn i Frankrig.
She explained that there aren't many homeless children in France.

Han sagde, at han ikke var træt.
He said that he wasn't tired.

(b) In spoken and informal written language it is increasingly common for an element other than the subject to follow the conjunction as a kind of 'topic' in this type of clause with inverted word order, i.e. main clause word order:

Hun forklarede, at i Frankrig er der ikke mange hjemløse børn.

(c) In colloquial use it is even possible for the clausal adverbial to follow the finite verb in reported speech without any 'topicalization', i.e. main clause word order:

Han sagde, at han var ikke træt.

In these cases **at** functions almost as a colon, and the second clause is regarded as a statement in direct speech. Compare:

Hun forklarede: "I Frankrig er der ikke mange hjemløse børn."
Han sagde: "Jeg er ikke træt."

1030 Conditional clauses

See also 517(e).

There are three main types of conditional clause:

(a) Clauses introduced by **hvis** (if):

Hvis du skriver til ham, (så) får du alt at vide om det.
If you write to him you'll find out everything about it.

Jeg skal nok ringe, hvis jeg får tid.
I'll certainly ring if I've the time.

These clauses usually occupy the 'F' or 'A' position in the sentence schema. If the **hvis**-clause comes first in the sentence it is often duplicated by the word **så** (see also 914(a)).

(b) Clauses with question word order

Some conditional clauses omit **hvis** and express the condition solely by means of inversion. In these clauses the finite verb comes first:

Kommer du i morgen, kan du hilse på hende.
If you come tomorrow you can meet her.
(cf. **Hvis du kommer i morgen, kan du hilse på hende.**)

Var jeg rig, kunne jeg købe huset.
If I were rich I could buy the house.
(cf. **Hvis jeg var rig, kunne jeg købe huset.**)

Such clauses with question word order are quite common in the spoken language. They always come first in the sentence and have main clause word order. The 'F' position is empty (as in questions without an introductory interrogative), and therefore such clauses have inverted word order (finite verb – subject). An inserted clausal adverbial will follow the finite verb and the subject, unlike in most subordinate clauses:

Kommer du ikke i morgen, så bliver jeg vred.
FV CA
If you don't come tomorrow I'll be angry.

Compare:

Hvis du ikke kommer i morgen, så bliver jeg vred.

This kind of inversion to indicate condition also occurs in written English, where conditionals formed with the subjunctive sometimes have inverted word order:

Had we but world enough, and time ...
Were he to agree to this, it would be disastrous.

(c) Imperative clauses

Condition can sometimes be expressed by means of an imperative clause. Such clauses have an empty 'F' position and take main clause word order as in (b) above. Note the obligatory use of the word **så** to duplicate the imperative/condition in the following clause:

Skriv til ham, så får du alt at vide om det.
Write to him, then you'll find out everything about it.

Kom her Preben, så skal du få en øl.
Come here, Preben, and you can have a beer.

1031 Independent clauses

There are four main types of clause in which the order is that of the subordinate clause, but in which there is no accompanying main clause. These may be called 'independent clauses'.

(a) Answers to questions using **fordi**:

> **(Hvorfor tager I ikke på ferie i år?) Fordi vi ikke har råd til det.**
> (Why aren't you going away this year?) Because we can't afford it.

(b) Clauses introduced by **mon** and **måske**:

> **Mon han nogensinde får tid til det.**
> I wonder if he'll ever have the time for it.

> **Måske han ikke havde tid til det.**
> Perhaps he didn't have the time for it.

This latter example represents a contraction of an earlier sentence:

> **Måske var det, fordi han ikke havde tid til det.**
> MC SC

Måske more commonly, however, introduces a main clause, causing inversion:

> **Måske havde han ikke tid til det.**

(c) Clauses expressing a wish. These are introduced by **bare/blot, gid** or **hvis + bare/blot** (see also 534(c)(i)):

> **Bare jeg ikke havde gjort det!**
> If only I hadn't done it!

> **Blot han ikke var kommet her!**
> If only he hadn't come here!

> **Hvis jeg bare/blot ikke havde snakket med hende om det!**
> If only I hadn't talked to her about it!

> **Gid jeg aldrig var født!**
> I wish I'd never been born!

(d) Clauses expressing an exclamation. A main clause verb may be understood in these constructions:

> **(Tænk at) / At han dog kunne gøre det!**
> (Imagine that) / That he could ever do it!

1032 Cleft sentences

(a) It is possible to focus on a particular element by using a construction of the type **Det er/var X, der/som/at ...** (It is/was X who/which/that ...)

> **Peter sendte mig to eksemplarer af bogen i sidste uge.**
>
> ⇨ **Det var *Peter*, der sendte mig to eksemplarer af bogen i sidste uge.**
> It was Peter who sent me two copies of the book last week.

This type of construction is known as a cleft sentence, and is formed in Danish in exactly the same way as in English. The subject in the base clause becomes the subject complement in a new main clause and is emphasized, while the remainder of the base clause is appended in the form of a relative clause. The original clause is thus cleft in two, the transformation involving both a kind of topicalization and an addition to the base clause. Elements of the base clause other than the subject may also be emphasized in this way:

> **Det var *to eksemplarer af bogen*, (som) Peter sendte mig i sidste uge.**
> (*direct object in base*)
>
> **Det var *mig*, (som) Peter sendte to eksemplarer af bogen i sidste uge.**
> (*indirect object in base)*
>
> **Det var *i sidste uge*, (at) Peter sendte mig to eksemplarer af bogen.**
> (*other adverbial in base*)

(b) In forming such constructions, **der** and **som** are used to refer to a non-adverbial noun phrase or pronoun, and **at** (unless omitted) is used to refer to to a time or place adverbial. As a basic rule of thumb, **der** and **som** are used whenever the English equivalent could have 'who(m)', 'which' or the relative 'that'; if they cannot be used in English, then **at** will be used in Danish:

> **Det var *i London*, (at) vi traf ham.**
> It was in London that we met him.

Det var *i går*, (at) vi traf ham.
It was yesterday that we met him.

Det var *min onkel*, (som) vi traf i London i går.
It was my uncle that [⇨ who(m)] we met in London yesterday.

Det var *os*, der traf ham i London i går.
It was we who met him in London yesterday.

(c) When a clause element is extracted in this way, it retains its original form, except for subject pronouns, which always assume their object form (cf. 403(a)(iii)). Thus:

Hun sang.	⇨	**Det var *hende*, som sang.**
She sang.		It was she who sang.

(d) When a prepositional phrase is involved, the whole phrase is usually moved:

Det var *på Færøerne*, at jeg lærte ham at kende.
It was in the Faroes that I got to know him.

When, however, the prepositional phrase is attached directly to the verb, the preposition may move with the noun it governs or remain stranded in the subordinate clause:

Det var *i det hus*, (at) vi boede.	That was the house we lived in.
Det var *det hus*, (som) vi boede *i*.	

(e) The cleft sentence is very common in questions:

Var det *ham*, som kritiserede regeringen?
Was it he who criticized the government?

Er det *dig*, der bestemmer?
Is it you who decides?

Er det *først på søndag*, (at) hun kommer?
Isn't it until Sunday that she's coming?

Er det *øl*, han drikker?
Is it beer he's drinking?

1033 Raising

(a) Raising is used to provide emphasis; an element is taken from a subordinate clause and placed in the 'F' position in the main clause, thereby 'raising' it from its original clause.

Jeg ved, at du kan lide ham.	Him I know you like.
⇨ ***Ham* ved jeg, at du kan lide.**	

In this case the object of the subordinate clause, **ham**, has been placed first in the sentence and is thereby emphasized. The word order is also changed from straight to inverted. This type of construction is common, especially in spoken Danish.

Raising frequently occurs in **at**-clauses and other clauses that are governed by the verbs: **sige**, say; **tænke**, think; **mene**, think; **vide**, know; etc.:

***Den mand* ved jeg ikke hvem er.**	I don't know who that man is.
(⇦ Jeg ved ikke, hvem den mand er.)	

***Det* mener hun ikke hun har noget at gøre med.**
(⇦ Hun mener, (at) hun ikke har noget at gøre med det.)
She doesn't think she's got anything to do with it.

(b) A certain kind of raising may also occur in cleft sentences (cf. 1032). In this instance the object may be raised to become the subject complement in the cleft sentence:

Base sentence: main clause:
Han har lånt hendes bil. ⇨
He has borrowed her car.

Cleft sentence:
Det er *hendes bil*, han har lånt.
It's her car he has borrowed.

Subordinate clause:
Jeg mener, det er hendes bil, han har lånt. ⇨
I think it's her car he's borrowed.

Raising:
Det er *hendes bil*, som jeg mener, han har lånt.
It's her car I think he has borrowed.

11 WORD FORMATION

1101 Introduction

(a) Many words in Danish are directly descended from Indo-European, Common Germanic or Common Norse from which Danish has developed. Examples of such indigenous words are:

mand, man; **kone**, wife; **fader**, father; **moder**, mother; **broder**, brother; **søster**, sister

Later words in Danish have arisen historically as a result of four main processes:

(i) Affixation, i.e. the addition of a prefix or suffix to an existing independent word (see 1102–08):

klar	⇨	***u*klar**	clear	⇨	unclear
god	⇨	**god*hed***	good	⇨	goodness
demokrati	⇨	**demokrati*sere***	democracy	⇨	democratize

(ii) Compounding, i.e. the joining together of two independent words into one (see 1109–16):

regering + chef	⇨	**regeringschef**	*lit.* government head
skrive + bord	⇨	**skrivebord**	writing desk

(iii) Abbreviation, i.e. the shortening of a word (see 1117–21) or the merging of two (shortened) words into one:

automobil	⇨	**bil**	car
elektrisk komfur	⇨	**elkomfur**	electric cooker

(iv) Borrowing, i.e. the introduction of a word from another language (see 1122–25):

English jazz	⇨	Danish **jazz**	jazz
French terrain	⇨	Danish **terræn**	terrain

(b) The *stem* of a word is an uninflected form onto which various word formation elements (prefixes, suffixes) and inflexional elements may be added:

In **afdelingerne**, the departments:	**del, afdeling** are stems
In **højeste**, highest:	**høj** is a stem
In **råbtes**, was shouted:	**råb** is a stem
In **uvenlighed**, unfriendliness:	**ven, venlig** are stems

Both *derivatives* and *compounds* can be formed from a stem:

u	+	**ven**	⇨	**uven**
prefix		*stem*		*derivative*
ungdom	+ s +	**ven**	⇨	**ungdomsven**
stem		*stem*		*compound*
childhood		friend		childhood friend

One kind of suffix already examined (in Chapters 1, 2 and 5) is inflexional endings:

In **afdelingerne**:	**+er, +ne**	are inflexional endings
In **højeste**:	**+est, +e**	are inflexional endings
In **råbtes**:	**+te, +s**	are inflexional endings

One inflexional ending, namely the genitive **-s**, is identical with the link which often joins compound nouns together:

cf. **et universitets rektor** a university's vice-chancellor	genitive **-s** (see 133)
en universitetsrektor a university vice-chancellor	s-link in noun compound

(c) Notice that the first element in a compound often modifies the second element: **tegltag, skifertag, stråtag** are all kinds of **tag** (roof). In both derivatives and compounds it is, of course, the second element to which the inflexional ending is attached, and consequently this element which determines the word class:

fritid	⇦	**fri**	+	**tid**	**uvant**	⇦	**u**	+	**vant**
noun		*adj*		*noun*	*adj*		*negative prefix*		*adj*
free time					unaccustomed				
rustfri	⇦	**rust**	+	**fri**	**godhed**	⇦	**god**	+	**hed**
adj		*noun*		*adj*	*noun*		*adj*		*noun suffix*
rust-free (stainless)					goodness				

This means that while prefixes never alter the word class (e.g. **vant** ⇨ **uvant**), suffixes are frequently used for this very purpose (e.g. **god** ⇨ **godhed**).

A AFFIXATION

1102 Danish and foreign affixes

(a) Chronology:

Old Danish had different means of forming words from those used nowadays. Many of these word formation elements disappeared during major linguistic developments as early as the Viking Age. Only a few of them have remained productive over the centuries, e.g.:

> **-ing** in Old Danish **viking, dronning**, or in more recent formations **gamling, opkomling**.

The number of affixes was severely reduced and many of them became non-productive. In medieval Danish new affixes developed to take their place, which were of two main kinds:

(i) Indigenous second elements in compounds became productive affixes (see 1103):

e.g. Old Danish
-dom = (meaning varies, abstract) in: **alderdom, sygdom**
-likær = 'body, figure, appearance' as **-lig** in: **kærlig, livlig**
-skab = 'form, type' in: **ondskab, venskab**

Other such productive elements include:

gen-	**gengæld**
mis-	**misforstå**
sam-	**samtale**
u-	**umulig**
van-	**vanvid**

(ii) A great number of words, and especially abstract terms, were borrowed from Low German in the Middle Ages, many of which provided productive affixes at that period:

an-	**ankomst, anse**
be-, bi-	**begynde, behagelig, bevare, bilægge, bistand**
for-	**foragt, fordærve, forsigtig, forstå**
und-	**undgå, undslippe, undsætte**

-agtig	**delagtig, livagtig**
-bar	**dyrebar, åbenbar**
-else	**bedrøvelse, forbindelse**
-er	**frelser, røver**
-eri	**frieri, tyveri**
-hed	**frihed, retfærdighed**
-inde	**fyrstinde, grevinde**
-ske	**løgnerske, sygeplejerske**

The prefix ge- was productive rather later, being borrowed originally in High German loans:

gebyr, gehør, gemen, gemytlig, gesandt

(iii) In more recent times Danish has received a fresh wave of productive affixes via words of French origin which have entered the language:

-abel	**kapabel**
-ade	**marmelade, maskerade**
-age	**bagage, lækage**
-al	**fatal, journal, liberal, original**
-ance	**assistance, leverance**
-ant	**bastant, elegant, kommandant, musikant**
-ar	**antikvar, kommentar**
-at	**apparat, desperat, privat, soldat**
-ens	**audiens, residens**
-ent	**agent, indifferent, insolvent, præsident**
-er	**officer, passager**
-ess(e)	**adresse, interesse**
-i	**akademi, garanti**
-isme	**calvinisme, egoisme**
-ist	**ateist, kapitalist**
-it	**favorit, kredit**
-ment	**dokument, fundament**
-or	**debitor, kreditor**
-sion, -tion	**information, pension**
-ur	**censur, korrektur**
-ut	**absolut, resolut**
-ør	**ambassadør, humør**
-øs	**dubiøs, religiøs**

(b) The addition to the language of foreign affixes often results in two word formation elements existing side by side in the lexicon with the same meaning. Approximately as in English, a major distinction can be made here between Germanic affixes (i.e. in indigenous words and German loans) and Romance affixes (mostly in Latin and French loans):

Prefixes

Germanic			*Romance*		
gen-	**genopbygge**	=	**re-**	**rekonstruere**	reconstruct
sam-	**samarbejde**	=	**ko-**	**kooperation**	cooperation
selv-	**selvlært**	=	**auto-**	**autodidakt**	self-taught
u-	**ulovlig**	=	**in- (il-, im-, ir-)**	**illegal**	unlawful

Suffixes

Verb	*Noun (person)*	*Noun (activity)*
Danish		
forsk*e*	**forsk*er***	**forsk*ning***
Romance		
inspic*ere*	**inspekt*ør***	**inspekt*ion***

Verb	*Noun (person)*	*Adjective*	*Noun (abstract)*
Danish			
tilvirk*e*	–	–	**tilvirk*ning***
Romance			
produc*ere*	**produc*ent***	**produk*tiv***	**produk*tivitet*** **produk*tion***

1103 Productive affixes and word elements

(a) A productive affix is one which when added to a word produces a derivative whose meaning is easily predicted from the meaning of the basic word, e.g.:

-bar is an adjective suffix meaning '**mulig at** x', originally borrowed in such words as **frugtbar** from Low German 'vruchtbar', but subsequently productive. So, using Danish stems, we can form:

læsbar = '**mulig at læse**'
vaskbar = '**mulig at vaske**'

Theoretically it should be possible to add a productive affix to any word of a particular grammatical or semantic type. Thus **-bar** is an adjective suffix which theoretically can be added to all transitive verb stems, although this does not always work in practice.

This must be contrasted with very frequent but non-productive affixes, which are only found with the loanwords they accompany, and as such do not give rise to any new formations in Danish, e.g.

kon- (⇦ Latin 'con-'): **konflikt, konservativ, konsonant**

(b) Some words frequently found in compounds may come to be regarded as productive affixes. This happened frequently in Old Danish (see 1102(a)(i)) and is still occurring. The meaning of the word usually becomes vaguer and more generalized when it is used as an affix, e.g.:

-venlig: originally in e.g. **børnevenlig** = '**venlig mod børn**' kind to children. Nowadays it is found in: **brugervenlig, fremskridtsvenlig, kundevenlig**, etc.

This process can be seen in words with the following affixes:

(i) **selv-** **selvfinansiere, selvkritisk, selvsikker**
-artet **fremmedartet, vanartet**
-dygtig **arbejdsdygtig, betalingsdygtig**
-fattig **blodfattig, vitaminfattig**
-fri **bakteriefri, krympefri**
-fuld **fantasifuld, smagfuld**
-løs **duftløs, statsløs**
-rigtig **brugsrigtig, moderigtig**

(ii) Amplifying prefixes (i.e. uptoners) often with a brief productive life:

aller- **allerbedst, allerstørst**
drøn- **drønfarlig, drøngod**
død- **dødkedelig, dødstille**
edder- **eddersmart, edderspændt**

hunde-	**hundekold, hundesulten**
kæmpe-	**kæmpeidiot, kæmpeskridt, kæmpestor**
rav-	**ravgal, ravjysk**
skide-	**skideflot, skidegod**
skrup-	**skrupforelsket, skruptosset**
smadder-	**smadderfuld, smaddergod**
smæk-	**smækfed, smækfuld**
splitter-	**splittergal, splitternøgen**
stang-	**stangdrukken, stangsmart**
stok-	**stokdøv, stokkonservativ**

See also 615(b),(c). Such prefixes formed from elements in compounds are marked in the table in 1105 thus: **/efter-/** in **efterskrift**.

(c) Some vogue affixes and word elements of recent years from the cultural and political debate are listed below. The meaning of such frequent elements is undergoing change:

anti- (⇦ Latin) Originally in: **antibiotikum, antipati, antitese.**
Recently in words denoting persons: **antiimperialist, antikommunist.**
Most recently in vogue words: **antihelt, antikonception.**

pseudo- (⇦ Greek) originally in: **pseudonym.**
Recently in: **pseudobegivenhed, pseudovidenskablig.**

-krati (⇦ Greek) originally in: **aristokrati, demokrati, plutokrati.**
New compounds are: **meritokrati, teknokrati.**

Other recent vogue word elements include:

bio-	**biocid, bioenergi**
discount-	**discountbutik, discountferie**
euro-	**eurocheck, eurokrat**
køns-	**kønsdiskriminering, kønsrolle**
mega-	**megabank, megastar**
miljø-	**miljøaktivist, miljøforurening**
multi-	**multikunst, multinational**
nær-	**nærbutik, nærmiljø**
øko- (⇦ **økologisk**)	**økolandbrug, økoteknisk**
-er	**behandler, layouter**
-eri	**dyneløfteri, formynderi**
-isme	**elitisme, maoisme**
-ist(isk)	**sexist(isk) (cf. sexisme)**

-log	**allergolog, kremlolog**
-nom	**agronom, datanom**

1104 Prefixes

A prefix is a morpheme which is added to the beginning of a word, but which is not itself a stem, e.g.:

u- + **ro** ⇨ **uro** (cf. English un- + rest ⇨ unrest)
prefix *stem* *derivative*

The same basic meaning may be expressed by more than one prefix. Thus, negation can be expressed by:

dis-: disharmoni; ikke-: ikkespredningsaftale; in-: intolerant; non-: nonkonformisme; u-: ulykkelig

See also 1105.

The same prefix may also occur in derivatives of a number of different word classes. Unlike suffixes, prefixes do not alter the word class (see 1106) e.g.:

u- + **dyr** ⇨ **udyr** — *neg. prefix* *noun* *noun*

u- + **lykkelig** ⇨ **ulykkelig** — *neg. prefix* *adjective* *adjective*

1105 Table of prefixes

In the table below prefixes are classified according to the way in which they modify the meaning of the stem to which they are added. This is not an exhaustive list. **Key**: / / = an independent word used as a prefix – see also 1103(b).

Group/prefix	*Meaning*	*Examples*
NEGATIVE & PEJORATIVE		
u-	not, opposite of	**ukonventionel, uven**
	bad	**uvane**
in-	not, opposite of	**intolerant**
il-	not, opposite of	**illegal**
im-	not, opposite of	**immobil**
ir-	not, opposite of	**irrelevant**
non-	not, opposite of	**nonkonformisme**

Group/prefix	*Meaning*	*Examples*
a-	not, opposite of	**amoralsk**
/ikke-/	not, opposite of	**ikkeryger**
/fejl-/	wrongly	**fejlskrivning**
mis-	wrongly	**misbruger**
	bad	**mislyd**
van-	wrongly	**vanskabt**
	bad	**vanrøgte**
des-	wrongly	**desillusion**
dis-	wrongly	**disharmoni**
PEJORATIVE		
kvasi-	false	**kvasividenskabelig**
pseudo-	false	**pseudoklassisk**
krypto-	secret	**kryptofascisme**
REVERSATIVE or PRIVATIVE		
de-	reverse action	**deeskalere**
des-	deprive of	**desinficere**
/af-/	deprive of	**affolke**
ATTITUDE		
kon-	together with	**kongenial**
kor-	together with	**korrespondere**
kom-	together with	**kompagnon**
kol-	together with	**kollaboratør**
ko-	together with	**koordinere**
sam-	together with	**samboer**
/med-/	together with	**medmenneske**
sær-	separate from	**særtilfælde**
anti-	against	**antikommunist**
/mod-/	resistance to	**modstand**
kontra-	against	**kontrarevolution**
pro-	favourable towards	**provestlig**
SIZE or DEGREE		
hyper-	beyond, extreme	**hyperfarlig**
super-	beyond, extreme	**superfosfat**
ultra-	beyond, extreme	**ultralyd**
ærke-	beyond, extreme	**ærkefjende**
mini-	little	**minigolf**
/over-/	too much	**overvurdere**
/under-/	too little	**underforsikre**
LOCATION (time or place)		
/før-/	before	**førægteskabelig**
/for-/	before	**forkundskab**
/efter-/	after	**efterskrift**
sub-	under	**subtropisk**
/under-/	under	**underetage**
bi-	beside, secondary	**bifag**

Group/prefix	*Meaning*	*Examples*
ur-	original	**urnordisk**
/middel-/	between	**middelklasse**
neo-	new	**neokolonialisme**
/ny-/	new	**nyfødt**
eks-	former	**ekskonge**
LOCATION or DIRECTION		
trans-	across	**transplantation**
/over-/	across	**overføre**
eks-	from	**ekskludere**
/ud-/	from	**udflytning**
DIRECTION (time or place)		
an-	to, towards	**ankomme**
/til-/	to, towards	**tilføre**
for-	away from	**fordrive**
/bort-/	away from	**bortlede**
/ind-/	in(to)	**insende**
/gennem-/	through	**gennemrejse**
und-	away from	**undslippe**
re-	back, again	**reetablere**
gen-	back, again	**genfinde**
fort-	further	**fortsætte**
/videre-/	further	**videreuddannelse**
/slut-/	end	**slutsum**
NUMBER		
mono-	one	**monoteist**
/en-/	one	**enrum**
bi-	two	**bilateral**
/to-/	two	**tostavelsesord**
tve-	two	**tvekamp**
/dobbelt-/	two	**dobbeltværelse**
/fler-/	many	**flerstemmig**
/mang(e)-/	many	**mangekantet**
pan-	all	**panamerikansk**
/al-/	all	**alsidig**
OTHERS		
auto-	self	**autobiografi**
/selv-/	self	**selvhjælp**
vice-	deputy	**vicedirektør**
pro-	instead of, deputy	**prorektor**
CONVERSION		
an- transitivizing	**råbe** ⇨	**anråbe**
be- transitivizing	**bo** ⇨	**bebo**
be- make into X	**fri** ⇨	**befri**
for- make into X	**ny** ⇨	**forny**

1106 Suffixes

(a) A suffix is a morpheme which is added to the end of a stem, but which is not itself a stem, e.g.:

barn + **lig** ⇨ **barnlig** (English child + -ish ⇨ childish)
stem *suffix*

Unlike prefixes, suffixes frequently alter the word class, e.g.:

barn +	**lig**	⇨	**barnlig**	**hvil**	+	**e**	⇨	**hvile**
noun	*adj. suffix*		*adj.*	*noun suffix*		*verb*		*verb*
				rest			⇨	to rest
fri +	**hed**	⇨	**frihed**					
adj.	*noun suffix*		*noun*					
free +	-dom	⇨	freedom					

The same suffix may in combination with different stems result in different meanings: **arbejder** = a worker (person), **viser** = a pointer (object). The converse is also true; the same basic meaningmay be expressed by more than one suffix, e.g.. **udvandr*er*, emigr*ant*, inspekt*or*, inspekt*ør*** are all people carrying out some activity. The same suffix may also occur in derivatives of a number of different word classes, e.g.:

-ing, -ling may be added to:	– nouns:	**ætling**	⇦	**æt**
		islænding	⇦	**Island**
	– adjectives:	**yngling**	⇦	**ung**
	– verbs:	**opkomling**	⇦	**komme op**

In the table in 1107 suffixes are classified according to the word class of the resultant derivative and further sub-classified according to the way they modify the meaning of either the stem to which they are added or the word class of the stem.

(b) In some cases the derivative may also have a different stem vowel from its base word:

(i) NOUN	⇨	NOUN	**udland**	**udlænding**
(ii) ADJECTIVE	⇨	NOUN	**lang**	**længde**
			tung	**tyngde**
			glad	**glæde**
(iii) ADJECTIVE	⇨	VERB	**tam**	**tæmme**
			tom	**tømme**
			fuld	**fylde**

1107 Table of suffixes

This is not an exhaustive list.
Key: V = verb, N = noun, A = adjective, e.g.. V-e = verb ending in **-e**, V-ere = verb ending in **-ere**, N-tion = noun ending in **-tion**, etc.

Group/Suffix	*Deriving from*	*Meaning*	*Examples*
NOUN-FORMING			
1 PEOPLE			
-iner			**fillipiner**
-ant	V-ere	person	**musikant**
-ent		person	**assistent**
-at		person	**demokrat**
-er		person	**snedker**
-er		agent of an action	**opvasker**
-er		nationality	**belgier**
-graf		person	**fotograf**
-ing, -ling, -ning		origin	**islænding, ætling, flygtning**
-iker	N-ik	occupation	**politiker**
-ist	V-e, N	hobby	**motionist**
-it		origin	**moskovit**
-log		occupation	**sociolog**
-or	V-ere	occupation	**illustrator**
-ær	V-ere	occupation	**missionær**
-ør	V-ere	occupation	**inspektør**
Feminine			
-inde			**værtinde**
-ske	V-e, N-er		**plejerske**
-esse	N		**prinsesse**
-øse	N-ør, V-ere		**massøse**
-trice	N-ør		**direktrice**
2 ACTIVITY			
-(n)ing	V-e	activity	**skrivning**
	V-e	activity	**udvikling**
-ende	V-e		**forehavende**
-else	V-e	activity	**følelse**
-sel	V-e	activity	**indførsel**
-(a)tion	V-ere	**inform/ere** ⇨	**information**
		fung/ere ⇨	**funktion**
-sion		**eksplod/ere** ⇨	**eksplosion**
-ition		**kompon/ere** ⇨	**komposition**
-grafi			**fotografi**
-ologi			**sociologi**

Group/Suffix	*Deriving from*	*Meaning*	*Examples*
Zero suffix	V-e		**duft, sult**
3 ABSTRACTIONS			
-ance, -ence, -ens			**elegance, kompetence, frekvens**
-dom	N, A		**sygdom**
-else			**fristelse**
-ende			**velbefindende**
-hed			**medlidenhed**
-ing			**afmagring**
-itet	A		**popularitet**
-isme			**socialisme**
-sel			**blusel**
-skab	N, A		**ondskab**
ADJECTIVE-FORMING			
1 FROM VERBS			
-at	V-ere		**separat**
-bar	V-e	possible	**vaskbar**
-et	V-e		**nystartet**
-et	V-ere		**indstuderet**
-lig	V-e	possible	**læselig**
-abel	V-ere	possible	**diskutabel**
-agtig	V, A	tendency	**løgnagtig**
-ibel	V-ere	possible	**disponibel**
-ig	V	inclination	**syndig**
-som	V, A	inclination	**arbejdsom**
-sk	V, A	inclination	**indbildsk**
-(t)iv	V-ere	inclination	**demonstrativ**
2 FROM NOUNS			
-agtig	N	characteristic of	**barnagtig**
-ant	N-ance/-ence		**elegant**
-el	N	belonging to	**kulturel**
-(e)lig	N	belonging to	**kristelig**
-en	N	which have X	**ulden**
-ent	N		**intelligent**
-et	N	which have X	**enarmet**
-ig	N	which have X	**smudsig**
-(i)sk	N	belonging to	**britisk, hollandsk**
-iv	N-tion/-sion		**aktiv**
-mæssig	N	in accordance with	**kontraktmæssig**
-ær	N		**litteræer**
-øs	N		**nervøs**
3 FROM ADJECTIVES			
-agtig	A	like	**livagtig**
-artet	A	having the property of	**godartet**
-laden	A	approximating to	**storladen**

Group/Suffix	*Deriving from*	*Meaning*	*Examples*
VERB-FORMING			
1 FROM NOUNS			
-e/-ere	N	add/provide with	**adressere, farve**
	N	remove	**støve, affugte**
	N	place in	**logere**
	N	do	**vaske**
			kritisere, cykle
	N	be, act as	**vikariere**
		(with prefix)	**forklare**
			amerikanisere
2 FROM ADJECTIVES			
-e	N, A	make, change into	**varme, tørre,**
		(with prefix)	**forbitre,**
		(with prefix)	**bemyndige**
-ne	A	become X	**gulne, mørkne**

1108 Back-formation

Usually nouns and adjectives are formed from verbs or other adjectives: **god ⇨ godhed; grøn ⇨ grønlig; lukke ⇨ lukket; ryge ⇨ rygning; skrive ⇨ skrivning**

But sometimes the process is reversed and verbs are formed from nouns or adjectives:

Concrete noun		*Abstract noun*		*Verb*
skrivemaskine	⇨	**maskinskrivning**	⇨	**maskinskrive**
typewriter		typing		type

Verb		*Abstract noun*		*Abstract noun*		*Verb*
ryge	⇨	**rygning**	⇨	**kæderygning**	⇨	**kæderyge**
smoke		smoking		chain-smoking		chain-smoke

This process is known as back-formation or retrogradation and is very common in newspaper style.

Some other examples are:

båndoptage, dagdrømme, databehandle, dybfryse, gæsteforelæse, hjernevaske, iscenesætte, lørdagslukke, nydanne, planlægge, støvsuge, sygemelde

B COMPOUNDING

1109 Introduction

(a) Compounds may be formed from all word classes. The final element determines the word class. Compound nouns are the most frequent type of compound, and nouns are the most frequent type of first element (FE) in these:

sol|skin *noun/noun*	sunshine

Nouns also form the most common FE in compound adjectives:

sol|brun *noun/adjective*	tanned (*lit.* sunbrown)

On occasion a phrase may form the FE in a compound: **to|etage|s|hus, hundred|år|s|fest**. An unusual group of noun compounds consist entirely of an imperative phrase: **et far|vel, en forglem|mig|ej**.

Combinations of word classes are found in 1110, 1113ff. For compound adverbs see 605.

(b) Compounds consist of two (or more) elements which may occur as independent words, but these do not often have equal importance. In most compounds there is a head word which indicates the basic meaning, usually the second element (SE), accompanied by a descriptive element, usually the first element (FE):

kurve|stol (wicker chair) is clearly a type of **stol** (chair) and the type is indicated by the FE **kurv**, basket(work). Other possible types of **stol** include: **drejestol, lænestol, pavestol, rullestol**, etc.

The main types of syntactic relationship between the elements are:

(i) Determinative, i.e. where one element determines or describes the type of head word as in **kurvestol** above. Here the compound may be replaced by the SE + a prepositional expression or a genitive:

træstol = stol af træ

(ii) Copulative, i.e. where the two elements are of equal status, e.g. **blå-gul, had-kærlighed**. Here the compound can be substituted by 'FE + SE':

blå-gul = blå + gul; had-kærlighed = had + kærlighed

(iii) A further type of compound is one which expresses some characteristic feature of a person or animal, providing a metonymic image (i.e. a part stands for the whole). These are sometimes called 'possessive compounds':

brunskjorte	=	**(menneske) som har brun skjorte** (i.e. Nazi)
gråben	=	**(dyr) som har grå ben** (i.e. wolf)
rødstjært	=	**(dyr) som har rød stjært** (redstart)
tusindben	=	**(dyr) som har tusind ben** (millipede)

Determinative compounding is most frequent among compound nouns and adjectives. Many compound verbs are not compounds proper but are formed by back-formation (see 1108). Many other compound verbs are separable compounds comprising a stressed particle + verb (see 546ff). For compound adjectives see also 236ff, and for compound adverbs see 605.

1110 Compound nouns, adjectives, verbs – forms

(a) Compound nouns may have as their FE a number of different word classes:

FE	*Example*
NOUN	**barneplejerske, møbelfabrik, skønhedsdronning**
ADJECTIVE	**centralvarme, fjernsyn**
PRONOUN	**jegroman, selvhjælp**
NUMERAL	**førsteklassesbillet, tiår**
VERB	**gågade, soveby**
PREPOSITION	**mellemrum, overklasse**
NOUN PHRASE	**allemandseje, femetageshus**
ADVERB	**fremtid, velstand**

(b) Some general guidelines apply to the form of the FE:

(i) Nouns are usually found in their uninflected form:

alperose	⇦	**Alperne + rose**
finanspolitik	⇦	**finanser + politik**

But see 118 for plurals of compound nouns and 1111 for vowel reductions and links.

(ii) Adjectives are usually found in their uninflected form:

gråvejr	⇦	**gråt vejr**
højland	⇦	**et højt land**
halvår	⇦	**et halvt år**
rødskægget	⇦	**med et rødt skæg**

But see also 236ff for compound adjectives.

Note 1 – There are some exceptions:

(1) A few adjectives agree in the neuter: **intetkøn, nytår**

(2) Some adjectives are in the definite form in **-e**: **førstehjælp, gulerod, Rundetårn, sortebroder**

(3) Some adjectives are in the plural form: **småbørn, småkage**

(4) Unstressed **-e** is usually retained, as in **kuldegrad, Stillehavet**, but may occasionally be dropped, as in **firben, flertal.**

(iii) Verbs are usually found in their infinitive form:

følgeseddel, skrivemaskine, spillemand

Note 2 – There are some exceptions where the final **-e** drops: **brushane, bygmester, drivfjeder**

(iv) Some compounds are formed with either an adjective or its equivalent adverb as FE, and thus have two alternative forms:

hård(t)frossen, sej(t)flydende, nær(t)beslægtet, grofthakket/ grovhakket

1111 Compound nouns – form of links

(a) In this paragraph and in 1112 only NOUN + NOUN compounds are discussed. See 1110(b) for other methods of linking. The linking of compound nouns is complex and no hard-and-fast rules exist; all that can be given are some general guidelines. Three main methods are employed:

(i) NOUN + NOUN

bog|bind, lampe|skærm, pige|skole, sommer|ferie

(ii). NOUN + **s** + NOUN

dag|s|rejse, fabrik|s|bygning, folketing|s|medlem, forsikring|s|præmie, år|s|tid

(iii) NOUN + **e** + NOUN

dreng|e|skole, jul|e|dag, seng|e|kant, stol|e|ryg

(b) It is only possible to provide general guidelines as to which of the three methods mentioned above is used with a specific FE:

(i) NOUN + NOUN:

1 When the FE ends in **-s**, in a stressed vowel or unstressed **-e**:

græs|plæne, industri|mand, klasse|kamp

2 When the FE ends in unstressed **-el**, **-en**, **-er**:

cykel|pumpe, forfatter|talent, køkken|kniv

3 When the FE is a loan from a Romance language and ends in **-al, -an, -ant, -ar, -el, -ent, -ik, -in, -iv, -log, -on, -or, -ur, -ær, -ør**:

ingeniør|firma, kollektiv|aftale, natur|fredning, rektor|bolig

(ii) NOUN + **s** + NOUN:

1 When the FE ends in one of the suffixes **-dom, -else, -hed, -(n)ing, -sel, -skab**:

kørsel|s|penge, storhed|s|vanvid, sætning|s|led, ungdom|s|herberg, videnskab|s|mand

Note 1 – English loans in **-ing** do not follow this rule: **marketing|chef**

2 When the FE is a loan from a Romance language ending in **-ion, -tion, -tet, -um**:

> **kommunikation|s|middel, station|s|forstander, universitet|s|bibliotek, museum|s|besøg**

3 When the FE is itself a compound:

> **en|gang|s|beløb, rød|vin|s|glas, skrive|bord|s|skuffe** (cf. **vin|glas, bord|skuffe**)

Note 2 – There are however many exceptions:

> **fodbold|dommer, tændstik|æske**

4 With certain frequent FEs, namely **alder-, andel-, arbejd-, embed-, erhverv-, handel-, rig-**:

> **alder|s|gruppe, andel|s|mejeri, arbejd|s|giver, erhverv|s|krise, rig|s|-ombudsmand**

Note 3 – Some frequent FEs possess different forms with different SEs:

aften-	**aften|skole** but: **aften|s|mad**
dag-	**dag|bog** but: **dag|s|lys**
gård-	**gård|ejer** but: **gård|s|karl**
land-	**land|mand** (farmer) but: **land|s|mand** (compatriot) and: **land|e|vej**
liv-	**liv|garde** but: **liv|s|forsikring**
mand-	**mand|drab** but: **mand|s|mod**

Note 4 – Some compounds in **-s** possess alternative forms without **-s**:

> **kartotek(s)kort, skade(s)forsikring, tid(s)nød**

Note 5 – In some modern officialese the **-s** is considered vulgar and is omitted:

> **enfamilie(s)hus, finanslov(s)debat, region(s)plan**

(iii) NOUN + **e** + NOUN:

The **e**-form appears to have many origins, including an original genitive ending (**jul|e|dag, natt|e|leje**) and a plural (**engl|e|skare, invalid|e|pension**). It occurs *inter alia* in the following cases:

1 When the FE ends in a consonant and the SE begins with a consonant:

barn|e|barn, dreng|e|forbund, eg|e|løv, havn|e|kaj, myg|ge|stik, mælk|e|leverandør, ost|e|mad, pil|e|våben, snaps|e|flaske, sogn|e|præst, sovs|e|skål, svin|e|foder

2 In words for living beings ending in **-ling** and **-(n)ing** (cf. (ii) above):

dronning|e|krone, kylling|e|bryst, viking|e|flåde, yngling|e|alder

3 In some cases **-e** replaces an old **og**:

hest|e|vogn, smør(r)|e|brød

Note 6 – Some compounds in **-e** possess alternative forms without **-e**:

hingst(e)føl, nat(te)himmel

(iv) A few nouns derived from German add **-en** when used as FE:

bakken|bart, børsten|binder, galgen|humor, rosen|busk

(v) A few nouns add **-er** when used as FE:

blomster|buket, gifter|mål, natter|gal, retter|gang, wiener|brød (from German)

Note 7 – Some compounds in **-er** possess alternative forms in **-e**:

fiske(r)kutter, male(r)arbejde, vandre(r)hjem

1112 Compound nouns – meaning

(a) The syntactic and semantic relationship between the FE and SE in a compound can be clarified by expanding the compound into a noun phrase (see also 1109), e.g.

skifertag = **tag af skifer**
(FE denotes material, content)

arbejdsområde = **område, hvor man arbejder**
(FE = adverbial of place)

barnegråd = **et barns gråd**
(FE is the subject of the activity in the SE)

(b) Various classifications can be made on this basis:

(i) Verbal activity in the SE:

FE is subject: **hundebjæf** = **hundens bjæf; at en hund bjæffer**
FE is object : **sygepleje** = **pleje af syge; at man plejer syge**
FE is adverbial: **toggrejse** = **rejse med tog; at man rejser med tog**

(ii) Verbal activity in the FE:

SE is subject: **rullestol** = **stol, som ruller**
SE is object : **bærepose** = **pose, som man bærer**
SE is adverbial: **skrivemaskine** = **maskine, som man skriver på**

(iii) No verbal activity in either the FE or the SE:

Adverbial relationship
place **skovsti** = **sti i skoven**
time **feriedag** = **dag i ferien**
means **damplokomotiv** = **lokomotiv, som drives ved hjælp af damp**

Material or content
bomuldskjole = **kjole lavet af bomuld**

Possessive relationship
arbejderkone = **en arbejders kone**

(iv) FE is an adjective:

FE is complement: **småbørn** = **børn, som er små**

For possessive compounds see 1109(b)(iii).

1113 Compound adjectives – forms

(a) Compound adjectives may have as their FE a number of different word classes:

FE	*Examples*
NOUN	**fabriksny, grydeklar, moderigtig**
ADJECTIVE	**dybfrossen, kortsigtet, mørk(e)blond**

VERB	**køreklar, læsesvag, strygefri**
PRONOUN	**selvoptaget**
ADVERB	**velholdt**
PREPOSITION	**underjordisk**

(b) For general rules applying to the form of the FE, see 1110(b), 1111ff.

1114 Compound adjectives – meaning

(a) FE is a noun:

(i) FE is the agent (SE is a participle): **fugtplettet = plettet af fugt**

(ii) FE is the object (SE is a participle): **opsigtsvækkende = som vækker opsigt**

(iii) FE functions as an adverbial

– time:	**aftenskole**	= **skole om aftenen**
– place:	**verdensberømt**	= **berømt i verden**
– cause:	**vandskadet**	= **skadet på grund af vand**
– degree, type:	**kulsort**	= **sort som kul**

(b) FE is an adjective (SE is a participle):

letlæst	= **let at læse**
enkeltsidet	= **som har en enkel side**

(c) FE is a verb:

SE is an adjective defining the FE: **køreklar = klar til at køre**

1115 Compound verbs

For separable compound verbs (e.g. **fremkalde/kalde frem**) see 546ff. For verbs formed by back-formation see 1108.

(a) Compound verbs may have as their FE a number of different word classes:

FE	*Example*
NOUN	**strejkelamme, vandkøle**
ADJECTIVE	**rengøre, umuliggøre, ødelægge**

NUMERAL	**fir(e)doble**
PREPOSITION	**overvurdere, underbelyse**
VERB	**sultestrejke**
ADVERB	**indramme, uddanne**

(b) For general rules applying to the form of the FE see 1110(b).

1116 Derivational compounding

A compound element may itself be a derivative of another word:

trykke|frihed	⇦	**trykke + frihed** *derivative* (under frihed)
ulykke|s|dag	⇦	**ulykke + dag** *derivative* (under ulykke)

One group of words is similar in type but differs in that the derived SE does not exist as an independent word:

arbejdstager, dobbeltdækker, femåring, mørkøjet, tomotoret, tre-hjulet

There are no words ***tager, *dækker, *åring, *øjet, *motoret, *hjulet**. These words are based on phrases: **med to dæk; som er fem år; med to motorer**; etc. They have been formed by a composite process of compounding and affixation.

Similar in type are: **fir(e)årig, gudfrygtig, lovmager(i), overnatte, overvintre, tosproget**.

C ABBREVIATION

1117 Clippings

Clipping involves the reduction of a morpheme or part of a morpheme at the beginning or end of a word, e.g. **bio** ⇦ **biograf**.

(a) Initial reduction (i.e. the beginning of the word disappears)

Reduction of a whole morpheme:	*Reduction of part of a morpheme:*
(bi)cykel	**(automo)bil**
	(frika)delle
	(omni)bus

(b) Final reduction (i.e. the end of a word disappears)

Reduction of a whole morpheme:	*Reduction of part of morpheme:*
abstinens(symptom)	**el(ektricitet)**
biograf(teater)	**fly(vemaskine)**
brugs(forening)	**krimi(nalroman)**
kilo(gram)	**memo(randum)**
mellem(skoleklasse)	**narko(tika)**
polio(myelitis)	**pop(ulærmusik)**
straffe(spark)	

1118 Acronyms

When the process of reduction (cf. 1117) leaves only an initial letter or letters in a word, the result is known as an acronym:

A/S (aktieselskab); edb (elektronisk databehandling); lix (læsbarheds-indeks); NESA (Nordsjællands Elektricitets og Sporvejs A/S); tb (tub-erkulose); VVS (varme, ventilation, sanitet)

Acronyms are of three kinds:

(a) Alphabetisms are words formed from initials and pronounced as the letters of the alphabet, e.g.:

LO ('Landsorganisationen') is pronounced as separate letters [ˈɛl ˈo:]

Other examples are: **bh ('brystholder'); DM ('danmarksmesterskab'); DSB ('Danske Statsbaner'); tv ('television'); ØK ('Østasiatiske Kompagni')**

(b) Acronyms formed from initials but pronounced as words in their own right:

NATO/Nato is pronounced [ˈna:to]

Others examples are: **BZ'er (besætter); RUC ('Roskilde Universitets-center'); SAS ('Scandinavian Airlines System'); UNESCO ('United Nations Educational, Scientific & Cultural Organization')**

(c) Hybrid forms:

a-kasse (arbejdsløsheds-); b-bombe (brint-); edb-behandling (elektronisk databehandling); p-pille (præventiv-); p-plads (parkerings-); s-sele (sikkerheds-); ubåd (undervands-); uland (udviklings-)

(d) Note the following on the morphology of abbreviations: Stops are normally found after each clipped word, e.g. **e.Kr. (efter Kristus); m.a.o. (med andre ord)**. The space is omitted between the letters of an acronym followed by a stop, e.g. **m.m. (med mere); cand.mag. (candidatus magisterii)**.

Note 1 – Two frequent cases where only one stop is found are: **dvs. (det vil sige); osv. (og så videre)**.

Note 2 – No stop is found in: **fx**, an alternative form to **f.eks. (for eksempel)**.

See also: for gender 108(a), stops 1205(b), apostrophe 1209(c)(ii). See also 1121 for a list of common abbreviations.

1119 Blends

When the middle of a word disappears this is known as a blend ('telescope' or 'medial' reduction):

Reduction of a whole morpheme:	*Reduction of part of a morpheme:*
tele(foto)linse	**m(er)oms(ætningsafgift)**
brand(korps)mand	**Eur(opa)asien**

1120 Familiarity markers

(a) Clipping (see (b) below and 1117) + **(er)en**

fjernsynet ⇨ fjerneren **fritidshjemmet ⇨ fritteren**

(b) First names have in many cases been derived from longer forms, some at an early date:

Birgitte ⇨ Gitte, Brit, Bibbi **Johannes ⇨ Hans**

Dorothea ⇨ Dorte, Thea
Edith ⇨ Ditte
Elisabet(h) ⇨ Lisbet(h), Lise, Lis, Bet(h)
Helene ⇨ Lene, Le
Jakob ⇨ Jeppe ⇨ Iep ⇨ Ib
Laurentius ⇨ Lars
Marie ⇨ Mia
Nikolaus ⇨ Niels
Margrethe ⇨ Grete, Grith
Ulrika ⇨ Ulla, Rikke

Nicknames include:

Ann ⇨ Nanny, Nella
Elisabet(h) ⇨ Bitten, Lissen, Litten, Misse, Mimi
Johannes ⇨ Johs
Vibeke ⇨ Vivi

1121 List of common abbreviations

What follows is not a full list, but a number of dictionaries of abbreviations are currently available. See 1118(d) for notes on forms.

adb	**automatisk databehandling**
adr.	**adresse**
AF	**arbejdsformidlingen**
afd.	**1 afdeling** **2 afdøde**
afg.	**afgang**
afs.	**afsender**
a.i.	**ad interim (indtil videre)**
alm.	**almindelig**
a.m.b.a.	**andelsselskab med begrænset ansvar**
ang.	**angående**
ank.	**ankomst**
anm.	**1 anmeldelse** **2 anmærkning**
apr.	**april**
ApS	**anpartsselskab**
art.	**1 artikel** **2 artium, e.g. mag.art.**
A/S, a/s	**aktieselskab**
ass.	**assistent**
ATP	**arbejdsmarkedets tillægspension**
aug.	**august**
att.	**attention (til)**
aut.	**1 automatisk** **2 autoriseret**
bd.	**bind**
bet.	**1 betalt** **2 betegne(lse)** **3 betydning**
bl.	**1 blad** **2 blandt**
bl.a.	**blandt andet/andre**
C	**Celsius**
c.	**cent**
ca.	**cirka**
cand.	**candidatus**
c.c.	**carbon copy (kopi til)**
cf.	**confer (jævnfør)**
cirk.	**cirkulære**
civiling.	**civilingeniør**
d.	**1 den** **2 død**
dat.	**dateret**
dav.	**daværende**
d.d.	**dags dato**
d.e.	**det er (det vil sige)**
dec.	**december**
dir.	**1 direkte** **2 direktorat** **3 direktør**
dir.	**4 dirigent**
div.	**1 diverse** **2 division**
DM	**danmarksmesterskab**
do.	**ditto**
dr.	**1 doctor, e.g. dr.phil.** **2 doktor** **3 drenge**
d.s.	**1 den/det/de samme** **2 dennes**
d.s.s.	**det samme som**
dvs.	**det vil sige**

d.y.	den yngre
d.æ.	den ældre
d.å.	dette år
edb	elektronisk databehandling
eftf.	efterfølger
eftm.	eftermiddag
egl.	egentlig
e.Kr.	efter Kristus
eks.	eksempel
ekskl.	eksklusive
ekspl.	eksemplar
e.l.	eller lignende
enk.	enkelt
EM	europamesterskab
em.	eftermiddag
etc.	etcetera
evt.	eventuel (-t, -le)
f	farve
f.	1 femininum
	2 for
	3 født
	4 følgende (side)
feb.	februar
ff.	følgende (sider)
fa.	firma(et)
fakt.	faktura
f.eks.	for eksempel
fhv.	forhenværende
fk.	fælleskøn
f.Kr.	før Kristus
fl.	flaske
flg.	følgende
flt.	flertal
fm.	1 formiddag
	2 fuldmægtig
F.M.	fredlyst mindesmærke
f.m.	foregående måned
fmd.	formand
f.n.	fra neden
f.o.	fra oven
f.o.m.	fra og med
forb.	1 forbindelse
	2 forbud
foreg.	foregående
forf.	forfatter
fork.	forkortelse, forkortet
form.	formiddag
forr.	forretning
forsk.	forskellig
forts.	fortsættelse, fortsættes
FP	førtidspension
fr.	1 fredag
	2 fru, frøken
frk.	frøken
f.t.	for tiden
f.v.t.	før vor tidsregning
fx	for eksempel

f.å.	foregående år
g	1 godt
	2 gram
	3 gymnasieklasse
g., gg.	gang(e)
gd.	gård
gdr.	gårdejer
gl.	1 gammel
	2 glas
g.m.	gift med
gn.	gennem
gnsn.	gennemsnit
gr.	1 grad
	2 gruppe
grdl.	grundlagt
G/S, g/s	gensidigt selskab
GT	Gamle Testamente
ha	hektar
henv.	1 henvendelse
	2 henvisning
hf	højere forberedelseseksamen
hf.	heftet, hæftet
hhv.	henholdsvis
hk	hestekraft
H.K.H.	Hans/Hendes Kongelige Højhed
hpl.	holdeplads
hr.	herre
i alm.	i almindelighed
ib.	indbundet
if.	ifølge
i henh. til	i henhold til
iht.	i henhold til
indb.	1 indbundet
	2 indbygger
ing.	ingeniør
inkl.	inklusive
instr.	1 instruktion, instruktør
	2 instrument
I/S, i/s	interessentselskab
istf., i st. for	i stedet for
itk.	intetkøn
jan.	januar
jf. (jvf.)	jævnfør
j. nr.	journalnummer
kap.	kapitel
kat.	1 katalog
	2 katolsk
kbh.	københavnsk
kgl.	kongelig
kl.	1 klasse
	2 klokken
kld.	kælder
km/t.	kilometer i timen
korr.	korrektur

kp.	**kogepunkt**
Kr.	**Kirke** (in place names)
kr.	**krone(r)**
K/S, k/s	**kommanditselskab**
kt.	**1 konto** **2 kontor**
kv.	**kvinde(lig)**
l	**liter**
l.	**linie, linje**
lb.nr.	**løbenummer**
lejl.	**lejlighed**
lgd.	**længde**
lign.	**lignende**
Ll.	**Lille** (in place names)
LM	**lønmodtagernes medejendomsret**
lok.	**1 lokal(nummer)** **2 lokale**
lø.	**lørdag**
m.	**med**
ma.	**mandag**
m.a.o.	**med andre ord**
mc	**1 motorcykel** **2 musikkassette**
md.	**1 mand** **2 måned**
mdl.	**1 mandlig** **2 månedlig**
mdtl.	**mundligt**
medd.	**meddelelse**
medflg.	**medfølgende**
medl.	**medlem**
MF	**medlem af Folketinget**
mfl., m.fl.	**med flere**
mgl.	**mangler, manglende**
mhp., m.h.p.	**med henblik på**
mht., m.h.t.	**med hensyn til**
mia.	**milliard(er)**
mio.	**million(er)**
m/k	**mand(lig)/kvinde(lig)**
ml.	**mellem**
m.m.	**med mere**
modsv.	**modsvarende**
modt.	**modtager**
mrs.	**marts**
mul.	**mulig(vis)**
mv., m.v.	**med videre**
N	**nord**
n.	**neutrum**
ndf.	**nedenfor**
ned.	**nederst**
nedenst.	**nedenstående**
nl.	**nemlig**
NM	**nordisk mesterskab**
NN	**nomen nescio** (=I do not know the name)
nord.	**nordisk**

nov.	**november**
Nr.	**Nørre** (in place names)
nr.	**nummer**
NT	**Ny Testamente**
nto.	**netto**
nuv.	**nuværende**
o.	**omkring**
o.a.	**og andet/andre**
obl.	**obligatorisk**
obs!	**observer!**
off.	**1 offentlig** **2 officiel**
ofl., o.fl.	**og flere**
og lign.	**og lignende**
okt.	**oktober**
OL	**Olympiske Lege**
o.l.	**og lignende**
o/m	**omdrejninger per minut**
o.m.a.	**og mange andre, og meget andet**
omg.	**1 omgang** **2 omgående**
omkr.	**omkring**
omr.	**område**
omtr.	**omtrent**
on.	**onsdag**
opg.	**opgang**
opl.	**1 oplag** **2 oplysning**
opr.	**1 oprettet** **2 oprindelig**
osfr., o.s.fr.	**og så fremdeles**
ovenn.	**ovennævnte**
ovenst.	**ovenstående**
ovf.	**ovenfor**
p-	**parkerings-, preventiv(pille)**
par.	**paragraf**
p.b.v.	**på bestyrelsens vegne**
pct.	**procent**
pg.	**piger**
pga, p.g.a.	**på grund af**
pk.	**pakke**
pkt.	**punkt**
Pl.	**Plads** (in place names)
pl., plur.	**pluralis**
PM	**promemoria**
P&T	**post- og telegrafvæsenet**
pr.	**per**
pr., prc.	**præcis**
pt.	**patient**
p.t.	**pro tempore** (for the time being)
p .... v.	**på ...s vegne**
på gr. af	**på grund af**

R	**rekommanderet** (letters)
rad.	**radikal**
red.	**redaktion, redaktør, redigeret (af)**
regn.	**regning**
repr.	**repræsentant**
resp.	**respektive**
S	**syd**
s	**sekund**
s.	**side**
sa.	**samme**
s.d.	**se denne (dette, disse)**
Sdr.	**Sønder, Søndre** (in place names)
sept.	**september**
sg.	**singularis**
s/h	**sort-hvid**
sing.	**singularis**
sj.	**sjælden**
Skt.	**Sankt**
s.m.	**samme måned**
sml.	**sammenlign**
sms.	**sammensætning**
sn	**sogn**
spec.	**specielt**
spm.	**spørgsmål**
spsk.	**spiseskefuld**
St.	**Store** (in place names)
st.	**1 station** **2 stuen (etage)** **3 størrelse**
stk.	**styk(ke)**
s.u.	**svar udbedes**
sø.	**søndag**
sædv.	**sædvanlig(vis)**
s.å.	**samme år**
såk.	**såkaldt**
t	**ton**
t.	**time**
tdl.	**tønde(r) land**
t.eks.	**til eksempel**
tg	**temmelig godt**
th., t.h.	**til højre**
ti.	**tirsdag**
tidl.	**tidligere**
tilf.	**1 tilfælde** **2 tilføjelse**
tilh.	**tilhørende**
tilsv.	**tilsvarende**
tlf.	**telefon**
to.	**torsdag**
t.o.m.	**til og med**
tsk.	**teskefuld**
tv., t.v.	**til venstre**
u.	**1 uden** **2 under**
uafh.	**uafhængig**
ubf.	**ubestemt form**
udb., udbet.	**udbetaling**
udd.	**uddannelse**
udg.	**udgave, udgivet (af)**
uds.	**1 udsendelse** **2 udsolgt**
undt.	**undtagen**
u.å.	**uden år**
V	**vest**
V.	**Vester** (in place names)
v.	**ved**
ved hj. af	**ved hjælp af**
vedk.	**vedkommende**
vedr.	**vedrørende**
vejl.	**vejledning**
VM	**verdensmesterskab**
vsa.	**ved siden af**
vvs	**varme, ventilation, sanitet**
vær.	**værelse**
Ø	**øst**
Ø.	**Øster** (in place names)
øv.	**øverst**
øvr.	**øvrige**
årg.	**årgang**
årh.	**århundrede**
årl.	**årlig**

D ASSIMILATION OF FOREIGN LOANS

1122 Types of foreign influence

(a) One may distinguish between quotations, i.e. foreign phrases (not inflected in Danish) retaining their foreign character, such as **Cheer up!**, **Sorry!** or **the Establishment**, and loans, i.e. words which remarkably quickly begin to be regarded as part of the Danish language, such as: **approach,**

computer or **management**. Assimilation of loans involves adaptation to Danish spelling and/or pronunciation and inflexion.

(b) Spelling and/or pronunciation

Until recent times loans were modified to adapt to Danish patterns of orthography and pronunciation:

Low German	*French*	*English*
handskemager	**butik**	**kiks**
(hantschemaker)	(boutique)	(cakes)
rådhus	**løjtnant**	**strejke**
(rathus)	(lieutenant)	(strike)

In recent times most Danes have acquired skills in foreign languages, and now words are often loaned in their original forms:

computer, deadline, playgirl, showbiz

But notice the respellings: **dekoder, eurokrat, fikse, fil** (computer file), **foto, overheadprojektor, pesticid, plak** (plaque), **padle**

(c) Inflexion

Direct loans are usually inflected according to Danish patterns:

carporten, containeriseret, interviewede

But see also 119ff.

(d) Calques

Calques involve borrowing the underlying ideas of a foreign word or phrase, often a compound or derivative, and translating these into the target language:

	Compare: *English*
jordskredssejr	landslide victory
kernefamilie	nuclear family
langhåret	long-haired, i.e. intellectual
nyhedsbrev	newsletter
tænketank	think tank
værkstedsteater	theatre workshop

	Compare:	*German*
fingerspidsfornemmelse		Fingerspitzengefühl
gummiparagraf		Gummiparagraph
gæstearbejder		Gastarbeiter
had-kærlighed		Haßliebe
udviklingsland		Entwicklungsland

	Compare:	*French*
caféteater		café théâtre
dokumentær		documentaire
ergoterapi		ergothérapie
landpostej		pâté de campagne
sort humor		humour noir
tredje verden		le troisième monde

(e) Semantic extension is the borrowing of a meaning from a foreign language and its addition to the existing meanings of an indigenous word. For example, **en due** and **en høg** in Danish meant 'a dove' and 'a hawk', that is two types of bird, but have recently gained the meanings 'peace-lover' and 'warmonger' from American English.

Other examples of semantic extension originating from English are:

	Original Danish meaning	*Added (loaned) meaning*
album	book for collecting	recording with several parts
græsrod	grass roots	general working population
høj	high	under the influence of drugs
massiv	solid	huge
varm kartoffel	hot potato	difficult problem

1123 Borrowings from Low German

(a) The total number of Low German words of all kinds borrowed into Danish, mostly in the 14th century, is very high, but loans tended to concentrate in the following fields:

trade:	**betale, fragt, købmand**
urban life:	**borgmester, rådmand**
crafts, guilds:	**bager, håndværk, værksted**
foodstuffs, goods:	**læder, sirup, sukker**
tools:	**høvl, værktøj**
courtly life:	**frue, frøken, fyrste, herre, hertug, slot**

(b) The influence led both to replacement of Old Danish words and to an enlargement of the lexicon:

e.g. **vorde** is replaced by **bli(ve)**; **genest** by **straks**; **børje** by **begynde**; **røne** by **prøve.**

(c) As significant as lexical borrowing is the introduction in many loans of frequent affixes which were later used to form new derivatives with indigenous stems.

an**mode,** ***be*****gynde,** ***for*****barme, bedrø*****velse*****, skriv*****eri*****, fyrst*****inde*** are German loans, while ***an*****tage,** ***be*****svare,** ***for*****vente, lign*****else*****, tigg*****eri*****, ejer*****inde*** are formations using indigenous stems.

See also 1102ff.

1124 Borrowings from French

(a) French loans entered Danish particularly in the 17th and 18th centuries, and tended to concentrate in the following fields:

diplomacy:	**ambassadør, konseil**
literature and theatre:	**atelier, ballet, maskerade, premiere**
food:	**bøf, delikatesse, dessert, frikassé, sovs**
furniture:	**møbel, persienne**
clothes, etc:	**bluse, frisure, negligé, parfume**
family:	**kusine, nevø, tante**
military:	**armé, infanteri, korporal, officer**
health care:	**ambulance, bandage, massage, sonde**
others:	**adjø, pæn, trist, vulgær**

(b) Many French loans still have end stress:

butik, brutal, engagement, hotel, idé, ingeniør, interessant

(c) Many French loans have retained their original spelling, but some adaptations have been made:

French		*Danish*	
hard c	⇨	k	**kabinet, karton, kroket**
silent -e	⇨	zero	**princip, trist, vag**
-que	⇨	-k	**bank, butik, fabrik**
ai	⇨	æ	**affære, egalitær, portræt, suveræn**

eu	⇨	**ø**	**guvernør, interiør, valør**
ou	⇨	**u**	**kusine, kuvert**

But notice the many words retaining largely unmodified French spelling:

applaudere, bourgeoisi, causeri, maitresse, mayonnaise (or **majonæse**), **ouverture, restaurant, voyeur**

1125 Borrowings from English

(a) English loans into Danish date back to the 17th century but most are from the last 100 years. They are found mainly in the following fields:

vehicles:	**bulldozer, cykel, jeep, truck**
clothing:	**bikini, blazer, cardigan, jeans, shorts, sweatshirt**
food, drink:	**bacon, bar, drink, juice, milkshake**
material:	**lambswool, nylon, tweed**
sport:	**back, drible, score, serve, sport**
work:	**boykot, job, strejke**
management:	**bestseller, briefe, goodwill, knowhow, teamwork**
communications:	**computer, container, radio, transistor**
others:	**baby, bus, film, interview, motel, pub, producer, smart, tank, teak, terminal, test(e)**

(b) Modern English loans in Danish may be categorized as follows:

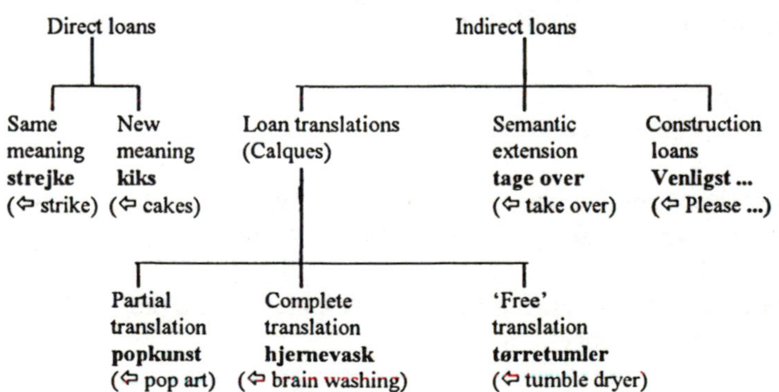

(c) Direct loans may be divided into:

(i) Loans that have the same meaning as the original: **image, team.**

(ii) Loans in which some semantic change has taken place: **city** in Danish refers only to the town centre, **drink** is used only of alcoholic drinks, **soul** is only a kind of music, **en butterfly** is a bow tie.

(iii) Loan phrases: **en dark horse**

(d) New English formations are those where a new formation in Danish is based on English patterns but does not originate from an English-speaking country: **en stationcar** is a station waggon or estate car; **en babylift** is a carry-cot; **en smoking** is not a smoking jacket but a dinner jacket or tuxedo.

(e) Indirect loans include loan translations, which may in their turn be:

(i) a partial translation: **backinggruppe, grapefrugt, holdingselskab, hårspray, interrailkort, intercitytog, popkunst, weltervægt**

(ii) a complete translation which is literal: **bananrepublik**, banana republic; **befolkningseksplosion**, population explosion; **ikkespredningsaftale**, non-proliferation treaty; **koldkrig**, cold war; **kæderyger**, chain smoker

(iii) a 'free' translation: **båndoptager**, tape recorder; **soveby**, dormitory town

(f) Semantic extension involves imparting a new (English) meaning to an existing word:

Det er ikke min hovedpine/kop te.
It's not my headache/cup of tea.

Det var op til dem selv at afgøre det!
It was up to them to decide the matter!

Man vil få kredit af det.
You can get some credit from it.

(g) Construction loans involve borrowing a structure type rather than a word or phrase, and there are several types in contemporary Danish.

(i) The incorrect use of the English apostrophe as a genitive marker in cases where Danish has no apostrophe:

***Jensen's hus** Jensen's house

(ii) The extension of use of the construction with an adjective + proper noun without front article (see 220(f)):

35-årige Svend Jørgensen 35-year-old Svend Jørgensen
(cf. the emotive use **kære/søde Lars**, dear/sweet Lars)

(iii) Verbs with a new intransitive sense:

Bilen sælger godt. The car is selling well.

(iv) The imparting of a new and generalized use to the pronoun **du**, which replaces the indefinite pronoun **man** (see 445):

Hvis du spiser meget engelsk mad, bliver du fed.
If you eat a lot of English food you get fat.

(h) Form of loans by word class

(i) Noun genders vary, see 108(b). Plural forms of nouns may be retained (**-s** plurals) or adapt to Danish inflexion:

checks, film, pullovere, trucker

See also 119–22.

(ii) Adjectives are in many cases easy to adapt to Danish patterns:

Some retain a form in '-y' and are indeclinable:

handy, sporty

Some past participles in '-ed' are retained or change to Danish **-et**:

filmminded; sophisticated ⇨ **sofistikeret**

(iii) Verbs are also very easy to adapt to Danish patterns:

briefe, flippe, guide

'-ate' ⇨ -ere: **deeskalere, indikere, indoktrinere**
'-ise' ⇨ -(is)ere: **institutionalisere, organisere, revolutionere**

12 PUNCTUATION

In many cases Danish and English practice is similar as regards punctuation. This section is largely a résumé of the most important points of usage, concentrating on the major differences between Danish and English. Paragraphs 1202–04 outline the two competing systems for the use of the comma in Danish.

1201 Punctuation marks

The names of the principle punctuation marks (**skilletegn**) used in Danish are:

.	**punktum**
,	**komma**
:	**kolon**
;	**semikolon**
-	**bindestreg**
–	**tankestreg**
( ) [ ] { }	**parentes**
” ” „ ” ’ ’ » «	**anførselstegn**
?	**spørgsmålstegn**
’	**apostrof**
!	**udråbstegn**
/	**skråstreg**
...	**prikker**

1202 The comma: the two systems

(a) Danish has two systems for employing the comma. Until recently, these were known as the 'grammatical comma' and the 'pause (or unitary) comma'. In 1996, *Dansk Sprognævn* (The Danish National Language Council) issued new guidelines for the correct use of the comma, and these were incorporated into the latest edition of *Retskrivningsordbogen* (1996).

There are still two systems. Because of strong resistance in some quarters to the idea of abolishing the 'grammatical comma', this has been preserved but renamed 'traditional comma'. In addition, a new integrated system - largely based on the 'pause comma' - has been created and dubbed the 'new comma'. Although both systems are thus officially acceptable, *Dansk Sprognævn* itself strongly recommends the use of the 'new comma'. However, it is important that one uses one system consistently and avoids a mixture of the two.

In practice, there are many cases where there is no difference between the two systems. The main similarities are set out in this paragraph, while 1203 and 1204 outline the two systems and their major differences.

(b) Similarities between the two systems

Both systems use a comma, or commas, in the following cases:

(i) Main clause + main clause

Det er varmt, og solen skinner.
It is warm and the sun is shining.

Jeg glæder mig til på søndag, for så rejser vi på ferie.
I look forward to Sunday because then we are going on holiday.

(ii) Subordinate clause + main clause

Da vi havde spist, gik vi i biografen.
When we had eaten, we went to the cinema.

Hvis du venter lidt, kan vi følges ad.
If you wait a moment, we can go together.

(iii) Parenthetical clause or expression

Jeg kender hendes bror, som nu arbejder i London.
I know her brother, who is working in London now.

Anden verdenskrig sluttede for længe siden, nemlig i 1945.
World War II ended a long time ago, viz. in 1945.

(iv) Parenthetical apposition

Danmarks højeste punkt, Yding Skovhøj, er 173 meter højt.
The highest point in Denmark, Yding Skovhøj, is 173 metres.

Min nabo, Peter Hansen, er pensionist.
My neighbour, Peter Hansen, is an old-age pensioner.

(v) Elements in extra positions (see 1025)

Morten, har du tid et øjeblik?
Morten, have you got a moment?

Han har ødelagt det hele, den store idiot.
He has ruined everything, the great idiot.

(vi) Interjections

Av, min guldtand!
Ow, my gold tooth!

Hold nu kæft, for fanden!
Now shut up, damn you!

(vii) Enumerations, though not before the last one

Soren, Mads, Maren og Mette går i samme klasse.
Soren, Mads, Maren and Mette are in the same class.

Vi købte kaffe, te, brød, ost og smør.
We bought coffee, tea, bread, cheese and butter.

(viii) Clarifying comment

Køb lige nogle blomster, og en flaske vin til middagen.
Just buy some flowers, and a bottle of wine for the dinner.

(ix) Before **men**

Middagen var dejlig, men dyr.
The dinner was lovely, but expensive.

1203 The traditional comma

This was previously called the 'grammatical comma' (see 1202(a)). In this system the comma is placed between clauses, whether these are main or subordinated clauses and irrespective of their order.

(i) Main clause + main clause

Manden løb, og konen cyklede.
The husband ran and the wife cycled.

(ii) Main clause + subordinate clause

Han sagde, at han ikke kunne holde det ud længere.
He said that he couldn't stand it any longer.

(iii) Subordinate clause + main clause

Da gæsterne var gået, ryddede de op.
When the guests had left, they cleared up.

(iv) Subordinate clause + subordinate clause

(De troede,) at det var en tyv, der havde taget pengene.
(They thought) that it was a thief who had taken the money.

This can lead to extensive use of commas, e.g.:

Grunden til, at Ole ikke kom, var, at han var syg.
The reason why Ole didn't come was that he was ill.

For other examples of the traditional comma see 1202(b).

1204 The new comma

This is a new integrated system, and the one that is officially recommended for use (see 1202(a)). Although it is mainly based on the previous 'pause comma', it is subject to more well-defined rules. The use of the new comma differs from that of the traditional comma on several points (cf. 1203).

No comma in the following cases:

(i) Main clause + subordinate clause

Han sagde at han ikke kunne holde det ud længere.
He said that he couldn't stand it any longer.

(ii) Subordinate clause + subordinate clause (but before main clause)

(De troede) at det var en tyv der havde taget pengene.
(They thought) that it was a thief who had taken the money.

Da han så hvor langt ned der var hvis han faldt, opgav han.
When he saw how far down it was if he fell, he gave up.

(iii) Before (but after) a restrictive relative clause

Kender du damen der står derovre?
Do you know the woman who is standing over there?

De børn der leger i haven, ser søde ud.
The children who are playing in the garden look sweet.

(Cf.: **Lise, der lige har været syg, ser træt ud.**
Lise, who has just been ill, looks tired.)

(iv) Around non-parenthetical appositions

Den berømte danske fysiker Niels Bohr fik Nobelprisen.
The famous Danish physisist Niels Bohr got the Nobel Prize.

(Cf. **Den længste danske å, Gudenåen, løber gennem Randers.**
The longest Danish river, the Gudenå, runs through Randers.)

Thus, where the traditional comma is employed mechanically, the use of the new comma is sensitive to the context in the case of parenthetical versus non-parenthetical constructions.

1205 The full stop

The full stop is used chiefly:

(a) At the end of a sentence

Jeg kører som regel i bil til arbejdet.
I usually drive to work.

Ræk mig lige saltet.
Pass me the salt.

Note 1 – The full stop is also used with incomplete sentences in some styles, and to emphasize a subordinate clause or part of a main clause in advertising language and informal journalism:

(Har du ikke set Peter?) Jo, for nogle minutter siden.
(Haven't you seen Peter?) Yes, some minutes ago.

Note 2 – The full stop may be used before **og** and **men**:

På mandag begynder hans ferie. Og det glæder han sig til.
On Monday he begins his holiday. And he's pleased about that.

Hun blev også bedt om at vaske op. Men det ville hun ikke.
She was also asked to wash up. But she didn't want to.

(b) In many abbreviations (see 1121)

kr.	**osv.**
m.m.	**bl.a.**
m.a.o.	**t. (time)**
mfl./m.fl.	**mv./m.v.**
Margrethe d. 2. (= den Anden)	

Note 1 – The stop is not found after metrical units:

5 l 250 g 100 km 50 kg 10 t (ton) 5 mm (millimeter) 100 dB

Note 2 – In a few cases the slash is used in abbreviations rather than the full stop:

A/S	**a/s**	**aktieselskab**	plc, limited company
G/S	**g/s**	**gensidigt selskab**	mutual company
I/S	**i/s**	**interessentselskab**	partnership
K/S	**k/s**	**kommanditselskab**	limited partnership
c/o			care of
s/h		**sort-hvid**	black and white
t/r		**tur-retur**	return

(c) In some numerical/mathematical expressions (see also 301 (Note 4), 1212)

kl. 07.45	**København, den 13.4.1995**
100.000 kr.	**7.000.000 indbyggere** (inhabitants)

(d) Note that the full stop is *not* used

(i) After book titles or names of newspapers and magazines or after chapter or section headings.

(ii) In lists and programmes:

INDHOLD	CONTENTS
Substantiver	Nouns
Verber	Verbs

(iii) After another full stop in an abbreviation:

Vi skal besøge flere storbyer: London, Paris, Berlin osv.
We will visit several large cities: London, Paris, Berlin, etc.

(iv) After other punctuation marks such as the exclamation mark, question mark, colon or dash:

Hold mund!	Shut your mouth!

(v) As a decimal point. Danish uses a comma instead:

14,5	14.5

1206 The exclamation mark

The exclamation mark is used after exclamations, greetings, commands (imperative verb forms, see 501, 533) and in introductions to letters:

Hej!	Hi!
På gensyn!	Be seeing you!
At I gider!	How could you be bothered!
Glædelig jul!	Happy Christmas!
Hænderne op!	Hands up!
Mine damer og herrer!	Ladies and gentlemen!
Kære hr. Hansen!	Dear Mr Hansen,
Det var som pokker/fanden!	Damn!
Ræk mig lige smørret!	Pass me the butter!
Der er han!	There he is!

Note 1 – After rhetorical questions either a question mark or an exclamation mark may sometimes be found:

Hvem kunne finde på at lære dansk!	Who would ever think of learning Danish!
Mon ikke!	I'll say!

Note 2 – In instructions, etc., where many imperatives are used, the exclamation mark is often omitted.

1207 Quotations

Both double and single quotations marks are used to indicate quotation:

” ”   ’ ’

Double quotations are the most common type. The guillemet » « is purely a typographical variant.

Single quotations are primarily used for a quotation within double quotes or to indicate a concept or meaning:

’Objection’ betyder på dansk ’indvending’.
‘Objection’ in Danish is ‘indvending’.

1208 Direct speech conventions

There are three ways of presenting a phrase in direct speech: with a dash **(tankestreg)**, quotation marks (see 1207) or without any convention (though often marked off from any lead verb by a comma):

– Der skal være lys!	"Let there be light!"
"Der skal være lys!"	"Let there be light!"
Gud sagde, Der skal være lys!	God said, "Let there be light!"

A colon is usually placed after the lead verb:

Gud sagde: "Der skal være lys!"
God said, "Let there be light!"

The guillemet is frequently found in Danish in printed text:

Gud Herren kaldte på Adam: »Hvor er du?«
God called to Adam: "Where are you?"

1209 The apostrophe

The apostrophe in Danish is a buffer which prevents the juxtaposition of letters that do not usually belong together and which may, therefore, prove confusing.

(a) The apostrophe is used to show that certain letters have been omitted in less common elisions:

Hva' si'r du?	What're you saying?
Go' mor'n!	'Morning!
På 'en igen!	Do it again!

(b) Unlike English, Danish does not normally use an apostrophe to indicate a possessor (i.e. genitive):

the dog's owner	**hundens ejer**
Eva's mother	**Evas mor**

Note – After proper nouns ending in **-s** and abbreviations an apostrophe may be found to indicate the genitive (see 131(c)):

Lars's/Lars' børn	Lars' children
SAS's/SAS' priser	SAS's prices

(c) The apostrophe is sometimes used to mark the inflexional ending:

(i) In foreign words (optional when the word ends in a silent consonant):

succesen or succes'en	the success
buffeten or buffet'en	the buffet

(ii) In abbreviations (without a full stop):

lp'en, the LP; **tv'et**, the TV; **wc'et**, the WC

(iii) In numerals:

1960'erne (nittenhundredetresserne)	the 1960s
90'erne (halvfemserne)	the 90s
en 7'er	a seven

(iv) In words not used in their normal context (citation words), and with words for letters or sounds:

Der er mange hvis'er i det, han sagde.
There are many 'ifs' in what he said.

Lars bruger mange og'er og men'er.
Lars uses many 'ands' and 'buts'.

Det sætter prikken over i'et.
That adds the finishing touch.

Man kan dårligt høre forskel på hendes u'er og y'er.
One cannot easily distinguish her u's from her y's.

1210 The hyphen

The hyphen shows that two words are linked (but see also 1313) and is used

(a) To replace **og** in compounds:

Slesvig-Holsten; Marxisme-Leninisme; den evangelisk-lutherske kirke

(b) To replace (**fra** ...) **til**:

åbent 10–12 **1939–45** **side 9–11** **færgen Dragør–Limhamn**

(c) To avoid repetition of the second element of a compound:

søn- og helligdage (i.e. **søndage og helligdage**)	Sundays and bank holidays
øre-, næse- og halssygdomme	ear, nose and throat complaints
olie- eller gasproduktion	oil or gas production

(d) Where one element in a compound is an abbreviation or in some cases a number (cf. 1209(c)(iii)):

tv-skærm, TV screen; **skole-tv**, school television; **edb-udstyr**, computer equipment; **1800-tallet**, the 19th century

(e) In group compounds where the first element is complex:

tag selv-bord, a buffet table; **en H.C. Andersen-entusiast**, a Hans Christian Andersen enthusiast; **gør det selv-metoden**, the DIY method

1211 Addresses

Danes use a four-figure postcode which precedes the name of the town:

3400 Hillerød **2300 København S**

In letters a straight left-hand margin and absence of punctuation is characteristic of the address:

To a private person:	*To a company:*
Marie Jensen	**Frugt og Grønt A/S**
Randersvej 101	**Rosenkålsvej 10**
1234 Vesterby	**5678 Sønderby**

Note 1 – If writing from abroad to an address in Denmark the nationality marker **DK-** should be added before the postcode:

DK-3460 Birkerød

Note 2 – The sender's address is written on the top of the back of the envelope or, on large envelopes, at top left on the front (recommended by the Danish Post Office), marked **Afs.** (= **Afsender**, sender).

Note 3 – The abbreviations **Hr.** (**herr**) and **Fr.** (**fru** or **frøken**) or a title are sometimes added above the addressee's name, though titles in particular are seldom used nowadays:

Bibliotekar
Marie Jensen

Note 4 – The house number always follows the street name.

Note 5 – The street name is best written out in full.

1212 Dates

(a) Traditionally the order in dates is day-month-year written either all in figures or in a mixture of figures and words:

14.4.1993 **14. april 1993**

The abbreviation **93** is acceptable if it is obvious that this refers to 1993 and not to, e.g., 1893).

It is still common (but now optional) to use the word **den** (abbreviated **d.**) in dates in running text:

den/d. 14. april 1993

In manuscripts people often use the slash for day/month:

14/4 1993

(b) International dates have the order year-month-day and are only expressed in figures:

1993-04-13

Note that two figures must always be used for month and day.

(c) Week numbers are used for reference in Denmark in business and industry. **Uge 1** (Week 1) is the first week of the year containing a Thursday.

13 ORTHOGRAPHY

A SYMBOLS AND SOUNDS

1301 Letters of the alphabet and their order

(a) The Danish alphabet comprises 29 letters:

a b c d e f g h i j k l m n o p q r s t u v w x y z æ ø å (aa)
A B C D E F G H I J K L M N O P Q R S T U V W X Y Z Æ Ø Å (Aa)

Notice that the three Nordic vowels **æ, ø, å** come at the end of the alphabet and that **v** and **w** are treated nowadays as separate letters, though earlier dictionaries and lists often merged the two.

On the use of small and capital letters see 1308–12.

In dictionaries and lists a word with a capital letter precedes one without, i.e. **Svend – svend**.

(b) In modern Danish **c, q, w, x, z** are only found in foreign words and, with the exception of **c**, have only a restricted use.

(c) Foreign characters are found in names and quotations from other languages (see also 1303). The following frequent foreign characters are alphabetized as follows:

ü as **y**   **ä** as **æ**   **ö** as **ø**

The Danish character precedes the foreign character, i.e. **Søren** precedes **Sören**.

(d) When the combination **aa** is pronounced as a single vowel, i.e. as long **a** or **å**, it comes at the end of the alphabet. Forms in **å** precede those in **aa**, i.e. **Skovgård – Skovgaard**. When (as happens rarely) it is pronounced as two vowels, e.g. **ekstraarbejder**, these are regarded as **a**'s. See also 1302.

Note – In dictionaries and lists before the spelling reform of 1948 **aa** was the first letter of the alphabet (see 1302).

1302 Aa, aa and Å, å

(a) In 1948 the letters **Å** and **å** officially replaced the spellings **Aa, aa** for the sound /å/ in Danish. By an oversight it was only in 1955 that a position in the alphabet was officially determined for **Å, å** (known to Danes as **bolle-å**) – it comes at the end of the alphabet. With the exception of a few place names and personal names (see (b)) the **å** is now general in Danish and ubiquitous in ordinary words: **åben, påstå**, etc. Before 1948 words beginning with **aa** came at the beginning of dictionaries and lists; they now come at the end (whether the form is changed to **å** or not) .

(b) In the debate prior to the change in 1948 supporters of **aa** argued on the basis of tradition and the position of the letter in the alphabet (at the beginning) which was understandable abroad. They claimed that the new letter **å** would not be understandable outside Denmark. **Å** was considered to be alien. One town's campaign slogan ran:

Byens Navn er Aabenraa uden svenske Boller paa.
The town's name is Aabenraa without Swedish balls on.

State organizations may now legally use either form. Business and private individuals may spell as they please, and traditional spellings of first and family names are protected in law, so one finds individuals with names such as **Baad** or **Aage Skovgaard**. Names ending in **-gaard** are the most common examples.

1303 Other diacritics

The letter **å** is not an accented letter but a distinct character (see 1301ff).

(a) Acute accent

The acute accent on **e**, i.e. **é**, is no longer obligatory in common words in Danish (*Retskrivningsordbogen 1986*), but does provide a useful way of indicating stress.

Note 1 – In proper names it is, of course, obligatory: **René, Tegnér.**

(i) The character **é** is found in approximately 70 foreign words, many of them loaned from French and all now optionally without the accent:

> **allé (alle)**, avenue; **café (cafe)**, café; **entré (entre)**, admission; **idé (ide)**, idea

The inflected and compounded forms also have an optional accentless form:

> **alléer (alleer)**, avenues; **armékorps (armekorps)**, army corps

The accented form may be useful on occasion to avoid confusion between stressed and unstressed **e**:

cf.	**allé**, avenue	and:	**alle**, all
	rosé, rosé wine	and:	**rose**, praise
	véd, know	and:	**ved**, by, at

Note 2 – The acute accent is unnecessary, and wrong, in: **kvarter**, 15 minutes; **passager**, passenger.

(ii) **Én** and **dér**

The acute accent is used to distinguish the unstressed indefinite article **en** (a) from the stressed numeral **én** (one) (for numerals see 301ff):

cf.	**Hun har en gammel bil.**	She has an old car.
	Hun har kun én bil.	She only has one car.

It is also used to distinguish the unstressed formal subject **der** (there) (see 407) from the stressed adverb of place **dér** (there):

Der var ingen elever i klassen, da læreren ankom.
There were no pupils in the classroom when the teacher arrived.

and: **Dér var ingen elever – de var alle gået.**
No pupils were there – they had all gone.

(iii) Imperatives in **-ér**

With verbs whose stems end in **-er** it may be useful to indicate the imperative form in **-er** by adding the acute accent:

kopiér, copy; **notér**, note

In these cases there are nouns with confusingly similar plural forms:

kopier, noter

(b) Grave accent

The grave accent is much rarer in Danish than the acute accent, and is only ever used above **a**, i.e. **à**, in approximately 15 words and phrases loaned from French. It is no longer officially used (cf. *Retskrivningsordbogen 1986*) but may occasionally still be found:

à la carte	**ris à l'amande**	**tête-à-tête**
à propos	**føre à jour**, bring up to date	**vis-à-vis**

Officially these are now spelt:

a la carte	**risalamande**	**tete-a-tete**
apropos	**føre ajour**	**vis-a-vis**

(c) Circumflex, cedilla, diaeresis, tilde

These are found only in a few words from other languages:

goût	**pêle-mêle**
garçon	**François**
Citroën	**Noël**
Dão	**mañana**

B SPELLING

1304 Introduction

The notorious lack of correspondence between written and spoken forms in Danish works both ways, like English but unlike languages such as German or Swedish.

For example: The letter 'd' corresponds to the sounds /d/, /ð/ or zero respectively in the words **skyldig**, **sidder**, **mand**. Conversely, the pronunciation /ˈbånə/ can be spelt either **bunde** or **bonde**.

The paragraphs below concentrate upon some of the specific problems of predicting the spoken from the written form.

1305 Vowel length

The following are rules of thumb for vowel length, to which there are, however, many exceptions.

(a) The consonant is doubled between vowels if the first vowel is short and stressed (ˈVCCV):

Long stressed vowel	*Short stressed vowel*
smile, smile	**lille**, small
høne, hen	**bønne**, bean
kæle, pet	**tælle**, count
læse, read	**læsse**, load
salaten, the salad	**katten**, the cat

Similarly, a short vowel precedes a consonant group: **læsk|e** has a short /æ/.

Note 1 – If the preceding vowel is unstressed the consonant may be either single or double:

cf. **a'lene** and: **bal'lon**

Note 2 – Some names have double vowels to indicate length:

Steen, Riis

(b) Danish words never double the consonant at the end of a word, which makes it difficult to predict vowel length in many cases:

Long stressed vowel	*Short stressed vowel*
pil, arrow	**pil!** fiddle!
ryg! smoke!	**ryg**, back

The final consonant is, however, usually doubled in inflected forms, thus revealing vowel length:

Long stressed vowel	*Short stressed vowel*
hus – huset, house	**bus – bussen**, bus

This also occurs after some short vowels with secondary stress, notably in words ending in **-dom, -som**:

ungdom	–	**ungdommen**, youth
morsom	–	**morsomme**, funny
bryllup	–	**bryllupet**, wedding

(c) If there is no consonant after the vowel this is often long:

ny, new; **bi**, bee

(d) Major exceptions:

(i) The letters **j** and **v** are never doubled even if the preceding vowel is short:

bajer, beer; **skoven**, the forest; **veje**, roads

(ii) A few words have double consonants after a long vowel:

bredde, breadth; **otte**, eight; **sjette**, sixth; **vidde**, width

(iii) Some words have a consonant group after a long vowel:

fart, speed; **faste**, fast; **hoste**, cough; **påske**, Easter; **skæbne**, fate; **ugle**, owl; **æble**, apple

These include a number of words in **-rd** where the **d** is silent:

bord, table; **fjerde**, fourth; **gård**, farm

Note – When **-rd** is pronounced /rd/ the preceding vowel is short:

hjord, herd; **lærd**, learned; **rekord**, record

(iv) Some words with a long vowel double the consonant only in inflected forms when the long vowel is retained:

læg – læggen, calf; **skæg – skægget**, beard; **væg – væggen**, wall; **æg – ægget**, egg; **æt – ætten**, lineage

(v) When monosyllabic words end in a vowel, this vowel is usually short:

de, they; **du**, you; **ja**, yes; **nu**, now; **så**, so

(vi) Many loan-words possess a short vowel and a single consonant:

ananas, pineapple; **britisk**, British; **cykel**, cycle

Some have a double final consonant: **boss, grill, jazz**

1306 Silent letters

Written Danish possesses a number of letters which are not pronounced:

(a) Initial **h** in **hv-, hj-**:

Many pronouns begin with a silent **h-** (**hv-** words, cf. English 'wh- words'):

hvad, what; **hvem**, who; **hver**, every; **hvilken**, which; **hvis**, whose; **hvorfor**, why

But there are many other examples:

hval, whale; **hvalp**, puppy; **hvide**, white of egg; **hveps**, wasp; **hvid**, white; **hvin**, squeal; **hvirvel**, whirl; **hviske**, whisper; **hvælv**, vault; **hvæse**, hiss; **hvæsse**, sharpen

Initial **hj-** occurs in about a dozen words:

hjelm, helmet; **hjem**, home; **hjerne**, brain; **hjerte**, heart; **hjord**, herd; **hjort**, deer; **hjul**, wheel; **hjælp**, help; **hjørne**, corner; **ihjel**, to death

(b) Final **-d** in **-ld, -nd**:

Although it is not pronounced, the **-d** does help to shorten the preceding vowel:

fald, fuld, gæld, held, kold, mild, skyld
brønd, kind, mand, mund, mænd, vind

(c) **-d** in **-rd, -ds** and **-dt**:

1 **-rd** after a long vowel: **færd, hård, jord, mord, nord, værd**
2 **-ds** after a long vowel: **buskads, kreds, lods, sejlads**
3 **-ds** after a short vowel: **gidsel, halvtreds, lakrids, plads, pludselig, tilfreds, trods**
4 **-dt** after a long vowel: **født, klædt, spredt**
5 **-dt** after a short vowel: **bidt, forladt, godt, hvidt, lidt**

(d) **-g** in **-gl, -rg**:

fugl, igle, kugle, ugle
spurgte, spørgsmål

(e) **-v** in **-lv**:

halv, gulv, selv, sølv, tolv

(f) Silent letters in foreign words, notably French loans:

-r **atelier, dossier, foyer**
-s **apropos, bourgeois, chassis, succes**
-t **camembert, debut, filet, kabaret**
p- in **ps-** **pseudonym, psykologi**

1307 Alternative spellings

Alternative spellings are possible for basic forms of words as well as for inflected forms (see Chapters 1, 2 for nouns and adjectives with alternative inflected forms). These forms are found in *Retskrivningsordbogen 1986.*

(a) They include both Danish words and loan-words:

Danish words with alternative spellings are relatively few, e.g.

balde/balle, hjerpe/jærpe, kigge/kikke, tredive/tredve, ærende/ærinde

Loan-words may exist in their original spelling and in a danicized version:

cognac/konjak, creme/krem, crepe/krep, ion/jon, mayonnaise/ majonæse, sporty/sportig, yoghurt/jogurt

(b) Among those words where the pronunciation of the alternatives is the same, two general problem areas are distinguishable:

(i) **æ** or **e**

There has been a tendency, with a few exceptions, in the last two editions of *Retskrivningsordbogen* (1955 and 1986) to change from **æ** spellings to **e** spellings in a number of words and to allow **e** spellings as alternatives in some others. Present-day alternatives include :

bjærge/bjerge, hæfte/hefte, jærpe/hjerpe

Some cases where only **æ** is allowed are: **kærne, skærme, værne, ærme**

(ii) Single or double consonant

Some alternatives are:

galopere/galoppere, karosseri/karrosseri, næbes/næbbes, penalhus/ pennalhus, skrupelløs/skruppelløs

C SMALL AND CAPITAL LETTERS

1308 Introduction

(a) The general rule in Danish is that capital initial letters are used in proper nouns (names) while small initial letters are used in common nouns:

cf.

Dér går Svend.	**Han er udlært som svend.**
There goes Svend.	He served his apprenticeship.

But, as explained in 1309, there may be some confusion about what exactly constitutes a proper noun and what a common noun.

(b) Two major differences between Danish and English are that Danish uses small letters where English has capitals in:

(i) Days of the week, months, national holidays:

tirsdag, Tuesday; **februar**, February; **påske**, Easter; **jul**, Christmas; **nytår**, New Year; **sankthansaften**, Midsummer Eve (Saint John's Night); **grundlovsdag**, Constitution Day

Note – Two cases where a name constitutes the first word: **Kristi himmelfartsdag**, Ascension Day; **Mariæ bebudelsesdag**, Feast of the Annunciation.

(ii) Nationality words, both nouns and adjectives:

en dansker, a Dane; **dansk**, Danish; **en englænder**, an Englishman; **engelsk**, English

(c) As part of punctuation, Danish, like English, uses a capital letter after a full stop:

Det ved jeg ikke rigtig. Måske er det ...
I don't really know. Perhaps it's ...

(d) After a colon practice may vary. Generally a capital is used, and it is obligatory if what follows is a sentence consisting of several clauses. With only one main clause the capital is optional. If what follows the colon is less than a clause a small letter must be used.

Herefter går vi over til noget andet: I en del tilfælde ...
Now we will turn to something different: In some cases ...

Jakkerne føres i tre størrelser: lille, middel og stor.
The jackets are available in three sizes: small, medium and large.

(e) In text headings usage varies, but capitals are generally used in contents lists in books and in numbered or lettered points where each point is rather long and consists of several clauses.

Sometimes capitals are used for main headings and small letters for sub-headings.

1309 The use of capital letters in simple proper nouns: **Er Dorte dansker?**

Most nouns are common nouns and have a small initial letter. Most proper nouns (names) are unproblematical in that they consist of a single word which then begins with a capital.

(a) Persons:

Mette, Jakobsen

This also applies in the plural: **Alle Larsener**, All the Larsens; **Der er tre Sørener i klassen**, There are three Sørens in the class.

It also applies to deities and mythological beings and creatures:

Allah; **Buddha**; **Djævelen**, The Devil; **Gud**, God; **Midgårdsormen**, the World Serpent; **Odin**; **Vorherre** (or **Vor Herre**), Our Lord; **Venus**

Note 1 – When such words are part of an oath they have a small initial letter:

for fanden! damn!; **gud bevares!** heavens!

Note 2 – When pronouns are used to refer to God or Jesus these no longer have capital letters even in the Bible or in hymnals:

Gud/Jesus – han/hans

Note 3 – When personal names are used as common nouns they have a small initial letter:

ampere, celsius, diesel, hertz, newton, ohm, røntgen, watt

Note also derivatives from personal names:

makadamisere, pasteurisering

(b) Animals, symbols, etc.:

Trofast (a dog); **Dannebrog** (the Danish flag)

(c) Places:

These include areas, seas, states, landscape regions, forests, lakes, rivers, mountains, towns, areas of towns, streets and other locations such as buildings:

Amerika, America; **Norden**, Scandinavia; **Skotland**, Scotland; **Alperne**, the Alps; **Rhinen**, the Rhine; **Børsen**, the Stock Exchange; **Christiansborg** (the palace housing the Danish Parliament)

Note – Exceptions: **ækvator**, the Equator; **den nordlige polarkreds**, the Arctic Circle

(d) Heavenly bodies:

Jupiter; Uranus; Karlsvognen, the Plough

But the following may have either: **Jorden/jorden**, the Earth; **Solen/solen**, the Sun; **Månen/månen**, the Moon

(e) Firms and institutions:

Baltica, Hafnia, Lego

Note – Exceptions: **forsvaret**, the defence forces; **hæren**, the army; **kirken**, the Church; **regeringen**, the government; **staten**, the state

(f) Book titles:

Bibelen, the Bible; **Hærværk**, Havoc; **Løgneren**, The Liar; **Rytteren**, The Riding Master; **Tine**, Tina

1310 The use of capital letters in compound nouns: Sønderjylland

The general rule is that compounds which are a proper noun begin with an initial capital letter. The second element then loses its capital.

1 Persons:

Helligånden, the Holy Spirit; **Menneskesønnen**, the Son of Man

2 Places:

Nordsverige, Northern Sweden; **Storkøbenhavn**, Greater Copenhagen; **Østamager**, Eastern Amager; **Andromedatågen**, the Andromeda Nebula; **Himmelbjerget**; **Sydpolen**, the South Pole

3 Institutions:

Folketinget (Danish Parliament); **Fremskridtspartiet**, the Progress Party; **Nationalmuseet**, the National Museum; **Verdensbanken**, the World Bank

4 Titles of works of art:

Måneskinssonaten, the Moonlight Sonata

Otherwise names have a capital initial letter, common nouns have a small initial letter:

Folketinget, the Danish Parliament
et folketingsvalg, a general election

However, when the compound contains a proper noun, but is not itself a proper noun, the use of the initial capital is optional:

en Churchilltale/churchilltale, a Churchill speech
en Middelfartborger/middelfartborger, a citizen of Middelfart
en Mozartentusiast/mozartentusiast, a Mozart enthusiast
en Stockholmsrejse/stockholmsrejse, a journey to Stockholm

In compounds of this kind that have become set expressions, and where the proper noun comes as first element, a small initial letter is used:

en danmarkshistorie, a History of Denmark; **en højesteretsdommer**, a High Court judge

Where the compound has lost the sense of the original proper noun, a small initial letter is used:

en dieselmotor, a diesel engine; **en karljohansvamp**, a Penny Bun bolete (mushroom); **en napoleonskage**, a Napoleon cake; **røntgenstråler**, X-rays; **sanktelmsild**, Saint Elmo's fire; **sankthansorm**, glow-worm

Note – Compounds whose first element is itself a compound or word group ('group compounds') employ a hyphen after the name:

en H.C. Andersen-specialist, a Hans Christian Andersen specialist	*common noun*
H.C. Andersen-Selskabet, the Hans Christian Andersen Society	*proper noun*

Common nouns derived from proper nouns have a small initial letter, unlike English (see 1308):

en grundtvigianer, a follower of Grundtvig; **en københavner**, a Copenhagener; **en marxist**, a Marxist

1311 The use of capital letters in phrases: **Forenede Nationer**

The general rule in an expression of more than one word constituting a proper noun is that the first word and any other significant words should have a capital initial letter.

This means that unimportant words such as conjunctions, prepositions and articles do not usually have a capital. The capital on the front article – which by definition is often the first word – is therefore optional:

det/Det Kaspiske Hav, the Caspian Sea
det/Det Kongelige Bibliotek, the Royal Library

When the front article is separated from the rest of the name by another word it has a small initial letter:

det forurenede Kaspiske Hav, the polluted Caspian Sea
det nymalede Kongelige Bibliotek, the newly painted Royal Library

(a) Persons:

Pia Andersen; **J.P. Jacobsen**; **Storm P.**; **Gorm den Gamle**, King Gorm the Old; **Margrethe den Anden**, Queen Margrethe the Second; **Valdemar Atterdag**

(b) Places:

Georg Brandes Plads; **Holmens Bro**; **Niels Juels Gade**; **Nørre Voldgade**; **Valby Bakke**; **Den Gamle By** (in Århus); **den/Den Persiske Golf**, the Persian Gulf

Note – Often, however, street names in **-vej** and **-gade** are compounded:

Amagerfælledvej, **Vermlandsgade**

(c) Institutions, firms, etc.:

Dansk Kirke i Udlandet, the Danish Church Abroad; **den/Den Europæiske Union**, the European Union; **Gladsaxe Kommune**, Gladsaxe Local Authority; **Ministeriet for Kulturelle Anliggender**, the Ministry for Cultural Affairs; **Det Radikale Venstre**, the Danish Social-Liberal Party; **Aarhus Universitet**, Aarhus University

Note – Even the unofficial names of such institutions have an initial capital letter:

Fællesmarkedet, the Common Market; **Sprognævnet** (= **Dansk Sprognævn**), the Danish Language Council

(d) Buildings:

Odense Rådhus, Odense Town Hall; **Statens Museum for Kunst**, the State Art Gallery

(e) Titles of works of art:

Figaros bryllup/Figaros Bryllup, the Marriage of Figaro

In these cases the front article must have a capital letter when it is the first word, cf. (c) above:

Gamle testamente/Gamle Testamente/Det gamle testamente/Det Gamle Testamente, the Old Testament
Ordbog over det Danske Sprog, Dictionary of the Danish Language
Den signede dag/Den Signede Dag, the Blessed Day (hymn)

(f) Forms of address and titles:

Generally speaking, small initial letters are used for titles, unlike English:

fru Jørgensen, Mrs Jørgensen; **hr. Pedersen**, Mr Pedersen; **dr. Lauritzen**, Dr Lauritzen; **dronning Margrethe**, Queen Margrethe; **onkel Tom**, Uncle Tom; **prinsen af Wales' gemalinde**, the Prince of Wales's Consort

However, royal and other exalted personages may be given a capital initial letter:

Hendes Majestæt, Her Majesty; **Prins Henrik**, Prince Henrik

Four pronouns also have a capital letter:

I, you (subject form, plural); **De**, you (subject form, polite); **Dem**, you (objective form, polite); **Deres**, your (polite)

(g) Historical periods and events:

Capital letters are optional in all words in groups such as the following that have become set phrases:

den franske revolution/Den Franske Revolution, the French Revolution
anden verdenskrig/Anden Verdenskrig, the Second World War

(h) Sports events:

Capitals are optional in cases such as the following that have become set phrases:

olympiske lege/Olympiske Lege, Olympic Games

1312 The use of capital letters in abbreviations: SAS

For a list of common abbreviations see 1121. The rules outlined in 1308–10 also apply in this case.

(a) Names of people, places and institutions, etc.:

Kbh.	**det/Det Kgl. Bibliotek**
Frp. (Fremskridtspartiet)	**Georg Brandes Pl.**
Skt. Jacob	

(b) Acronyms (see 1118)

(i) When they are pronounced as separate letters they are written in capitals:

DSB, EU, FN, USA

(ii) When acronyms can be read as a word, they either have an initial capital or are written entirely in capitals:

Nato/NATO, **Opec/OPEC**, **Unesco/UNESCO**

(iii) Some acronyms that are common nouns have capitals:

A/S (or a/s), plc.; **FM**, fm; **ID-kort**, identity card; **MF**, member of the Danish Parliament

Others begin with a small letter:

en bh, a bra; **cand.mag**, M.A.; **edb**, electronic data processing; **en lp**; **p-piller**, contraceptive pills; **et tv**, a TV; **et uland**, a developing country; **et wc**

Note 1 – When the letter illustrates a shape a capital letter is used:

T-shirt, U-rør

Note 2 – When the letter denotes order or quality or a group or type a capital letter is used:

A-skat, B-indkomst, Opgang F

(c) Abbreviations of titles and common nouns with a full stop (see 1121, 1205(b)) have a small initial letter:

frk. (**frøken**, Miss); **hr.** (**herr**, Mister); **osv.** (**og så videre**, etc.); **tlf.** (**telefon**, telephone)

(d) Abbreviations for chemical elements begin with a capital:

Na, Cl, Na, Cl

(e) Abbreviations for musical notation vary according to major or minor key:

a-mol, A minor; **D-dur**, D major

D MISCELLANEOUS

1313 Hyphenation (word division)

It is best to avoid dividing words at the end of a line, but it is useful to have a basic knowledge of the principles involved.

(a) Compound words are divided into their separate elements (see 1101):

bil-fabrik, skole-børn, elsk-værdig

(b) Derivatives can be divided according to their prefix or suffix:

an-give, be-tale, dis-kvalificere, for-stå, u-gerne
far-lig, lys-ne, prins-esse, viden-skab, yng-ling

(c) Words which are not compounds divide according to the number of consonants involved:

– one or two consonants: one consonant goes to the new line:

bo-gen, bus-sen, sta-den, vil-la, øl-let

– two or more consonants: a consonant group may move to the new line if it is a group that normally begins a Danish word:

bis-pen or **bi-spen, eksem-pler, tas-ke** or **ta-ske, æ-ble**

Consonants that belong in the same syllable cannot be separated:
cf.

***kno-gle, knog-le; *te-knik, tek-nik**

Note that the link **-e** or **-s** belongs on the first line:

fugle-rede, storebælts-færge

(d) Inflexional endings can be divided from the stem:

bøg-erne, hurtig-ere, student-en, vent-ede

(e) Two vowels coming together can be divided if they belong to separate syllables:

di-alekt, ekstra-arbejde, revoluti-onen

1314 Figures or letters?

(a) As a general rule it may be said that numbers up to ten are best written in words. In some cases, particularly when the writer wishes to appear precise, figures are used even for numbers under ten.

(b) The following are usually written as figures:

(i) Large numbers:

Året har 365 dage.	The year has 365 days.
Januar har 31 dage.	January has 31 days.
Byen har 564.321 indbyggere.	The town has 564,321 inhabitants.

(ii) Numbers in abbreviations:

2 kg   6 %   5 km   § 42, stk. 6   7 kr.

(iii) Numbers in decimals and fractions:

10,56   ¾

(iv) Telephone numbers, street numbers, etc.:

Jeg bor Havnegade 42 og har telefonnummer 99 12 34 56.
I live at 42 Havnegade and my telephone number is 99 12 34 56.

(v) Dates, times, etc.:

Han er født den 10. december 1944 kl. 11.55.
He was born on 10 December 1944 at 11.55 a.m.

(vi) Prices, etc.:

Det koster 95, 50 kr.	It costs 95 kroner 50 øre.

(vii) Measurements:

5 kg smør	5 kg of butter

Note 1 – Very large numbers often have a mixture of figures and words involving **millioner (mio.)**, **milliarder (mia.)**.

Note 2 – Names of rulers, popes, etc. can be given in several different ways:

1 Arabic numerals:	**Margrethe den 2.**
2 Roman numerals:	**Margrethe II**
3 Words:	**Margrethe den Anden**

Notice that the ordinal number is often written as a figure with a following full stop when Arabic numerals are used, but without the stop when Roman numerals are used.

1315 One word or two?

Compounds are common in Danish. They may be written either as one word or two. Even native speakers often find it difficult to choose the right form.

(a) Compounds

The pronunciation (i.e. number of main stresses) indicates whether these should be one word or two. Compounds with two main stresses must be written as two words. In the examples below ´ marks main stress and ` secondary stress:

Compare:

One word:	*Two words:*	*Meaning:*
en ´billig`bog	**en ´billig ´bog**	paperback/ cheap book
´rød`vin	**´rød ´vin**	red wine
´stor`magt	**´stor ´magt**	world power/ great power

(b) Uptoners, including amplifying prefixes and other words sometimes used as prefixes

These are often written as one word: **allerbedst, dødkedelig, smadderærgerligt**.

The same principle applies here as in (a):

en ´kæmpe`succes a great success	**en ´kæmpe ´succes**
en ´halv`flaske a half bottle/half a bottle	**en ´halv ´flaske**
et ´femkroners`frimærke a five kroner stamp	**et ´fem ´kroners ´frimærke**
en ´fireværelses`lejlighed a four-room flat	**en ´fire ´værelses ´lejlighed**

(c) Adverbs and prepositions

When used as prepositions a number of compounds are found as two separate words, but when used as adverbials the same expressions are compounded. Compare the following cases:

Han er her fra byen. **Det er ikke langt herfra.**	He is from this town. It is not far from here.
Bolden var inden for linien. **Kom indenfor!**	The ball was inside the line. Come in!
Huset ligger over for stationen. **Det er huset overfor.**	The house is opposite the station. It is the house opposite.

(d) Numerals

Numbers under 100 are written as one word, numbers over 100 as several words.

(e) Common problem words

Always one word:	*Always two words:*	*Either one or two words:*
alting	**af sted**	**etcetera/et cetera**
derimod	**frem for**	**gudbevares/gud bevares**
derudover	**for længst**	**herregud/herre gud**
førend	**i alt**	**ingenting/ingen ting**
ifølge	**om end**	**nogensinde/nogen sinde**
langtfra (= slet ikke)	**på ny**	**selvom/selv om**

Always one word:	*Always two words:*	*Either one or two words:*
medmindre (=hvis ikke)	**rundt om**	**simpelthen/simpelt hen**
tilsammen	**i dag**	**stadigvæk/stadig væk**
tværtimod	**i morgen**	**tillykke/til lykke**
	i går	
	i øvrigt	

LINGUISTIC TERMS

This list comprises terms that may not be familiar to a student of language or that are not already explained in the text. Users should also consult the Index for references in the text.

ABSTRACT NOUNS refer to unobservable notions, e.g. **musik, påstand, vanskelighed** (music, assertion, difficulty).

ABSTRACT SENSE is found when the literal sense has been extended so far that it is no longer transparent, e.g. the locative prepositions **i** and **på** in **i særdeleshed**, in particular; **på må og få**, at random. Abstract sense is usually associated with ABSTRACT NOUNS.

ADJECTIVE PHRASES consist of an adjective or a participle with optional words which modify its meaning, e.g. **Han er *(utrolig) energisk***, He is (incredibly) energetic.

ADVERB PHRASES consist of an adverb with optional words which modify its meaning, e.g. **Han kørte *(temmelig) hurtigt***, He drove (quite) fast.

ADVERBIALS (see CLAUSAL ADVERBS) are words, phrases or clauses that function as adverbs. Adverbs, noun phrases, prepositional phrases and subordinate clauses can all be adverbials of different kinds (manner, place, time, condition, etc.), e.g. **Hun sang *smukt*** (adverb, manner), She sang beautifully; **Hun sang *hele aftenen*** (noun phrase, time), She sang the whole evening; **Hun sang *i Det Kongelige Teater*** (prep. phrase, place), She sang in the Royal Theatre; **Hun sang kun, *hvis hun havde lyst*** (sub. clause, condition), She only sang when she felt like it.

AFFIX is a prefix added to the beginning or a suffix added to the end of a word, e.g. ***u*lykkelig**, unhappy; **god*hed***, goodness.

AGENT is the person or thing carrying out the action of the verb. It also appears in passive constructions, e.g. **Zebraen jages *af loven***, The zebra is chased by the lion.

AGREEMENT is a way of showing that two grammatical units have a certain feature in common, e.g. **min*e* hund*e***, my dogs; **slott*et* er stor*t***, the castle is big.

ANALYTIC (or PERIPHRASTIC) REALIZATION means using two or more words in sequence to show tense or case, in contrast to SYNTHETIC REALIZATION, where the tense or case is shown by an inflexional ending. Thus the perfect tense is realized analytically in Danish (and English), e.g. **Jeg har syndet** (I have sinned) but synthetically in Latin, 'peccavi'. Both realizations are found in Danish passive constructions, e.g. **Varerne hentes kl. 5** (synthetic)/**Varerne bliver hentet kl. 5** (analytic), The goods will be picked up at 5 o'clock.

ANAPHORIC reference means that a word refers back to a previous word or words, e.g. **Ib er syg. *Han* har drukket for meget**, Ib is ill. He (i.e. Ib) has drunk too much.

APPOSITION is where two consecutive noun phrases separated only by a comma describe the same phenomenon, e.g. ***Ib*, *min bror*, er syg**, Ib, my brother, is ill.

ATTRIBUTIVE is used to describe adjectives or pronouns that precede a noun and modify it, e.g. **et *stort* hus**, a big house; ***min* bil**, my car.

BLENDS are new words formed by omitting part of an existing word, e.g. **meromsætningsafgift** ⇨ ***moms***, VAT.

CLAUSAL ADVERBS are adverbs that modify the sense of the clause as a whole, e.g. **Han er *ikke* dum**, He's not stupid; **De er *sjældent* hjemme**, They are rarely at home.

CLAUSE is a syntactic unit that usually consists of at least a finite verb and a subject (though the subject may be understood, as in most imperative clauses, e.g. **Skyd ikke budbringeren!**, Don't shoot the messenger!). There are two major types of clause: main clauses (MC) and subordinate clauses (SC), e.g. **Middagen stod på bordet** (MC), **da jeg kom hjem** (SC), The dinner was on the table when I got home. (Cf. SENTENCE.)

CLIPPINGS are new words formed by omitting the beginning or end of a word, e.g. **automobil** ⇨ ***bil***, car; **biograf** ⇨ **bio**, cinema.

COLLECTIVE NOUNS are nouns whose singular form denotes a group, e.g. **familie**, family; **hold**, team; **kvæg**, cattle.

COMMON NOUNS are all nouns that are not PROPER NOUNS, e.g. **en hund**, a dog; **et træ**, a tree.

COMPLEMENTS express a meaning that adds to (or complements) that of the subject or object. They can be either an ADJECTIVE PHRASE or a NOUN PHRASE, e.g. **Dorthe og Sven er *intelligente*. De er *gode venner***, Dorthe and Sven are intelligent. They are good friends; **De slog ham** ***bevidstløs***, They knocked him unconscious. (For 'prepositional complement' see PREPOSITIONAL PHRASE.)

COMPLEX VERBS have two or more parts: **Jeg** ***har spist*** **snegle**, I have eaten snails; **Cyklen** ***er blevet stjålet***, The bike has been stolen.

COMPOUND VERBS are verbs consisting either of a STEM and a prefix or PARTICLE, which may be inseparable or separable from the stem, e.g. ***be*****tale**, pay, but ***del*****tage/tage** ***del***, take part; or of two stems, e.g. **plan|lægge**, plan.

CONGRUENCE (= AGREEMENT)

CONJUGATION denotes the way a verb is inflected, its pattern of endings, and also the different groups of verbs with the same endings, e.g. past tenses in: Conj. I **leve – levede**, live; Conj. II **spise – spiste**, eat.

COPULAS link a subject complement to the subject, e.g. **Eva** ***er*** **læge**, Eva is a doctor; **Peter** ***blev*** **skuffet**, Peter was disappointed.

COPULATIVE means 'linking'.

COUNT NOUNS are nouns that denote individual countable entities and therefore usually possess a plural form (including zero-ending), e.g. **bog – bøger**, book-s; **dreng – drenge**, boy-s; **æg – æg**, egg-s.

DECLENSION denotes the different ways of INFLECTING count nouns in the plural, e.g. **bil*****er***, **krig*****e***, **flag**, cars, wars, flags. It also denotes adjective inflexion, e.g. **en rød bil**, a red car, **et rød*****t*** **hus**, a red house; **den rød*****e*** **bil**, the red car.

DEFINITE refers to a specified entity, cf. ***Tyven*** **har stjålet uret**, The thief has stolen the clock. INDEFINITE refers to a non-specified entity, e.g. ***En tyv*** **har stjålet uret**, A thief has stolen the clock.

DEICTIC REFERENCE (from Greek 'deixis' meaning 'pointing') is dependent on the context of the utterance in space and time, e.g. the referent of the pronoun **ham** and the exact meaning of the adverbs **derovre** and **nu** in the sentence **Ham derovre burde gå nu** (Him over there ought to go now) depend entirely on the actual situation, time and place when the words are spoken (the speaker may point or give a nod in the direction of the man in question). (Cf. ANAPHORIC REFERENCE.)

DERIVATIVE refers to a word derived from a STEM, usually by the addition of an AFFIX, e.g. ***an*****gå** (concern), ***fore*****gå** (take place), and ***under*****gå** (undergo) are all derivatives of the verb **gå** (go).

DIRECT OBJECT denotes a noun phrase, a pronoun or a clause governed by a (transitive) verb, e.g. **Drengen hentede *bolden/sin søster,*** The boy fetched the ball/his sister; **Hun sagde, *at hun var træt***, She said that she was tired.

DUPLICATION involves the repetition of a subject, object or adverbial, usually in the form of a pronoun or adverb, e.g. ***Jens, han* er ikke dum**, Jens, he isn't stupid.

ELLIPSIS involves the omission of a word or word group in the sentence, e.g. **Må jeg ryge? Nej, du må ikke** */ryge/*, May I smoke? No, you may not /smoke/.

FIGURATIVE SENSE is when the literal sense has been extended but is still somehow transparent, e.g. **Han fulgte i sin faders fodspor**, He followed in his father's footsteps. (Cf. ABSTRACT SENSE.)

FINITE VERB is a verb form which in itself shows tense (and sometimes mood and/or voice). There are three finite verb forms in Danish: the present tense, the past tense and the imperative, e.g. **Jeg venter, Jeg ventede, Vent!**, I'm waiting, I waited, Wait! (Cf. NON-FINITE VERB.)

FORMAL SUBJECT is **der** or **det** in cases when the REAL SUBJECT is postponed, e.g. ***Der*** (FS) **sidder *en gammel mand*** (RS) **på bænken**, There's an old man sitting on the bench; ***Det*** (FS) **er synd, *at du ikke kan komme til festen*** (RS), It's a pity that you can't come to the party.

FRONT is the position at the beginning of all main clause STATEMENTS and **hv**-questions. It is usually occupied by the subject, e.g. ***Vi/Forfatterne* kan lide øl**, We/The authors like beer. But non-subjects, especially ADVERBIAL expressions of time or place, often occupy the front position, e.g. ***I morgen* skal jeg spille fodbold**, Tomorrow I'm playing football.

GENDER may indicate sex: **drengen - *han*, pigen - *hun*** (the boy - he, the girl - she) or grammatical gender: ***et* barn, *et* hus, *en* stol**, (a child, a house, a chair).

HOMONYM is a word that is identical in form to another word, e.g. **en frø** = a frog, **et frø** = a seed.

IDIOM(ATIC) indicates a usage that is not readily explicable from the grammar.

IMPERATIVE is a finite verb form identical in Danish with the stem of the verb, expressing command, warning, direction or the like, e.g. **Kom!**, Come on!; **Vend om!**, Turn round!

IMPERSONAL CONSTRUCTIONS do not involve a person but usually **det** or **der**, e.g. **Det sner**, It's snowing; **Der snydes meget**, There's a lot of cheating.

INDECLINABLE describes words that do not INFLECT, e.g. the adjectives **moderne**, good; **fælles**, common, mutual, which take no endings for gender or plural: **et moderne hus**, a modern house, **fælles venner**, mutual friends. Whole word classes may be indeclinable, e.g. conjunctions and prepositions.

INDEFINITE (see DEFINITE)

INDIRECT OBJECT usually denotes a person or an animal 'benefiting' from an action (i.e. the recipient), e.g. **Vi gav *ham* pengene**, We gave him the money.

INFINITIVE PHRASE is a phrase consisting of an infinitive (optionally) accompanied by one or more phrases, e.g. **at skrive et brev**, to write a letter.

INFLECT means to change the form of a word by means of endings, vowel change(s) or in other ways, e.g. the verb **skrive** (write) inflects **skriv**, **skriv*e***, **skriv*er***, **skr*e*v**, **skrev*et***, etc.

INFLEXIBLE (= INDECLINABLE)

INFLEXION (see INFLECT)

INTERROGATIVE is used of questions, e.g. interrogative pronouns and adverbs introduce a question: ***Hvem* var det?**, Who was that?; ***Hvorfor* kom du ikke?**, Why didn't you come?

INVERTED word order denotes verb – subject order, e.g. **Idag *rejser vi***, Today we are leaving.

MATRIX is that part of a complex sentence that remains when the subordinate clause is removed, e.g. ***Birthe lovede,* at hun ville skrive til os**, Birthe promised that she would write to us.

MORPHEME is the smallest part of a word expressing meaning: in the word **bilerne** (the cars) there are three morphemes: ***bil*** ('car'), ***er*** (plural morpheme), ***ne*** (definite plural morpheme).

MUTATED VOWEL ('Umlaut', cf. Danish 'omlyd') is one that changes when a noun or adjective is inflected, e.g. **o ⇨ ø** in **f*o*d – f*ø*dder** (foot – feet); **u ⇨ y** in ***u*ng – *y*ngre** (young – younger). Vowel change in verbs, usually strong verbs, is known as 'Ablaut' (cf. Danish 'aflyd'), e.g. **s*y*nger, s*a*ng, s*u*nget**.

NOMINAL means a word or phrase functioning as a noun, e.g. ***Bogen* er interessant**, The book is interesting; ***At læse* er interessant**, Reading is interesting.

NON-COUNT NOUNS are nouns that cannot describe individual countable entities. They may be either singular words with no plural form, usually denoting substances ('mass-words'), e.g. **luft**, air; **mel**, flour; **sand**, sand; or they may be plural words with no equivalent singular form, e.g. **klæder**, clothes; **penge**, money; **shorts**, shorts.

NON-FINITE VERB forms are those not showing tense, namely infinitive and participles, e.g. **(at) løbe**, (to) run; **løbende**, running; **løbet**, run.

NOUN PHRASES consist of a noun (optionally) accompanied by one or more modifiers which may precede or follow the noun, e.g. **en *dejlig* dag**, a lovely day; **en dag, *som jeg aldrig vil glemme***, a day I shall never forget.

NUMBER is a collective term for singular and plural; the latter is usually marked by an inflexional ending, e.g. **en blyant**, a pencil; **to blyant*er***, two pencils.

PART OF SPEECH means word class, e.g. noun, adjective, verb, conjunction, etc.

PARTICLE is an adverb or preposition appearing together with a verb to form a single unit of meaning, e.g. **ned** in **skrive *ned***, write down; **til** in **lægge *til***, add.

PARTITIVE denotes a part of a whole or of a substance, e.g. ***en del af* pengene**, some of the money; ***en flaske* vin**, a bottle of wine; ***et kilo* kartofler**, a kilo of potatoes.

PEJORATIVE means deprecating, e.g. **Dit fjols!** You idiot!

PERIPHRASTIC REALIZATION (see ANALYTIC REALIZATION)

POSTMODIFIER follows the word or phrase it modifies (i.e. is subordinate to), e.g. in the way that a relative clause follows the NOUN PHRASE it modifies, as in **Hunden, *som leger med kodbenet* ...**, The dog that is playing with the bone ... (Cf. PREMODIFIER.)

POSTPOSITIONED or POSTPOSED means coming after another sentence element.

PREDICATE is the central part of the clause, excluding the subject. The predicate comprises the verb plus any object, complement or adverbial: **Han *spiller (klaver hver dag)*,** He plays (the piano every day).

PREDICATIVE indicates a position that is found after the verb.

PREDICATIVE COMPLEMENT is a noun phrase or adjective phrase in the PREDICATE complementing (i.e. filling out) the subject or object: **Ib er *min bror.* Han er *seks år gammel*,** Ib is my brother. He is six years old.

PREMODIFIER precedes the word or phrase it modifies (i.e. is subordinate to), e.g. in the way that the adjective **hyggelig** premodifies the noun **aften** in **en hyggelig aften**, a pleasant evening; or in the way that the adverb **meget** premodifies the adjective **farlig** in **Løven er meget farlig**, The lion is very dangerous. (Cf. POSTMODIFIER.)

PREPOSITIONAL PHRASE consists of a preposition plus a prepositional complement (a noun phrase, a pronoun, an infinitive (phrase) or a clause), e.g. **pigen *med det lange hår*,** the girl with the long hair; **pigen tænkte *på ham*,** the girl thought of him; **pigen gik *uden at sige farvel*,** the girl left without saying goodbye; **pigen sørgede *for, at bordet blev dækket*,** the girl saw to it that the table was set.

PREPOSITIONED or PREPOSED means coming in front of another sentence element.

PRODUCTIVE implies that a word class or method of word formation can still produce new words, e.g. the suffix **-bar** in **vaskbar**, washable.

PROPER NOUNS are names of specific people, places, occasions, events, books, etc., e.g. **Jørgen, Randers, *Guldhornene.***

RAISING is the movement of an element from a subordinate clause to the FRONT of the main clause, e.g. ***Det* sagde Hans, at vi ikke skulle gøre**, Hans said that we should not do that.

REAL SUBJECT is the postponed subject, e.g. **Det er dejligt *at drikke vin*,** It's nice to drink wine. (Cf. FORMAL SUBJECT.)

RECIPROCAL or RECIPROCATING indicates a mutual activity expressed either in the pronoun, e.g. **De elsker *hinanden*** (They love one another), or in the verb, e.g. **Vi *ses* i morgen** (See you tomorrow).

SEMANTIC denotes the meaning of words, phrases, etc.

SENTENCE is a syntactic unit that contains a complete meaning and consists of one or more clauses (cf. CLAUSE). Thus the following three examples are all sentences: **Se der!**, Look there!; **Hun tager bussen, når det regner**, She takes the bus when it rains; **Hvis du tror, at jeg kan huske, hvad han sagde, da vi besøgte ham i sidste uge, tager du fejl**, If you think that I can remember what he said when we visited him last week, you're wrong.

SIMPLE VERBS consist of one word only (a FINITE VERB), e.g. ***Hjælp!***, Help!; **(Han)** ***sover***, (He) sleeps; **(Han)** ***gik***, (He) went.

STATEMENT is a sentence or clause conveying information, as distinct from a question, a command or an exclamation.

STEM is the part of the verb onto which the inflexional endings are added, e.g. **dans*e*, dans*er*, dans*ede*, dans*et***.

SYLLABLE consists of a vowel and usually one or more consonants, e.g. **ø, dø, rør, rødt, in-du-stri-ar-bej-de-re**.

SYNTHETIC REALIZATION (see ANALYTIC REALIZATION)

TAG QUESTION is a phrase attached to the end of a STATEMENT which turns it into a question: **Han kan lide laks, *ikke sandt*?**, He likes salmon, doesn't he?

VERB PHRASES consist of a FINITE VERB form (optionally) accompanied by one or more NON-FINITE VERB forms in a chain, e.g. **Han *sover***, He is sleeping; **Han *må kunne løbe***, He must be able to run.

VOICED indicates a consonant produced with vibration of the vocal cords, e.g. **l, m, n, v**. All vowels are voiced.

VOICELESS indicates a consonant produced without vibrating the vocal cords, e.g. **p, t, k, f, s, h**.

SHORT BIBLIOGRAPHY

Unless otherwise stated, works are published in Copenhagen.

GENERAL ON DANISH

Nyt fra Sprognævnet

Danske studier

Mål og Mæle

Erik Hansen, *Magister Stygotii betænkninger over det danske sprog*, 1973

Erik Hansen, *Rigtigt dansk*, 2nd ed., 1993

Erik Hansen, *Sprogiagttagelse*, 1970

Henrik Galberg Jacobsen and Peter Stray Jørgensen, *Politikens Håndbog i nudansk*, 3rd ed., 1997

Per Anker Jensen, *Principper for grammatisk analyse*, 1985

Ord til andet. Iagttagelser og synspunkter 2, 1980

Peter Skautrup, *Det danske sprogs historie*, I-IV, 1944ff

Sprog i Norden

Sprog og samfund

Sproget her og nu (eds. Erik Hansen and Jørn Lund), Dansk Sprognævns skrifter 14, 1988

Sprognævnet på skærmen

DANISH DICTIONARIES

Erik Bruun, *Dansk sprogbrug. En stil- og konstruktionsordbog*, 1980

B. Kjærulff Nielsen, *Engelsk–dansk ordbog*, 4th ed., 1991

Ordbog over det danske sprog, 1918–54

Politikens Nudansk ordbog, 15th ed., 1992

Politikens slangordbog, 1982

Retskrivningsordbogen, 1996

Pia Riber Pedersen, *Nye ord i dansk 1955–1975*, 1984

Hermann Vinterberg and C.A. Bodelsen, *Dansk–Engelsk Ordbog*, 3rd ed., 1990

DANISH GRAMMAR

Otto Afzelius *et al.*, *Dansk grammatik for udlændinge*, 8th ed., 1986

Elias Bredsdorff, *Danish. An Elementary Grammar and Reader*, Cambridge, 1965 (and subsequent editions).

Paul Diderichsen, *Elementær dansk grammatik*, 3rd ed., 1962

Aage Hansen, *Moderne dansk I–III*, 1967

Aage Hansen, *Vort vanskelige sprog*, 1965

Gunnar Hansen, Per Mogens Hansen and Ragna Lorentzen, *Dansk sproglære for seminarier*, 1971

Henrik Galberg Jacobsen, *Erhvervsdansk, Opslagsbog*, 1990

Henrik Galberg Jacobsen and Peder Skyum-Nielsen, *Erhvervsdansk, Grundbog*, 1990

Henrik Galberg Jacobsen and Peder Skyum-Nielsen, *Dansk sprog. En grundbog*, 1996

W. Glyn Jones and Kirsten Gade, *Danish. A Grammar*, 1981

H.A. Kofoed, *Teach Yourself Danish*, London, 1958

Jørgen Lomholt, *Le Danois Contemporain*, 1982

Kr. Mikkelsen, *Dansk ordföjninglære. Med sproghistoriske tillæg. Håndbog for viderekomne og lærere*, 1911 (reprinted 1975)

Annelise Munck Nordentoft, *Hovedtræk af dansk grammatik. Ordklasser*, 2nd ed., 1972

Palle Spore, *La Langue Danois*, Odense, 1965

V. Vestergaard (ed.), *Dansk sprog: hjælpebog for den højere undervisning*, 1965

H.G. Wivel, *Synspunkter for dansk sproglære*, 1901

MORPHOLOGY

Baglænsordbog, Dansk Sprognævns skrifter 15, 1988

Danske dobbeltformer. Valgfri former i retskrivningen, Dansk Sprognævns skrifter 18, 1992

Henrik Holmboe, *Dansk Retrograd-ordbog*, 1978

Allan Karker, *Nordiske talord i dansk. Historie og vejledning*, Dansk Sprognævns skrifter 2, 1959

WORD FORMATION

Jørgen Eriksen and Arne Hamburger, *Forkortelser i hverdagen*, Dansk Sprognævns skrifter 13, 1988

Pia Jarvad, *Nye ord. Hvorfor og hvordan?*, 1995

Jørn Lund, *Okay? Amerikansk påvirkning af dansk sprog*, 1989

Bo Seltén, *Svengelsk ordbok*, Växjö, 1987

Knud Sørensen, *Engelske lån i dansk*, Dansk Sprognævns skrifter 8, 1973

Knud Sørensen, *Engelsk i dansk. Er det et must?*, 1995

SYNTAX

Erik Hansen, *Dæmonernes port. Støttemateriale til undervisningen i nydansk grammatik*, 4th ed., 1997

Lars Heltoft and John E. Andersen, 'Sætningsskemaet og dets stilling – 50 år efter', *NyS* 16–17, 1986

Annelise Munck Nordentoft, *Hovedtræk af dansk grammatik. Syntaks*, 3rd ed., 1982

ORTHOGRAPHY AND PUNCTUATION

Britta Christensen and Christian Dreyer, *Om retstavning*, 1986

Henrik Galberg Jacobsen, *Sæt nyt komma. Regler, grammatik, genveje og øvelser*, Dansk Sprognævns skrifter 25, 1996

Aage Hansen, *Om moderne dansk retskrivning*, 1969

Aage Hansen, *Pausekommaet*, Dansk Sprognævns skrifter 1, 1957

Erik Hansen and Bodil Haar, *Om pausekomma*, 1976

Erik Hansen, *Skrift, stavning og retstavning*, 2nd ed., 1991

Eva Heltberg, *Støj på ledningen. Stave- og sprogfejl – regler og forklaringer*, 1990

Komma – hvornår og hvorfor? En debatbog om kommatering, Dansk Sprognævns skrifter 20, 1993

Gunnar Nissen, *Ska det i et eller flere ord?*, 1986

ENGLISH GRAMMAR

Bertil Johanson and Michael Stevens, *Gads Grammatik - Engelsk*, 1990

Randolph Quirk, Sidney Greenbaum, Geoffrey Leech and Jan Svartvik, *A Comprehensive Grammar of the English Language*, London, 1985

Poul Steller and Knud Sørensen, *Engelsk grammatik*, 1966

Torben Vestergaard, *Engelsk grammatik*, 1985

INDEX

English words are in *italics* and Danish words are in **bold**. The Danish order of the alphabet is used, namely **a ... z, æ, ø, å**. References are to paragraphs, not pages; those in bold are to the main paragraphs on the subject.